Heidinger/Hubalek
Anglo-amerikanische Rechtssprache

Anglo-amerikanische Rechtssprache

Praxis-Handbuch für Rechtsanwälte,
Wirtschaftsjuristen
und Wirtschaftstreuhänder

von

MMag. Franz J. Heidinger, LL.M. (Virginia)
Rechtsanwalt
Partner der Kanzlei Alix Frank Rechtsanwälte KEG Wien

und

Andrea Hubalek
Staatlich geprüfte Übersetzerin
Translex Wien

Wien 1996

Die Deutsche Bibliothek – CIP-Einheitsaufnahme

Heidinger, Franz J.:
Anglo-amerikanische Rechtssprache : Praxis-Handbuch für
Rechtsanwälte, Wirtschaftsjuristen und Wirtschaftstreuhänder /
Franz Heidinger/Andrea Hubalek. KPMG Austria. – 2.,
überarb. und wesentlich erw. Aufl. – Wien : Orac, 1996
   ISBN 3-7007-0808-4
NE: Hubalek, Andrea:

Information an unsere Leser

Das vorliegende Buch wurde auf
    chlorfrei gebleichtem Umweltschutzpapier Bio Top 3
gedruckt.
Auch die Plastikfolie, in die unsere Bücher eingeschweißt sind, ist ein
    umweltfreundliches Produkt.
Sie ist aus Polyäthylen
    chlor- und schwefelfrei
hergestellt und verbrennt in Müllverbrennungsanlagen
    völlig ungiftig;
sie zerfällt unter Lichteinfluß langsam, verhält sich auf Mülldeponien
grundwasserneutral und ist
    voll recyclingfähig.

ISBN 3-7007-0808-4

Verlag Orac, Wien

Hersteller: Druckerei Robitschek & Co. Ges.m.b.H., Wien

VORWORT
ZUR ZWEITEN AUFLAGE

Seit dem Erscheinen der ersten Auflage der Anglo-amerikanischen Rechtssprache sind nunmehr gut vier Jahre vergangen. Als wir die erste Auflage fertiggestellt hatten, waren wir uns wohl bewußt, wie unvollständig und bruchstückhaft unser Buch war. Was wir nicht wissen konnten ist, daß wir mit dem Buch und den sich daraus ergebenden Tätigkeiten selbst am Beginn der Entwicklung einer neuen Disziplin standen. Kurz nachdem unser Buch als „Erstling" zum Thema englische Rechtssprache erschienen war, wurden auch in England zwei Bücher, die sich mit dem Thema befaßten, publiziert. Während die nach unserem erschienenen Bücher primär sprachlich orientiert und damit unserer Erfahrung nach für Juristen und Praktiker schwerer zugänglich waren, hat sich der Ansatz der Anglo-amerikanischen Rechtssprache bewährt. Die strenge Orientierung an praxisrelevanten Themen und Musterdokumenten ist von Praktikern, aber auch bei in Ausbildung stehenden Juristen höchst positiv aufgenommen worden.

Mit dieser zweiten Auflage haben wir den Versuch unternommen, einige „Kinderkrankheiten" zu beseitigen. Das Buch ist mit Ausnahme der Einleitungskapitel grundsätzlich einsprachig angelegt, wobei jedoch Musterdokumente und vor allem Glossare selbstverständlich zweisprachig gehalten sind. Die Glossare sind nach wie vor nach Sachgebieten gegliedert, wobei jedoch eine Untergliederung vermieden wurde und die jeweiligen Glossare streng alphabetisch geordnet sind. Dies wird zur besseren Übersichtlichkeit und leichteren Verwendbarkeit in der Praxis führen.

Themenmäßig haben wir in dieser zweiten Auflage dem Wunsch vieler Benützer entsprechend die Kapitel Steuern und Rechnungslegung massiv aufgewertet bzw. neu aufgenommen und konnten dafür einen der besten Partner auf diesem Gebiet, nämlich die *KPMG Österreich*, gewinnen. Wir möchten an dieser Stelle Herrn *Dr. Robert Reiter* und *Frau Mag. Regina Reiter*, die für die Kapitel "Tax Law" und "Accounting" verantwortlich zeichnen, herzlich danken. Das Kapitel "The Law of Business Organisations" wurde um eine konzise Einführung in die gesellschaftsrechtlichen Grundlagen nach englischem, amerikanischem und österreichischem Recht ergänzt, das Kapitel "Insurance" erhielt eine interessante Überblicksdarstellung. Für beide Ergänzungen möchten wir Herrn *Mag. Michael Pramberger*, Wien, aufrichtig Dank sagen. Ein weiteres neues Kapitel beschäftigt sich mit "Trusts in English Law", einer in der Praxis wichtigen und für das anglo-amerikanische Rechtssystem so charakteristischen Rechtsfigur, die unserem Rechtssystem fremd ist. Für die Erstellung dieses Kapitels möchten wir Herrn *Owen McIntyre*, Manchester, herzlich danken. Weiters gebührt Dank Herrn *John Robbins*, Washington D.C., für die Erstellung der „Doctrine" zum Vertragsrecht.

Für die kritische Durchsicht unseres Manuskripts danken wir Frau *Nicola Armstrong*, Oxford. Ferner wäre die Erstellung dieser zweiten Auflage ohne die (computermäßige) Unterstützung durch Herrn *Dr. Peter Hubalek*, Wien, nicht möglich gewesen.

Auch im Zusammenhang mit dieser zweiten Auflage würden wir uns über Ihre Anregungen und Kritik freuen und stehen Ihnen darüber hinaus für Ihre fachsprachlichen Anliegen auch über unser Büro *H & H Translex* (siehe auch Informationskasten am Ende des Buches) sowie für Anfragen im Zusammenhang mit österreichischen und internationalen Rechtsfragen über die Kanzlei Alix Frank Rechtsanwälte KEG Wien jederzeit gerne zur Verfügung.

Wien, im April 1996

Andrea Hubalek   **Franz J. Heidinger**

VORWORT

Mit diesem Lehr- und Handbuch haben wir den Versuch unternommen, eine Überblicksdarstellung der anglo-amerikanischen Rechtssprache für den Bereich des Zivil- und Wirtschaftsrechts zu geben, um damit insbesondere Studenten und Rechtsanwendern in der Praxis eine Arbeitshilfe zu bieten.

Wir waren uns der Tatsache bewußt, daß eine Aufgabe dieser Größe nur bruchstückhaft und nur aufgrund rigoroser Beschränkung in der Auswahl der Sachthemen und Dokumente angegangen werden konnte. Ungeachtet dessen hoffen wir, die wichtigsten praxisrelevanten Fachbereiche abgedeckt zu haben.

Die Erstellung dieses Buches wäre ohne die hilfreiche Unterstützung von *Frau Jane Nitsche-Shapiro*, die uns bei der Durchsicht der englischsprachigen Textteile mit wertvollem Rat zur Seite stand, nicht möglich gewesen.

Weiters möchten wir Herrn *Univ.-Prof. Dr. Peter Bierbaumer*, Universität Graz, danken, der seit der Gründung des Internationalen Sprachzentrums an der Universität Graz insbesondere auch die juristische Fachsprache gefördert hat.

Weiterer Dank gilt der Rechtsanwaltskanzlei *Weiss-Tessbach, Galle & Benn-Ibler*, Wien, wo wir zwischen 1988 und 1991 unsere Kenntnisse in der Praxis anwenden und verbessern konnten.

Obwohl wir bei der Zusammenstellung der Texte, Muster und Glossare mit größter Sorgfalt vorgegangen sind, möchten wir jedoch darauf hinweisen, daß die in diesem Buch enthaltenen Aussagen nur zur Information dienen. Die Musterdokumente sind lediglich als Anregung für die Konzeption eigener Dokumente gedacht. Im Einzelfall sind sowohl die Expertise eines Rechtsanwaltes als auch eines gerichtlich beeideten Dolmetschers unumgänglich.

Für Anregungen und Kritik sind wir dankbar.

Wien, im Sommer 1991

Andrea Hubalek   **Franz J. Heidinger**

VIII

INHALTSVERZEICHNIS

I. EINLEITUNG

1. ZUR IDEE DIESES BUCHES

Die Idee, ein Praxishandbuch für Juristen über die englische Rechtssprache zu schreiben, entstand aus zwei Überlegungen:

Der Autor *Franz J. Heidinger* hat seit dem Herbst 1987 an der Universität Graz und seit dem Herbst 1988 zusätzlich an der Universität Wien sowie seit ebenfalls Herbst 1989 für die Gesellschaft für juristische Fortbildung (welche die Ausbildungsveranstaltungen für Rechtsanwaltsanwärter zur Vorbereitung auf die Rechtsanwaltsprüfung veranstaltet) Fachsprachkurse „Englisch für Juristen" abgehalten. Im Zuge dieser Lehrtätigkeit wurde klar, daß ein ständig wachsender Bedarf an einer Zusatzfachsprachausbildung für Juristen herrschte, welcher aufgrund mangelnden Angebotes nicht abgedeckt werden konnte. Einschlägige Literatur oder Unterrichtsmaterialien waren nur äußerst spärlich vorhanden und, soweit dies der Fall war, kaum praxisrelevant. Aus dieser Situation wurde die Idee geboren, ein Lehrbuch zu schaffen, welches sowohl den Anforderungen der Fachsprachvermittlung wie auch jenen eines Fachbuches aus dem Bereich des angewandten Rechts gerecht werden konnte.

Die Problematik dabei war jedoch die Einschränkung des Umfanges eines solchen Lehr- und Handbuches auf einen bestimmten Sachbereich. Bedarfs- und Kursbewertungsanalysen, welche im Zuge der an den Universitäten sowie für die Rechtsanwaltskammer abgehaltenen Seminare durchgeführt wurden, zeigten eine Diskrepanz der Interessen und des Bedarfs zwischen Studenten und Juristen, welche bereits in der Praxis standen. Während bei den Studenten im Zuge der Bedarfserhebung über die abzudeckenden Fachrechtsbereiche an erster Stelle allgemeines Zivilrecht, knapp gefolgt von Strafrecht und öffentlichem Recht und erst an vierter Stelle Wirtschaftsrecht angegeben wurden, sah die Prioritätenliste bei den Rechtsanwälten und Rechtsanwaltsanwärtern so aus, daß die drei wichtigsten Fachrechtsgebiete Vertragsrecht, Gesellschaftsrecht und allgemeines Zivilrecht waren.

Aufgrund dieser Tatsache, nämlich daß offensichtlich gerade für die Rechtsanwender wirtschaftsrechtliche Fachbereiche von besonderer Bedeutung und Wichtigkeit waren, entstand der Entschluß, den Themenbereich dieses Buches auf das (ohnedies breite) Gebiet des Wirtschaftsrechtes zu beschränken.

Neben den Erfahrungen aus dem Fachsprachenunterricht sowie den daraus erlangten Erkenntnissen über die Bedarfsstruktur hat aber auch die gemeinsame Tätigkeit der Autoren, *Franz J. Heidinger* und *Andrea Hubalek*, in Wiener Anwaltskanzleien mit internationaler Klientel und einem Schwerpunkt auf der Abwicklung internationaler Transaktionen sowie im Rahmen ihrer Beschäftigung in dem von ihnen gegründeten Büro für juristische

Fachübersetzungen *H&H TRANSLEX* wesentlichen Anteil an der Entwicklung der Idee zu diesem Handbuch gehabt. Gerade diese Erfahrung aus der Praxis, ob im Umgang mit ausländischen Klienten und insbesondere mit solchen aus dem anglo-amerikanischen Raum oder in der Darstellung österreichischer Transaktionen gegenüber Ausländern (Übersetzung, Erläuterung), ebenso wie die Teilnahme an der Konzeption und Durchführung internationaler Transaktionen, hatten maßgeblich Einfluß darauf, daß das vorliegende Buch in erster Linie zu einem Praxishandbuch geworden ist.

2. ZUR KONZEPTION – AUFBAU UND INHALT

Wie bereits aus der vorangehenden Darstellung hervorgeht, basiert die Konzeption des Buches auf zwei Dingen. Zum einen soll das Buch als Lehrbuch im Fachsprachenbereich dienen, zum anderen soll es ein Handbuch für den Rechtsanwender in der Praxis sein. Sachlich und thematisch ist das Buch beschränkt auf die wichtigsten Teilrechtsgebiete des Wirtschaftsrechts, dem wichtigsten Bereich der internationalen Wirtschafts- und Rechtsbeziehungen. Die beiden größten Kapitel des Buches sind die Kapitel über das Vertragsrecht und über das Gesellschaftsrecht, wobei bei letzterem insbesondere auf das Recht der Kapitalgesellschaften im Rechtsvergleich zwischen England, USA und Österreich Bezug genommen wurde. Neben diesen beiden Schlüsselkapiteln werden die Bereiche Versicherung, Schiedsgerichtsbarkeit, Steuerrecht, Rechnungslegung und Immaterialgüterrecht abgedeckt.

Der Aufbau der einzelnen Kapitel ist zwar im Detail unterschiedlich, dennoch folgt er im wesentlichen einem einheitlichen Schema, nämlich einer Einleitung, in welcher je nach Relevanz aus der Praxis ein Rechtsgebiet entweder nach unserer, oder aber nach der englischen bzw der amerikanischen Rechtslage dargestellt wird, ohne daß jedoch diese Darstellung einen Anspruch auf Vollständigkeit erhebt. Ziel dieser Einleitung ist vielmehr, den Leser mit der typischen Terminologie des Fachbereiches vertraut zu machen, um ihm einerseits die unterschiedlichen rechtlichen (und somit sprachlichen) Konzepte im anglo-amerikanischen Rechtskreis und im eigenen darzustellen, und andererseits, um ihn so in die Lage zu versetzen, ausländischen Klienten gegenüber die eigenen Konzepte vor allem sprachlich so darzustellen, daß sie dem fremdsprachlichen Klienten/Partner verständlich werden.

Den Einleitungskapiteln folgen in der Regel eine Anzahl von Dokumenten oder Mustern, welche in der Praxis eine entsprechende Rolle spielen, wobei diese Dokumente entweder authentische Dokumente aus dem anglo-amerikanischen Rechtskreis bzw aus unserem Rechtssystem sind (versehen mit Annotationen bzw Randnoten), Dokumente mit Übersetzungen oder Mischdokumente (Hybridformen), in welchen bestimmte Sachverhalte bzw Rechtsverhältnisse in eine Dokumentenform gegossen werden, ohne dabei auf die Eigenheiten eines Rechtssystems (weder auf die rechtlichen noch auf die sprachlichen) einzugehen.

Dieser Praxisteil wird gefolgt von einem umfangreichen Vokabelteil, wobei jeweils ein Teil davon ein englisches Glossar mit Übersetzung und Erläuterung, der andere jeweils ein deutschsprachiges Glossar ist.

Zu den Kapiteln im einzelnen:

Im Kapitel über das Vertragsrecht werden im allgemeinen Teil die wesentlichen Grundlagen des anglo-amerikanischen Vertragsrechts dargestellt, gefolgt von einer kurzen Präsentation der typischen (und für unser Rechtssystem oft ungewohnten) Aspekte und Schritte, welche bei internationalen Vertragsabschlüssen berücksichtigt bzw. gesetzt werden (müssen). Dieser Darstellung folgt eine kurze Beschreibung der wichtigsten Bestandteile eines typischen anglo-amerikanischen Vertrags und eine kurze Abhandlung über die typische vertragsrechtliche Sprache.

Diesem Einleitungskapitel folgt eine Vielzahl von Beispielen, wobei ein ausgewogenes Verhältnis zwischen authentischen anglo-amerikanischen Dokumenten, deutschsprachigen Dokumenten mit Übersetzung und neutralen Dokumenten besteht.

Im folgenden Kapitel, *Cut & Paste* genannt, werden die wichtigsten, immer wiederkehrenden Vertragsklauseln (sogenannte *boiler plates*) aufgelistet, welche durchaus als Muster für die Konzeption (*drafting*) von Verträgen in englischer Sprache bzw Form verwendet werden können. Die Struktur der Glossare folgt im wesentlichen der Unterteilung des Kapitels, wobei ein eigenes Unterkapitel mit typischen Vertragsrechtsfloskeln vorgesehen wurde.

Gesellschaftsrechts-
kapitel

Im Kapitel über das Gesellschaftsrecht wird zunächst ein Überblick über die wesentlichsten Gesellschaftsformen nach dem Recht der Bundesstaaten der USA, nach englischem und nach österreichischem Recht gegeben. Anschließend wird versucht, anhand eines konkreten Szenarios alle wichtigen Dokumente, welche im Zusammenhang mit gesellschaftsrechtlichen Transaktionen gebraucht werden, darzustellen. Im folgenden Abschnitt (*Cut & Paste*) sind Bausteine für alle wichtigen Spezialvollmachten und Gesellschafterbeschlüsse vorgesehen. Englische und deutsche Glossare runden das Kapitel ab.

Kapitel über Versiche-
rungsrecht und
Schiedsgerichtsbarkeit

In den folgenden Kapiteln über Versicherung und Schiedsgerichtsbarkeit werden nach einer kurzen Einleitung Musterdokumente und entsprechende Glossare präsentiert.

Steuerrechtskapitel

Im Kapitel Steuerrecht wurde versucht, anhand einer Darstellung der wichtigsten amerikanischen, englischen und österreichischen Steuern die wesentliche Steuerrechtsterminologie abzudecken. Gleiches gilt für das Kapitel über die Rechnungslegung.

Kapitel über
Immaterialgüterrecht

Das Kapitel über die Immaterialgüterrechte ist dreigeteilt, und zwar in die Gebiete Markenrecht, Patentrecht und Urheberrecht, wobei jedem dieser Unterkapitel eine kurze Darstellung der Situation in den Vereinigten Staaten von Amerika vorangeht, gefolgt von wichtigen Musterdokumenten und schließlich von den jeweiligen Glossaren.

3. ARBEITSMETHODE

Als Lehrbuch kann das vorliegende Buch sowohl zum Selbststudium als auch als Grundlage für ein Kursprogramm dienen, wobei ein *"Cover to Cover"*-Studium den Leser in die Lage versetzen müßte, alle wesentlichen terminologischen und konzeptiven Anforderungen aus dem Bereich des Zivil- und Wirtschaftsrechts abzudecken.

Selbststudium
Lehrbuch

Für den Rechtsanwender in der Praxis soll das Buch jedoch andere Funktionen erfüllen. Dies sei anhand von zwei kurzen Beispielen erläutert:

Anwendungsbeispiele

1. Ein deutschsprachiger Anwalt bekommt von einem Kollegen aus Amerika eine Anfrage über einen steuerrechtlichen oder markenrechtlichen Sachverhalt und muß diese innerhalb kürzester Zeit möglichst kurz und präzise (entweder durch ein Telefonat oder ein Telefax) beantworten.

   In diesem Fall kann ein 10- bis 15minütiges Studium der entsprechenden Abschnitte des Buches sowie ein Blick in das jeweilige Glossar den Rechtsanwender in die Lage versetzen, die von ihm zu erteilende Auskunft auch unter Zuhilfenahme des notwendigen Fachvokabulars und der dem anglo-amerikanischen Klienten geläufigen Konzepte zum Ausdruck zu bringen.

2. Der deutschsprachige Anwalt muß innerhalb kurzer Zeit ein Vertragsdokument oder zB eine Spezialvollmacht in englischer Sprache oder in anglo-amerikanischer Form konzipieren, verfügt aber im konkreten Fall über kein geeignetes Muster.

   In einer solchen Situation kann er unter Zuhilfenahme der einschlägigen *Cut & Paste*-Abschnitte alle jene Formulierungen, die Standardfloskeln sind (*boiler plates*), übernehmen (und entsprechend anpassen) und seine (limitierte) Zeit auf die Ausgestaltung der wesentlichen inhaltlichen Punkte konzentrieren.

Zu beachten ist bei der Verwendung bzw beim Studium von Originaldokumenten/Mustern und insbesondere bei den Übersetzungen, daß sich in vielen Bereichen die Konzepte des anglo-amerikanischen Rechts und ihre begriffliche Ausgestaltung mit den entsprechenden deutschsprachigen Gegenstücken nicht zu 100% decken. In diesem Fall wurde sowohl bei den Annotationen/Marginalien wie auch im Glossar jeweils ein Vermerk („*") angebracht. Dies ist als Hinweis auf die konzeptionellen Unterschiede ebenso wie auf den Umstand, daß es sich bei der Übersetzung lediglich um eine Oberflächenübersetzung handelt, zu verstehen. Obwohl man in der Regel mit dieser das Auslangen finden kann, wird bei näherer Befassung eine weitergehende Erklärung des Begriffs bzw des dahinterstehenden rechtlichen Konzepts unumgänglich sein. Wo immer daher das Zusatzzeichen * verwendet wurde, wird zur Vorsicht bei der Verwendung von 1:1-Übersetzungen geraten.

* = Kennzeichnung
von nicht deckungs-
gleichen Konzepten
und Begriffen

Der Aufbau der Glossare erfolgte (in Unterkapiteln) jeweils in alphabetischer Form, so daß sowohl das Auffinden von englischen als auch deutschen Ausdrücken erleichtert wird.

4. ZUR GENERELLEN PROBLEMATIK DER RECHTSSPRACHE/RECHTSSPRACHEN-ÜBERSETZUNG

Bisher gab es nach unserer Erfahrung keine wissenschaftlich komparatistische Aufarbeitung der Fachsprachenspezifika der englischen und deutschen Rechtssprache. Wohl gibt es einige wenige Betrachtungen über die Eigenheiten der deutschen Rechtssprache (insbesondere von **Schönherr**), die jedoch mehr von der juristischen als von der linguistischen Seite das Phänomen der Rechtssprache kritisch untersuchten (mit Schwerpunkt auf dem Gebiet der Legistik), ebenso wie eine größere Anzahl von Arbeiten über die englische Rechtssprache (die eher von der Seite der Linguistik kamen), jedoch gibt es bisher weder allgemeines komparatistisches Schrifttum noch Arbeiten, die dem Rechtsanwender, der sich in einer fremden Sprache und unter Zuhilfenahme fremder/andersartiger Begriffe und Konzepte zurechtfinden muß, bzw dem Fachübersetzer in der Praxis Hilfe bieten.

Das vorliegende Buch erhebt keinesfalls Anspruch, in die erste der vorgenannten Kategorien, nämlich die allgemein komparatistische, zu fallen, zumindest jedoch nicht, etwas zu sein, das als eine wissenschaftliche (rechtsvergleichende oder linguistische) Aufarbeitung zu bezeichnen wäre.

Ungeachtet dessen haben wir eine praxisrelevante, intersystematische Gegenüberstellung versucht, wobei hinsichtlich wesensverwandter Sachverhalte zumindest ein für das Rechtssystem typisches Dokument seinem Pendant in der anderen (Rechts-)Sprache gegenübergestellt wurde. Durch diese Methode können ebenfalls allgemeine, vergleichende Konzepte gewonnen werden. Die zugrundeliegende Idee ist jedoch, durch das ganzheitliche Verstehen einer konkreten Sachverhaltslösung in fremden Rechtssystemen, insbesondere in der fremden Rechtssprache, kontrastiv wertvolle Erkenntnisse für den eigenen Umgang mit der fremden Rechtssprache zu erlangen. Neben den durchaus vorhandenen, aber nur durch Selbststudium zu erlangenden allgemeinen komparatistischen Ansätzen verfolgt dieses Buch aber hauptsächlich die Idee, dem Rechtsanwender wie dem Fachübersetzer konkrete Hilfestellungen für häufige wirtschaftsrechtliche Sachverhalte zu bieten. Egal, ob es sich um einen gesellschafts- oder vertragsrechtlichen Sachverhalt handelt oder um die Präsentation einer Thematik aus dem Bereich des Immaterialgüterrechtes, findet der Leser die dokumentarisch ausgestalteten Unterlagen (in Übersetzung der eigenen oder in musterhafter Präsentation jener aus dem jeweils anderen Rechtssystem) und kann sich so direkt vom anderen System bzw der dort üblichen strukturellen und sprachlichen Ausgestaltung eines rechtlichen Sachverhalts ein Bild machen bzw vorliegende Muster (*Cut & Paste* Abschnitte) auch als Arbeitsbasis für eigenes Konzipieren (*drafting*) heranziehen.

intersystematische Gegenüberstellung

ganzheitliches Verstehen der sprachlich-dokumentarischen Darstellung rechtlich relevanter Sachverhalte innerhalb eines Systems

7

Das Phänomen der Rechtssprache tritt im täglichen Leben in unzähligen Formen auf und kann nur schwer insgesamt erfaßt werden.

charakteristische Elemente der Rechtssprache

Die charakteristischen Elemente der Rechtssprache und die damit zusammenhängenden Probleme in der Fachsprachenübersetzung, mit denen der Rechtsanwender, der in zwei Sprachen, hinter welchen noch dazu verschiedene Rechtssysteme stehen, konfrontiert ist, lassen sich im wesentlichen auf drei Ebenen darstellen, nämlich auf der lexikalischen, der semantischen und der syntaktischen Ebene.

lexikalische Ebene

Phänomene der englischen Rechtssprache auf **lexikalischer Ebene** sind insbesondere:

antiquierte Ausdrücke

– antiquierte/obsolete Morpheme/Ausdrücke Bedeutungsveränderung/-verengung
  zB *merchant, servant* (für *employee*), *set forth, to undertake* (sich verpflichten*), *this day* (für *today*), *landlord* (für *lessor*), *witnesseth, bill of lading* (für *loading*)

Spezialbedeutung

– spezielle Bedeutung allgemeinsprachlicher Ausdrücke (sa Semantik)
  zB *consideration, public policy*

Kollokationen

– Wortkreationen/-kollokationen
  (Adverbialpräfixe, Präfixverdoppelung)
  zB *hereby, hereunder, aforementioned, hereinafter*

Gerundiv

– Gerundivkonstruktionen
  zB *sums payable* (für *sums to be paid*)

Einzelfälle

– spezielle Bedeutung der Wörter *thus, so, such* und *said*
  zB *thus/so rendered* (für *that has been rendered*), *such payment/the said payment* (unmittelbarer Bezug auf vorangehende Textstelle/Definition)

Repetition

– Repetition, Enumeration, Redundanz (tautologische Erscheinungen)
  zB *to covenant, agree and contract; representations and warranties; whether express or implied; lawful authority; mutually agreed; by and between; for and on behalf of; due diligence;*

shall

– besondere Verwendung des Hilfsverbs "*shall*"
  s Semantik

semantische Ebene

Auf **semantischer Ebene** weist die englische Rechtssprache folgende Besonderheiten auf:

Bedeutungskonzentration

– Bedeutungsdichte (Konzentration eines breiten juristischen Bedeutungsfelds in einem oder mehreren Begriffen)
  zB *consideration*
  public policy
  contra bonos mores

Bedeutungswandel

– Bedeutungsveränderung/-verengung bestimmter Begriffe, Versteinerung antiquierter Begriffe/Abweichung von der Normalsprache (sa lexikalische Ebene)

Scheinredundanz

– Phänomen der Scheinredundanz (Enumeration scheinbar deckungsgleicher Ausdrücke, die in der Normalsprache als re-

dundant erscheinen, in der Rechtssprache jedoch aufgrund der Kasuistik rechtshistorisch gewachsen und somit notwendig geworden sind)
zB *at any reasonable time or times,*
all normal and reasonable expenses,
for and on behalf of,
representations and warranties

- Phänomen der Umschreibung (*circumlocution*)   **Umschreibung**
zB *A agrees to transfer and B agrees to accept; A undertakes to deliver X/to employ B*
- besondere Bedeutung/Verwendung des Hilfsverbs "*shall*" (kein   **shall** Futurum, sondern Ausdruck der Verpflichtung)

Syntaktische Besonderheiten der englischen Rechtssprache sind: syntaktische Ebene
- komplizierte Satzkonstruktionen mit zahlreichen Verschachte-   diffizile Satzkonstruk- lungen (in Abweichung von der Gemeinsprache)   tionen
- logisch-normativer Satzbau (Sachverhalt/Tatbestand –> Rechts-   logisch-normativer folge)   Satzbau
zB *in the event of breach/buyer's default A shall ...;*
for the purposes of this Agreement asbestos shall mean ...;
- Wegfall (Elision) des konjugierten Hilfsverbs "*to be*" im Bedeu-   **Elision** tungsfeld von müssen (*shall*), soweit diese Konstruktion wiederholt auftritt (Enumeration)
zB *A to provide certain services and to supply certain goods* (für *A is to provide ...* mit der Bedeutung "*shall*"/müssen)
- syntaktisch neutralisierte Verwendung der allgemeinsprachlich   **Whereas** kontrastierenden Konjunktion "*whereas*" in Präambeln
zB *WHEREAS A is engaged in the business of manufacturing cars;*
WHEREAS B is engaged in the business of manufacturing certain tools and machinery;
(...)
NOW THEREFORE ...

Zweifelsohne sind eine Reihe der dargestellten Phänomene auch in der deutschen Rechtssprache präsent. Die vorstehend angeführten Konzepte der englischen Rechtssprache erheben keinen Anspruch auf Vollständigkeit, sondern sind vielmehr ein Versuch, die wichtigsten Abweichungen der englischen Rechtssprache von der Normalsprache darzustellen. Eine weitere Analyse kann aufgrund der im Praxisteil dieses Buches vorliegenden Muster erfolgen.

II. THE LAW OF CONTRACT

1. DOCTRINE

1.1. General Introduction

Contract law, the very heart of contemporary business law, is predominantly concerned with commercial transactions between two or more parties. A contract may be defined as an agreement between at least two parties which the law will enforce. There is no single code or statute regulating contract law in England or the United States. Instead, there is case law by means of which various general principles of contract law have been developed. There are, of course, some statutory provisions and regulations that apply to certain aspects of contract law ranging from consumer protection to the unfair terms of trading provisions, and there is the very important Uniform Commercial Code ("U.C.C.") in the USA which applies in commercial matters. Generally speaking, however, contract law is dominated by case law. The following is an introduction to some of the general principles of contract law.

case law

U.C.C.

1.2. The Formation of a Contract

1.2.1. The Offer

offer

A valid offer requires an expression of present intent to enter into a contract; that the offeree have actual knowledge of this intent; a definite description of the subject matter, e.g., in real estate a description of the land and its price or in the sale of goods the quantity; and reference to how long the offer is valid either stated in the offer or for a reasonable time if no reference to duration is stated in the offer. Furthermore, there is a requirement that the offer be believable from the point of view of a reasonable person. An offer is considered effective upon receipt and may be revoked any time before acceptance so long as the revocation is received by the offeree. The U.C.C. contains some exceptions to this requirement where the sale of goods is concerned.

intent
offeree
subject matter

1.2.2. The Acceptance

acceptance

The acceptance must agree in content with the offer, i.e., the acceptance must "mirror" the terms of the offer. Otherwise, the acceptance is treated as a counteroffer under case law. Under the U.C.C., any additions or modifications in the acceptance are treated as offers for an additional contract, but the acceptance is considered valid for those items which agree with the offer. Also under the U.C.C., additions made by merchants may become part of the contract automatically if the offeror fails to make a timely objection.

counteroffer

offeror

Unlike the offer, the acceptance is effective upon dispatch (*mail box rule*), not upon receipt by the offeror. The offeree, however, is

mail box rule

11

required to use a means of communication at least as quick as that used by the offeror. It is important to remember that the offeror always has the ability to control the manner and content of the acceptance by express stipulation in which case the foregoing would not apply.

consideration

1.2.3. The Doctrine of Consideration

The third and final element of a contract is consideration. This doctrine requires there to be a bargained for exchange between the

promisor, promisee

promisor and the promisee, and either a benefit to the promisor or a detriment to the promisee. A bargained for exchange simply means the existence of any bargaining, and does not include gifts or moral consideration. The benefit to the promisor need not have a certain economic value, i.e., the monetary value is irrelevant. Even a peppercorn would satisfy this benefit requirement, so long as the promisor receives something in the exchange for his/her promise. The detriment requirement is satisfied by the promisee performing an act s/he is not legally obligated to perform, or by the promisee forbearing from asserting a good faith claim s/he would otherwise have the right to assert.

writing requirement

Statute of Frauds

1.2.4. The Writing Requirement and the Statute of Frauds

The Statute of Frauds, which dates back to 1677 England, contains a general requirement of a writing only for certain types of contracts. This Statute is still in force in all states in the USA. The following contracts fall under the Statute: (1) promises to pay the debts of another; (2) promises in consideration of marriage; (3) promises of administrators to pay the debts of a decedent from their own property; (4) promises in contracts requiring more than one year to perform; (5) contracts involving real property; and (6) sales contracts exceeding $ 500. According to the Statute, a suit can be brought only if there exists a writing by the party to be charged, i.e., a writing by the defendant specifying his/her obligation. It is therefore possible that a contract is enforced against only one party due to the absence of a writing specifying the obligation of the other contracting party. Regarding the sale of goods, the Statute can be satisfied by the buyer making a partial payment or by the buyer receiving the goods.

parol evidence rule

1.2.5. The Parol Evidence Rule

Except for the types of contracts falling under the Statute listed above, a contract need not be in writing. If the parties make a written contract, however, what is known as the Parol Evidence Rule applies. This rule states that when parties have produced a writing

final expression of
parties' intent

which they consider to be the final expression of their intent to enter into a contract, any previous or simultaneous agreements may no longer be considered. In such a case, the content of the contract is defined exclusively by the writing.

1.2.6. Invalidity

An otherwise valid contract can be invalidated or rescinded under certain circumstances. For example, if one or both parties lack capacity; where the agreement is based on a mistake; where the contents of the contract are contaminated by illegality; and where consent of one of the parties was obtained by fraud, misrepresentation, or duress. The notion of unconscionability can also invalidate a contract. Arising from case law and adopted by the U.C.C., unconscionability exists when a party exploits its overwhelming economic strength resulting in "unconscionable" conditions on the other party.

invalidity

lack of capacity
mistake
illegality
fraud, misrepresentation, duress

unconscionability

1.3. Assignment

assignment

Except for cases where the identity of the party is important for the contract, claims can be assigned. Future claims, however, may not be assigned in many states although some exceptions exist, e.g., future wage claims.

Like a contract, an assignment requires consideration, and the same defenses concerning performance owed exist against the assignee as they would have against the assignor. Notice of an assignment to the debtor is not required.

assignee
assignor

1.3.1. Delegation of contractual duties

delegation of contractual duties

A third party may assume contractual duties with the same exception for highly personalized duties as noted above. If a duty is delegated, the performance requirement of the contract is satisfied by the delegate's performance of the contractual duty. If the delegate fails to perform the delegated duty, the creditor can bring a claim against the delegator, and in some cases against the delegate as well.

performance requirement

1.4. Third Party Beneficiary Contracts

Third party beneficiaries have a direct claim against the promisor. It is therefore unnecessary for a third party beneficiary to bring a claim against the promisee first. In deciding whether or not one qualifies for third party beneficiary status, U.S. courts focus on whether the party was an intended beneficiary. Such contracts are made usually for purposes of making a gift or for the payment of a debt.

third party beneficiary

1.5. Performance, breach, and other forms of satisfying the contract

performance, breach of contract

The obligations under a contract are satisfied by performance of the terms of the contract. The terms of the contract must be met regardless of whether the terms are expressed or implied in the

substantial perfor-
mance

contract. Such strict compliance is required with the exception of what is known as substantial performance. It provides some relief from strict compliance with the contract's terms and can be found in both case law and the U.C.C. Under the doctrine of substantial performance, a debtor who deviates from the requirements of the contract would have his/her claim reduced by the cost required to correct the deviations.

termination of contract

1.5.1. Termination

mutual recission

new contract

A contract can be terminated by mutual recission. In order to do so, however, it is normally required that each party still has to ful-fill part of its contractual obligations. An alternative to recission is the formation of a new contract. If the new contract is meant to re-place the original contract, the new contract would be a substitu-ted contract. If satisfaction of the original contract depends on performance of the new contract, the new contract would be refer-red to as an "accord and satisfaction." In this case, both the origi-nal and new contracts bind the parties until performance of the new contract is satisfied.

If obligations under a contract are delegated (see above section IIIa), the delegating party is relieved from his/her obligations only if the other party to the original contract approves the delegation.

impossibility

1.5.2. Impossibility

objective i.

subjective i.

There are two kinds of impossibility, namely, "objective" and "subjective." Objective impossibility results from circumstances for which the party is not at fault and, therefore, releases the party from its contractual obligation. Examples of this include cases where death or illness prevent the rendering of personal services; performance of the contract is illegal; or when the objective of the contract cannot be achieved. On the other hand, "subjective" im-possibility does not release the party from its obligations. An example would be a party's inability to render services on time.

frustration of contracts

Under the English system, a doctrine known as "frustration of contracts" was developed which moved the English courts away from the notion of strict compliance. This doctrine allows the court to assume an implied term that terminates the contract or al-lows for rescission. Although this doctrine also exists under U.S. law, American courts rarely apply it.

breach of contract

1.5.3. Breach of Contract

nonperformance
without excuse

repudiation

Breach is defined as nonperformance without excuse and gives rise to a claim for damages (a more in depth discussion of dama-ges follows). Defective and delayed performance can also be con-sidered a breach. In cases where one party declares his/her inten-tion not to perform, i.e., "repudiation," it may be possible to estab-lish a breach.

14

The notion of partial breach also exists. For example, when only a portion of the contracted delivery is made. This may constitute a partial breach entitling a party to damages. If the partial breach affects the value of the entire contract, the plaintiff may stop his/her own performance and sue for damages for a total breach.

partial breach

1.6. Remedies

remedy

1.6.1. Damages

damages

Money damages are the normal remedy for breach of contract. The intent of money damages is to put the nonbreaching party in as good a position as if the promise had been performed in full as originally agreed. Damages are calculated by taking into account actual damages including lost profits, reasonably foreseeable or consequential damages, as well as incidental damages. It is important to remember that damages are only a remedy for breach of contract. In the case of recission as discussed above, no action for damages is available.

money damages

The nonbreaching party is required to mitigate any damages s/he may be subjected to, i.e., the nonbreaching party would not be compensated for damages s/he could have avoided. For example, the builder of a bridge could not simply ignore a repudiation, continue to build the bridge, and then sue for the total contract value. Although, as a matter of principle, s/he is entitled to the full contract value, s/he would be under an obligation to mitigate damages and avoid any cost which can be avoided.

1.6.2. Specific Performance

specific performance

Contrary to many continental legal systems where specific performance constitutes the primary remedy for breach of contract, Anglo-American contract law doctrine views specific performance as a special remedy for breach of contract which is ordinarily available only when damages would be inadequate. For example, when the transaction involves real property or unique or irreplaceable goods which cannot be sufficiently compensated by the awarding of money damages.

1.6.3. Restitution and Quasi-Contract

restitution, quasi-contract

Restitution is defined as the return or repayment of a performance and, where appropriate, the payment of the value of any unjust enrichment which may have occurred, i.e., restitution quasi ex contractu. Both restitution and the payment of unjust enrichment may be obtained in cases of a total breach of contract. As an example, suppose A contracted with B for the sale of goods, but A erroneously delivered the goods to C. Restitution would consist of the return of the goods to A, while quasi contract relief would mean the restitution of any unjust enrichment of C as a result of the er-

payment of unjust enrichment

erroneous delivery

roneous delivery. In the latter case, the calculation of unjust enrichment would not be limited by the total contract value. It would be based on the value to C of the erroneous delivery, which could exceed the value of the total contract.

U.C.C.

1.7. The Uniform Commercial Code (U.C.C.)

The provisions of the U.C.C. apply mainly to merchants and, in most cases, govern the sale of goods. All states have adopted its provisions although several states have adopted it only with certain exceptions or amendments to apply. To insure uniformity, a permanent editorial board regularly reviews case law from the member states and recommends amendments which would help avoid different interpretations and applications. As a statute, the U.C.C. is subject to interpretation by the courts.

conditions

1.8. Conditions

A condition is defined as an occurrence or nonoccurrence of events which limit the duty to perform. In most cases, the failure of the condition or conditions would discharge the obligation of the promisor to fulfill his/her promise. Conditions are usually express, i.e., written, but also may be constructive, i.e., read into the contract in the interest of fairness. Conditions precedent are defined as conditions which have to occur or be fulfilled before the contractual obligation becomes binding or comes into force whereas conditions subsequent are conditions which would cause an obligation to cease as soon as they have been fulfilled.

express conditions
constructive conditions
c. precedent

c. subsequent

2. ANGLO-AMERICAN CONTRACTS IN INTERNATIONAL BUSINESS

2.1. Introduction

Due to the increase in international relations over the last few years and decades, German-speaking lawyers, legal counsels and businesspersons are increasingly faced with the necessity of having to deal with national and international transactions which are being carried out in a language different from their mother tongue. In such cases, the lawyer or businessperson involved will encounter very specific problems which require certain skills.

increase in international relations

language different from mother tongue

In order to cope with such situations and handle them successfully, the tasks to be performed have to be analyzed and the degree of involvement of the German-speaking lawyer/counsel in the transaction has to be determined first of all. The first step of the analysis is therefore to ask

transaction

(A) what type of transaction am I dealing with: (Is it a national or international transaction? Which law is to govern the transaction to be carried out? Which languages will be used in the negotiations and in the contracts, etc.);

law
language

(B) what role am I going to play in the said transaction: (Will I have to do the structuring of the transaction myself or am I only going to be a local counsel in the international transaction?).

role of counsel

The most important distinction is to be drawn between the organization/structuring of the transaction, according to the principles of one particular legal system/jurisdiction (from negotiations via documentation to final drafting of contracts), and the language to be used for the transaction. Nowhere does the inherent relationship between the language and the legal system become more obvious than in the case of the organization, execution and written documentation of national and international transactions in a language different from your own mother tongue.

organization/ structuring

In what case is the German-speaking lawyer or economic advisor actually confronted with the situation where s/he has to carry out a transaction in English? Basically, we have to distinguish between two different situations:

(1) The first situation is where an exclusively national transaction is to be structured and carried out pursuant to Austrian or German law, involving a person/party who does not speak German. In such a case a contract will usually be drafted in German, according to German or Austrian law, and will be translated into English (or any other language) afterwards. The problems arising in such a case are usually in the translation and explanation, since concepts and institutions typical of the German or Austrian legal system have to be explained to the non-German speaker. Apart from

national transaction involving a non-German speaker

translation and explanation

translations, explanations are a suitable means of communication for this purpose (since translations are often merely superficial due to different concepts in different legal systems).

In order to avoid misunderstandings and miscommunication it will depend on the skills of the German-speaking lawyer/counsel to explain such terms and concepts to the English-speaking client/colleague, and above all to describe the particularities of German or Austrian law.

Examples:

* acquisition of land in Austria

   things to be explained: Ausländergrunderwerb, Grundbuch

* formation of a subsidiary in Austria

   things to be explained: Firmenbuch, difference AG-Ges.m.b.H.

   Ausländergrundverkehr

(2)   If legal counsels are confronted with contracts in English and of an Anglo-American structure, the requirements are totally different from those in the first case. Above all, this will apply in the case of multinational or transnational transactions, however, it could also apply if clients from Anglo-American legal systems want to have transactions structured in Austria, Germany or third countries (e.g. Central or Eastern European countries), according to the structure they are familiar with and if, for the purpose, they more or less force their counsels to use Anglo-American standards.

multinational or transnational transactions

As for this second case, we again have to distinguish between three different situations:

(2.1.)   The simplest case of this type of situation is where a German-speaking counsel acts as expert in an international transaction to point out the implications of a transaction that has already been fully structured as far as his/her country or legal system is concerned. In most cases, this is done in the form of a "legal opinion", in which the counsel usually only confirms that – as far as his/her country/legal system is concerned – the proposed transaction is legal and enforceable. In this case, the German-speaking counsel's function is reduced to giving his/her opinion. Usually, however, this rendering of a legal opinion will be preceded by consultations, in which the German-speaking counsel may draw the attention to structural problems, if any, concerning his/her own legal system and may thus slightly affect or influence the final drafting of contracts.

expert in international transactions

legal opinion

(2.2.)   The second and much more complex situation is where a German-speaking lawyer is asked to structure an international transaction according to his/her country's law, which at the same time, however, has to be carried out with Anglo-American partners. In such a case, it normally happens that the organization and structure of the transaction becomes Anglo-American and thus takes precedence over national practice. This "**hybridization**" is a phenomenon which has become increasingly common and has gained more and more importance over the last few years. It actually affects our legal system, which is shown by the fact that you can find an increasing number of specimen contracts with typical Anglo-American features or characteristics in German textbooks or collections of specimen contracts (e.g. in case of agreements for the purchase of businesses).

structuring of an international transaction according to local laws

hybridization

It cannot be denied that this phenomenon of "hybridization" is a matter of fashion, which not only occurred due to the influence by Anglo-American clients/counsels on the organization of international transactions (although drafted pursuant to national German or Austrian law), but also because German-speaking counsels quite willingly started to use the structure and form of Anglo-American contracts. This may be explained by the fact that Anglo-American type documents are impressive as regards their design as well as their attention to detail, and also by the fact that the choice of this form brought about the flair of internationality.

(2.3.) The third case is more or less the second one taken a stage further, i.e. German-speaking lawyers are asked to organize transactions in third countries (as, for instance, in the former Eastern block countries). In this case there is even more hybridization, since German/Austrian legal institutions are often applied to changing civil law systems, some of which are still partly socialist and some of which are new. In addition to this, Anglo-American examples written in English are used. Only the future will show what results this complete merger of different legal systems, structures and contents is going to produce; however, we have to anticipate that this way of carrying out transactions has already become indispensable for the legal practitioner. That is why it is essential for him/her to be able to communicate in English, in particular, legal English, as well as to understand the structure of Anglo-American contracts.

organizing of transactions in third countries

changing systems

2.2. Typical structure of Anglo-American negotiations

structuring

When structuring international transactions following Anglo-American samples, as well as when structuring national transactions in which parties from the Anglo-American system are involved, it is first of all necessary to be familiar with the usual steps to be taken in the preliminary talks, organizing, structuring and execution of such a transaction, as well as to know what the documentation should look like.

documentation

preliminary
negotiations

In most cases, the legal counsel will only be asked for assistance after preliminary negotiations between the partners (mostly businessmen) have been concluded successfully. Normally, legal counsels and tax counsels will only be asked to structure the project after the transaction has become concrete. Usually, counsels will already be confronted with preliminary documents that constitute the essential parts of the transaction and show the understanding between the parties. Such documents may be called

letters of intent
memorandum of
understanding
term sheet

* letters of intent,

* memoranda of understanding, or

* term sheets.

due diligence

Documents of that kind usually also contain mutual promises made by the parties regarding loyalty and confidentiality. When the counsel is asked to come in, the structuring of the transaction starts, i.e. the lawyer is asked to start drafting the contracts. Apart from drafting, a "due diligence" procedure will usually be commenced (especially in the case of acquisitions) in the course of which the parties examine each other; depending on the type of transaction, the result of these investigations (the due diligence report) usually provides substantial information about the partner (an overall description of the economic and legal situation of the partner). In general terms, the purpose of such a due diligence is to check on certain preconditions that are important for the conclusion of the transaction.

opinion letter

The drafts constitute the subject-matter of the negotiations that will follow. However, even at this stage structural adjustments in the concept of the transaction can still be made. When the contracts/agreements have been negotiated, the partners normally request opinion letters from the legal counsel of the other party or even from other lawyers from all countries directly or indirectly involved in the transaction.

signing/preclosing

closing

When all essential problems regarding the contracts have been solved, it comes to the (ceremonial) signing and preclosing, during the latter of which the legal counsels involved give the final touch to the contracts and supervise relevant actions of the parties that are necessary for the execution of the transaction. Eventually, the last step is the so-called closing by means of which the transaction is being formally concluded, and all steps are being taken in order to start performance of the contract.

2.3. Structure of Anglo-American contracts

2.3.1. General characteristics of Anglo-American contracts

Anglo-American contracts are usually very complex, have a sophisticated structure and tend to explain all circumstances in great
detail. As for their appearance, they are mostly standardized,
which makes a general description of the typical structure of such
contracts comparatively easy. Various reasons may be given for
the fact that Anglo-American contracts are very complex and detailed. The two most important reasons are:

sophisticated structure

complex and detailed

  * the basic opinion that a document has to describe a transac-
    tion as precisely as possible, and that the contract should
    give an answer to or solution for any kind of situation one
    can think of.

precise

  * The second reason lies in the Anglo-American legal system.
    As it is based mainly on decisions (case law), the Anglo-
    American system is not familiar with codifications, as is the
    case with Continental European legal systems. Although
    there are codes for various fields in the individual U.S.
    states, as well as in the federal system, and also in Great
    Britain (above all in the field of commercial law we have to
    mention the Uniform Commercial Code, which is now ef-
    fective in all U.S. states), the contracting parties generally
    prefer to finally regulate all issues by means of the docu-
    mentation, although this is sometimes even done against
    codified regulations. Any possible further development re-
    sulting from case law will also be taken into account when
    drafting the documentation, namely by including decisions
    in the wording of the contract, as well as by trying to antici-
    pate future legal developments and to take them into ac-
    count – as far as possible – when drafting the contract.

*decisions, case law
no codification*

Additional reasons for the complexity of Anglo-American contracts
are the specialization of Anglo-American lawyers (and therefore the
special knowledge and expertise in certain fields), as well as the fact
that Anglo-American legal counsels can make use of manpower,
which is totally unknown to Continental Europeans (i.e. law firms
with several hundred legal staff are not unusual), as well as of prac-
tically inexhaustible collections of specimen contracts.

specialized lawyers

2.3.2. The typical elements of Anglo-American contracts

(A) The preamble (recitals/opening clauses/"whereas" clauses)

The preamble's function is to describe the background of the transaction as well as the intention of the parties. Depending on the
scope of the transaction, the preamble might consist of two lines but
may also cover several pages. It is important to know that the preamble itself does not belong to the contents of the contract and is
thus not binding on the parties; however, it may be used as a means
for the interpretation of the parties' intentions in case of disputes.

*description of trans-
action's background*

*not binding
means of interpretation*

(B) Consideration

The principle of consideration is one of the major principles of the Anglo-American law of contract. In order to create a contractual liability, or rather in order to make such obligation enforceable, both parties to a contract have to give something in order to get something in return: both parties have to take on obligations.

contractual obligation

The idea behind this is the mutuality of legal transactions or the concept of a bargain, respectively. Section 71 of the so-called Restatement of Contracts, Second (which is a quasi-codification of the law of contract in the U.S., which, however, is not binding) defines the prerequisite of consideration as follows:

mutuality concept of bargain

Section 71: Requirements of Exchange; Types of Exchange:

performance return promise

(1) To constitute consideration, a performance or a return promise must be bargained for.

(2) A performance or return promise is bargained for if it is sought by the promisor in exchange for his promise and is given by the promisee in exchange for that promise.

(3) The performance may consist of (a) an act other than a promise or (b) a forbearance, or (c) the creation, modification or destruction of the legal relation.

(4) The performance or return promise may be given to the promisor or to some other person. It may be given by the promisee or by some other person.

In the course of the centuries, the principle of Consideration has undergone a substantial change. Apart from the fact that the existence of consideration became unnecessary due to the fact that certain formalities were adhered to when a contract was concluded (execution of a Deed or using the so-called Seal), the contents of consideration itself were also carved out because of/by means of case decision. In simple terms: it is not being checked whether the consideration is adequate; ever very little consideration may lead to the validity and enforceability of the contract.

Deed, Seal

The phenomenon is reflected by the fact that the so-called "Whereas clauses" are followed by standardized clauses (so-called "boiler plates"), which stipulate the existence of consideration. These clauses usually read: "NOW THEREFORE, in consideration of the promises and mutual covenants herein contained, the Parties agree as follows:".

(C) Definitions

The preamble and the consideration clause are – at least in the case of more complex agreements – usually followed by a list of definitions. By using definitions, contracts become shorter and simpler (thus avoiding unnecessary repetitions), and complicated terms will be defined right from the beginning. Note that defined words and terms are usually capitalized or emphasized in some other way.

definition of complicated terms

(D) Conditions precedent

Definitions are usually followed by the actual description/explanation of contents. The description of the conditions that have to be fulfilled in order for the contract to become legally effective and binding is an essential part of every documentation. The conditions precedent will usually have to be fulfilled at closing.

(E) Representations and warranties

Historically speaking, the distinction between representations (which are statements regarding certain circumstances which are essential for the conclusion of the contract, and which are made by the respective other party) and warranties (which are declarations giving reasons for the warranty of one party vis-à-vis the other) was essential. However, this distinction has lost its significance and nowadays only becomes obvious by the fact that often similar lists of binding declarations regarding facts or circumstances are stated once under the title representations and a second time under the title warranties.

If a contract is concluded subject to Austrian or German law, the legal qualification of the representations and warranties has to be defined as to the legal consequences which may result if one of these essential declarations is breached.

(F) Covenants

Apart from the representations and warranties (which are statements regarding certain existing or non-existing circumstances), covenants are essential. By means of these covenants the contracting parties agree to perform certain tasks.

The distinction must be drawn between affirmative covenants (e.g. an obligation to report, making declarations, etc.) and negative covenants (e.g. declarations that one will not assume other obligations, etc.).

affirmative covenants
negative covenants

The systematic distinction between representations and warranties on the one hand and covenants on the other is very important, and sometimes hard for Austrian and German lawyers to understand.

In short: representations and warranties specify the presence/existence or absence of certain facts, factual aspects and circumstances/qualities of or in relation to a given transaction.

In contrast to that

covenants do not address facts or circumstances, but obligations to act (affirmative covenants) or to refrain from doing something (negative covenants).

(G) Defaults and remedies

Under this title, the parties agree what actions shall constitute a breach of contract (default) and what legal consequences (reme-

breach of contract

23

legal consequences
event of default

dies) each individual breach shall cause. In the case of an "event of default", the parties normally agree to inform the respective other party about the default s/he is accused of, and also agree on a period of time within which the party who is accused of the default may make it good. Such stipulations regarding defaults can be found, above all, in loan agreements of any kind.

For Austrian or German lawyers it is recommended that a detailed remedies clause be included in any agreement which addresses representations and warranties in order to clearly define the legal consequences of any infringement or breach of representations and warranties on the one hand, and covenants on the other. This, of course, only applies to contracts which are subject to Austrian or German law.

(H) Indemnification

indemnify

The promise to indemnify the other party to a contract is another important clause which is directly related to the abovementioned stipulations relating to representations, warranties and covenants.

(I) Term/Duration/Termination

contractual relationship

The next central clause to be discussed is the one regulating the term/duration of the contractual relationship, as well as the termination of a contract. The termination clause is also closely connected with the abovementioned clauses regarding a breach of contract (default).

(J) Force majeure

Anglo-American contracts usually contain numerous definitions of cases of force majeure, as the definition of events of force majeure is normally up to the parties. This is due to the absence of a respective statutory provision.

(K) Assignment/Succession

This clause regulates rights and duties regarding the assignment of rights, as well as legal succession.

(L) Notices

notification

Anglo-American contracts often contain stipulations regarding the notification of the other party; usually, the notification has to be served not only upon the party him/herself, but also upon his/her legal counsel in order for the notification to become legally valid.

(M) Waivers

This clause stipulates that failure to give notice of a breach of contract to the respective other party does not mean a waiver of the rights to which the other party is entitled in that case.

(N) Entire agreement/Merger clause

By means of this provision, the parties state that the entire agreement regarding their intentions has been laid down in the final contract and that no further agreements have been made. Furthermore, this clause, in most cases, contains the statement that all preliminary agreements made before the actual agreement have been incorporated into the final document. Merger clauses commonly regulate amendment proceedings.

(O) Severability

The severability clause demands that the legal invalidity of one single stipulation does not result in the invalidity of the entire contract.

invalidity of one stipulation

(P) Counterparts

This clause regulates that the contract will be executed in a certain number of counterparts.

(Q) Governing law clause

By means of this clause the applicable or governing law is being agreed upon.

applicable law

(R) Jurisdiction/Forum

By means of this clause the parties agree on the jurisdiction/forum; at the same time they normally agree on a process agent (a person entitled to accept writs of action/complaints), and exclude possible objections against the competence of a court.

process agent

competence of a court

(S) Arbitration clause/Alternative dispute resolution

Under this clause all kinds of arbitration clauses or agreements regarding alternative dispute resolution are being agreed upon.

(T) Languages

If the contract is executed in more than one language, or if the parties authorize the production of translations, it is recommendable to address the issue of which of the versions shall be the prevailing one for future interpretation in construction.

prevailing version

3. MUSTERVERTRÄGE

3.1. Kaufvertrag über eine bewegliche Sache (anglo-amerikanisch)

AGREEMENT FOR THE SALE OF A CAR MERCEDES 240 D/CHANGE OF OWNERSHIP

Kaufvertrag über ein Auto

This agreement for the sale of a Mercedes 240 D with Chassis and Engine Number as ... is made on this ... day of ..., 1990 between John Miller of 224 Charleston Road, Mississauga, Ontario, Canada, now referred to as the Seller on the one part, and Daisy Smith of 106 Broadway, Los Angeles, now referred to as the Buyer.

parties definitions/ abbreviations

WHEREAS

recitals

The Seller is a businessman and deals in importation/exportation and sale of motor cars.

seller's business

The said Mercedes 240 D was imported/exported by the Seller from West Germany, where he resided.

object of the sale

The Seller has agreed to sell the said Car to the Buyer for her absolute use without any incumbrances.

unrestricted rights (full ownership)

The Buyer is a staff member of First Western Continental Bank Ltd. with head office at 227 Market Square, Westwood, Cal.

details on buyer

The Buyer shall take delivery of the said Mercedes 240 D on the payment of the agreed sum of U.S. $ 6,500 (six thousand five hundred U.S. Dollars only).

delivery upon payment of purchase price

NOW IT IS AGREED AS FOLLOWS:

binding stipulations obligation to sell the specified object

That the Seller shall sell and the Buyer shall buy the said Mercedes 240 D with Chassis and engine number as ... and registered at Westwood County, licensing office as ....

That the price of the said Mercedes 240 D is agreed between the Seller and the Buyer at U.S. $ 6,500 (six thousand five hundred U.S. Dollars only).

agreement on price

That the Seller has now received the said U.S. $ 6,500 (six thousand five hundred U.S. Dollars only) from the Buyer as the future beneficial owner of the car (the receipt of which is hereby acknowledged by the Seller).

receipt of payment

That the Buyer, Ms. Daisy Smith, shall take all necessary steps and is duly authorized by the Seller, Mr. John Miller, to effect change of ownership of the said car.

effecting the transfer of ownership

That the Seller, Mr. John Miller, hereby covenants with the Buyer, Ms. Daisy Smith, that he will at all times well and truly keep indemnified the Buyer against all expenses and losses occasioned or

indemnification

27

defective title
(warranty of good
title)

arising as a result of this sale by reason of any defect in the title of the Seller or from the acts of any person or persons rightfully claiming through the Seller.

signatures
of parties

IN WITNESS WHEREOF THE PARTIES HAVE HEREUNTO SET THEIR HANDS AND SEAL THE DAY AND YEAR FIRST ABOVE WRITTEN.

... (Seller)

... (Buyer)

signatures
of witnesses

IN THE PRESENCE OF

(1) Name ...
    Address ...
    Occupation ...

(2) Name ...
    Address ...
    Occupation ...

(3) Name ...
    Address ...
    Occupation ...

3.2. Handelskauf (international)

AGREEMENT FOR SALE OF CEMENT

commercial sales
agreement

Agreement made this 27th day of October, 1990 between XY S.A., of Paris, France, a corporation organized and existing under the laws of France, herein referred to as Seller, and FH, Inc., of Chicago, Illinois, a corporation organized and existing under the laws of the State of Delaware, herein referred to as Buyer.

identification of
parties

1. Sale. Seller hereby agrees to sell and deliver and Buyer agrees to buy, receive, and pay for during the term hereof and in accordance with the provisions of this contract, the quantity set forth below of the products named below and at the prices hereinafter specified.

2. Products. In the performance of their respective obligations, seller will deliver and buyer will receive and pay for the following grades and/or brands of products of the kind and quality marketed by the seller at the time and place of delivery or as determined by seller:

product specification

Ordinary Portland Cement BSS 10/88

3. Quantities and Commencement. 100,000 metric tons (plus 10% or minus 10%) over a period of 10 months at about 8,000 – 12,000 metric tons per month (plus or minus 10%). Deliveries to commence during December 1990 and to continue for the fixed term until end of October 1991.

quantity,
commencement of
delivery

4. Price, U.S. $ ... per metric ton net FOB STOWED. Price is fixed for deliveries until July 31, 1991.

price

5. Method and place of delivery. FOB STOWED Marseille, France.

delivery terms

6. Territory. Buyer's distribution of products purchased hereunder without Seller's written consent, extend beyond the limits of the following territory: city limits of Chicago, Illinois.

territory

This provision shall not be deemed to give Buyer any exclusive territorial rights or any other exclusive rights of any nature whatsoever.

no exclusivity

7. Terms of payment. Seller agrees to execute L/C opened at prices higher than U.S. $ ... per metric ton and return the difference to the Buyer and/or to the party named in L/C provided, however, that if credit is extended and if at any time Buyer's financial responsibility shall become impaired or unsatisfactory to Seller, advance cash payment of satisfactory security shall be made or given by Buyer on demand by Seller, which may withhold further deliveries until such payment or security is received or on any failure to receive same, Seller may at its option terminate this contract.

terms of payment
L/C = letter of credit

requirement for
additional
security in case of
buyer's financial
problems

Discounts for cash, if any, shall not be allowed from or applied to or computed upon taxes or freight.

discounts

duration

8. Duration of contract. This contract shall continue in effect for a period of twelve months from October 27, 1990.

termination upon
default

In addition to all other available remedies, Seller may terminate this contract forthwith upon any default by Buyer hereunder. Any termination shall be without prejudice to accrued rights of Seller.

suspension of
deliveries

All rights and remedies of Seller are cumulative. Without prejudice to other rights or remedies, Seller may, during any default by Buyer, suspend deliveries.

cooperation

9. Cooperation. Buyer shall try to notify Seller of the expected loading dates for each month period one month ahead of each period.

All scheduling and nominations shall be arranged in the spirit of cooperation bearing in mind Buyer's needs and Seller's ability to perform.

approval
requirement
amendments

10. Approval. This contract shall not be binding on Seller unless signed by an officer or manager of Seller; likewise no modification shall be binding on Seller unless in writing and similarly signed. Commencement of performance prior to compliance with the preceding sentence shall not be construed as a waiver hereof.

In witness whereof, the parties have executed this agreement at Paris the day and year first above written.

Signatures

3.3. Liefervereinbarung (deutsch mit Übersetzung)

LIEFERVEREINBARUNG

zwischen

Stahlwarenhandelsgesellschaft,
5000 Köln

– nachstehend „Köln" genannt –

und

Austria Stahlproduktions-
Gesellschaft m.b.H.,
8010 Graz

– nachstehend „Graz" genannt –

1. Vertragsgegenstand

Köln wird für die Laufzeit dieser Vereinbarung von Graz nachstehend genannte
Teile, soweit diese von Graz herstellbar
sind und von Köln für deren Gesamtpro-
duktion benötigt werden, mit der Maßgabe der Wettbewerbsfähigkeit, ausschließlich beziehen:

. . .

. . .

. . .

Sofern Teile wegfallen oder hinzukom-
men, werden die Vertragspartner eine
entsprechende Vereinbarung treffen.

Graz verpflichtet sich, die von Köln bestellten Teile in der geforderten Qualität
gemäß den übergebenen Unterlagen und
zu den gewünschten Terminen zu liefern.

2. Preise

Die Preisliste, welche als Anlage 1 diesem Vertrag beigefügt ist, beinhaltet die
vereinbarten Notierungen bis zum
31. 12. 1990. In der Folge werden die
Vertragspartner vom 1. 1. 1991 bis
31. 12. 1991 und darüber hinaus jeweils
für 12 Monate eine Preisvereinbarung
treffen.

Es handelt sich immer um Festpreise für
den vorgesehenen Zeitraum. Die Notierungen haben sich an den Marktpreisen
zu orientieren.

SUPPLY CONTRACT

between

Stahlwarenhandelsgesellschaft,
5000 Cologne

– hereinafter called "Cologne" –

and

Austria Stahlproduktions-
Gesellschaft m.b.H.,
8010 Graz

– hereinafter called "Graz" –

1. Object of the Contract

For the life of this agreement, Cologne
will use Graz as their exclusive supplier
for the parts listed below, to the extent
that they can be manufactured by Graz
and are needed by Cologne for their
overall production, under the condition
of competitiveness:

. . .

. . .

. . .

If parts are deleted or added, the parties
to the contract shall enter into an appro-
priate agreement.

Graz agrees to furnish the parts ordered
by Cologne in the required quality in ac-
cordance with the supplied documenta-
tion and at the specified time.

2. Prices

The price list added as Enclosure 1 to
this contract contains the agreed prices
up to December 31, 1990. Thereupon,
the parties to the contract shall reach a
price agreement from January 1, 1991 –
December 31, 1991 and thereafter for
periods of 12 months each.

These prices will always be fixed for the
specified period. The prices shall be tied
to the market prices.

31

Sollten sich die Materialpreise derart verändern, daß diese in der Folge zu allgemeinen Teuerungszuschlägen führen, sind neue Preise zu vereinbaren. Sofern die Preise und Konditionen, welche Graz fordert, nicht wettbewerbsfähig sein sollten, ist dies von Köln nachzuweisen. Ein solcher Nachweis ist erbracht, wenn Köln Wettbewerber benennen kann, deren allgemeine Liefer- und Preiskonditionen bei sonst vergleichbarer Qualität günstiger sind als die von Graz. Tritt ein solcher Fall ein, so kann Graz entweder in die Preise leistungsfähiger Wettbewerber eintreten oder auf die Lieferung der entsprechenden Teile verzichten. Der Nachweis darf sich nicht nur auf einzelne Positionen des Lieferumfangs beschränken.

Wird von Graz ein Lieferverzicht ausgesprochen, hat Graz die Teile noch drei Monate zu den alten Preisen und Konditionen zu liefern, danach kann vereinbart werden, daß Graz die Werkzeuge, die sich im Eigentum von Graz befinden, zur Miete oder zum jeweiligen Zeitwert Köln überläßt.

3. Preisstellung

Die Preise verstehen sich frei Werk Köln, unverzollt. Die Kosten für die Ausfuhr-Zollabwicklung trägt Graz.

4. Zahlungsbedingungen

Die Rechnungen werden bei Lieferung in der Zeit vom 1.–15. am 30. des laufenden Monats, vom 16.–30. bzw 31. am 15. des Folgemonats mit 2% Skonto (Bedingung: telegrafische Anweisung) bezahlt.

5. Verpackung

Eine sachgerechte, mit Köln abgestimmte Verpackung ist vorgesehen. Die Kosten hierfür sind in den vereinbarten

Should the material prices change to an extent that they lead to general price increases, new prices shall be negotiated. If the prices and terms demanded by Graz are not competitive, this fact must be proved by Cologne. Such proof shall be considered as given if Cologne is able to name competitors whose general prices and terms for goods of comparable quality are more favourable than those of Graz. In such case Graz shall have the option of either supplying goods at the competitors' prices, or of declining to supply the respective parts. The proof shall not be limited to individual terms of the total order.

If Graz declines to supply goods, Graz shall continue to supply the goods at the old prices and terms for a period of three months. After that an agreement may be made that Graz shall lease or sell at current value to Cologne the tools which are the property of Graz.

3. Prices

All prices are ex works Cologne, excluding customs duty. The cost for export customs duties shall be paid by Graz.

4. Terms of Payment

For deliveries made between the 1st and the 15th of a given month, invoices shall be paid on the 30th of that month. For deliveries made between the 16th and the 30th or the 31st, the invoices shall be paid on the 15th of the following month, with 2% discount (condition: telegraphic transfer).

5. Packing

An appropriate packing approved by Cologne shall be provided. The costs for this are included in the agreed prices. A

Preisen enthalten. Im Zusammenhang mit einer Neuordnung der Lagerorganisation ist eine erneute Abstimmung erforderlich.

reorganization of the stock system shall require a review of the agreement.

6. Werkzeuge und Vorrichtungen

Die Werkzeuge und Vorrichtungen, die zur Herstellung der von Köln benötigten Teile erforderlich werden, sind zum Zeitpunkt des Vertragsabschlusses uneingeschränktes Eigentum von Graz, bis auf die auf der in der Anlage beigefügten Liste enthaltenen Werkzeuge, für die jeweils ein Leihvertrag abgeschlossen ist/wird.

Alle neuen Werkzeuge bzw Neubestückung von Werkzeugen der X-Klasse werden von Graz angeschafft bzw bezahlt und sind somit Eigentum von Graz. Graz verpflichtet sich, aus diesen Werkzeugen und Vorrichtungen Köln zu beliefern.

Graz ist verpflichtet, die Werkzeuge und Vorrichtungen auf seine Kosten in gebrauchsfähigem Zustand zu erhalten,

insbesondere

– die Werkzeuge und Vorrichtungen sach- und fachgerecht zu behandeln und für deren Wartung und Pflege zu sorgen

– die erforderlichen Instandsetzungsarbeiten unverzüglich sach- und fachgerecht zu seinen Lasten vorzunehmen.

Die vorgenannten Maßnahmen haben mindestens bis zum Erreichen der vereinbarten Kapazität Gültigkeit.

Schäden an den Werkzeugen und Vorrichtungen sind Köln unverzüglich mitzuteilen.

Graz teilt Köln rechtzeitig mit, dh unter Berücksichtigung der üblichen Lieferfrist, zu welchem Zeitpunkt der Ersatz der entliehenen Werkzeuge und Vorrichtungen in Folge normaler Gebrauchsnutzung erforderlich werden wird. Graz trägt die Kosten für den Ersatz der Werkzeuge und Vorrichtungen, die in Verlust

6. Tools and installations

The tools and installations which are necessary for the manufacture of the parts required by Cologne are the unrestrictet property of Graz at the time when this Contract becomes effective, with the exception of those listed in the enclosure, for which a lease agreement has been/shall be signed.

All new tools or replacement tools for the X series shall be provided or paid for by Graz, thus becoming the property of Graz. Graz agrees to supply Cologne from these tools and installations.

Graz agrees to keep the tools and installations in serviceable condition, at its own expense,

in particular

– to treat the tools and devices appropriately and with care, and to provide service and maintenance

– to carry out necessary repairs appropriately, without delay, at their own expense.

These measures shall be valid at least until the agreed capacity has been reached.

Cologne shall be informed without delay of damage to tools and installations.

Graz shall inform Cologne in time, i.e. taking into account the usual delivery schedule, at which point in time the replacement of the leased tools and installations will become necessary due to normal wear. Graz shall pay the costs for the replacement of tools and installations that have been lost or have become

geraten oder durch Umstände unbrauchbar geworden sind, die Graz zu vertreten hat.

Köln trifft die Entscheidung, ob Werkzeuge oder Vorrichtungen der Klassen Y – Z in gleicher Weise oder mit Rücksicht auf technische Änderungen in anderer Weise herzustellen sind. Für Werkzeuge sind folgende Hersteller freigegeben:

Graz kann bei Beschaffung von Werkzeugen für Teile für Köln unter diesen Herstellern wählen, sofern Technik und Preis mit Köln abgestimmt sind. Sollte ein Hersteller gewählt werden, der oben nicht erwähnt ist, so ist dies mit Köln abzustimmen.

Graz wird aus Werkzeugen, welche zur Herstellung von Teilen für Köln notwendig sind, Dritte nicht beliefern, sofern dazu von Köln nicht eine ausdrückliche Genehmigung vorliegt.

7. Technische Ausführung

Graz verpflichtet sich, die von Köln bestellten Teile in der geforderten Qualität, gemäß den übergebenen Unterlagen, zu liefern.

8. Lieferunfähigkeit

Für den Fall der Lieferunfähigkeit, aus welchem Grund auch immer, verpflichtet sich Graz, sofort die notwendigen Werkzeuge und Betriebseinrichtungen, die zur Herstellung der von Graz zu liefernden Teile notwendig sind, Köln für den Zeitraum bis zur uneingeschränkten Lieferfähigkeit gegen eine Mietgebühr, abzüglich der anfallenden Transportkosten, zur Verfügung zu stellen. Für Werkzeuge, die sich im Eigentum von Köln befinden, kann keine Miete erhoben werden.

Die Mietkosten errechnen sich wie folgt:

Die in der beigefügten Preisliste angeführten Werkzeugkosten-Anteile pro Stück, abzüglich der Zuschläge für Ver-

unserviceable due to circumstances for which Graz is at fault.

Cologne shall decide whether tools or installations of the Y to Z series shall be made in the same way or differently, in consideration of technical changes. For the tools, the following manufacturers have been approved:

When acquiring tools for parts to be produced for Cologne, Graz may choose among these manufacturers, provided technology and price have been approved by Cologne. If a manufacturer is chosen who is not listed above, Cologne's approval is required.

Graz agrees not to supply third parties from tools which are necessary to manufacture parts for Cologne, unless Cologne has given its express approval.

7. Technical Design

Graz agrees to furnish the parts ordered by Cologne in the required quality and in conformity with the furnished documentation.

8. Inability to deliver

In case of an inability to deliver, for whatever reasons, Graz agrees to make the necessary tools or installations for the manufacture of the parts to be supplied by Graz immediately available to Cologne in exchange for a rent fee, minus the transportation cost, for the period until the unrestricted ability to deliver is restored. A rent fee cannot be charged for tools which are the property of Cologne.

The rent fees are calculated as follows:

The shares of tools' cost shown in the enclosed price list, minus the surcharge for administration and distribution, cur-

waltung und Vertrieb, derzeit 4%, multipliziert mit der Ausbringung während der Mietdauer.

9. Wareneingangskontrolle

Die Vertragsgegenstände werden bei Eingang Stichproben unterzogen. Falls Teile nicht den Zeichnungen oder Spezifikationen entsprechen oder sonstige Mängel oder das Fehlen zugesicherter Eigenschaften festgestellt werden, wird Graz unverzüglich mittels Kontrollbericht Mitteilung gemacht. Über Ausbesserung und Nacharbeiten, die auf Kosten von Graz durchgeführt werden, muß zuvor mit Graz Einigung erzielt werden.

Für solche beanstandeten Teile ist Köln berechtigt, neben den gesetzlichen Möglichkeiten termingerechte, kostenlose Ersatzlieferung zu verlangen.

Graz hat das Recht, die mangelhaften Teile zu untersuchen, bzw sich Teile zusenden zu lassen, kann aber davon die gegebenenfalls kurzfristig notwendig werdende Ersatzlieferung nicht abhängig machen.

Die Rücksendung der beanstandeten Teile erfolgt auf Kosten und Gefahr von Graz.

Sollten Teile die Wareneingangskontrolle passiert haben und nachträglich vorher nicht erkennbare Mängel auftreten, so haftet hierfür ebenfalls Graz bis zur Auslieferung der Endprodukte durch Köln.

Bei versteckten Mängeln, die weder bei der Wareneingangsprüfung noch bei Prüfung des Endproduktes durch Köln erkennbar sind, haftet Graz längstens zwölf Monate ab Fertigungsdatum.

Für Ersatzlieferungen und reparierte Teile haftet Graz in gleichem Umfang, wie für die ursprünglich geschuldeten Lieferungen. Für Ersatzlieferungen beginnt die Gewährleistungsfrist neu zu laufen.

rently 4%, multiplied by the output during the rent period.

9. Inspection at Delivery

The contractual products shall be inspected upon delivery by means of random samples. If parts do not conform to the drawings or specifications, have other defects or are found not to have promised qualities, Graz shall be informed immediately by means of an inspection report. Repairs or reworking at Graz's expense requires Graz's prior consent.

For such defective parts, Cologne is entitled to demand, besides the rights granted by law, replacement free of charge and in compliance with the delivery schedule

Graz shall have the right to examine the rejected parts or to have the parts sent to them. However, they shall not make this a condition for the delivery of replacement parts, which may become necessary at short notice.

The rejected parts shall be returned at the expense and risk of Graz.

If the parts have passed the inspection at delivery, and are then found to have defects which were not noticeable before, Graz shall also be liable until the finished products are delivered by Cologne.

In case of hidden defects which were not noticeable during the inspection at delivery of the parts, nor during the inspection of the finished product by Cologne, Graz shall be liable for a period not exceeding 12 months after the date of completion.

For replacements and repaired parts, Graz shall be liable to the same extent as for the originally owed shipments. For replacements, the warranty period starts anew.

10. Höhere Gewalt

Höhere Gewalt, wie zum Beispiel Krieg, Streik, Aussperrung und Naturkatastrophen entbinden Graz für die Dauer der Behinderung von der Lieferpflicht

Höhere Gewalt entlastet Graz nur, wenn Graz die Umstände, welche sie begründen, Köln so rechtzeitig mitteilt, wie Graz dazu in der Lage ist.

11. Geheimhaltung

Die Vertragspartner sind verpflichtet, alle ihnen während oder aus Anlaß der Zusammenarbeit anvertrauten oder bekanntgewordenen Unterlagen und Informationen, die von dem anderen Vertragsteil als geheimhaltungsbedürftig bezeichnet werden, sowie alle Geschäfts- und Betriebsgeheimnisse streng geheimzuhalten und nicht an Dritte weiterzugeben. Dies gilt auch für die Zeit nach Beendigung dieses Vertrages, jedoch für maximal zwei Jahre. Jeder Vertragspartner wird alle zur Geheimhaltung erforderlichen Vorsichtsmaßnahmen ergreifen, insbesondere seine Arbeitnehmer und sonstigen Mitarbeiter zur Geheimhaltung verpflichten und jeglichen Mißbrauch verbieten.

12. Vertragsdauer

Dieser Vertrag tritt mit seiner Unterzeichnung in Kraft. Er kann von jedem Vertragspartner unter Einhaltung einer Kündigungsfrist von 12 Monaten zum Ende eines Kalenderjahres mittels Einschreibebriefes gekündigt werden. Für die Rechtzeitigkeit der Kündigung ist das Postaufgabedatum maßgebend. Eine ordentliche Kündigung ist erstmalig zum 31. 12. 1995 möglich. Jeder Vertragspartner hat das Recht zur fristlosen Kündigung aus wichtigem Grund. Als wichtiger Grund gilt insbesondere:

10. Force Majeure

In case of Force Majeure or Acts of God, such as war, strike, lock-out, natural disasters, etc., the contractual obligation shall be suspended for the duration of the impediment.

Force Majeure or Acts of God, however, shall only release Graz from contractual obligations if Cologne is informed as soon as possible of these circumstances.

11. Confidentiality

The parties to the contract are obligated to keep strictly secret all information and documents which they were given or became acquainted with during or on occasion of this cooperation, and which were designated confidential by the other party to the contract, as well as all business and trade secrets, and not to reveal them to third parties. This shall also apply for the time after the expiration of this contract for a maximum of two years. Each of the parties to the contract shall take all precautionary measures that are necessary to preserve the confidentiality. In particular he shall require the preservation of the confidentiality from all his employees and other members of his company, and forbid any kind of misuse.

12. Duration of Contract

This contract shall come into force upon signing. It may be terminated by registered letter by either of the parties to the contract, with a notice of twelve months at the end of a calender year. The date of the postmark shall determine the timeliness of the cancellation. The first date for a regular cancellation is December 31, 1995. Each party to the contract has the right to a termination without notice for reasonable cause. Reasonable causes include but are not limited to:

– wenn einer der Vertragspartner eine wesentliche Vertragspflicht verletzt und dieses vertragswidrige Verhalten trotz schriftlicher Aufforderung durch den anderen Vertragsteil und Setzung einer angemessenen Nachfrist nicht einstellt;
– Eröffnung des Konkurs- oder Vergleichsverfahrens;
– Einstellung des regelmäßigen Geschäftsbetriebes.

Ein Wechsel der Gesellschafter der Vertragspartner ist kein wichtiger Grund zur fristlosen Kündigung.

13. Erfüllungsort

Erfüllungsort für die Lieferung und Leistung ist Köln am Rhein.

14. Anwendbares Recht/Gerichtsstand

1. Für alle Rechtsbeziehungen aus dem Vertragsverhältnis gilt das Recht der Bundesrepublik Deutschland.

2. Für sämtliche aus diesem Vertragsverhältnis entstehenden Rechtsstreitigkeiten wird Köln als Gerichtsstand vereinbart.

15. Schlußbestimmungen

Es gelten nur schriftliche Vereinbarungen. Mündliche Nebenabreden sind ungültig. Änderungen und Ergänzungen dieses Vertrages sind demgemäß nur wirksam, wenn sie schriftlich vereinbart und als Vertragsänderung bzw -ergänzung bezeichnet werden.

Eine Übertragung der mit diesem Vertrag begründeten Rechte und Pflichten durch einen Vertragspartner bedarf zu ihrer Wirksamkeit der Zustimmung des anderen Vertragspartners.

Sollten einzelne Bestimmungen ganz oder teilweise unwirksam oder nichtig sein oder werden, so wird die Gültigkeit

– if an essential contractual obligation is violated by one of the parties to the contract, and if said party continues to act in violation of the contract despite a written demand to desist and the granting of a reasonable time by the other party to the contract;
– the opening of bankruptcy proceedings;
– discontinuation of regular business operations.

A change of the shareholders/partners of one of the parties shall not be a reasonable cause for a cancellation without notice.

13. Place of Performance

The place of performance for supply and performance is Cologne on the Rhine.

14. Applicable Law/Competent Court

1. The laws of the Federal Republic of Germany shall apply to all legal relations arising in connection with this contract.
2. Cologne shall be the venue for all legal disputes arising from this contract.

15. Concluding Clauses

Only written agreements as to this transaction are valid. Oral supplementary agreements are invalid. Consequently, modifications of or amendments to this contract shall only be effective if they have been agreed on in writing and have been designated as contract modification or amendment.

In order to become effective, a transfer of the rights and obligations arising from this contract by one of the parties to the contract requires the approval of the other party to the contract.

If individual terms of this contract are or become ineffective and/or void, either as a whole or in part, this fact shall have

des Vertrages im übrigen davon nicht berührt. Die Vertragspartner verpflichten sich, die unwirksame bzw nichtige Regelung durch eine solche zu ersetzen, die dem Vertragszweck möglichst nahe kommt.

Dieser Vertrag wird in zwei Ausfertigungen errichtet, von denen jeder Vertragspartner eine erhält.

Köln, den ...
Stahlwarenhandelsgesellschaft
Graz, am ...
Austria Stahlproduktions-
Ges.m.b.H.

no effect on the validity of the remainder of the contract. The parties to the contract agree to replace the ineffective/void term by one which serves the purpose of the contract as closely as possible.

This contract shall be executed in two counterparts, of which each of the parties to the contract shall receive one.

Cologne, this ... day of ..., 19
Stahlwarenhandelsgesellschaft
Graz, this ... day of ..., 19
Austria Stahlproduktions-
Ges.m.b.H.

3.4. Alleinvertriebsvertrag (amerikanische Form)

EXCLUSIVE MARKETING AGREEMENT

Alleinvertriebsvertrag

This Exclusive Marketing Agreement (the "Agreement"), dated as of ..., 1990, is made and entered into between the ABC Group, Inc., an Arkansas corporation ("ABC"), and XYZ GmbH, a German corporation ("XYZ").

agreement
date
parties

RECITALS:

recitals

A. XYZ owns all rights to a gadget used for washing potatoes (commonly known as the "Potatoe Washer"). The Potatoe Washer is based upon intellectual property rights owned by XYZ, including plans, specifications, patents, pending patents, trade secrets, and other related confidential documents and intellectual property (collectively, the "Technology"), some of which is further described in Exhibit A attached to this Agreement.

to own rights to

intellectual property rights, patents pending patents, trade secrets, confidential documents

B. ABC desires to obtain from XYZ, and XYZ desires to grant to ABC, exclusive marketing rights to the Potatoe Washer and to all improvements made by XYZ to its design. For the purpose of this Agreement, "XYZ Products" means and is limited to the Potatoe Washer and all later improvements in the design of the Potatoe Washer.

to obtain from
to grant to
exclusive marketing rights, improvements

C. ABC also desires to obtain from XYZ, and XYZ desires to grant to ABC, the right of first refusal for exclusive marketing rights on similar technology designed to clean other agricultural products such as beets and roots.

right of first refusal

AGREEMENTS:

Now, therefore, in consideration of the recitals and mutual covenants contained in this Agreement, the parties agree as follows:

recitals, mutual covenants

1. Grant of Exclusive Marketing Rights. XYZ grants to ABC and ABC accepts from XYZ the exclusive right to market, distribute and sell XYZ Products in the United States, Mexico and Canada (together the "Licensed Territories").

to market, distribute and sell, licensed territories

1.1. As used in this Agreement, "exclusive right to market, distribute and sell" means that XYZ shall not market, distribute or sell XYZ Products in the Licensed Territories except pursuant to the terms of this Agreement, and shall not authorize or license any other person or entity to do so, during the term of this Agreement.

pursuant to the terms of the Agreement
to authorize or license somebody

1.2. The terms "exclusive right to market, distribute and sell" include ABC's rights to (a) sublicense its rights pursuant to this Agreement to other persons or entities and (b) repackage and rename XYZ Products sold in the Licensed Territories. However,

to sublicense
to repackage
to rename

39

trademarks, trade names, copyrights term of agreement	*XYZ grants to ABC a license to use XYZ's trademarks, trade names and copyrights for the term of this Agreement if ABC chooses to use such trademarks, trade names and copyrights.*
right of first refusal	***2. Right of First Refusal.** XYZ grants to ABC and ABC accepts from XYZ the right of first refusal for the exclusive right to market, distribute and sell XYZ's Similar Technology in the Licensed Territories.*
marketing distribution to notify, availability	*2.1. If any Similar Technology becomes available for marketing and distribution in any of the Licensed Territories, XYZ agrees to notify ABC within ... days of such availability.*
receipt, notification	*2.2. ABC shall have ... days from the receipt of notification to negotiate with XYZ for the exclusive rights to market, distribute and sell such Similar Technology in the Licensed Territories. If for any*
to agree on terms less favorable terms	*reason ABC and XYZ are unable to agree on terms, XYZ shall not grant such rights to any other person or party on terms more favorable than offered by ABC.*
to exercise a right provisions, to apply to to negotiate	*2.3. If ABC elects to exercise its right of first refusal, all provisions of this Agreement shall apply to the new agreement except that the parties shall negotiate the prices to be paid for the Similar Technology.*
option manufacturing rights	***3. Option for Exclusive Manufacturing Rights.** XYZ grants to ABC, and ABC accepts from XYZ, an option for the exclusive right to manufacture XYZ Products and Similar Technology for distribution and sale in the Licensed Territories.*
	3.1. The option granted to ABC by XYZ includes the right of ABC to sublicense the manufacture of the XYZ Products or Similar Technology to other persons or entities.
to give notice to exercise an option	*3.2. ABC shall give XYZ ... days notice of its election to exercise its option to manufacture XYZ Products or Similar Technology, after which the parties shall negotiate the terms of an exclusive manufacturing agreement.*
price, shipment	***4. Price and Shipment of Products.** ABC shall pay the prices for XYZ Products contained in the schedule attached to this Agreement as Exhibit B or such other price as may be agreed on by the parties from time to time. All prices shall be stated in U.S. Dollars.*
day of payment	*4.1. If XYZ requests payment in German Marks, the rate of exchange shall be the rate of exchange from U.S. Dollars to German Marks quoted by ... Bank on the day of payment.*
irrevocable letter of credit payable in full	*4.2. ABC shall provide XYZ with written purchase orders specifying quantity and requested date of delivery. Every purchase order shall be accompanied by an irrevocable letter of credit from ... Bank in ... in favor of XYZ in the full amount of the purchase price for that order, payable in full upon delivery to ABC of the documents required by the letter of credit terms.*

4.3. XYZ shall ship to ABC by (method of transport) all XYZ Products or Similar Technology within ... days of the receipt of an order from ABC.

4.4. XYZ shall replace defective XYZ Products or Similar Technology returned within ... days of receipt.

5. Title and Risk of Loss. *Title and risk of loss shall pass from XYZ to ABC upon delivery by XYZ to ABC or ABC's designee.*

> title, risk
> designee

6. Term and Termination. *The initial Term of the Agreement shall be from the date of this Agreement through ..., 1993.*

> term, termination

6.1. XYZ grants to ABC an option to extend the Term for a period of ... years if ABC is not then materially in default of its obligations pursuant to this Agreement. To exercise such option, ABC must notify XYZ at least ... days prior to the scheduled termination date.

> in default of
> obligations

6.2. If either party is or becomes insolvent, or enters into an agreement with its creditors, or if a receiver is appointed for it, or either party files any petition or application under any bankruptcy laws or acts, an involuntary proceeding is filed in which a party is named a bankrupt, or either party is adjudicated a bankrupt, then the other party shall have the right to terminate this Agreement upon giving notice pursuant to section 8 of this Agreement.

> insolvency
> agreement with
> creditors, receiver,
> petition/application
> for bankruptcy, to be
> adjudicated a
> bankrupt

7. Covenants.

> covenants

7.1. During the Term of this Agreement, XYZ agrees that it will neither offer nor sell XYZ Products or Similar Technology in the Licensed Territories to any person or entity other than ABC nor negotiate with any person or entity other than ABC concerning any right to purchase or market XYZ Products or Similar Technology, except as otherwise contemplated by this Agreement.

7.2. XYZ shall take all reasonable action to enforce territorial restrictions of other licensees and distributors with whom it has contracted or with whom it may contract in the future.

> enforcement of
> territorial restrictions
> (protection of
> exclusivity)
> referral

7.3. XYZ shall immediately refer to ABC any person or entity that approaches XYZ to discuss the purchase of any XYZ Products or Similar Technology for use in any of the Licensed Territories ("Potential Customer"), and shall notify ABC within ... days of any such contact with a Potential Customer. XYZ shall disclose in writing to ABC the identity of any Potential Customer (including the name, address, telephone number and employer) and the content of any discussions with the Potential Customer.

> no direct sales
>
> disclosure of potential
> customers

7.4. XYZ shall maintain an ongoing manufacturing control program that will emphasize achieving a "zero defect" level of manufacturing quality.

> continuing quality
> control program to
> keep defect level low

7.5. XYZ shall provide ABC with engineering change notices, which shall be serially numbered, within ... days after they become effective.

> engineering change
> notices

protection of existing intellectual property rights

7.6. XYZ shall maintain in full force and effect, to the extent possible, its present rights to use the trade names, trademarks, copyrights and pending and licensed patents associated with XYZ Products and any Similar Technology.

indemnification for damages (broad definition) incurred due to

defects
fraud, breach of contract
infringements

*8. **Indemnity.** XYZ indemnifies ABC, its customers and its sublicensees from and against all debts, liabilities, damages, costs, demands, expenses, interest and charges, including attorneys' fees and costs, caused or arising out of or attributable to (a) alleged defects in XYZ Products or Similar Technology, (b) XYZ's wilfull misconduct, fraud, negligence, or breach of this Agreement or that of its servants or agents or (c) alleged infringement of any licensed patents, trade names, trademarks, copyrights or other protected rights of other parties in Germany or any of the Licensed Territories based upon ABC's exercise of its rights granted pursuant to this Agreement.*

default, termination aggrieved party notification to remedy/cure a breach

immediate termination procedure for winding up the business relationship after termination

*9. **Default and termination.** In the event either party is in breach of this Agreement, the aggrieved party shall be entitled to serve notice on the other party. The party in breach shall have ... days to remedy the indicated breach. If, after such period, the breach has not been remedied to the aggrieved party's reasonable satisfaction, such party shall be entitled to serve notice on the other party immediately terminating this Agreement. In such event, XYZ shall complete the sales to ABC for any orders which shall have been received by XYZ prior to the termination date and ABC shall have the right to dispose of all its XYZ Products and Similar Technology in the regular course of ABC's business. Failure to take any of the actions specified in this section does not constitute a waiver or condonation of any breach by either party.*

waiver/condonation

continuing waiver

*10. **Waiver.** The waiver by either party of any breach of this Agreement shall not be deemed to be a continuing waiver or a waiver of any subsequent breach.*

choice of law clause

*11. **Applicable law and language.***
11.1. The parties to this Agreement agree that German law shall apply in the interpretation of this Agreement.

prevailing/binding/ governing version

11.2. The parties to this Agreement agree that this Agreement shall be written in both English and German and that the English version shall be binding.

notices, to be deemed effective

mode of changing addresses

*12. **Notices.** Notices to any party to this Agreement shall be deemed effective when sent to the party by certified mail or when received by the party by personal delivery or facsimile transmission. The addresses to be used for notices are stated below. The parties may change such addresses by written notice to the other party and the change of address shall be effective if received within ... days prior to the mailing of the notice.*
12.1. XYZ
...
...

12.2. The ABC Group, Inc.

…

…

13. Attorneys' fees. *If any arbitration or litigation to enforce the terms of this Agreement is commenced, the prevailing party shall be paid by the other party all costs, including attorneys' fees, incurred as a result of legal action.*

legal fees, allocation of expenses for dispute resolution

14. Miscellaneous Provisions.

miscellaneous

14.1. XYZ shall take all actions necessary to maintain its patent rights in Germany and the Licensed Territories.

14.2. The parties shall cooperate in taking all actions necessary to obtain any requisite licenses, authorizations, approvals or consents in any jurisdiction, including, without limitation Germany and the Licensed Territories to permit ABC to market, distribute and sell XYZ Products or Similar Technology in the manner contemplated by this Agreement.

undertaking to cooperate in obtaining necessary approvals

14.3. If any clause in this Agreement is found to be invalid, that clause shall be separable and shall not affect the validity or enforceability of the remaining portions of the Agreement.

severability/partial invalidity

14.4. Neither party shall be liable to the other for failure to perform an obligation to the other under this Agreement if such delay or failure to perform is due to any Act of God, acts of the other party, acts of civil or military authority, labor disputes, fire, riots, civil commotions, sabotage, war, embargo, blockage, floods, epidemics, delays in transportation or when due to governmental restrictions. In the event of any such delay or failure, the party shall have an additional period of time equal to the time lost by reason of the foregoing acts in which to perform under this Agreement.

force majeure clause

14.5. This Agreement may be executed in counterparts and each counterpart executed by the parties shall be deemed an original for all purposes.

counterparts

14.6. This Agreement contains the entire understanding of the parties with respect to the subject matter of the Agreement and supersedes all prior agreements, written or oral, between the parties. This Agreement may be amended only by a written instrument signed by the party against whom it is sought to be enforced.

entire agreement/ merger clause/ integration clause

14.7. The various headings in this Agreement are inserted for convenience only and shall not affect the meaning or interpretation of any provisions of this Agreement.

headings

IN WITNESS WHEREOF, the parties have executed this Agreement as of this … day of …, 1990.

The ABC Group, Inc.   *XYZ GmbH*

By: …   *By: …*

   President   *Geschäftsführer*

3.5. Mietvertrag (österreichisch mit Übersetzung)

MIETVERTRAG

Der Eigentümer der Liegenschaft Salzburg, Denisgasse 19/14 als Vermieter einerseits und Herr Volker Wagner als Mieter andererseits schließen den folgenden

MIETVERTRAG

I.

Gegenstand dieses Mietvertrages ist die Eigentumswohnung top 14 im Haus Salzburg, Denisgasse 19, bestehend aus zwei Zimmern, Küche, Bad und WC.

Der Mietgegenstand darf nur zu Wohnzwecken verwendet werden.

II.

Das Mietverhältnis beginnt am 1. 8. 1990 und endet am 31. 7. 1992

Der Mietvertrag erlischt durch Ablauf der bedungenen Zeit. Einer Kündigung bedarf es hierzu nicht.

Der Vermieter räumt dem Mieter das Recht ein, das Mietverhältnis durch schriftliche Erklärung bis längstens 31. 12. 1992 zu verlängern. Diese Erklärung muß beim Vermieter bis zum 30. 6. 1992 eingelangt sein

III.

Der Mietzins besteht aus dem Hauptmietzins, den auf das Bestandobjekt entfallenden Betriebskosten und öffentlichen Abgaben, dem auf den Mieter entfallenden Anteil an der Erhaltung und dem Betrieb der folgenden, der gemeinsamen Benützung der Bewohner dienenden Anlage des Hauses: Aufzug.

Der Mieter ist zur Zahlung der Umsatzsteuer, die vom Mietzins zu entrichten ist, verpflichtet.

LEASE AGREEMENT

The owner of the plot/property located at Denisgasse 19/14, A-5020 Salzburg, as lessor on the one hand, and Mr. Volker Wagner, as lessee on the other hand, enter into the following

LEASE AGREEMENT

I.

Condominium flat no. 14 of the house Denisgasse 19, A-5020 Salzburg, consisting of two rooms, kitchen, bathroom and toilet shall be the object of this Agreement.

The object may only be used for residential purposes.

II.

The Agreement shall commence on August 1, 1990 and shall terminate on July 31, 1992.

The Agreement shall expire by termination of the stipulated period. No notice of termination shall be necessary

The lessor shall grant the lessee the right to prolong the Agreement by written declaration until December 31, 1992. Such declaration shall be served upon the lessor not later than June 30, 1992.

III.

The consideration to be paid by the lessee shall consist of the rent, a proportion of running expenses and public charges for the flat, and a proportion of the maintenance and running costs for the parts of the house used by all inhabitants: the lift.

The lessee shall be obliged to pay value-added tax on the rent.

Als Hauptmietzins wird gemäß § 16 (1) MRG ein angemessener Betrag in der Höhe von S 5.000,– monatlich vereinbart. An den Betriebskosten und öffentlichen Abgaben nimmt der Mieter derzeit mit S 1.222,22 teil. Der Mietzins zuzüglich 10% Umsatzsteuer ist monatlich im vorhinein am Ersten eines Monats in der vom Vermieter bekanntgegebenen Art (zB durch Einziehungsauftrag) in einem Betrag zu entrichten. Im Verzugsfalle sind Zinsen in der Höhe von 4% über der Bankrate zu bezahlen.

The parties agree on a rent (*) in the amount of Austrian Schillings 5,000 per month which shall be deemed adequate in accordance with Para 16 (1) of the Austrian Rent Act (Mietrechtsgesetz, MRG). At present, the lessee's portion of running expenses and public charges amounts to ATS 1,222.22. The rent, plus 10% VAT, shall be paid monthly in advance on the first day of the month; the payment shall be rendered in the way determined by the lessor (e.g. by collection order) and the amount shall be paid in one portion. In case of default or delay in payment interest in the amount of 4% above the bank rate shall be paid.

IV.

Der Hauptmietzins ist wertgesichert. Er verändert sich in dem Verhältnis, das sich aus der Veränderung des vom Österreichischen Statistischen Zentralamt verlautbarten Verbraucherpreisindex 1986 oder dessen Nachfolgeindex ergibt.

Ausgangsbasis ist die für den Monat 10/90 verlautbarte Indexzahl. Vergleichsbasis sind die folgenden Monatsindizes. Änderungen sind zu berücksichtigen, sobald sie jeweils 5% des ursprünglich vereinbarten Hauptmietzinses erreichen oder überschreiten.

Erhöhungen aus der Wertsicherung hat der Vermieter durch eine Abrechnung nachzuweisen, die spätestens sechs Monate nach Vorschreibung des erhöhten Mietzinses vorzulegen ist.

IV.

The rent (*) shall be subject to a stable-value clause. It shall be adapted in accordance with the fluctuations of the Consumer Price Index of 1986 published by the Austrian Central Statistical Office or the successive index thereto.

The index figure published for October 1990 shall be the basis for calculation. The following monthly indexes shall constitute the standards for comparison. Fluctuations shall be taken into account when they reach or exceed 5% of the originally stipulated rent.

Increases in the rent due to the stable-value clause shall be proved by the lessor by a statement that has to be submitted not later than six months after the rent increase.

V.

Ein Verzicht auf die Benützung der der gemeinsamen Benützung der Bewohner des Hauses dienenden Anlagen befreit den Mieter nur von dem auf ihn entfallenden Kostenanteil, wenn der Vermieter zustimmt und die übrigen Mieter den auf den Verzichtenden entfallenden Kostenanteil übernehmen. Die hiezu notwendigen Erklärungen sind vom Mieter auf seine Kosten einzuholen.

V.

If the lessee waives his right to use such parts of the house designated for common use by all lessees, the lessee shall only be released from paying his portion of the running expenses for such parts if the lessor agrees and the remaining tenants assume the portion of the said lessee. The lessee shall provide at his expense for the declarations required in such case.

Der Mieter erklärt, aus zeitweiligen Störungen oder Absperrungen der Wasserzufuhr, Gebrechen oder Absperrungen des Personenaufzugs, an den Gas-, Licht-, Kraft- und Kanalisierungsleitungen, Mängeln der Waschküche und dergleichen keinerlei Rechtsfolgen abzuleiten.

Der Mieter hat die vorübergehende Benützung und Veränderung des Mietgegenstandes ohne Ersatzanspruch zu dulden, wenn dies zur Beseitigung ernster Schäden des Hauses oder zur Durchführung von Erhaltungs- und Verbesserungsarbeiten am Haus notwendig oder zweckmäßig ist.

Die vorübergehende Benützung und Veränderung seiner Wohnung zur Durchführung von Veränderungen in anderen Bestandobjekten hat der Mieter zu dulden, wenn ihm dies bei Abwägung aller Interessen zumutbar ist. In diesem Fall ist der Mieter für die Beeinträchtigung seines Gebrauchsrechtes angemessen zu entschädigen.

Schäden im Bestandobjekt, die als ernste Schäden des Hauses anzusehen sind, hat der Mieter unverzüglich schriftlich dem Vermieter anzuzeigen.

VI.

Der Vermieter ist nach seiner Wahl berechtigt, von der Möglichkeit der Jahrespauschalverrechnung gem § 21 (3) MRG Gebrauch zu machen oder den auf den Mietgegenstand entfallenden Anteil an Betriebskosten und öffentlichen Abgaben nach Maßgabe ihres tatsächlichen Anfalles vorzuschreiben.

Der Nachweis der Höhe der Betriebskosten und öffentlichen Abgaben erfolgt in diesem Fall durch fristgerechte Auflage der Rechnungsbelege in der Kanzlei des Hausverwalters.

Ferner erklärt sich der Mieter damit einverstanden, daß der auf den Dienstneh-

The lessee hereby declares that the following events shall not give rise to a claim of any kind and thus waives his right to seek remedial action in connection therewith (*): temporary disturbances or cutting-off of water supply, defects of the lift, the gas and lighting mains, sewer pipes, defects in the laundry room or any similar defects.

The lessee shall be obliged to permit temporary use and possible changes of the object without compensation if such use should become necessary or reasonable for repair of serious defects of the house or for maintenance or improvement works relating to the house.

The lessee shall be obliged to permit temporary use and possible changes of his flat for the purpose of making changes in other flats if upon due consideration of all interests involved such measure may be asked of him. In such case the lessee shall be paid an adequate compensation for impairment of his right to use the object.

The lessee shall immediately notify the lessor of serious damage to the flat which has to be considered serious damage to the house.

VI.

The lessor shall at his choice be entitled to either make use of the annual flat-rate calculation set forth in Para 21 (3) of the Austrian Rent Act or to demand payment of the proportion of running expenses and public charges at the time they actually become due.

In the second case the proportionate amount of running expenses and public charges shall be proved by the house administrator by means of making the relevant invoices available in his office within the stipulated period.

In addition, the lessee agrees to bear the portion of the social security contribu-

mer entfallende Anteil der Sozialversicherung des Hausbesorgers von ihm nach Maßgabe des Betriebskostenschlüssels mitgetragen wird.

tion for the janitor to be paid by the employee (i.e. by the janitor him-/herself) in accordance with the scheme for allotment of the running expenses.

VII.

Der Mieter erlegt bei Unterfertigung des Vertrages eine Kaution in der Höhe von S 30.000 in bar oder durch Übergabe einer Bankgarantie über den genannten Betrag.

Der Vermieter ist berechtigt, aus der Kaution alle aus diesem Vertrag sich ergebenden Forderungen abzudecken.

Wird die Kaution während des aufrechten Vertragsverhältnisses auch nur teilweise verwendet, ist der Mieter verpflichtet, die Kaution unverzüglich auf ihre ursprüngliche Höhe zu ergänzen oder eine neue Bankgarantie vorzulegen.

Die Kaution ist binnen drei Monaten nach Beendigung des Mietvertrages abzurechnen

VII.

When signing this Agreement, the lessee shall deposit a security deposit in the amount of ATS 30,000 in cash or submit a bank guarantee for the said amount.

The lessor shall be entitled to cover all claims arising out of or in connection with this Agreement out of such deposit.

If the security deposit should be used during the term of the Agreement – even if only in part – the lessee shall be obliged to supplement the deposit up to the original amount or to submit a new bank guarantee.

This security deposit shall be accounted for within three months of termination of the Lease Agreement.

VIII.

Der Mieter bestätigt, das Bestandobjekt in ordnungsgemäßem Zustand übernommen zu haben, und verpflichtet sich, es in einem ebensolchen Zustand zu erhalten.

Etwaige nach Übergabe der Wohnung hervorkommende Mängel, die die Brauchbarkeit der Wohnung oder eines Ausstattungsmerkmales der Wohnung beeinträchtigen, sind dem Vermieter unverzüglich schriftlich anzuzeigen.

Behebt der Vermieter diese Mängel binnen angemessener Frist, ist der Mieter nicht berechtigt, weitere Ansprüche zu stellen, oder Rechtsfolgen abzuleiten.

Veränderungen des Mietgegenstandes dürfen nur mit Zustimmung des Vermieters durchgeführt werden.

Bei Zurückstellung des Mietgegenstandes hat der Mieter den vorherigen Zustand herzustellen.

Macht der Mieter gemäß § 10 MRG Ersatzansprüche für Aufwendungen in der

VIII.

The lessee confirms that he has taken over the object in proper condition and agrees to maintain such condition.

The lessee shall immediately notify the lessor in writing of defects that impair the use of the flat or equipment thereof and which were detected only after its transfer.

If the lessor repairs such defects within a reasonable time, the lessee shall not be entitled to assert further claims or seek remedial action.

Changes of the object may only be made with the lessor's consent

When returning the object the lessee shall reinstate the previous condition.

If the lessee in accordance with Para 10 of the Austrian Rent Act, claimed com-

gemieteten Wohnung geltend, so ist der Vermieter auf Kosten des Mieters berechtigt, den Wert dieser Aufwendungen durch einen Sachverständigen feststellen zu lassen.

pensation for expenses incurred in connection with the flat, the lessor shall be entitled to have the value of such expenses determined by an expert at lessee's cost.

IX.

Jede Untervermietung des Bestandobjektes ist verboten.

IX.

The lessee shall not sublet the apartment.

X.

Als Kündigungsgrund, der im Sinne des § 30 (2) Z 13 MRG als wichtig und bedeutsam anzusehen ist, wird die Änderung des vertraglich festgelegten Verwendungszweckes vereinbart.

X.

The parties agree that a change in the mode of using the flat as stipulated hereby shall constitute an important reason for termination of the Agreement within the meaning of Para 30 (2) 13 of the Austrian Rent Act.

XI.

Der Vermieter oder ein von ihm Beauftragter ist aus triftigem Grund und bei Gefahr in Verzug jederzeit, sonst gegen vorherige Anmeldung, berechtigt, das Bestandobjekt zu betreten.

XI.

The lessor or a representative of his shall be entitled to enter the premises upon prior notification to the lessee; in case of imminent danger and for good cause he shall be entitled to do so at any time.

XII.

Der Mieter ist zur Einhaltung der Hausordnung verpflichtet.
Die Haltung von Tieren ist nur mit Zustimmung des Vermieters gestattet.

XII.

The lessee shall be obliged to comply with the house rules.
Pets shall only be allowed with the lessor's consent

XIII.

Das Bestandsobjekt enthält die in der angeschlossenen Inventarliste angeführten Gegenstände

XIII.

The object comprises all items listed on the attached inventory.

XIV.

Der Mieter ist nicht berechtigt, Forderungen gegen den Vermieter mit dem Mietzins aufzurechnen oder den Mietzins ganz oder teilweise zurückzubehalten, es sei denn, daß der Vermieter zahlungsunfähig ist oder daß die Forderung mit dem Mietverhältnis zusammenhängt, gerichtlich festgestellt oder vom Vermieter anerkannt wurde.

XIV.

The lessee shall not be entitled to offset claims against the lessor against the rent or to entirely or partially retain the rent unless the lessor is insolvent, the claim is related to the Agreement, or the claim was approved of by court or by the lessor.

XV.

Alle wie immer gearteten Änderungen des Mietvertrages bedürfen der schriftlichen Form. Mündliche Zusagen sind ungültig, solange sie nicht schriftlich bestätigt werden.

Ebenso bedarf das Abgehen von dieser Formvorschrift der Schriftform.

XV.

Any amendments to this Lease Agreement shall be made in writing in order to be effective. Oral promises shall be ineffective until confirmed in writing.

If the above formal requirement was amended or changed, such amendment or change has to be made in writing, too, in order to be effective.

XVI.

Die Vertragsteile stellen einvernehmlich fest, daß keine wie immer gearteten Nebenabreden neben diesem Vertrag bestehen, sondern daß dieser Vertrag abschließend alle Rechte und Pflichten der Vertragsteile enthält.

XVI.

The contracting parties unanimously state that no other agreements of any kind exist but that this Agreement contains all rights and duties of the contracting parties.

XVII.

Die Kosten der Errichtung dieses Mietvertrages trägt der Mieter.

XVII.

All costs arising in connection with the setting-up of this Agreement shall be borne by the lessee.

XVIII.

Dieser Mietvertrag wird in drei Ausfertigungen errichtet, wovon jeder Vertragsteil eine erhält; eine Ausfertigung ist für das Finanzamt für Gebühren und Verkehrsteuern bestimmt.

Wien, am ...
Unterschriften ...

XVIII.

This Lease Agreement shall be made in triplicate, in order that each contracting party and the Finanzamt für Gebühren und Verkehrssteuern (i.e. the competent tax office) shall receive one.

Vienna, ...
Signatures ...

3.6. MIETVERTRAG (HYBRIDFORM)

MIETVERTRAG

LEASE CONTRACT

1. Frau Beate Müller, wohnhaft in 5000 Köln 21, Mühlenweg 3 (im folgenden als „Vermieter" bezeichnet)

vermietet an

Herrn Hubert Meier (im folgenden als „Mieter" bezeichnet)

eine unmöblierte Wohnung in 5060 Bergisch-Gladbach 3, Reuterstraße 6.

Aufgrund dieses Vertrages hat der Mieter auch das Recht, die gemeinschaftlichen Räumlichkeiten und Einrichtungen des Gebäudes zu benützen

2. Der Mietgegenstand besteht aus drei Zimmern, Küche, Bad, WC und einem Kellerabteil.

Eine Liste der vom Vermieter beigestellten und vom Mieter übernommenen Gegenstände und deren Zustand zum Zeitpunkt der Übernahme ist diesem Vertrag als Anhang beigefügt.

3. Der Mieter erklärt sich bereit, dem Vermieter als Miete monatlich DM 1.080,– im voraus am Ersten jeden Monats zu bezahlen. (Bankkonto Nr.: ...)

4. Kosten für Strom, Wasser und Heizung sind nicht in der Miete enthalten und werden vom Mieter getragen.

5. Keinerlei andere Ausgaben, Gebühren und Steuern irgendwelcher Art außer den in diesem Vertrag vereinbarten werden vom Mieter getragen

6. Der Mieter übernimmt den Mietgegenstand mit allem Zubehör und allen Einrichtungsgegenständen für einen Zeitraum von zwei Jahren beginnend mit dem 1. April 1990.

7. Dieser Vertrag kann vom Mieter und Vermieter mit dreimonatiger Frist schriftlich gekündigt werden.

8. Der Mieter bestätigt, daß er die Wohnung und alle im Anhang angeführten

1. Mrs. Beate Müller, residing at 5000 Cologne 21, Mühlenweg 3 (hereinafter referred to as "lessor")

agrees to let to

Mr. Hubert Meier (hereinafter referred to as "lessee")

an unfurnished apartment at 5060 Bergisch-Gladbach 3, Reuterstrasse 6.

Rights under this lease include the right to use the common areas and facilities of the building.

2. The premises as defined by this contract consist of three rooms, a kitchen, a bathroom, a toilet and a cellar compartment.

A list of items furnished by lessor and the condition in which they are taken over by lessee are contained in an Annex to this contract.

3. Lessee agrees to pay to lessor a rent of DM 1,080 per month, payable in advance on the first day of every month. (Bank Account No.: ...)

4. Expenses for electricity, water and heating are not included in the rent and shall be the responsibility of the lessee.

5. No other expenses, fees or taxes of any kind, except those stipulated in this contract, shall be borne by lessee.

6. Lessee shall hold the said premises with all appurtenances and furnishings for a term of two years to commence on April 1, 1990.

7. This contract may be terminated by lessee and lessor on three months' written notice.

8. Lessees confirms that the apartment and all items listed in the Annex have

Gegenstände in gutem Zustand übernommen hat, soweit nicht auf der zur Zeit seines Einzuges in die Wohnung aufzustellenden Bestandliste anders angegeben.

9. Der Mieter ist für die Behebung aller Schäden verantwortlich, die von ihm bzw von Angehörigen seiner Familie oder seines Haushalts in der Wohnung verursacht wurden, sowie für die normale Instandhaltung der Wohnung während der Dauer des Mietverhältnisses.

10. Für Reparaturen von baulichen Schäden bzw an den Gas- und Stromhauptleitungen, Installationen, der Kanalisation und der Zentralheizung sowie aller anderen Reparaturen, die über die normale Instandhaltung hinausgehen, ist nicht der Mieter verantwortlich, es sei denn, daß sie durch ihn verursacht wurden. Wenn solche Reparaturen notwendig werden, hat der Mieter unverzüglich den Vermieter zu verständigen.

11. Der Mieter verpflichtet sich, die Wohnung und die beigestellten Gegenstände schonend zu benützen und sie dem Vermieter, abgesehen von der normalen Abnützung, in dem übernommenen Zustand zurückzustellen; der Vermieter erhebt keinen Anspruch auf etwaige Renovierungskosten. Ohne Zustimmung des Vermieters hat der Mieter keine vom Vermieter beigestellten Gegenstände aus der Wohnung zu entfernen.

12. Abänderungen und Zusatzvereinbarungen zu diesem Vertrag bedürfen der schriftlichen Form.

Datum: 21. März 1990

Vermieter

Mieter

Zeuge

been taken over by him in good condition unless otherwise stated on the inventory to be established at the time when lessee moves into the apartment.

9. Lessee shall be responsible for repair of any damage to the apartment caused by him or members of his family or of his household as well as for normal maintenance of the apartment during the period of the lease.

10. Repairs of structural damage, damage to the mains of gas and electricity, piping, drainage and central heating systems or any other repairs beyond regular maintenance etc. are not the responsibility of lessee unless caused by him. Lessee shall inform lessor promptly whenever repairs of this kind become necessary.

11. Lessee agrees to take good care of the apartment and items furnished and return them to lessor in the condition in which they were taken over, except for normal wear and tear. Lessor will not claim any ensuing renovation costs. Lessee will not remove any objects furnished by lessor from the apartment without consent of lessor.

12. Any amendments and additions to this contract shall be agreed upon in writing.

Date: March 21, 1990

Lessor

Lessee

Witness

3.7. Mietvertrag (amerikanisch)

STANDARD LEASE NUMBER – 2345

agreement

THIS AGREEMENT made this 25th day of April, 1986 by and between OLD ILY LIMITED PARTNERSHIP ... (lessor) and the following named individual(s):
Harry B., Franz H., Jayshree P. (lessee(s))

WITNESSETH

lessor, to rent, lessee, apt (= apartment), furnished, term

to expire

That the lessor hereby rents to the lessees Apt. 112-02 ILY DRIVE, OLD ILY ... APARTMENTS; CHARLOTTESVILLE, VA 22901 2-D FP RGP (FURNISHED) for a term to begin at 4:30 P.M. on the 12th day of JULY, 1986 and to expire at 10:00 A.M. on the 11th day of JULY, 1987.

lease, renewable

new lease
termination of the lease
rental payable

installments

This lease is NOT automatically renewable. Lessee(s) desiring to remain in this apartment for another year should discuss the possibility of NEGOTIATION of a NEW LEASE at least 90 days prior to termination of this lease.

Yearly rental for the above defined term shall be $ 6,360.00, payable at OLD ILY ... RENTAL OFFICE, 100 ILY DRIVE, CHARLOTTESVILLE, VA 22901 in monthly installments of ...

due and payable

late fee

default in payment, rent, complaints premises, breach of covenant, Act of God

security deposit

The first installment becoming due and payable on the 12th day of JULY, 1986, with each succeeding installment becoming due on the 1st day of each of the succeeding 12 months. Each installment is subject to a $ 25.00 late fee if more than four (4) days past due. The lessor may terminate the lease and re-enter for four (4) days' default in payment of any part of installment of rent or for substantiated complaints of any undue noise or improper behavior on the premises or for the breach of any other covenant herein contained. Acts of God or fire rendering premises unusable for a substantial period shall automatically terminate the lease. Required and agreed Security Deposit $ 300.00.

private residence
to assign, to sublet

joint and several liability

Premises shall be used for private residence purposes only and lessee(s) shall not assign or sublet all or any part of the premises without the written consent of the lessor. NO PETS ALLOWED and only 3 named lessee(s), or authorized substitute sublessee(s), shall occupy the premises. No pianos, water beds, or other heavy objects allowed on premises. Joint and several liability applies.

reasonable
negligence

bill(-s)

Premises shall be kept in reasonable repair by the lessor, except that repairs or service calls made necessary by the negligence of the lessee(s) shall be paid for by the lessee(s). Electric bills shall be paid by lessee(s); water bills by lessor.

Lessor and his agents shall have the right of entry at any reasonable time for inspection, repair, redecoration, or re-rental without prior notice and any such entry shall not constitute termination or constructive eviction of lessee(s).

Other Agreements: (1) Lessee(s) agree to all provisions of both pages one and two of this lease and to abide by all Rules & Regulations of the lessor as and when issued. (2) Breach of NO PETS covenant by lessee(s) shall constitute an EMERGENCY for the lessor and the lessee(s) agree that the lessor or his agents shall have the right to enter the premises without notice and to remove the pet permanently as a trespasser.

All provisions of this lease (page 1 & 2) are covenants of the parties as WITNESS THE FOLLOWING SIGNATURES AND SEALS:

lessee	*(SEAL)*
lessee	*(SEAL)*
lessee	*(SEAL)*
lessor/Owner	*OLD ILY PARTNERSHIP*
	(SEAL)

NAME   *TITLE*

Page Two

RESPONSIBILITIES TO BE ASSUMED BY THE LESSEE(S) BEFORE VACATING APARTMENT:

1. Clean apartment thoroughly, including balconies, closets and patios.

2. Stove, burners, oven, oven racks and broiler pans must be well cleaned. Leave oven door open.

3. Refrigerator and freezer must be cleaned thoroughly. Leave refrigerator off and door open.

4. All non-carpeted floors must be cleaned and waxed. Do NOT put wax on top of dirt. All carpets must be clean and free of spots, which will require "steam-clean" shampooing.

5. Clean bathroom fixtures and walls (especially in shower/tub area).

6. Remove ashes from fireplace and clean thoroughly.

7. Damaged premises (including furniture, fixtures and appliances), must be repaired or replaced if repair is not feasible.

8. All keys (including mailbox and patio door) must be returned or replaced by lessee(s).

Failure to comply with any of the above items or to return the apartment in the same general condition as received will result in a charge to the lessee(s) which will be deducted from lessee(s) Security Deposit. Check out inspection will be made at the earliest convenience of the lessor after lessee(s) [or sublessee(s)] have paid their rent IN FULL, turned in all keys and have no further need to occupy the apartment for any reason. Security Deposits

---

Margin notes:

agent(-s), right of entry for inspection prior notice, to constitute termination, constructive eviction

to abide by, rules & regulations, breach, covenant, emergency

to remove permanently, trespasser

covenants, witness, signatures, seals

to assume a responsibility

furniture, fixtures, appliances, feasible

failure to comply with condition, charge

at the earliest convenience, to pay in full

at somebody's option	*will NOT be applied to rent, except at the lessor's option on breach of lease only. Security Deposits will be returned by mail only, within thirty (30) days after the expiration of the lease.*
expiration	*In case of lessee(s) breach of any covenant of this lease agreement, the lessor or his agents shall have the right to:*
notice, legal proceedings	*(a) take immediate possession of, or prohibit lessee(s), their legal assigns, sublessee(s) or guests from the leased premises without notice or legal proceedings;*
assign, trespass conversion	*(b) remove all persons and/or their property (INCLUDING PETS) from the premises without liability to the lessee(s), sublessee(s), assigns, guests or anyone else for any manner of trespass, conversion or other damage or injury;*
liquidated damages right to sue eviction	*(c) retain lessee(s) deposit as liquidated damages for breach of lease, and right to sue for actual damages and other costs not covered thereby, notwithstanding the fact that an eviction may have already occurred.*
	Special Agreements: (1) Separate "damage list" furnished to lessee(s) is hereby made a part of this lease. (2) Separate maintenance inspection furnished to lessee(s) stating that smoke detector is present, has a working battery and is in good working order.
to initial	*Initialed* *Initialed* *Initialed* *By:* *By:* *By* *Lessor* *Lessee* *Lessee*

3.8. Geschäftsführerdienstvertrag (österreichisch mit Übersetzung)

GESCHÄFTSFÜHRERDIENST-
VERTRAG

zwischen der Firma XYZ Gesellschaft m.b.H., 1010 Wien, Kärntnerstraße 17, vertreten durch ihre Generalversammlung (im folgenden kurz Dienstgeberin bzw Gesellschaft genannt)

und

Herrn Peter Müller, geboren am 1. 5. 1945, 1190 Wien, Cobenzlgasse 17 (im folgenden kurz Dienstnehmer bzw Geschäftsführer genannt)

wird folgender Vertrag geschlossen:

PRÄAMBEL

Mit Gesellschafterbeschluß vom heutigen Tage wurde Herr Peter Müller zum einzelvertretungsbefugten Geschäftsführer der Gesellschaft bestellt. Herr Müller hat diese Bestellung angenommen.

I.
Verantwortungsbereich

Der Dienstnehmer ist als handelsrechtlicher Geschäftsführer der Dienstgeberin als leitender Angestellter im Sinne des § 1 (2) Z 8 Arbeitszeitgesetz anzusehen.

Der Geschäftsführer leitet die Gesellschaft eigenverantwortlich unter Einhaltung der Vorschriften und Beschränkungen, die die Gesetze, der Gesellschaftsvertrag, die Generalversammlungsbeschlüsse und der Aufsichtsrat fordern, sowie mit der Sorgfalt eines ordentlichen und gewissenhaften Geschäftsführers.

EXECUTIVE SERVICE AGREEMENT

XYZ Gesellschaft m.b.H., 1010 Vienna, Kaerntnerstrasse 17, represented by its general shareholders meeting (hereinafter called Employer or Company)

and

Mr. Peter Mueller, born May 1, 1945, 1190 Vienna, Cobenzlgasse 17 (hereinafter called Employee or Managing Director)

have entered into the following contract of employment:

PREAMBLE

By shareholders' resolution of today Mr. Mueller has been appointed Managing Director of the Company with full power of representation. Mr. Mueller has accepted his appointment.

I.
Scope of responsibility

The Employee holding the position of a managing director as defined by the Austrian Commercial Code („handelsrechtlicher Geschäftsführer") is to be regarded an executive employee within the meaning of sec. 1 subsec. 2 lit 8 of the Statutory Working Time Regulations (Arbeitszeitgesetz).

The Managing Director shall be solely responsible for managing the Company in compliance with the provisions and restrictions as set forth by law, the Articles of Association, the shareholders' resolutions, as well as by the Supervisory Board; moreover he shall act with the care of an orderly and diligent managing director.

In die Verantwortung und den Tätigkeitsbereich des Geschäftsführers fallen insbesondere:

- Die Abstimmung der Geschäftspolitik der Gesellschaft mit den Vorgaben der Konzernmutter/der Gruppe;
- die gesamte Betreuung der Kunden; bei internationalen Kunden ist die Abstimmung mit den Schwestergesellschaften oder der Konzernmutter zwingend;
- die Akquisition von Neukunden zur Ausweitung des Geschäfts;
- die Inanspruchnahme der Beratungsdienste der Gruppe.

Above all, the Managing Director shall be in charge of the following tasks:

- *harmonization of the Company's business policies with the objectives set forth by the holding/group;*
- *overall customer service; coordination with fellow subsidiaries of / or the holding company, respectively, shall be mandatory if international customers are concerned;*
- *soliciting of new customers in order to expand business;*
- *utilization of the advisory services of the group.*

II.
Tätigkeitsbereich

Über den Punkt I hinaus hat der Geschäftsführer insbesondere auch die diesem Vertrag beigelegte Geschäftsordnung in der jeweils gültigen Fassung zu beachten. Die jederzeitige Abänderung oder Erweiterung der Geschäftsordnung bleibt der Gesellschaft vorbehalten

Die Abänderung des im Punkt I angeführten Verantwortungsbereiches ist jederzeit durch einseitige Verfügung der Dienstgeberin möglich, sofern der neu zugewiesene Bereich der Ausbildung und den Fähigkeiten des Dienstnehmers und den Erfordernissen der Dienstgeberin entspricht und dem Dienstnehmer zumutbar ist. Dies insbesondere dann, wenn der Dienstnehmer als Geschäftsführer der Gesellschaft abberufen wird oder zurücktritt.

II
Scope of Services

Apart from the responsibilities described in para I the Managing Director shall comply with the Internal Rules attached to this Agreement as amended from time to time. The Company shall be entitled to amend such Rules at any time.

Amendment to or modification of the responsibilities under para I shall be admissible at any time by means of unilateral disposition of the Employer provided that the newly imposed responsibilities correspond to education and abilities of the Employees, meet the demands of the Employer and may reasonably be requested from the Employee. This shall above all be the case if the Employee is discharged or resigns from his office as Managing Director.

III.
Sorgfaltspflicht

Der Dienstnehmer verpflichtet sich, seine Pflichten aus diesem Vertrag mit äußerster Sorgfalt wahrzunehmen. Der Dienstnehmer wird seine ganze Kraft darauf verwenden, die Interessen der

III.
Obligation to take care

The Employee agrees to fulfill his obligations as laid down in this Agreement with the utmost care possible. The Employee shall undertake all he can do to promote the interests of the Employer

Dienstgeberin zu fördern und allfällige Nachteile von ihr abzuwenden.

and to avert possible disadvantages to the Employer.

IV.
Dauer des Vertrages

Das Dienstverhältnis ist für die Zeit bis zum 30. 9. 1992 abgeschlossen.

Die Vertragsteile werden spätestens bis zum 31. 12. 1991 Verhandlungen über eine Verlängerung des Dienstverhältnisses aufnehmen. Werden solche Verhandlungen nicht rechtzeitig aufgenommen, so ist das Dienstverhältnis nur unter Einhaltung einer mindestens sechsmonatigen Kündigungsfrist zum Kalenderquartal, frühestens zum 30. 9. 1992 aufkündbar.

Werden Verhandlungen über eine Verlängerung des Dienstverhältnisses rechtzeitig aufgenommen und führen sie zu keinem einvernehmlichen Ergebnis, so daß der Geschäftsführerdienstvertrag am 30. 9. 1992 endet, stehen dem Dienstnehmer alle Ansprüche nach den Bestimmungen des Angestelltengesetzes so zu, als wäre das Vertragsverhältnis zu diesem Zeitpunkt durch die Dienstgeberin aufgekündigt worden.

IV.
Duration of Agreement

This Agreement has been entered into for a limited period of time and shall expire on September 30, 1992.

The parties agree to commence negotiations about the continuation of this employment relationship not later than December 31, 1991. If such negotiations are not commenced in due time, this Service Agreement may only be terminated upon six months' notice before the end of each quarter of the calendar year, however, not earlier than September 30, 1992.

If negotiations concerning the continuation of this Service Agreement have been commenced in due time but have not led to a result acceptable for both parties, which means that this Agreement will be terminated on September 30, 1992, the Employee shall be entitled to all claims and benefits as set forth by the provisions of the Statute on Employees (Angestelltengesetz) just as if this Agreement were terminated by the Employer as of that date.

V.
Urlaub

Dem Dienstnehmer steht ein jährlicher bezahlter Urlaub von einer Dauer zu, die fünf Tage über dem jeweiligen gesetzlichen Urlaubsausmaß liegt.

Eine Erhöhung dieses Urlaubsanspruchs ist nur nach Maßgabe der gesetzlichen Bestimmungen bzw über ausdrückliche schriftliche Vereinbarung möglich.

Der Dienstnehmer hat hinsichtlich des Zeitpunktes des Urlaubsantrittes auf die betrieblichen Verhältnisse Rücksicht zu nehmen, so daß die Geschäftslage und die Dringlichkeit der vorliegenden Aufgaben berücksichtigt sind.

V.
Annual leave

The Employee shall be entitled to a fully paid annual leave entitlement which exceeds the statutory provisions, as amended, by five days per year.

An increase in the annual leave entitlement shall only be possible in accordance with the statutory provisions or by explicit written agreement.

When choosing the point of time of his annual leave, the Employee shall take into consideration the business conditions and the urgency of the orders to be processed at that time.

VI.
Entgelt

Für seine Tätigkeit erhält der Dienstnehmer

a) ein Jahresgehalt von S ... Mio brutto, aufgeteilt auf zwölf Monatsgehälter und zwei Sonderzahlungen im Ausmaß je eines Bruttomonatsgehaltes;

b) die ihm mit der Ausübung der Tätigkeit außerhalb des Sitzes der Dienstgeberin verbundenen Spesen gegen Abrechnung.

Die Monatsgehälter sind jeweils am Letzten eines jeden Monats im nachhinein zur Zahlung fällig. Die beiden Sonderzahlungen (13. und 14. Gehalt) sind jeweils mit dem für Juni und November fälligen Monatsgehalt zu bezahlen.

Durch das vereinbarte Entgelt werden alle Überstundenleistungen abgegolten. Es ist davon auszugehen, daß der Geschäftsführer monatlich jedenfalls 20 Überstunden zu leisten haben wird. Eine gesonderte Überstundenentlohnung ist ausgeschlossen.

Sonstige Arbeitsleistungen können nur geltend gemacht werden, wenn diese von den Gesellschaftern oder deren Vertretern angeordnet wurden und im Umfang/Zeitvolumen auch schriftlich festgehalten und genehmigt worden sind.

Sämtliche Ansprüche auf Spesenersatz sind vom Dienstnehmer spätestens bis zum Ende des der Erbringung der Leistung folgenden Monats bei sonstigem Verfall des Anspruches schriftlich geltend zu machen.

VII.
Wettbewerbsverbot, Konkurrenzklausel

Während des aufrechten Bestandes des Dienstvertrages ist es dem Dienstnehmer untersagt, ohne ausdrückliche schriftliche Bewilligung der Dienstgeberin Ne-

VI.
Salary

For his services the Employee shall receive

(a) a yearly salary of AS ... million, gross, divided into twelve monthly payments plus two extra payments in the amount of one monthly gross salary each;

(b) expenses incurred in connection with services rendered outside of the Company's offices against production of receipts.

The monthly salary shall be due and payable in arrears on the last day of each month. The two extra payments (13th and 14th salary) shall be paid together with the monthly salaries for June and November.

The agreed salary shall also settle all overtime claims. It has to be assumed that the Managing Director will have to work an average of 20 hours overtime per month. No extra overtime pay shall be granted.

Settlement of other services rendered may only be claimed if they were ordered to be done by the shareholders and their representatives, respectively, if details thereof were put down in writing and approved of.

All claims for reimbursement of expenses have to be made by the Employee in writing not later than by the end of the month following the month in the course of which the services were rendered; otherwise the claim shall be forfeited.

VII.
Prohibition to compete; exclusive service clause

For the term of this Agreement, the Employee shall be prohibited from taking on, in addition to the work for his Employer, secondary occupations or from

benbeschäftigungen oder selbständige Unternehmungen, gleichgültig welcher Art immer, neben der Tätigkeit für die Dienstgeberin zu betreiben, insbesondere ist es auch untersagt, im Geschäftszweig der Dienstgeberin für eigene oder fremde Rechnung Geschäfte zu tätigen.

Der Dienstnehmer ist verpflichtet, bis zum Ablauf eines Jahres ab Beendigung dieses Vertrages sich weder selbständig noch unselbständig noch in irgendeiner anderen Form im Geschäftsbereich der Dienstgeberin zu betätigen. Von diesem Konkurrenzverbot sind auch Beteiligungen, in welcher Weise auch immer, an Unternehmen im Geschäftsbereich der Dienstgeberin umfaßt.

Weiters verpflichtet sich der Dienstnehmer im Falle der Beendigung des Dienstverhältnisses unabhängig von den Gründen der Beendigung, innerhalb eines Jahres weder in ein Anstellungsverhältnis zu einem Kunden der Dienstgeberin oder dessen Mutter-, Tochter- und Beteiligungsgesellschaft zu treten; er wird weder sonstige Verträge, die die Geschäftsbeziehungen der Dienstgeberin in irgendeiner Weise berühren könnten, für sich oder für Dritte eingehen, noch um solche Verträge werben, weder in sonstiger Weise Aktivitäten setzen, die das Abwandern der Kunden zur Folge haben könnten.

engaging in independent enterprises – regardless of kind – without explicit written consent of the Employer; above all, he shall be prohibited from doing business on his own or on someone else's account in the branch of industry of the Employer.

The Employee shall be excluded from working in the branch of industry of the Employer whether as employee, freelancer or in any other form for one year after termination of this Agreement. This prohibition to compete also includes investments of any kind in enterprises of the branch of industry of the Employer.

In case of termination of this Agreement and regardless of the reasons for termination the Employee agrees for the period of one year not to conclude an employment contract with any customer of the Employer nor with the parent company, subsidiary or holding company of any customer; he agrees not to conclude any other contracts on his or on a third person's behalf that might affect the Employer's business relations in any way; he agrees not to solicit such contracts, nor to do anything that might result in customers abandoning the Company.

VIII.
Geheimhaltungspflicht

Der Dienstnehmer nimmt zur Kenntnis, daß aufgrund der bestehenden Vertrauensverhältnisse zwischen der Dienstgeberin und deren Kunden die absolute Geheimhaltung aller Geschäfts- und Betriebsbelange sowohl der Dienstgeberin als auch von deren Kunden strengstens zu befolgen ist.

Die Offenbarung von Geschäfts- und Betriebsgeheimnissen der Dienstgeberin als auch von deren Kunden durch den

VIII.
Obligation to maintain secrecy

The Employee shall take notice of the fact that due to the confidentiality of the relationship between the Employer and its customers he shall comply with the obligation to maintain absolute secrecy concerning all business matters of the employer as well as of its customers.

Any kind of disclosure of business matters of the Employer as well as of its customers by the Employee to third per-

Dienstnehmer an dritte Personen, welcher Art immer, stellt einen Grund für die sofortige vorzeitige Auflösung des Dienstverhältnisses durch die Dienstgeberin dar. Der Dienstnehmer verpflichtet sich, die Dienstgeberin für jeden daraus entstandenen Schaden schadlos zu halten. Die Dienstgeberin ist berechtigt, ohne Nachweis eines konkreten Schadens für jeden Verletzungsfall vom Dienstnehmer eine Konventionalstrafe im Betrag von S 100.000,– für jeden Übertretungsfall zu verlangen. Dies unbeschadet des Rechtes, einen höheren Schadensbetrag geltend zu machen.

Der Dienstnehmer nimmt weiters zur Kenntnis, daß alle ihm zur Kenntnis gelangenden Daten von Kunden sowie der Dienstgeberin unter die Bestimmungen des Datenschutzgesetzes fallen und über solche Daten absolute Verschwiegenheit zu bewahren ist. Der Dienstnehmer unterwirft sich insbesondere sämtlichen Bestimmungen des Datenschutzgesetzes und verpflichtet sich, alle diese Daten absolut geheim zu halten und keinem Dritten weiterzugeben. Auch für den Fall des Zuwiderhandelns gegen diese Vertragsverpflichtung verpflichtet sich der Dienstnehmer, die Dienstgeberin für jede Inanspruchnahme schad- und klaglos zu halten. Die Verpflichtung zur absoluten Geheimhaltung besteht auch gegenüber anderen Mitarbeitern der Firma der Dienstgeberin, wenn diese mit den betreffenden Geschäftstätigkeiten aufgrund ihrer Stellung nicht befaßt sind. Diese Pflicht besteht nach Beendigung dieses Vertrages fort.

sons shall constitute a cause for immediate premature termination of the Agreement by the Employer.

The Employee agrees to indemnify the Employer against all losses due to such disclosure.

The Employer shall be entitled to demand from the Employee a stipulated penalty (liquidated damages) in the amount of AS 100,000 for any breach of secrecy without having to produce evidence of actual losses.

This, however, shall not exclude the Employer from asserting claims exceeding the stipulated penalty.

Furthermore, the Employee takes notice of the fact that all data of the customers as well as of the Employer known to him are subject to the regulations of the Data Protection Statute* and that absolute secrecy shall be maintained in connection therewith. The Employee submits to the regulations of the Data Protection Statute and agrees to maintain secrecy about said data as well as to refrain from passing them on to third persons.

Also in case of breach of this stipulation, the Employee agrees to indemnify and hold harmless the Employer against all claims arising therefrom.

The obligation to maintain absolute secrecy shall also exist vis-à-vis other employees of the Company, if, due to their respective positions, they are not concerned with such business activities.

This obligation shall also continue after termination of this Agreement

IX.
Übergabe der Geschäftsunterlagen

Bei Beendigung des Dienstverhältnisses – aus welchem Grund auch immer – ist der Dienstnehmer verpflichtet, unverzüglich sämtliche Geschäftsunterlagen einschließlich Kopien an die Dienstgeberin zu übergeben.

IX.
Obligation to surrender documents

Upon termination of this Agreement, and regardless of the cause of such termination, the Employee shall be obliged to immediately surrender all business documents including copies thereof to the Employer.

X.
Sonstiges

Im übrigen finden die jeweiligen Bestimmungen des Gesetzes über die Gesellschaften mit beschränkter Haftung, des Handelsgesetzbuches und des Angestelltengesetzes in der jeweiligen Fassung Anwendung

Die diesem Vertrag beigelegte Geschäftsordnung bildet einen integrierten Bestandteil dieses Vertrages.

Beide Vertragsteile bestätigen, daß außer diesen Vertragsbedingungen keine weiteren Vereinbarungen getroffen wurden. Abänderungen dieses Vertrages sind nur dann gültig, wenn diese schriftlich erfolgen und von beiden Vertragsteilen unterzeichnet sind.

XI.
Gerichtsstand und anzuwendendes Recht

Für alle Streitigkeiten aus diesem Dienstverhältnis wird zwischen den Vertragsteilen die ausschließliche Zuständigkeit des Arbeits- und Sozialgerichtes Wien vereinbart; es ist österreichisches Recht anzuwenden.

Wien, am 22. April 1990

X.
Miscellaneous

Moreover, the respective regulations of the Statute on GmbH-Companies*, the Commercial Code* as well as the Statute on Employees* (as amended from time to time) shall apply.

The Internal Rules annexed to this Agreement shall form an integral part of this Agreement.

Both contracting parties confirm that except for the stipulations of this Agreement no additional agreements were entered into. Amendments to this Agreement shall only be effective if made in writing and upon signature of both contracting parties.

XI.
Governing law and forum

All disputes arising from or relating to this Agreement shall be subject to the exclusive jurisdiction of the Court for Labor and Social Matters Vienna*. Austrian law shall govern.

Vienna, April 22, 1990

4. CUT & PASTE

The following clauses have been taken from the above specimen contracts („Musterverträge").

4.1. Opening Phrases

1.

THIS AGREEMENT *is made this 7th day of July 1990 BETWEEN COMPANY (U.K.) LIMITED whose Registered Office is at 17, Winston Road, Kent (hereinafter called "the Company") on the one part and PETER MAYER of Fleet Street, City of London, England (hereinafter called "Mr. Mayer") on the other part.*
WHEREBY IT IS AGREED AS FOLLOWS:
(...)

agreement, to make an agreement, date, parties, on the one part, hereinafter called, on the other part (for details relating to corporations **see** the section on **Corporate Law-Terminology**)

2.

THIS AGREEMENT *is made the 7th day of July one thousand nine hundred and ninety:*
BETWEEN
X HOLDINGS LTD. *whose Registered Office is situated at 17, Winston Road, Kent, England (hereinafter called "X" or "the Lessor") of the one part and PETER MAYER, D-5000 Köln 91, Bahnhofstraße 1, Federal Republic of Germany (hereinafter called "the Lessee") on the other part:*
WHEREBY IT IS AGREED AS FOLLOWS:
(...)

date

parties

abbreviations, definitions, addresses

3.

This Exclusive Marketing Agreement (the "Agreement"), dated as of July 7, 1990, is made and entered into between Miracle Computers, Inc., a Delaware Corporation ("Miracle"), and Mayer Ges.m.b.H., an Austrian corporation ("Mayer").
(...)

specification of contract, date, parties

4.

PURCHASE AGREEMENT

entered into between Mr. Jack Emerson, born October 28, 1943, A-3021 Preßbaum, Goethestraße 8, as seller on the one part and Mrs. Carol Robins, born April 8, 1964, 425 Seaview Drive, Melbourne, Australia, as purchaser on the other part as follows:
(...)

purchase agreement

parties
particulars

5.

THIS *contract, made on this seventh day of July 1990 by and between Fantasia Industrial Corporation, a corporation orga-*

contract, parties

nized under the laws of Delaware and having its principal place of business at 1234 Franklin Drive, Washington D.C., United States of America (hereinafter called "FIC") and P & Q, Ltd., a corporation organized and existing under the laws of the state of Delaware and having its principal place of business at 209 Ivy Road, Charlottesville, VA, U.S.A. (hereinafter called "P & Q") as the one part and ABC Gesellschaft mit beschränkter Haftung, organized under the laws of Austria and having its principal place of business at Kahlenberger Straße 59, A-1190 Wien, Austria (hereinafter called "ABC") as the other part.
WITNESSETH:
(...)

6.

agreement date

This AGREEMENT ist made as of July 7, 1990, by and between FALSTAFF Ges.m.b.H. & Co. KG. an Austrian limited partnership having its registered office at Rathausstraße 17, A-1010 Vienna, Austria ("FALSTAFF") and MIRACLE COMPUTERS INC., a Delaware corporation having its registered office at 1234 Franklin Street, Washington D.C., U.S.A. ("MIRACLE"). The Partners of Falstaff are the General Partner, FALSTAFF Ges.m.b.H., an Austrian corporation, and the Limited Partners, SCHNEIDER Ges.m.b.H., an Austrian corporation ("SCHNEIDER") and MIRACLE Ges.m.b.H., an Austrian corporation, and a wholly-owned subsidiary of MIRACLE ("MIRACLE AUSTRIA").
(...)

4.2. Preamble/Recitals/Preliminary Statements

1.

A. *Mayer owns all rights to a computer software controlled device (commonly known as "Mayer Master") used for the control and operation of snow-removal equipment. The "Mayer Master" is based upon intellectual property rights owned by Mayer, including plans, specifications, patents, pending patents, trade secrets, and other confidential documents and intellectual property (the "Technology"), some of which is further described in Exhibit A attached to this Agreement.*

general description of the parties, their respective capacity and their intentions with respect to the proposed transaction; these so-called recitals do not form part of the contract itself and are thus not binding on the parties

B. *Miracle desires to obtain from Mayer, and Mayer desires to grant to Miracle, exclusive marketing rights for the Mayer Master and for all improvements made by Mayer to its design. For the purpose of this Agreement, "Mayer Products", means and is limited to the Mayer Master and all later improvements in the design of the Mayer Master.*

C. *Miracle also desires to obtain from Mayer, and Mayer desires to grant to Miracle, the right of first refusal for exclusive marketing rights on similar technology designed to alleviate the strains of the winter. For purposes of this Agreement, "Similar Technology" includes any technology, other than Mayer Products, designed to alleviate the burdens of the winter.*

(...)

2.

WHEREAS, FIC is engaged in the business of manufacture of snow-removal equipment, including special products as listed in Exhibit A hereto and as amended from time to time by FIC and of parts and accessories therefor (hereinafter collectively called "Products") and desirous of exporting Products to Austria (hereinafter called "Territory"); and

WHEREAS, P & Q has been appointed by FIC as its export agent; and

WHEREAS, ABC is engaged in the business of sale and marketing of merchandise, including the items covered by the Products in the Territory; and

WHEREAS, both parties desire to make a contract for the sale of the Products to users and customers in the Territory.

(...)

(assembly agreement)   *3.*

Letter of Intent
(L.o.I.) negotiations
definitive contracts

WHEREAS, MIRACLE and SCHNEIDER have entered into a Letter of Intent on July 7, 1990 by which SCHNEIDER and MIRACLE agreed to negotiate definitive contracts for FALSTAFF to assemble computer hardware for purchase by MIRACLE;

to conclude
negotiations

WHEREAS, SCHNEIDER and MIRACLE have concluded these negotiations;

(for details on corpo-
rate law terminology
see the respective section on **Corporate
Law-Terminology**)

WHEREAS, SCHNEIDER and MIRACLE AUSTRIA have established FALSTAFF for the purpose of producing computer hardware, replacement parts and accessories under contract for MIRACLE; and

WHEREAS, SCHNEIDER and MIRACLE AUSTRIA have established the General Partnership for the sole purpose of managing FALSTAFF;

(…)

4.3. Consideration Clauses

1.

(exklusive marketing agreement)
boiler plate
(Standardklausel)

Now, therefore, in consideration of the recitals and mutual covenants contained in this Agreement, the parties agree as follows:

(…)

2.

(exklusive distributor contract)
promises, mutual covenants

NOW THEREFORE, in consideration of the promises and mutual covenants herein contained, the parties hereto agree as follows:

(…)

3.

(assembly agreement)

NOW THEREFORE, in consideration of these promises and the mutual covenants contained in this Agreement, FALSTAFF and MIRACLE hereby agree to the following terms:

(…)

4.4. Materielle
Bestimmungen

4.4. Main Provisions

The actual contents of the core of the contracts will have to be determined in accordance with the specific requirements of the individual agreements. For reference to sample contracts see special section on INDIVIDUAL CONTRACTS in the third part of this chapter.

4.5. Individual Stipulations

4.5.1. Definitions, General

As used in this Agreement, the following terms, in both their singular and plural forms, shall have the meaning set forth below. Defined terms appearing in this Agreement will be capitalized.

capitalization
(Großschreibung)

4.5.2. Sample definitions

4.5.2. Musterdefinitionen

A. *"Party": X and Y, or both of them when used in the plural.*

Vertragsparteien

B. *"Settlement day": The day for regular settlement of accounts between the Parties as set forth in section ... of this Agreement.*

Verrechnungtag

C. *"Federal Republic of Germany" means the Federal Republic of Germany, its territories, its possessions and all areas subject to its jurisdiction.*

Landesdefinition

D. *"Business Day": shall mean a day on which banks are open for business in London, Frankfurt and Vienna.*

Werktag

E. *"Person" shall mean any person, firm, company, corporation or state entity or any association or partnership (whether or not having separate legal personality) of two or more of the foregoing.*

Person

F. *"AS" and „Austrian Schillings" shall mean the lawful currency of the Republic of Austria.*

Währungsdefinition

G. *"Subsidiary" shall mean a corporation of which more than 50% of the outstanding voting stock, as the case may be, is owned, directly or indirectly, by a Company (separate definition) or by any one or more other subsidiaries of a Company. For the purpose of this definition, "voting stock" means stock which ordinarily grants voting power for the election of directors, whether at all times or so long as no senior class of stock has such voting power by reason of any contingency.*

Tochterunternehmen

4.5.3. Headings

4.5.3. Überschriften

Article and section headings in this Agreement, except for the definitions, are included for convenience and reference only and will not constitute a part of this Agreement for any other purpose.

Überschriften dürfen nicht zur Auslegung herangezogen werden

4.5.4. Representations and Warranties

4.5.4. Verbindliche Zusicherungen und Garantien(*)

Sample A (Excerpt)

The Company and the Guarantor respectively represent and warrant that:

69

Garantie(*) des auf-
rechten Bestandes
einer Kapitalgesell-
schaft, Verfügungs-
berechtigung

(i) *the Company is a corporation duly incorporated and validly existing under the laws of the state of Delaware and the Guarantor is a corporation duly incorporated and validly existing under the laws of Switzerland, each with power to own its property and assets and to transact the business in which they are engaged or propose to engage and are duly licensed or qualified as a foreign corporation in every jurisdiction in which the nature of the business in which they are engaged make such qualification or license necessary;*

Berechtigung zum
Abschluß dieser
Vereinbarung

(ii) *the Company and the Guarantor each have the corporate power to enter into this Agreement and/or the Guarantee and/or the Power of Attorney and to exercise their rights and perform their respective obligations hereunder, under the Guarantee, under the Power of Attorney, and all corporate and other action required to authorize the execution of this Agreement by the Company and by the Guarantor and of the Power of Attorney by the Company and of the Guarantee by the Guarantor and the performance by the Company and of the Guarantor of their respective obligations herunder, under the Power of Attorney and under the Guarantee has been duly taken.*

...

Sample B

verbindliche Zusiche-
rung darüber, daß
keine für die Gesell-
schaft nachteiligen
Verfahren jedweder
Art anhängig sind

The Company represents and warrants that there are no actions, suits or proceedings pending, or to the knowledge of the Company threatened, against or affecting the Company before any court of law or before any governmental or administrative body or agency which might result in any material adverse change in the operations, business, property or assets or in the condition (financial or otherwise) of the Company.

Sample C

Zusicherung der
Fehlerfreiheit
der Produkte

Garantie(*)anpas-
sungsregelung

A warrants that all Products to be supplied hereunder will be free from all defects in design, material and workmanship and will conform with the specifications for the period that A warrants the Products to its customers. A may change its current warranty coverage from time to time to remain at the same level or better than warranties for competitive products.

4.5.5. Schad- und
Klagloshaltung

4.5.5. Indemnification

Sample A

ABC shall indemnify and hold harmless FIC and/or P & Q from any responsibility and/or liability for any claims and/or suits by third parties with respect to the Products.

70

Sample B

The Company undertakes to indemnify X Corporation against any expense (including legal fees), reasonably incurred and costs or loss incurred as a direct consequence of any default by the Company in the performance of any of the obligations expressed to be assumed by it in this Agreement.

4.5.6. Covenants

4.5.6. Verbindliche Zusicherungen und Garantien(*) (Exclusive Marketing Agreement)

Sample A (Excerpt)

1. During the Term of this Agreement, XYZ agrees that it will neither offer nor sell XYZ Products or Similar Technology in the Licensed Territories to any person or entity other than ABC nor negotiate with any person or entity other than ABC concerning any right to purchase or market XYZ Products or Similar Technology, except as otherwise contemplated by this Agreement.

Exklusivität für die Dauer des Vertrages

2. XYZ shall take all reasonable action to enforce territorial restrictions of other licensees and distributors with whom it has contracted or with whom it may contract in the future.

Verteidigung des Gebietsschutzes

3. XYZ shall immediately refer to ABC any person or entity that approaches XYZ to discuss the purchase of any XYZ Products or Similar Technology for use in any of the Licensed Territories ("Potential Customer"), and shall notify ABC within ... days of any such contact with a Potential Customer. XYZ shall disclose in writing to ABC the identity of any Potential Customer (including the name, address, telephone number and employer) and the content of any discussion with the Potential Customer.

Weiterleitung von Informationen betreffend potentielle Kunden für das Vertragsgebiet

4. XYZ shall maintain an ongoing manufacturing control program that will emphasize achieving a "zero defect" level of manufacturing quality.

Zusicherung von Kontrollen betreffend die Produktqualität

5. XYZ shall provide ABC with engineering change notices, which shall be serially numbered, within ... days after they become effective.

Verständigung über technische Änderungen

6. XYZ shall maintain in full force and effect, to the extent possible, its present rights to use the trade names, trademarks, copyrights and pending and licensed patents associated with XYZ Products and any Similar Technology.

Bestandgarantie für Immaterialgüterrechte

Sample B (Excerpt)

(Loan Agreement)

Kreditvertrag

The Borrower covenants and agrees that so long as this Agreement is in effect, it will, unless the Agent and, unless otherwise provided, the Bank waive compliance in writing, such waiver not to be unreasonably withheld:

Verbindliche vertragliche Zusicherungen des Kreditnehmers

71

Verwendung:

1. Use of Proceeds and Revenues

des zugezählten
Kredits

(a) Proceeds. Deposit the Proceeds of the Loan in the Account and use them solely to pay Project Costs.

der Einnahmen aus
dem Projekt

(b) Revenues. Deposit all Project Revenues in the Operating Account and apply them solely for purposes and in the order and manner provided in Section ... of the Agreement.

Rückzahlung

2. Payment. *Pay all sums due under this Agreement according to the terms hereof.*

Verständigungspflicht
bei:

3. Notices. *Promptly, upon acquiring notice or knowledge or giving notice, as the case may be, give written notice to the Agent of:*

Gerichtsverfahren
(anhängig oder
drohend)

(a) Any litigation pending or, to the knowledge of the Borrower, threatened against the Borrower involving claims against the Borrower or the Project in excess of $ ... in the aggregate:

Streitigkeiten zwischen Kreditnehmer
und Behörden

(b) Any substantial dispute or disputes which may exist between the Borrower and any government, governmental regulatory body or law enforcement authority and which involve claims against the Borrower which in the aggregate exceed $ ... or any Liens for taxes due but not paid;

wesentlichem
Vertragsbruch

(c) Any event of Default;

jedwedem Schaden im
Vermögen des Kreditnehmers

(d) Any casualty, damage or loss, whether or not insured, through fire, theft, other hazard or casualty, or any act or omission of the Borrower, its employees, agents, contractors, consultants or representatives, or any other person if such casualty, damage or loss affects the Borrower or the Project, in excess of $ ... for any one casualty or loss or an aggregate of $ ... for any one calendar year;

Änderung der Versicherungsdeckung

(e) Any cancellation or material change in the terms, coverages or amounts of any insurance;

jedweder Verschlechterung der finanziellen
Lage des Kreditnehmers

(f) Any matter which has resulted or is likely to result in any material adverse change in the Borrower's financial condition or operations;

bei Übernahme einer
Verpflichtung gegenüber Dritten durch den
Kreditnehmer

(g) Any act by the Borrower to become a surety, guarantor or endorser for a third party;

(...)

Buchführung

4. Books, Records, Access thereto. *Maintain adequate books, accounts and records with respect to the Borrower and the Project and prepare all financial statements required hereunder in accordance with generally accepted accounting principles and in compliance with the regulations of any governmental regulatory body having jurisdiction over the Borrower and the Project, and permit employees or agents of the Agent at any reasonable time and upon reasonable prior notice to inspect all the Borrower's properties,*

Verpflichtung zur
ordentlichen Buchführung

Recht zur Einsichtnahme durch Kreditgeber

including the Site, and to examine or audit all of the Borrower's books, accounts and records and make copies and memoranda thereof.

5. Compliance with Laws. *At its expense, promptly (i) comply, or cause compliance, in all material respects, with all laws, rules, regulations and legal requirements, including without limitation laws, rules, regulations and legal requirements, relating to pollution control, environmental protection, equal employment opportunity and employee safety, with respect to the Borrower or the Project; and (ii) procure, maintain and comply, or cause to be procured, maintained and complied with, in all material aspects, all Permits required for any use of the Project or any part thereof.*

Einhaltung gesetz-
licher Vorschriften

Erwerb aller notwen-
digen Konzessionen/
Genehmigungen

4.5.7. Secrecy

4.5.7. Geheimhal-
tungsklausel

Sample A

During the term of this Contract and for a period of 36 months after termination thereof, X shall not, orally or in documented form, disclose to any third party, including its customers, commission agents and/or subdistributors, any knowledge concerning techniques, design, pricing details or any other matters whether commercial or technical, relating to the Products which X has received from Y.

Geheimhaltungsklau-
sel mit Nachwirkung
über das Vertragsende
hinaus

Sample B

During the term of this Agreement, upon expiration or termination thereof and at all times thereafter, the parties will hold all confidential information concerning the other party obtained in connection with carrying out this Agreement as confidential and will release such information to third parties only to the extent essential for the performance of work hereunder and only upon prior notice to and consent of the other party. The parties will take all reasonable steps to maintain confidentiality in their relations with their subcontractors and their suppliers. Upon termination of this Agreement, the parties will return to the other any and all confidential material which each may have received from the other party.

Sample C

All technical and business information (including drawings and documents but not including sales literature intended to be distributed to potential purchasers of the Products) supplied by the Manufacturer to the Distributor shall be deemed to be confidential and so kept (and not disclosed to any third party) by the Distributor during and after the term of this Agreement. All such information and documents shall remain the exclusive property of the Manufacturer and shall not be used, copied or reproduced by the Distributor without the consent of such party.

Other than is necessary to fulfill its obligations pursuant to this Agreement, the Distributor shall not reveal, use to its financial benefit or utilize to the financial detriment of the Manufacturer any trade secrets or other similarly protected confidential information of the Manufacturer during the term of this Agreement or after the termination of this Agreement.

4.5.8. Konkurrenz-
verbot

4.5.8. No Competition Clause

X shall not, directly or indirectly or in any manner whatsoever, sell, buy, handle or deal in any products similar to or competitive with the Products without prior written consent of Y.

4.5.9. Vertragsdauer

4.5.9. Term/Duration

Sample A

Vertragsbeginn
Vertragsende

This Agreement will come into force as of July 7, 1990 and will last until July 6, 1995 unless terminated earlier as provided for herein.

Verlängerung der Ver-
tragsdauer durch Par-
teienvereinbarung

At least twelve (12) months prior to the expiration date, the parties hereto shall meet in order to discuss and evaluate a possible renewal, provided, however, that nothing herein contained shall be deemed to create or imply a duty upon either party hereto to renew this Agreement and that neither party will be entitled to damages against the other for failure of such other party to renew this Agreement.

Sample B

This Agreement will take effect on the first date above-written. Unless earlier terminated in accordance with the provisions of this Section, this Agreement will continue in effect until the end of 1995. This Agreement will be extended only by the mutual consent of the parties as evidenced by formal amendment to this Agreement.

Sample C

unbestimmte Dauer

The term of this Agreement shall continue indefinitely unless terminated by either party.

4.5.10. Vertrags-
beendigung

4.5.10. Termination

Sample A

sofortige/vorzeitige/
außerordentliche
Vertragsauflösung
Insolvenzfälle

Either party may immediately terminate this Contract by notice in writing to the other party

(a) in the event that the other party is adjudicated a bankrupt, becomes insolvent or makes an assignment for the benefit of creditors;

(b) in the event that any party should breach any term or condition of this Contract or fail to perform any of its obligations or undertakings hereunder and such default is not rectified within 30 days after notice by the non-defaulting party to the defaulting party specifying the nature of the breach.

Vertragsbruch

Leistungsverzug

mangelnde Heilung

Termination of this Contract for any reason shall not entitle either party to compensation, reimbursement or damages on account of loss of prospective profits on anticipated sales or on account of expenditure, investments, losses of commitments in connection with the business of either party. The Distributor, however, shall not be relieved of any obligation for any unpaid balances for the Products shipped prior to termination or ordered by the Distributor which are in the process of manufacture or from any other obligation which from the context hereof are intended to survive the termination of this Contract.

Haftungsbegrenzung

Einschränkung der Haftungsbegrenzung

Sample B

Either party may terminate this Agreement for cause if the other (the "Defaulting Party"):

1. defaults in its material obligations under this Agreement, and fails to remedy such default and give adequate assurance of future performance within three (3) months after such default has been called to its attention by notice from the other party; or

2. files a petition in bankruptcy, makes a general assignment for the benefit of its creditors or otherwise acknowledges insolvency, is adjudicated a bankrupt, has an involuntary petition filed against it in bankruptcy, which petition is not discharged within forty-five (45) days of the filing thereof, goes into, or is placed in a process of complete liquidation other than for an amalgamation or reconstruction, or is otherwise wound up and dissolved, or suffers an appointment of a receiver for any substantial portion of its business, who is not discharged within forty-five (45) days after his appointment.

In any such event, the party not in default may immediately terminate its obligations to the Defaulting Party under this Agreement upon notice to the Defaulting Party. Termination pursuant to this section will be in addition to, and not in place of, a party's other rights or causes of action.

Sample C

(a) Either party may terminate this Agreement at any time, without cause, by giving written notice of termination to the other party at least three (3) months prior to the effective date of such termination in the event that the termination is effective on or before the second anniversary of this Agreement, and thereafter such notice must be given at least six (6) months prior to the effective date of such termination;

(b) While it is the hope and expectation of the parties that this Agreement will create an enduring and mutually profitable and satisfactory relationship, it is recognized that circumstances may arise making it necessary for the Manufacturer to take steps to protect its business or making it impracticable for this Agreement to continue, and under which it should be immediately terminated. In order that those circumstances and the Manufacturer's rights in connection therewith may be clearly understood, it is agreed that, notwithstanding the provision of sub-section (a) hereof, the Manufacturer may at its option terminate this Agreement, effective at once, if any of the following events occurs:

(i)   the Distributor fails to cure a Default under this Agreement within thirty (30) days after the Manufacturer has given written notice of and demand for cure;

(ii)   there is any change in the principal officers, directors, management, or stock ownership of the Distributor, which will effect a substantial change in the operation, management, or control of the Distributor;

(iii) the Distributor admits insolvency or there is instituted with respect to the Distributor any voluntary or involuntary proceeding in bankruptcy or under other insolvency law, or for an arrangement with creditors or for corporate reorganization or for receivership or dissolution of the Distributor;

(iv)   there is any dispute, disagreement, or controversy arising between or among the principals, managers, officers, or stockholders of the Distributor which may adversely affect the operation, management, reputation, business or interest of the Distributor or the business or interest of the Manufacturer or the reputation of the Manufacturer's Products;

(v)   any officer or principal of the Distributor is convicted of any crime, which adversely affects the interest of the Distributor or the Manufacturer; or

(vi)   any officer of the Distributor presents false records or reports to the Manufacturer.

Abwicklungs-
bestimmung

(c) Termination of this Agreement shall not affect the right of the parties existing on the date of termination in relation to Products, the order for which was accepted by the Manufacturer pursuant to Section ... hereof prior to the date of termination, including, without limitation, the obligation of Distributor to pay the purchase price for all Products shipped by the Manufacturer.

ausdrücklicher
Verzicht seitens des
Vertragshändlers

(d) The Distributor hereby expressly waives any rights it may have to recover any payments from the Manufacturer as a result of the termination of this Agreement and any other rights which it may have against the Manufacturer as the result of the termination of this Agreement.

(e) During the period from the notice of termination of this Agreement until the effective date of the termination, the Distributor shall have the right to purchase no more than one hundred and fifty percent (150%) of the value of Products purchased during an equivalent period of time immediately preceding the notice of termination, and such Products shall be paid under an irrevocable letter of credit covering the full purchase price thereof which the Distributor shall cause to be opened in favor of the Manufacturer and confirmed by a U.S.-bank before the shipment of such Products by the Manufacturer.

Vorratsbestellungs-
beschränkung für
Abwicklungsstadium

4.5.11. Force Majeure

4.5.11. Höhere Gewalt

Sample A

Neither the Manufacturer nor the Distributor shall be responsible for any losses resulting therefrom to the other party, or to third parties, if fulfillment by it of any terms or provisions of this Agreement (other than provisions requiring the payment of money), or any order, is delayed or prevented by revolution or other disorder, war, acts of enemies, strike, fire, flood, labor dispute, riot, insurrection, accident, storm, inability to obtain materials or supplies, act of God, act of any government, or other cause not within the control of the Manufacturer or the Distributor, as the case may be. Where only part of the Manufacturer's capacity to perform shall have been excused under this paragraph, the Manufacturer shall use its best efforts to allocate deliveries among its customers, including the Distributor, in a commercially fair and reasonable manner. Where such allocation has been made, reasonable notice of the estimated quota to be made available to Distributor shall be given.

Diese Bestimmung ist
in Ermangelung einer
gesetzlichen Regelung
in anglo-amerikani-
sche Verträge aufzu-
nehmen, so eine dies-
bezügliche Regelung
gewünscht wird. Die
Aufzählung der
Anlaßfälle für höhere
Gewalt erfolgt regel-
mäßig in Katalogform,
was sich aus der
üblichen Kasuistik
ergibt.

Sample B

If performance of this Agreement or of any obligation hereunder is prevented, restricted or interfered with by reason of Force Majeure, the Party so affected, upon giving prompt notice to the other Party, will be excused from such performance to the extent of such prevention, restriction or interference; provided that the Party so affected will use its best efforts to avoid or remove such causes of non performance and will immediately continue performance hereunder whenever such causes are removed.

Force Majeure will mean damage or delay caused by acts of God; acts, regulations or decrees of any government (de facto or de jure); natural phenomena; shipwrecks; strikes; freight embargoes; lockouts; or other causes whether forseeable or not, beyond the reasonable control of the Parties.

Definition der
Anlaßfälle

If Force Majeure prevents any performance of a Party's obligation under this Agreement, the Party claiming Force Majeure will notify the other Party in writing as soon as possible and in any event

Benachrichtigungs-
pflicht

within five (5) days. The notice will state the beginning and, if possible, the ending times of such case of Force Majeure and describe the circumstances thereof.

Vertragsbeendigung in
Fällen langanhaltender
höherer Gewalt

Notwithstanding the above provisions of this Article, if Force Majeure prevents either Party from performing its obligations under this Agreement for more than fifty (50) days, the other Party shall have the right to elect to terminate this Agreement by providing the non-performing Party with written notice of its intention to terminate.

Sample C

Kurzformel mit
offener Gestaltung der
Anlaßfälle

No Party hereto shall be held liable or responsible to the other Party hereto for failures or delays in delivery of the Products in fulfilling this Contract or any order received, in case such failure or delay is caused by a reason beyond its reasonable control, including but not limited to, acts of God, riots, wars, hostilities, strikes, lockouts, and/or labor disputes, embargoes, shortage of supply of raw materials, unavailability of loading or transportation facilities, laws and regulations of governments.

4.5.12. Abtretung/
Rechtsnachfolger

4.5.12. Assignment/Succession

Sample A

Abtretungsverbot

This Contract shall not be assigned by X to any other party without the prior consent in writing by Y.

Sample B

Rechtsnachfolger

This Contract shall be binding upon and shall inure to the benefit of the successors of the respective parties hereof.

Sample C (combined clause)

Kombinierte Klausel

This Agreement will be binding upon and will inure to the benefit of and be enforceable by the Parties and their respective successors and permitted assigns. A may not assign this Agreement, in whole or in part, except with the prior written consent of B. B will be entitled to assign its rights or delegate its duties hereunder, in whole or in part, to any affiliated company of B. Any other assignment will require the consent of A.

4.5.13. Benachrichti-
gungen

4.5.13. Notices

Sample A

Art der Verständigung

Any notices required or permitted to be given pursuant to this Agreement will be given in writing and sent by telex or sent postage prepaid by certified or registered air mail, return receipt requested, and addressed as follows:

If to A:	*...(name)...*
	...(address)...
	attention:...
If to B:	*...(name)...*
	...(address)...
	attention:...
with a copy to:	*...(name)...*
	...(address)...
	attention: (counsel)

Either Party may change its address or addresses for notices by notice given in writing in accordance with this Section.

Adressenänderung

Any notice to B must be given in English.

All notices given hereunder will be deemed given upon receipt by the Party to whom sent as indicated by the date of the signature on the return receipt.

Zustellung durch tatsächliche Übernahme

Sample B

Any notice or request to be given by either party to the other hereunder shall be given in writing, shall be sent by registered air mail, postage prepaid, or, at the option of the person giving such notice, by prepaid cable or telex. Whenever a notice or request is required to be given at or prior to a particular time, such notice or request must be actually received by the party to whom it is requested to be given at or prior to such time. Notices shall be addressed to the respective parties at the following addresses or to such other addresses as either party may hereinafter from time to time designate in writing to the other party for the reception of notices:

Zustellungsmodalität

Adressenänderung

If to Manufacturer: ...

If to Distributor: ...

4.5.14. Waivers

4.5.14. (Kein Verzicht) auf Geltendmachung von Rechten

Sample A

No failure to exercise, nor any delay in exercising on the part of either party, any right or remedy hereunder shall operate as a waiver thereof, nor shall any single or partial exercise of any right or remedy prevent any further or other exercise thereof or the exercise of any other right or remedy. The rights and remedies herein provided are cumulative and not exclusive of any rights or remedies provided by law.

Nichtausübung bzw nicht sofortige Ausübung von Rechten bedeutet nicht den Verzicht

Kumulation mit gesetzlichen Vorschriften

Sample B

No waiver by either party of any breach or default hereunder of the other party or the giving of time for performance shall be deemed to be the waiver of any subsequent breach or default.

Nicht-Beanstandung von Vertragsbruch, Nicht-/Schlechterfüllung sowie das Setzen einer Frist bedeuten nicht Verzicht

4.5.15. Keine Neben-
abreden/Ergänzungen

4.5.15. Entire Agreement/Amendments

Sample A

Keine zusätzlichen
Vereinbarungen; Vor-
rang gegenüber älteren
Vereinbarungen
jedweder Art. Schrift-
form für Ergänzungen/
Nachträge/Änderun-
gen

*This Contract contains the entire agreement between the parties
with respect to the subject matter hereof and supersedes any prior
or contemporaneous agreements and understandings, whether
oral or written, relating to the subject matter hereof. This Contract may be amended only by written instrument executed by both
parties hereto which expressly states that it is intended to constitute an amendment to this Contract.*

Sample B

Schriftform für
Änderungen

*No Amendment to this Agreement shall be effective unless the
same shall be in writing and signed by the Parties.*

4.5.16. Teilnichtigkeit
(Salvatorische Klausel)

4.5.16. Severability/Partial Invalidity

Sample A

teilweise Ungesetz-
lichkeit, Undurchsetz-
barkeit

Vertragsergänzung
durch Interpretation

*If any one or more of the provisions of this Contract should be
found to be illegal or unenforceable, then all other provisions
shall be given effect separately therefrom and shall not be affected
thereby. If any covenants set forth are illegal or unenforceable, it
is the intention of the parties that such covenant shall not thereby
be terminated but shall be deemed amended to the extent necessary to render it valid and enforceable.*

Sample B

Bezugnahme auf die
gesetzliche Situation
in den involvierten
Rechtssystemen

*If at any time any provision hereof is or becomes illegal, invalid or
unenforceable in any respect under the law of any jurisdiction,
neither the legality, validity, nor enforceability of the remaining
provisions hereof nor the legality, validity, or enforceability of
such provision under the law of any jurisdiction shall in any way
be affected or impaired thereby.*

Sample C

*If any of the provisions hereof is held to be invalid or unenforce-
able, it shall be considered severed from this agreement and shall
not serve to invalidate the remaining provisions hereof.*

4.5.17. Ausfertigungen

4.5.17. Counterparts

Sample A

Vertragserrichtung in
zwei (mehreren) Aus-
fertigungen, die beide
(alle) als Originale
gelten

*This Contract may be executed in two or more counterparts, each
of which shall be deemed an original and all of which shall evidence the same agreement, and it shall not be necessary in making proof of this agreement to produce or account for more than
one such counterpart.*

Sample B

This agreement has been executed in two (2) counterparts, each of which shall be deemed an original.

4.5.18. Governing law

Sample A

This contract shall be governed by and interpreted in accordance with the laws of the state of New York.

Rechtswahlklausel

Sample B

This agreement, including any contract provided for herein, shall be governed by and construed in accordance with the laws of Austria.

4.5.19. Jurisdiction/Forum

4.5.19. Gerichtsstand

Sample A

Each of the parties hereto irrevocably agrees for the benefit of each of the other parties hereto that the competent courts in the City of Vienna, Austria, shall have jurisdiction to hear and determine any suit, action or proceeding, and to settle any disputes which may arise out of or in connection with this Agreement and for such purpose submits to the non-exclusive jurisdiction of such courts.

unwiderrufliche Gerichtsstands- vereinbarung

Unterwerfung unter die nicht ausschließ- liche Zuständigkeit der vorgenannten Gerichte

The parties irrevocably waive any objection which they may have now or hereafter to such courts as are referred to in the preceding provision of this clause, being nominated as the forum to hear and determine any suit, action or proceeding, and to settle any disputes, which may arise out of or in connection with this Agreement and any claim that any such court is not a convenient or appropriate forum.

Verzicht auf Geltend- machung von Ein- reden den Gerichts- stand betreffend

The parties hereby irrevocably appoint Mr. ..., currently at ..., to be their agent for service of process ("Process Agent") for the purpose aforesaid.

Ernennung eines Zu- stellbevollmächtigten

Such service shall be deemed completed on delivery to the Process Agent by registered mail, by hand delivery, by courier, or in accordance with the Austrian "Zustellgesetz" ("Act on the Service of Process") independent of whether or not such service has been actually effected to the other party itself. If for any reason such Process Agent ceases to be able to act as such or no longer has an address in ..., the parties irrevocably agree to appoint a substitute Process Agent with an address in ... and to deliver to the Agent an original copy of the new agent's acceptance of the appointment within thirty (30) days.

Zustellungs- bestimmung Art der Zustellung

Nachfolgeregelung für den Zustellungs- bevollmächtigten

Nothing herein shall affect the right to serve process in any other manner permitted by law.

Andere Formen der Zustellung zulässig

Sample B

A and B irrevocably agree that the competent courts of the First District of Vienna, Austria shall have jurisdiction to hear and determine any suit, action or proceeding, and to settle any disputes which may arise out of or in connection with this Agreement and for such purposes irrevocably submit to the non-exclusive jurisdiction of such courts. (...)

Ausbauklausel für den Fall, daß die Gerichtsstandsvereinbarung nur für zwei der mehreren Parteien anwendbar ist

Sample B – extended (several parties, choice of forum only applies to two of them)

(...)

The submission to the said jurisdiction shall not (and shall not be construed so as to) limit the rights of other parties hereto or any of them to take proceedings against A and/or B in any other court of competent jurisdiction nor shall the taking of proceedings in any one or more jurisdiction preclude the taking of proceedings in any other jurisdiction, whether concurrently or not.

Zulässigkeit von Parallelverfahren

4.5.20. Schiedsgerichtsbarkeit (siehe auch das Kapitel über **Schiedsgerichtsbarkeit**)

4.5.20. Arbitration

Sample A

Schiedsklausel UNCITRAL-Regeln

Any dispute, controversy or claim arising out of or in connection with this Agreement, or the breach, termination or validity thereof, shall be settled by final and binding arbitration in accordance with the UNCITRAL Arbitration Rules as presently in force (UNCITRAL = United Nations Commission on International Trade Law).

Zusammensetzung des Schiedsgerichts

Auswahl des Vorsitzenden

The tribunal shall consist of three arbitrators, one selected by each party, and a presiding umpire selected by the two party-appointed arbitrators. In selecting the presiding umpire of the tribunal the party-appointed arbitrators shall not select a person who is of the same nationality as either party or of the same nationality as either party-appointed arbitrator. Failing selection of the presiding umpire within thirty (30) days of request by a party for arbitration, or in the event of a vacancy or inability of any person to serve, within thirty (30) days thereafter, the presiding umpire shall be selected by the President of the Vienna Commercial Court (Handelsgericht Wien).

Ersatzwahl durch den Präsidenten des Wiener Handelsgerichtes

Tagungsort des Schiedsgerichtes

The place of arbitration shall be Vienna/Austria, and the award shall be deemed an Austrian award.

Sprache

The English language shall be used in the arbitral proceedings, submissions, documents, and other correspondence.

Währung

The award shall be made and shall be payable in Swiss Francs free of any tax or any other deduction.

Zinsenregelung

The award shall include interest from the day of any breach or other violation of this Agreement. The arbitrators shall also fix an appropriate rate of interest from the date of the breach or other vi-

olation to the date when the award is paid in full. In no event, however, should that interest rate be lower than the prime commercial interest rate announced by X-Bank, at its principal office in ... for ...-day loans for responsible and substantial commercial borrowers.

Obergrenze für Zinssatz

The parties agree that the award of the arbitral tribunal will be the sole and exclusive remedy between them regarding any and all claims and counter-claims presented to the tribunal. However, the foregoing shall be without prejudice to the right of a party to resort to a court or other tribunal to obtain interim, injunctive or other relief to the extent necessary to enforce the terms of this Agreement or the other party's compliance therewith, including but not limited to compelling arbitration enjoining disclosure or unauthorized use of the products and protecting and preserving A's interests in the products, whether before or during the pendency of the arbitration proceeding; or to enforce an arbitration award thereafter.

Vereinbarung der endgültigen Schlichtung

Zulässigkeit der Anrufung von Gerichten und anderen Institutionen für einstweilige Maßnahmen zur Durchsetzung des Vertrages sowie zum Schutz der (jeweiligen) Partei; auch während offenem Verfahren

The arbitrators shall determine the matters in dispute in accordance with the law of the United States, or the State of New York, depending on the nature of the claim.

anwendbares materielles Recht

All notices to be given in connection with the arbitration shall be in writing. All notices shall be effected in accordance with section ... of this Agreement.

Verständigung

Sample B

The parties agree to submit any and all disputes arising under this Agreement to arbitration in the city of Zurich, Switzerland.

Schiedsklausel

The arbitration tribunal will have three members. Each party will choose one arbitrator, and these two arbitrators will then choose the third arbitrator. If the two arbitrators cannot agree, the third arbitrator may be appointed by a cantonal court of Zurich upon application of either arbitrator or either party. The arbitrators will be Swiss nationals who are either attorneys or certified public accountants or auditors.

Zusammensetzung des Schiedsgerichts

The cost of arbitration will be shared equally by the parties. The language of the arbitration will be English.

fixe Kostenaufteilung
Sprache

The arbitrators will decide the dispute according to principles of equity and will not be bound by particular provisions of any country's law, except that any matters which, in order to be enforced in ..., must be decided in accordance with ...'s law. The arbitration tribunal will develop its own rules of procedure. In the event of this Agreement, the Arbitration Rules of the International Chamber of Commerce (ICC) will apply. The arbitration tribunal will be empowered to call witnesses and examine documents.

Entscheidung nach Billigkeit, ohne Berücksichtigung eines bestimmten Rechts, mit Ausnahme solcher Angelegenheiten, zu deren Durchsetzung die Anwendung einer bestimmten Rechtsordnung geboten ist

The tribunal must render its decision within three months from the date of submission of the case. The tribunal will decide the case by majority vote. The decision of the tribunal will be in writing

Entscheidungspflicht binnen drei Monaten, durch Mehrheit

endgültige Ent-
scheidung, Rechts-
mittelausschluß, Voll-
streckbarkeit
ordentlicher Rechts-
weg durch einver-
nehmlichen Verzicht
auf Schiedsgerichts-
barkeit

and signed by the arbitrators who voted in favor of the decision. The tribunal will communicate the decision to the parties. The decision will be binding on the parties and not subject to appeal. The arbitral award may be enforced by any court of competent jurisdiction.

The parties may by mutual agreement waive arbitration and submit the case to litigation in the courts of the canton of Zurich, Switzerland.

Sample C

Schiedsgerichtsklausel
der Internationalen
Handelskammer

Any dispute arising in connection with this Agreement shall be finally settled under the Rules of Conciliation and Arbitration of the International Chamber of Commerce by a court of arbitration appointed in accordance with said Rules.

The arbitration shall take place in Geneva, Switzerland.

4.5.21. Sprache

4.5.21. Languages

Sample A

authentische Version/
Vorzug gegenüber der
zweiten Vertrags-
sprache

This Contract has been executed in German and English. The parties hereto agree that the German version shall be the authentic one and shall thus prevail over the English one for all matters of interpretation and construction.

Sample B

authentische Version
mit Übersetzung, Aus-
legungsneutralität

This Agreement has been executed in both English and Hungarian. The English version shall be deemed the original and the Hungarian version shall only be deemed a translation thereof. Thus, the parties agree that the Hungarian version shall not be used for the construction and interpretation of the meaning of the English original.

4.6. Closing phrases

Sample A

IN WITNESS WHEREOF the Parties have caused this Agreement to be executed by their duly authorized representatives in the manner legally binding upon them as of the date first above-written.

A, Ltd.   *B, Inc.*
by: ...   *by: ...*
    (Name)   *(Name)*

Unterfertigung des Vertrages durch die befugten Vertreter in rechtsverbindlicher Weise

Sample B

IN WITNESS WHEREOF, the parties have caused this Contract to be executed in triplicate by their duly-authorized representatives as of the day first above-written.

FIC: ...   *(President)*
P & Q: ...   *(Vice President)*
ABC: ...   *(Managing Director)*

Unterzeichnung von drei Ausfertigungen

Sample C

IN WITNESS WHEREOF the parties hereto have hereunto set their hands and seals on the day and year first above written.

     A INDUSTRIES, INC. (Manufacturer)
SEAL   *By: ...*
       Name: ...
       Title: ...
     ABC Ges.m.b.H. (Distributor)
       By: ...
       Name: ...
       Title: ...

Unterschrift und offizielles Firmen-siegel; entspricht firmenmäßiger Zeichnung

86

VERTRAGSRECHTS-TERMINOLOGIE

TERMINOLOGY OF CONTRACTS

Abfertigung	*severance pay, redundancy pay*
Abnutzung	*wear and tear*
abtreten	*to assign*
Abtretungsvertrag	*contract of assignment, assignment contract*
am unten angesetzten Tage (abgeschlossen ..)	*entered into this ... day of ... 19..*, at the date first above* written*
anbieten	*to offer*
Anbot	*offer*
andererseits	*on the other hand/part*
ändern	*to amend, to modify*
Änderung	*amendment to (a contract), modification of (a contract)*
Anerkenntnis	*acknowledgement*
angestellt sein als	*to be employed as, to serve the company as*
Angestellter	*employee, white-collar worker*
Anhang	*annex, attachment, exhibit*
Annahme (eines Anbots)	*acceptance (of an offer)*
annehmen (ein Anbot)	*to accept (an offer)*
Antrag	*application, request, motion*
Anwalt	*attorney(-at-law), solicitor, counsel, [lawyer*]*
Anweisungen befolgen	*to comply with directives, to obey directives*
anwendbares Recht	*applicable law, governing law*
Arbeiter	*worker (blue-collar worker)*
Arbeitslosigkeit	*unemployment*
Arbeitsunfähigkeit	*incapacity*
auf Anforderung von jmdm	*upon request by so., at so.'s request, on demand of so.*
auf Kosten von jmdm	*at so.'s expense*
Aufgabenbereich	*scope of responsibilities/tasks/duties*
Auftrag	*order, instruction*
Ausfertigung (eines Schriftstückes)	*counterpart*
Ausgleich (Insolvenz)	*assignment to the benefit of one's creditors, settlement*
auslegen	*to construe, to interpret*
Auslegung (eines Vertrages)	*interpretation (of a contract), construction*
Austritt	*voluntary retirement (D); immediate termmnation of employment by employee (A)*
Barauslage(n)	*expenses, expenditure*
bedarf der Schriftform	*shall be in writing*

87

Beginn	*commencement date*
beginnend mit	*beginning with, commencing with*
Beilage	*annex, attachment, exhibit*
berechtigt sein	*to be entitled to*
Beschwerde	*complaint*
bestellen (jmdn zum Geschäftsführer ...)	*to appoint so. managing director*
bestellt werden (zum Geschäftsführer)	*to be appointed managing director*
Bestellung	*appointment*
(zum Geschäftsführer)	*(as managing director);*
(i.S.v. Auftrag)	*order*
Betriebskosten	*running expenses, running costs, maintenance fee*
Betriebskostenschlüssel	*scheme for allotment of running expenses/running costs/maintenance fee*
bezahlter Urlaub	*paid leave*
bezugnehmend auf	*with reference to, referring to*
Buchhalter	*book-keeper, accountant*
Buchhaltung	*book-keeping, accounting*
Buchprüfer	*auditor*
Buchprüfung	*audit*
Courtage	*brokerage*
Dauer	*term, period, duration*
Definitionen	*definitions*
Delogierung	*eviction*
Dienstgeber	*employer*
Dienstnehmer	*employee*
Dienstvertrag	*service agreement, employment contract*
Dritter	*third party*
Durchführung (eines Vertrages)	*implementation*
durchsetzbar sein	*to be enforceable*
Durchsetzbarkeit	*enforceability*
Eigenbedarf	*requirement for one's own use*
einerseits	*on the one hand/part*
einhalten	*to comply with, to adhere to, to abide by*
Einhaltung	*compliance with, adherence to*
Eintrittsrecht	*right to succeed an existing lodger/ tenant, right to enter into an existing lease agreement, subrogation*
einvernehmliche Auflösung	*termination by mutual agreement*
Entlassung (vorzeitige)	*dismissal (immediate)*
erfüllen	*to perform, to fulfil*
Erfüllung (eines Vertrages)	*performance (of a contract)*
ergänzen	*to amend*
Ergänzung	*amendment*
Erhalt	*receipt*

Erhaltung	*maintenance*
erheblich nachteiliger Gebrauch	*materially adverse use*
errichten (einen Vertrag)	*to enter into (a contract), to conclude (a contract), to execute (a contract)*
Errichtung (eines Vertrages)	*conclusion, execution (of a contract)*
Ersterer	*the former*
Erwerbsunfähigkeit	*incapacity*
Exportvertreter	*export agent*
fällig sein/werden	*to be/to become due*
Fälligkeit	*due date, maturity*
Fälligkeitstag	*due date*
Fehler	*defect*
fehlerhaft	*defective*
Fehlverhalten (schweres)	*misconduct (serious)*
Firmenwagen	*company car*
Form	*form*
Formalitäten	*formalities*
Formerfordernisse	*formal requirements*
Funktion	*capacity*
für die Dauer dieses Vertrages	*for the term of this contract, for the duration of this contract, during the term of this contract*
Garantie	*guarantee*, warranty***
garantieren	*to guarantee, to warrant**
Gebiet (Vertrags-)	*territory, area*
gegen die guten Sitten	*contra bonos mores*, violating public policy*
Gehalt	*salary*
gemäß	*pursuant to, according to, in accordance with, due to, subject to, in compliance with*
gemäß den gesetzlichen Bestimmungen	*as required by law, in accordance with the statutory provisions*
gemeinsame Benützung	*joint use*
Gerichtsstand	*forum, [jurisdiction*]*
Geschäftsführer	*managing director*, manager**
Gesellschaftsvertrag	*articles/memorandum of association*
gewährleisten	*to represent*, to warrant**
Gewährleistung	*representation*, warranty**
Gewinnspanne	*rate of profit, profit margin*
guter Zustand	*good condition, proper condition*
haften	*to be liable for*
Haftung	*liability*
Haftung zur ungeteilten Hand	*joint and several liability*
Handelsreisender	*(travelling) salesman*
Hausmeister	*janitor (US), house-keeper (UK)*
Höhere Gewalt	*Acts of God, force majeure**

im Anhang	*attached*
im Auftrag von	*on behalf of, upon demand by, upon instruction by, for*
im erforderlichen Ausmaß	*to the extent necessary, to the extent required*
im Ermessen von	*at the discretion of*
im Hinblick auf	*with respect to, regarding, in respect of, as regards*
im nachhinein (zahlbar)	*(payable) in arrears*
im Namen und im Auftrag von	*in the name and on behalf of*
im Sinne von	*within the meaning of, pursuant to*
im Verhältnis (z.B. ihrer Anteile)	*pro rata (their respective stakes), in proportion to, proportionate to*
im Verhältnis zu	*in relation to, relating to*
im voraus (zahlbar)	*(payable) in advance*
in der derzeit gültigen/geltenden Fassung	*as amended*
in der jeweils gültigen Fassung	*as amended from time to time*
in gebrauchsfähigem Zustand erhalten	*to keep/maintain in good/proper condition/ working order/reasonable repair*
in Kraft sein	*to be in effect, to be in force*
in Kraft treten	*to enter into effect, to enter into force, to become effective*
insbesondere	*including without limitation, in particular, above all, especially*
Inventar	*inventory*
Irrtum	*mistake*
jede der Parteien	*either (of the) party (-ies)*
jedenfalls	*in any event, in any case*
Karenz	*leave**
Kaufpreis	*purchase price*
Kaufvertrag	*purchase agreement, contract of purchase*
Kaution	*security deposit*
Keller (-abteil)	*cellar, basement (compartment)*
Klausel	*clause, stipulation, provision*
Klient	*client*
Kollektivvertrag	*collective bargaining agreement, collective labour agreement*
konkurrieren mit	*to compete with*
Kosten	*costs*
Krankenstand	*sick leave, sickness leave*
Kunde	*customer*
Kündigung	*termination upon notice, notice to terminate*
Kündigungsausschluß	*exclusion of grounds for terminating (a lease agreement)*

Kündigungsbeschränkung	*limitation on right to terminate*
Kündigungsfrist	*period of notice*
Kündigungsgrund	*cause/ground(s) for termination*
Kündigungstermin	*effective date of termination*
Kündigungsverzicht	*waiver of right of termination,*
	waiver of right to terminate
leitender Angestellter	*executive, senior employee, senior officer*
Letzterer	*the latter*
Lieferbedingungen	*terms of delivery*
Lieferung	*delivery, shipment*
Lieferverzug	*delay in delivery*
Lohn	*wage*
Maklerprovision	*broker's commission, broker's fee,*
	brokerage
Mangel	*defect*
mangelhaft	*defective*
Meinungsverschiedenheiten	*disagreements*
Miet(zins)rückstand	*unpaid rent*
Miete	*rent*
Mietenerhöhung	*rent increase*
Mieter	*tenant, lessee, lodger*
Mietrechtsgesetz (MRG)	*Austrian Rent Act**
Mietvertrag	*lease agreement, rental agreement*
Mietzins	*rent*
Mietzinsbeschränkung	*statutory limitation on rents*
	(maximum amounts)
Mietzinserhöhung	*rent increase*
Mietzinskategorien	*classes of maximum rents (assessed on*
	the basis of the condition of the flat)
mit Ausnahme von	*except for*
möbliert	*furnished*
Mutterschaftsurlaub	*maternity leave*
nach besten Kräften	*best efforts, best endeavours*
nachstehend	*hereinafter, hereunder, in the following,*
	as follows
Nachtrag	*amendment*
namens	*in the name of, on behalf of*
namens und auftrags	*in the name and on behalf of*
Nebenabrede	*additional agreement, subsidiary*
	agreement, subsidiary understanding,
	side agreement
Nebenvereinbarung	*side agreement*
Nichterfüllung	*failure to perform, non-performance,*
	non-fulfilment
Notariatsakt	*notarial deed**
Nutzungsrecht	*right to use*

offene Salden	*outstanding balances*
ohne Einschränkung	*without limitation*
ohne Präjudiz	*without prejudice*
Partei	*party*
Parteienwille	*intention/intent/understanding of the parties*
Pensionsanspruch	*entitlement to a pension*
Personal	*personnel, staff*
Pflichten	*obligations, duties*
Pflichten nicht mehr erfüllen können	*to become incapable of performing/ fulfilling one's duties*
Pflichterfüllung	*performance/fufillment of one's duties*
Präambel	*preamble*
Preisminderung	*reduction in price*
private Wohnzwecke	*private residential purpose, private residential use*
Produkte	*products*
Provision	*commission*
räumen	*to evict, to move out, to vacate*
Räumung	*eviction*
Räumungsaufschub	*deferred eviction*
Räumungsklage	*action for eviction*
Recht	*right, title, power, authorization*
Recht durchsetzen (ein ...)	*to enforce a right*
Recht geltend machen (ein ...)	*to assert a right*
Recht haben (ein ...)	*to be entitled to, to have a right*
Rechtsbehelf	*remedy*
Rechtsmangel	*defective title*
Rechtsnachfolger	*(legal) successor, assign*
Rechtsstreit	*litigation, (court) case*
Rechtsstreitigkeit	*legal dispute, litigation*
rechtsverbindlich	*(legally) binding*
Reisekosten	*travel(ling) expenses*
Reisekostenersatz	*reimbursement of travel(ling) expenses*
Rohstoffknappheit	*shortage of raw material*
Rücktritt (vom Vertrag)	*repudiation (prior to performance), recission (upon performance), cancellation*
Saldo	*balance*
schad- und klaglos halten	*to indemnify and hold harmless*
Schad- und Klagloshaltung	*indemnification*
Schadenersatz	*damages*
Schiedsgericht	*arbitration tribunal, arbitral tribunal*
Schiedsgerichtsbarkeit	*arbitration*
schriftlich	*in writing, in written form*
seitens	*on the part of*

sittenwidrig	*contra bonos mores*, violating public policy*
Sorge tragen für	*to ensure, to take care, to arrange for*
Spesen	*(out-of-pocket) expenses*
Stimmrechtsbevollmächtigter	*person holding proxy*
Stimmrechtsvollmacht	*proxy*
Streitigkeiten	*disputes*
Tierhaltung	*keeping of pets*
Transportmöglichkeiten	*transport(ation) facilities*
über Aufforderung von	*on demand of, upon request of*
Übereinkunft (mündliche)	*arrangement, agreement (oral)*
übernehmen (eine Wohung)	*to take over, to move in*
Umsatz	*sales, turnover*
unbeschadet	*notwithstanding*
unbezahlter Urlaub	*unpaid leave*
undurchsetzbar	*unenforceable*
Undurchsetzbarkeit	*unenforceability*
ungesetzlich	*illegal, unlawful*
unleidliches Verhalten	*serious misconduct, improper behaviour*
unmöbliert	*unfurnished*
unter der Voraussetzung, daß	*provided that, on condition that, subject to, under the provisio that/of*
unterfertigen	*to sign, to execute*
Unterfertigung	*signing, signature, execution*
Untermiete	*sublease*
Untermieter	*sublessee*
untervermieten	*to sublet*
Urkund dessen	*IN WITNESS WHEREOF, WITNESSETH*
Urkunde	*document*
Urlaub	*holidays (UK), vacation (US), annual leave*
Urlaubsgeld	*vacation pay, holiday bonus*
Vaterschaftsurlaub	*paternity leave* (A)*
Verbraucherpreisindex	*Consumer Price Index*
vereinbaren	*to agree, to covenant, to stipulate*
Vereinbarung	*agreement; covenant; stipulation*
Verfahren	*procedure; proceedings*
Verfahrensregeln	*rules of procedure*
verhandeln	*to negotiate*
Verhandlungen (Vertrags-)	*negotiations*
Verkäufe	*sales*
Verkaufsförderung	*sales promotion*
Verkaufsleiter	*sales manager, director of sales*
Verkaufsrepräsentant	*sales representative*

Verkürzung über die Hälfte (laesio enormis)	*Continental European concept of voidability of a given contract if the consideration given in exchange for a certain thing is worth more than twice as much as the good bargain for**
Verlademöglichkeiten	*loading facilities*
Verladen	*loading*
Verlust (Gewinn-)	*loss (of profits)*
Vermieter	*lessor, landlord, landlady*
Vermietung	*lease, rental, letting*
vernachlässigen	*to neglect*
verpflichtend	*binding*
verpflichtet sein	*to be bound, to be obliged, to be under an obligation*
Verpflichtung	*obligation, commitment, undertaking*
Verständigung	*notification, notice*
Vertrag	*contract, agreement*
Vertrag errichten	*to conclude (a contract, an agreement)*
Vertrag schließen	*to enter into, to conclude (a contract, an agreement)*
Vertragsabschluß	*conclusion of (a contract, an agreement)*
Vertragsänderung	*amendment to, modification of (a contract, an agreement)*
Vertragsauflösung	*termination of (a contract, an agreement)*
Vertragsbeendigung	*termination of (a contract, an agreement)*
(sofortige)	*(immediate)*
(begründete)	*(for cause)*
Vertragsbestimmungen	*terms, conditions, provisions, clauses, stipulations*
Vertragsbruch	*breach of contract*
Vertragsergänzung	*amendment to (a contract, an agreement)*
Vertragshändler	*distributor, authorized dealer*
Vertragsklauseln	*clauses, provisions (of a contract, an agreement)*
Vertragsparteien	*contracting parties*
Vertragsverlängerung	*renewal (of a contract)*
Vertragsverletzung	*default under a contract/an agreement*
Vertreter	*representative, agent*
vertretungsberechtigt	*to be authorized to represent*
Vertretungsberechtigter	*authorized representative, authorized agent*
Vertretungsbevollmächtigter	*authorized representative*
Vertriebshändler	*distributor*
Vertriebsvertrag	*distributor contract, distributorship agreement*
Verzicht	*waiver*

94

verzichten	*to waive*
Verzug	*delay*
Vollmacht	*power of attorney*
Vollmachtsinhaber	*person holding power of attorney*
vom ... (Datum) an (z.B. in Kraft treten)	*(e.g. to become effective) as of ... (date)*
von einer Pflicht befreit werden	*to be relieved from an obligation*
Vordienstzeiten	*periods of prior employment*
vorgenannt	*(herein)abovementioned*
vorstehend	*hereinbefore, hereinabove, abovementioned, decribed/listed/stated above*
Wandlung	*cancellation of contract*
Ware	*commodity*
Waren	*goods, commodities*
Weihnachtsgeld	*Christmas bonus*
Wertsicherungsklausel	*stable-value clause*
wie (bereits) vereinbart	*as (previously) agreed upon*
wie folgt	*as follows*
wie oben angeführt	*hereinbefore mentioned, abovementioned*
wie unten angeführt	*as set forth below*
Wiedervermietung	*re-rental*
Wohnung	*flat (UK), apartment (US)*
zahlbar	*payable*
Zahlungsbedingungen	*terms of payment*
Zahlungsverzug	*delay in payment*
zu ungeteilter Hand	*joint(ly) and severable(-ly)*
Zubehör	*fixtures, fittings, appurtenances, appliances*
Zugeständnis	*concession, acknowledgment*
Zuhaltung des Vertrages	*performance pursuant to the terms of the contract/the agreement*
zumutbar	*that can be asked of so., appropriate, reasonable*
zur Gänze oder teilweise	*in whole or in part*
zurücktreten (von einem Vertrag)	*to repudiate, to rescind, to cancel (a contract)*
Zustandekommen (eines Vertrages)	*conclusion (of a contract)*
zuteilen	*to allot*
Zutrittsrecht	*right of entry*
zuweisen	*to allot, to distribute*
Zwangsräumung	*eviction*
zwischen (abgeschlossen)	*(entered into) by and between*

TERMINOLOGY OF CONTRACTS

VERTRAGSRECHTS-TERMINOLOGIE

abide by	einhalten, sich halten an
abovementioned	vorstehend, vorgenannt, obgenannt
acceptance	Annahme (eines Anbots)
according to	gemäß, nach
accountant	Buchhalter
accrue	auflaufen, entstehen (Kosten, Zinsen etc.)
acknowledgement	Anerkenntnis, Zugeständnis
act in the name of so.	im Namen von jmdm handeln
act jointly with	gemeinsam mit jmdm handeln
act on behalf of so.	im Auftrag von jmdm/für jmdn handeln
Acts of God	Höhere Gewalt*, inbesondere Naturkatastrophen
affected thereby	davon berührt
affiliated company	Beteiligungsgesellschaft
see also the chapter on Business Organisations	
agent	Bevollmächtigter, Handelsvertreter*
agree to negotiate	vereinbaren, in Verhandlungen einzutreten
agreement	Vereinbarung, Vertrag, Einigung, Absprache, Übereinkunft
agreement for the sale of ...	Kaufvertrag über ...
allot	zuteilen, zuweisen, zusprechen
amend	ändern, ergänzen
amendment	Änderung, Ergänzung, Nachtrag
amounts due	geschuldete/fällige Beträge
annex	Anhang, Beilage
anticipated sales	erwartete Verkäufe/Umsätze
apartment (US)	Wohnung, Appartement
appearing in this agreement (terms)	die in diesem Vertrag aufscheinenden Bedingungen
appendix	Anhang
application	Antrag
appointed	bestellt
appurtenances	Bestandteile, Zubehör
arbitral tribunal	Schiedsgericht
arbitration	Schiedsgerichtsbarkeit
area	Gebiet
arrange for	Sorge tragen, daß
as agreed upon	wie vereinbart, gemäß Vereinbarung
as amended (from time to time)	in der (jeweils) gültigen Fassung
as at ... (date)	per ... (Datum)
as evidenced by	wie sich aus ... ergibt
as follows	wie folgt
as of ... (date)	vom ... (Datum)
as otherwise authorized	wie anderweitig/sonst gestattet

as provided for in (section, etc.)	wie in ... (Paragraph etc.) vorgesehen/ geregelt
as required by law	gemäß den gesetzlichen Bestimmungen
as set forth below	wie unten ausgeführt
as set forth in (section)	wie in (Paragraph) ausgeführt
as soon as possible (asap)	so schnell wie möglich
as soon as practical	sobald die Voraussetzungen gegeben sind
as used in this agreement	im Sinne dieser Vereinbarung
assign	Rechtsnachfolger
assign	abtreten
assignment	Abtretung
assignment contract	Abtretungsvertrag
assignment for the benefit of one's creditors	Vergleich/Ausgleich (im Insolvenzrecht)
at all times (during the term of this agreement)	zu jeder Zeit (während der Dauer dieser Vereinbarung)
at all times thereafter	zu jeder Zeit/jedem Zeitpunkt danach
at any reasonable time or times	zu jedem angemessenen Zeitpunkt
at so's request	über jmds Aufforderung/Anforderung/ Verlangen
at so.'s expense	auf Kosten von jmdm
at the discretion of	im Ermessen von
attached hereto	im Anhang
attachment	Anhang, Beilage
attorney	Anwalt
attorney-at-law	Rechtsanwalt
audit	Buchprüfung
audit	prüfen (die Bücher)
auditor	Buchprüfer
authorized representative	bevollmächtigter Vertreter
be considered (A shall ...)	von A wird angenommen, daß ... (Fiktion)
become due and payable	fällig und zahlbar werden
beginning with	beginnend mit
best efforts/endeavours	nach besten Kräften
beyond one's reasonable control	außerhalb des Einflußbereiches
binding upon	verpflichtend, verbindlich
breach	(einen Vertrag) brechen
breach of contract	Vertragsbruch
brokerage	Maklerprovision, Courtage
business and affairs of the company	die Geschäfte und Angelegenheiten der Gesellschaft
by and between	zwischen
by and large	im großen und ganzen
capacity	Funktion, Eigenschaft
capitalization	Kapitalisierung, Aktivierung, Kapitalausstattung, aber auch: Großschreibung

capitalization of defined terms	Großschreibung definierter Begriffe
carry on business	Geschäfte tätigen
cause an arrangement to be executed	die Unterfertigung eines Vertrages veranlassen
cellar compartment	Kellerabteil
certified mail (US)	Einschreibebrief, Einschreibesendung
certified public accountant (CPA) (US)	beeideter Buchprüfer, Wirtschaftsprüfer
chartered accountant (UK)	beeideter Buchprüfer, Wirtschaftsprüfer
check-out inspection	Abnahme anläßlich des Auszugs
clause	Klausel, Vertragsbestimmung
commencement date	Beginn
commencing with	beginnend mit
commission	Provision
commission agent	Vertreter auf Provisionsbasis
commit an act of bankruptcy	in Konkurs gehen
commitment	Verpflichtung
commodity	Ware
common use	gemeinsame Benützung
communication	Informationsfluß, Mitteilung
company	Gesellschaft
see the chapter on Corporate Law	
compensation	Wiedergutmachung, Ersatz
compete with (to)	in Konkurrenz stehen mit, im Wettbewerb stehen mit
compliance	Einhaltung
comply with directives	Anweisungen befolgen
conclude contracts	Verträge abschließen
condition	Bedingung
condition precedent	aufschiebende Bedingung
condominium (US)	Eigentumswohnung*
confidentiality	Vertraulichkeit
consent	Zustimmung
consideration	Gegenleistung* **(siehe auch Einleitung zum Vertragsrecht)**
constitute	begründen (z.B. ein Recht)
construe	auslegen
Consumer Price Index	Verbraucherpreisindex
contained herein	in diesem Dokument enthalten
continue in effect	in Kraft bleiben
continuing throughout	aufrecht bleiben während ...
contract	Vertrag
contract of assignment	Abtretungsvertrag
corporation	Kapitalgesellschaft
see the chapter on Corporate Law	
cost(s)	Kosten
counterpart(s)	Ausfertigung(en)
covenant	vereinbaren
covenant(s)	Vertrag, Vertragsbestimmung, Klausel, Vereinbarung

cover an area	ein Gebiet abdecken
CPA (certified public accountant) (US)	beeideter Buchprüfer, Wirtschaftsprüfer
cure	Heilung (von Vertragsbrüchen)
customer	Kunde
date first above written	(entspricht „am unten angesetzten Tage")
de facto	de facto
de jure	de iure
deemed (e.g. effective)	angesehen werden (z.B. als rechtswirksam) (Fiktion)
default	Vertragswidrigkeit, Schlechterfüllung, Leistungsstörung (insb. Zahlungsverpflichtungen nicht nachkommen)
defect	Fehler, Mangel
defective title	Rechtsmangel (Titel, Eigentum)
defined terms	definierte Begriffe
definitions	Definitionen
delay	Verzug
delay in delivery	Lieferverzug
delay in payment	Zahlungsverzug
delegate one's duties	Verpflichtungen abtreten
deliver (a document)	zustellen, übergeben (eine Urkunde)
deliver goods	Waren liefern
delivery	Lieferung
delivery terms	Lieferbedingungen
desirous of (e.g. A is desirous of selling X to B)	(z.B. A möchte X an B verkaufen*)
disagreement(s)	Meinungsverschiedenheiten
disputes	Streitigkeiten
disputes arising out of/under this agreement	Streitigkeiten aus diesem Vertrag
distributor	Vertriebshändler, Vertragshändler
distributor contract	Vertriebsvertrag
distributorship agreement	Vertriebsvertrag
divulge information	Informationen preisgeben
document	Urkunde, Dokument, Unterlage
due to	gemäß, aufgrund
duly executed	ordnungsgemäß gezeichnet
duly incorporated	ordnungsgemäß eingetragen/registriert (Gesellschaften)
duly signed	ordnungsgemäß unterfertigt
during the continuance of this agreement	für die Dauer dieses Vertrages
during the term of (this agreement)	für die Dauer (des Bestands dieser Vereinbarung)
each such ... (e.g. order)	jeder ... (z.B. Aufträge)
either party	jede der Parteien
electric bill	Stromrechnung

embargo(-es)	Embargo(s)
empowered to do something	ermächtigt sein zu
enforceable	durchsetzbar
engaged in the business of (manufactu-ring cars)	ein (Autohersteller) sein
ensure	sicherstellen
enter into (an agreement)	abschließen (eine Vereinbarung)
entire agreement	Vertragsklausel, die die abschließende Regelung aller zwischen den Parteien getroffenen Vereinbarungen bestätigt (keine Nebenabsprachen)
entitled to	berechtigt
establish a corporation/company **see also the chapter on Business Organisations**	eine Gesellschaft errichten/gründen
evict	zwangsweise räumen, delogieren
eviction	Zwangsräumung, Delogierung
except as specified in this section	mit Ausnahme der Bestimmungen dieses Punktes
except for	mit Ausnahme von
exclusive	exklusiv, ausschließlich, Allein-
executed	unterfertigt
exercise a right	ein Recht ausüben
exercise powers	Kompetenzen ausüben, Rechte ausüben
exhibit	Anlage, Beilage
expenditures	Barauslagen
export agent	Außenhandelsvertreter, Exportvertreter
F will cause A to do	F wird A dazu anhalten, .../ F wird veranlassen, daß A ...
failure	Unterlassung, Nichterfüllung
failure (to perform)	Nichterfüllung
feasible	angemessen, angebracht
fixtures, fittings and appliances	Wohungs-/Grundstückszubehör, fest eingebaute Anlagen etc.
flat (UK)	Wohnung
for a period of	für die Dauer/den Zeitraum von
for a term to begin on .. and to expire on ...	für einen Zeitraum von ... bis ...
for any reason (whatsoever)	aus welchem Grund auch immer
for the purpose of	zum Zwecke
for the time being	derzeit, jetzt
force majeure	Höhere Gewalt*
foregoing paragraph (the)	der vorstehende Absatz
form	Form
former (the)	Ersterer
forthwith	zukünftig, von ... an
forum	Gerichtsstand
found to be (e.g. illegal)	sich als (z.B. gesetzeswidrig) heraus-stellen

from time to time	jeweils
from time to time (as amended from t. to t.)	jeweils (in der jeweils geltenden Fassung)
fulfil an obligation	einer Verpflichtung nachkommen
furnished	möbliert
good condition	guter Zustand
goods	Waren
governed by and interpreted/construed in accordance with (the laws of)	(dem Recht von) unterliegen und gemäß diesem ausgelegt werden
governing law	anwendbares Recht
guarantee	garantieren*
guarantee (UK) / guaranty (US)	Garantie*
have the meaning as defined hereunder	nachfolgende Bedeutung haben
have the meaning set forth below	nachfolgende Bedeutung haben
have the right to	das Recht haben, berechtigt sein
headings	Überschriften
hence	somit
henceforth	von jetzt an
hereby	hiermit
hereinafter (referred to as X)	nachstehend (X genannt)
hereinbefore	vorstehend
hereincontained	in diesem Dokument enthalten
hereof	hievon, davon
hereto	hiezu
hereunder	im folgenden
hold sb. harmless	jmdn schadlos halten
holding company	Holdinggesellschaft
if (and when) required	falls gewünscht/erforderlich/notwendig
if accepted	im Fall der Annahme
if necessary	falls erforderlich
illegal	ungesetzlich, illegal
impairment of one's right to use	Beeinträchtigung des Rechts auf ungestörte Nutzung
improper behaviour	unleidliches Verhalten
improve and extend business	den Geschäftsgang verbessern und ausweiten
in accordance with	in Übereinstimmung mit, gemäß
in addition to and not in place of	zusätzlich zu und nicht anstatt von
in advance	im voraus
in any event	jedenfalls
in arrears	im nachhinein
in both their singular and plural forms (terms)	(Begriffe) in der Einzahl und Mehrzahl
in consideration of ...	als Gegenleistung für
in good working order	in funktionstüchtigem Zustand

in proportion to	verhältnismäßig
in relation to	im Verhältnis zu
in the event of	im Falle von
in the presence of	in Gegenwart von
in the proper course of duties	im Rahmen des Aufgabenbereichs
in whole or in part	zur Gänze oder teilweise
IN WITNESS WHEREOF	URKUND DESSEN
in writing	schriftlich
inapplicable to	nicht anwendbar auf
incapacitated from performing one's duties (to become)	seine Pflichten nicht mehr erfüllen können
incapacity	Arbeitsunfähigkeit, Erwerbsunfähigkeit
including without limitation	insbesondere, einschließlich, aber nicht beschränkt auf
incur expenses	Barauslagen haben
indemnify	schad- und klaglos halten
independent of	unabhängig von
infra	nachstehend, unten
inspection	Kontrolle
instal(l)ments	Raten (-zahlungen)
intend	beabsichtigen
intention of the parties	Absicht/Wille der Parteien
inure to the benefit of	zum Vorteil gereichen
inventory	Inventar
janitor (US)	Hausmeister
joint and several	zur ungeteilten Hand*
joint and several (liability)	Haftung zur ungeteilten Hand*
jointly	gemeinsam
keep in reasonable repair	in gebrauchsfähigem Zustand erhalten
keep sb. indemnified against	jmdn für/gegen etwas schad- und klaglos halten
labour disputes	arbeitsrechtliche Konflikte
landlady	Vermieterin
landlord	Vermieter
late fee	Verspätungszuschlag
latter (the)	Letzterer
law(s)	Recht, Gesetz(e)
lease	Miete
lease agreement	Mietvertrag
legally binding	rechtsverbindlich
lessee	Mieter
lessor	Vermieter
litigation	Rechtsstreit
lock-out	Aussperrung

made as of ... (date) (this agreement is ...)	(dieser Vertrag wurde) am ... errichtet, abgeschlossen
mains	(Haupt-) Leitung(en)
maintenance	Erhaltung
maintenance fees	Betriebskosten
make commitments, representations or warranties	verbindliche Zusicherungen machen (z.B. hinsichtlich Umsatz, Abnahmemengen etc.)
manager	Geschäftsführer*, Geschäftsleiter*
manner (legally-binding)	(rechtsverbindliche) Form
may include without limitation	kann insbesondere enthalten
modification	(Ab-) Änderung
modify	(ab-) ändern
monthly instalments	Monatsmiete
mutual covenants	wechselseitige Vereinbarungen
mutually agree upon	wechselseitig übereinkommen
negligence	Fahrlässigkeit, Vernachlässigung
negotiations	Verhandlungen
no pets allowed	Tierhaltung verboten
no waiver	kein Verzicht
non-assignment	Nichtübertragung
normal wear and tear	normale(r) Abnutzung, Verschleiß
nothing herein contained (shall be construed as)	keine Bestimmung dieses Vertrages (soll so ausgelegt werden, daß)
notice	Verständigung, Mitteilung
notwithstanding	unbeschadet
NOW THEREFORE	**siehe Cut & Paste – Recitals**
obligation	Verpflichtung
of ... (company address)	mit der Geschäftsanschrift ...
of whatsoever nature/kind	welcher Art auch immer
offer	An(ge)bot
offset claims against the rent	Ansprüche gegen die Miete aufrechnen
on an ongoing basis	auf dauerhafter Basis/Grundlage, auf Dauer
on behalf of	für, namens/auftrags von
on demand	über Aufforderung
on the one part	einerseits
on the other part	andererseits
on the part of	seitens
on the premises	in den Räumlichkeiten
on these grounds	aus diesen Gründen
or such longer time as may be required	oder in angemessener Zeit
order	Auftrag, Bestellung
original	Original(dokument)
other than	außer
out-of-pocket expenses	Barauslagen, Spesen
owing to	aufgrund von, durch, gemäß

paid holiday	bezahlter Urlaub
parties have hereunto set their hands and seals	die Parteien haben dieses Dokument ordnungsgemäß gefertigt*
party	(Vertrags-) Partei
payment terms	Zahlungsbedingungen
perform duties	Pflichten erfüllen
performance	Erfüllung, Leistung
postage prepaid	freigemacht, Porto bezahlt
power	Ermächtigung, Berechtigung, Kompetenz
power of attorney	Vollmacht
preamble	Präambel
preclude	ausschließen
preliminary statements	einleitende Feststellungen
premises	Räumlichkeiten, Betriebsstätte
press on regardless (por)	ohne Rücksicht auf Verluste
prevail over	vorgehen
principles of equity	Grundsätze des Law of Equity* (vgl. Auslegung nach Billigkeit)
private residence purposes	private Wohnzwecke
pro rata	anteilig, verhältnismäßig
products similar to or competitive with	ähnliche (Konkurrenz-) Produkte
promote sales	Umsatz/Verkauf fördern
proper condition	ordentlicher Zustand
prospective profits	erwartete Gewinne
provided that	vorausgesetzt, daß
provisio	unter der Voraussetzung, daß
provision	(Vertrags-) Bestimmung
purchase agreement	Kaufvertrag
purchase price	Kaufpreis
pursuant to	gemäß
rate of profit	Gewinnspanne
re-rental	Wiedervermietung
reasonably required	über angemessenes/zumutbares Verlangen
receipt	Erhalt
recitals	formelle Vertragseinleitungsklauseln **siehe Cut & Paste**
redecoration	Ausmalen, Anstreichen, Tapezieren
redundancy payments	Abfertigung, Abfindung*
regarded as cumulative (sick leave, prior periods of service)	zusammengezählt werden (bezahlter Krankenstand, Vordienstzeiten)
regardless of	unabhängig von
registered mail	Einschreibebrief, Einschreibesendung
registered office	Sitz einer Gesellschaft, Firmensitz*
regulation	Bestimmung
reimburse sb. his/her expenses	jmdm seine Kosten ersetzen

relating to	in bezug auf
remedy	Rechtsbehelf
remuneration	Bezahlung, Vergütung, Entschädigung
render premises unusable	den Mietgegenstand unbenutzbar machen
renewable	verlängerbar
rent	Mietzins, Miete
rent increase	Mietzinserhöhung
rent to sb.	vermieten
rental	Mietzins, Vermietung
repair	Reparatur
represent	verbindlich zusichern, gewährleisten*
representations	verbindliche Zusicherungen, Gewähr-leistungen*
representative	Vertreter
requested (minimum) stocks	Mindestlagermenge, Mindestabnahme-menge
residential purposes	Wohnzwecke
residing at	wohnhaft in ...
retain copies of documents	Kopien von Dokumenten/Unterlagen behalten
return receipt	Rückschein
right	Recht
right of entry	Zutrittsrecht
right to use	Nutzungsrecht
rules of procedure	Verfahrensregeln
running expenses	Betriebskosten
said ... (the)	(der, die, das) genannte ...
salary	Gehalt
scheme for allotment of the running expenses	Betriebskostenschlüssel
section	Paragraph, Punkt, Abschnitt
security deposit	Kaution
seek	beabsichtigen
separate and severable obligation	selbständige Verpflichtung
separately therefrom	unabhängig/getrennt davon
serious misconduct	schweres Fehlverhalten
serve a company as ...	angestellt sein als ...
service agreement	Dienstvertrag
severability	Trennbarkeit (vgl. Teilnichtigkeit) **siehe Cut & Paste**
share costs	Kosten aufteilen
ship products	Waren versenden, liefern
shortage of supply of raw materials	Rohstoffknappheit
sign	unterzeichnen, unterfertigen
signature	Unterschrift
so as to	um zu
sole purpose	ausschließlicher Zweck

specification	nähere Reglung/Bestimmung
stable-value clause	Wertsicherungsklausel
stipulate	vereinbaren
stipulations	Vereinbarungen, Bestimmungen
subdistributor	Vertreiber, mit dem ein Vertragshändler in untervertraglicher Beziehung steht
subject matter	Gegenstand (der Vereinbarung)
subject to	abhängig von; unter der Voraussetzung, daß
sublet	untervermieten
submit disputes to	Streitigkeiten vor ... austragen
subsidiary **see chapter on Business Organisations**	Tochtergesellschaft
substantial complaints	begründete Beschwerden
succession	(Rechts-) Nachfolge
successor	(Rechts-) Nachfolger
such (e.g. company)	die genannte (z.B. Gesellschaft)
supersede	ersetzen, ablösen
supersede prior and contemporaneous agreements and understandings	ältere und andere gleichzeitig getroffene Vereinbarungen ersetzen/ablösen
supplier	Lieferant
supply	liefern
supra	oben
take over	übernehmen
tenant	Mieter
terminate upon	auf ... hin beenden, nach .. beenden
termination	Beendigung
terms of an agreement	Vertragsbedingungen
terms of delivery	Lieferbedingungen
terms of payment	Zahlungsbedingungen
territory	(Vertrags-) Gebiet
thereafter	danach
thereof	davon
thereon	danach
thereupon	danach
to the extent necessary	im erforderlichen Ausmaß
tolerate sb. to do sth.	zulassen, daß jmd. etwas tut
travel(l)ing expenses	Reisekosten, Reisespesen
unavailability of loading or transportation facilities	Nichtverfügbarkeit von Verlade- oder Transportmöglichkeiten
under contract	aufgrund des Vertrages
under the laws of (country)	nach dem Gesetz von (Staat)
under this agreement	gemäß dieser Vereinbarung
undertake to do sth.	sich zu einer Handlung verpflichten
unenforceable	undurchsetzbar
unfurnished	unmöbliert

106

unless provided to the contrary	wenn nicht anderweitig/anderwärtig bestimmt
unpaid balances	offene Salden
unreasonably withheld	grundlos vorenthalten
upon delivery	bei Lieferung
upon expiration or termination of	nach Ablauf/Auslaufen oder Beendigung
upon notice to	nach Mitteilung/Verständigung von
upon termination	bei Beendigung
utilities	laufende Betriebskosten
vacate	räumen
validly existing	in aufrechtem Bestand
waiver	Verzicht
warrant	garantieren*
warranty	Garantie*
water bills	Wasserrechnungen
whatsoever	wie auch immer
WHEREAS	**siehe Cut & Paste – Recitals**
WHEREBY IT IS AGREED AS FOLLOWS	**siehe Cut & Paste – Recitals**
wholly-owned	im 100%igen Eigentum stehend
wilful breach of one's obligations	bewußte Verletzung von Verpflichtungen
willfully neglect to perform one's duties	bewußt verabsäumen, die Pflichten zu erfüllen
with respect to	im Hinblick auf
within ... days of ...	innerhalb von ... Tagen nach ...
within the meaning of	im Sinne von
without limitation	ohne Einschränkung
without reference to	ohne Bezugnahme auf
without so's prior written consent	ohne jmds vorherige schriftliche Zustimmung
WITNESSETH	URKUND DESSEN

III. LAW OF BUSINESS ORGANISATIONS

1. TYPES OF BUSINESS ORGANISATIONS

1.1. United Kingdom

The law of the United Kingdom recognises four main types of business organisations:

(a) the sole trader — sole traders

(b) the partnership — partnerships

(c) companies limited by shares — companies limited by shares

(d) branch of an overseas company in the U.K. — branches of overseas companies

Other forms of business organisations, e.g. unlimited companies and old trading companies incorporated by royal charter, also exist, but are not very common. Statutory companies are used to run public utilities. These other types are not a subject of this book.

1.1.1. The Sole Trader
sole trader

The sole trader is a very simple way of running a business undertaking. S/He is an individual businessperson, a one-person firm — one-person firm *that has no separate legal existence from the business s/he runs or from the services s/he provides. The sole trader brings the capital into the business and makes all the profit. In comparison to the companies limited by shares the sole trader's liability is unlimited:* — unlimited liability *if her/his business does not succeed s/he is liable for all her/his business debts.*

The sole trader must hold records for value added tax, but otherwise there are no regulations forcing her/him to keep books.

In general, this type of business organisation is favoured for small undertakings, e.g. crafts and retailers. They do not require large amounts of capital and are easy to establish.

1.1.2. Partnership
partnership

A partnership may be founded by two or more persons or corporate bodies who intend to carry on a business together with a view to making a profit. It is not legally distinct from its constitutive members and is thus considered a conduit entity. — conduit entity

According to United Kingdom law, two kinds of partnerships are possible:

(a) the ordinary partnership under the Partnership Act 1890 and — ordinary partnership

(b) the limited partnership under the Limited Partnership Act 1907. — limited partnership

The ordinary partnership may be set up without any formalities, even by tacit agreement. In such a case the structure, rights and duties of the partners are regulated by the Partnership Act 1890. — tacit agreement

109

However, large partnerships usually draw up an express partnership agreement stipulating the rights, powers and duties of the partners as well as the division of capital and profits between them. Such an agreement only governs the relationship between the partners and does not affect the rights of third parties.

ordinary partnership
unlimited liability

The main legal characteristic of an ordinary partnership is the fact that the partners have unlimited liability: they may be called upon, individually or jointly, to meet all obligations of the partnership.

Each partner of an ordinary partnership is the agent of the same and may thus enter into transactions obliging the partnership as a whole, provided that such activities fall within the ordinary course of the business.

limited partnership
registration

The limited partnership is governed by the Limited Partnership Act 1907, which lays down regulations for registration at the Companies Registry. The registration of such a partnership must contain:

name

(a) the name of the company

nature of business

(b) the nature of the business

place

(c) the place of business

names of partners

(d) the full name of each partner

duration

(e) the duration of the partnership

date of commencement

(f) the date of its commencement

statement of limited liability
limited partners

(g) a statement of the limited liability of the partnership and

(h) a list of the limited partners.

Not every partner's liability is limited. There must always be at least one partner who is personally fully liable for all the debts and obligations of the partnership with all her/his private belongings. Also, the partnership's liability may not be limited. In order to benefit from the limitation of their liabilty vis-à-vis creditors, limited partners must register the amount of capital contributed, otherwise they will be considered as ordinary partners with full liability.

A partner with limited liability does not have many possibilities of playing an active role in the business of the partnership: s/he may neither take part in the management, nor have the power to oblige the undertaking. If s/he did, s/he would risk losing the protective shield of limited liability.

Limited partnerships are rather rare in the United Kingdom, and are usually chosen for tax reasons. (See the chapter on tax law for more details).

limited companies

1.1.3. Companies Limited by Shares

The Companies Act 1985, as amended by the Companies Act 1989, governs the major part of the law on public and private companies limited by shares. Voluntary and compulsory liquidations are regulated under the Insolvency Act 1986. The Financial

110

Act 1986 governs investment business and investor protection in the United Kingdom.

In addition to this statute-based corporate law, the courts in the United Kingdom have established a considerable body of case law, which – in addition to the above mentioned statutes – applies to companies limited by shares.

The two types of companies limited by shares are:

(a) the Public Limited Company (PLC) and

(b) the Private Company Limited by Shares (Limited/Ltd.).

public limited company

private limited company

A. Public Limited Company

A public limited company is a company whose shares can be acquired by the general public. In order to facilitate the transfer of shares public companies can be listed at the London Stock Exchange. But there are also public companies which are not publicly quoted. They are usually smaller companies and sell their shares privately.

acquisition of shares by the public

The share capital must not be less than £ 50,000 of which at least 25 per cent must be paid before the company may be incorporated. The name of every public limited company must end with „public limited company" or with the abbreviation „PLC". The foundation document must state that the company is to be a public limited company. A public company must have a minimum of two shareholders.

share capital

B. Private Company Limited by Shares

A private company is a company registered under the Companies Act which is not a public company. The main difference is that its shares are not offered to the public, but are owned by a designated number of shareholders such as the members of a family or employees of the company.

shares are not offered to the public

There must be at least two shareholders, but there is no minimum capital required for private companies.

no minimum capital

C. Incorporation

incorporation

Every private and public company must be set up in accordance with the provisions of the Companies Act, and must therefore fulfil certain formal requirements. This is done by the Memorandum of Association, the foundation document, which is supplemented by the Articles of Association.

Memorandum and Articles of Association

The Memorandum of Association is the basis of a company's existence. The fundamental provisions of the memorandum must include:

(a) the name of the company; in the case of a private company, the company name must end with the word „limited" or „Ltd"; in the case of a public company, the company name must end with the words „public limited company" or „PLC".

111

registered office	*(b) where the registered office of the company will be situated: in England and Wales, or in Scotland.*
objects	*(c) the objects of the company (objects clause).*
limited liability	*(d) the limited liability of the shareholders.*
share capital number of shares	*(e) the amount of the share capital in Pounds Sterling and the number of shares the capital is divided into.*

The last section is followed by the names, addresses and descrip-
subscribers *tions of the subscribers plus the number of shares taken by each subscriber. The number of shares taken must be listed opposite the name of each subscriber. Every subscriber must subscribe to at least one share.*

If the company is a public company this must be stated in the memorandum. In the following, the memorandum is signed by each subscriber in the presence of a witness. The witness attests that the signatures on the memorandum are those of the subscribers.

Registrar of
Companies
The Memorandum of Association must be submitted to the Registrar of Companies for England and Wales. In addition to that, a statement of the identity of the first directors and the secretary of the company must also be delivered to the Registrar.

The Articles of Association govern the conduct of the internal affairs, the management and the administrative structure of the company. The articles must be divided into paragraphs and signed by the subscribers.

The articles state:

share capital	*(a) the amount of share capital with all the rights and liabilities attached to the shares;*
issuance of shares	*(b) the right to issue and transfer shares as well as what will happen to unissued shares;*
shareholders' meetings	*(c) proceedings at shareholders' meetings;*
directors	*(d) amount, appointment and removal of directors, their powers, duties and remuneration;*
general provisions	*(e) general provisions on administrative and financial matters.*

Existing model regulations show how the Articles of Association can be set up and what they can contain. Such a model regulation
Table A *is the so-called "Table A" to the Companies Act 1989, which a company may refer to or even adopt in its articles. Often companies do adopt Table A but with certain modifications depending on their size and objects.*

Board of Directors
D. The Board of Directors

A public company must have at least two directors. A private company may only have one director as long as s/he is not the secretary of the company at the same time.

The subscribers of the memorandum appoint the first directors. It is common that the subsequent directors are appointed by both the

*incumbent directors and at the general meeting, unless the Arti-
cles of Association stipulate otherwise. The office of a director can
end through her/his resignation or through removal by ordinary*   resignation or removal
*resolution of a general meeting (a simple majority of the votes in
favour is required). The board of directors also has the power to
remove a director (depending on the articles: either by simple majority or by qualified majority). Table A sets out the possibility
that one third of the directors shall retire by rotation at general*   rotation
*meetings. The Articles of Association usually exclude retirement
by rotation.*

The board of directors must meet regularly in order to pass reso-   regular meetings
*lutions which are then implemented by the management of the
company. Quite often one or more directors also serve as execu-
tives and are then responsible for the management of the company. The day-to-day decisions are usually taken and the routine
work is performed by these executive directors or managers.*

*Generally speaking, the directors' task is to conduct and control
the company's business for the benefit and in the interest of the
shareholders. This can also be seen in the personal liability of a director to the shareholders. Furthermore, s/he can be made liable if
s/he breaches any of the duties imposed on her/him or acts outside
of the company's objects, and therefore abuses her/his power.*

E. Meetings of Shareholders

*The first type of meeting is the Annual General Meeting of the
shareholders (AGM) in each calender year. Proper notice must be*   notice of the meeting
*given at least 21 days before the AGM is held. A meeting without
a notice cannot be conducted properly. The notice states the date,
time, place and agenda of the meeting.*

AGMs are held to discuss and pass resolutions on the ordinary   resolutions
*business of the company, e.g. appointment and removal of direc-
tors, appointment and remuneration of auditors and consideration
of accounts and dividends.*

*The second form of meeting is the Extraordinary General Meeting
(EGM). An EGM is any meeting which is not an AGM and is held
whenever necessary. 14 days notice is required for an EGM.*

*Most AGMs and EGMs are called by the directors. Shareholders
also have the right to request an EGM from the directors. The
shareholders may directly convene such a meeting only if the directors fail to comply with such a request. All shareholders of a
company may attend and vote, unless they hold shares with no
voting rights. At general meetings resolutions are passed. These
fall into four categories:*

*(a) ordinary resolutions requiring a simple majority of votes in fa-
vour;*

*(b) special resolutions requiring 21 days notice and a three-quar-
ter majority;*

(c) extraordinary resolutions only requiring 14 days notice, but also needing a three-quarter majority;

(d) elective resolutions being passed at general meetings of private companies in order to exclude certain company law regulations.

In certain cases, private companies may also pass written resolutions. They must be signed by all shareholders. The advantage is that it is not necessary to hold a formal meeting when a written resolution will be passed.

keeping of minutes

Minutes must be kept of every general meeting.

shares

F. Shares

classes of shares

The memorandum and the articles state the classes of shares and the rights of the holders. The articles also determine the rank of the different classes for the distribution of any dividend. The most common shares are:

(a) convertible shares

(b) deferred shares

(c) non-voting shares

(d) ordinary shares

(e) preferred shares

(f) redeemable shares

As mentioned before, a public company must have a minimum capital of £ 50,000 whereas there is no minimum for private companies. £ 12,500 must be paid in full at the time of incorporation of a public company. A further distinction is to be made between bearer shares, which belong to the holder who possesses the share certificates, and registered shares, which are made out to the respective doner.

1.1.4. Branch of an Overseas Company in the United Kingdom

A foreign company – incorporated outside the United Kingdom – may establish a place of business in the United Kingdom, as long as it complies with U.K. company law and has office premises. If this is the case, an overseas company has set up a branch in the United Kingdom.

The following documents must be submitted to the Registrar of Companies within one month of establishing the branch:

(a) the articles of association or similar byelaws in the form of certified copies;

(b) a document on the internal organisation, such as a list of the directors and secretary;

(c) a list of United Kingdom citizens authorised to receive any notice on behalf of the company (service agent);

(d) the date of establishment.

114

When doing business an overseas company has to make it clear to any business partner that it is acting as an overseas company rather than a U.K. entity: it must show its name and the name of the country where its headquarters are set up on letterheads, publications and at its place of business.

1.2. United States

1.2.1. Sole Proprietorship

sole proprietors

The sole proprietor is the simplest form of a business organization in the U.S.A. and belongs to the group of unincorporated businesses which have no legal identity of their own. The liability of

unlimited liability

the owner cannot be limited: the sole proprietor must bear all debts of her/his business.

On the other hand, the proprietor gains all the profits because it is her/his money which is invested and her/his risk. S/he does not pay any corporate income tax but only personal income tax on the profits made.

There are not many legal requirements concerning the establishment and conduct of a sole proprietorship.

partnerships

1.2.2. Partnerships

A partnership is an association of two or more persons acting as co-owners of a profit-making business, and is governed in many

Uniform Partnership Act

states by the provisions of the Uniform Partnership Act (UPA). All profits and losses are shared between the partners in accordance with the respective provisions of the partnership agreement which may, inter alia, be based on the amount of capital they have invested or other contributions they may have made.

There are two main types of partnerships:

(a) (General) Partnership

(b) Limited Partnership

general partnership
unlimited liability

The main characteristic of a (general) partnership is that all partners are general partners, meaning that all partners have unlimited liability: all partners, individually and jointly, must be liable for all the obligations of the partnership.

Partnerships can be set up by written or oral contract, but can even be informally inferred by joint activity or conduct of several people doing business. All the rights and duties of the partners are usually specified in the „articles of partnership" or „partnership agreement", otherwise they are governed by the Uniform Partnership Act (UPA). The UPA determines the internal relationship of the partners, eg. the equal sharing of profits and losses, the influence in the control of the partnership and the right to inspect the books. Several states have already enacted the Revised Uniform Partnership Act (RUPA) which has introduced several changes to the law of partnerships.

Every partner is the agent of the partnership and can bind the same in business transactions with third parties as long as s/he is not exceeding the ordinary course of the business.

termination

A partnership ends

– with the death of a partner; the remaining partners may establish a new partnership;

– *by judicial dissolution;*
– *by voluntary dissolution through all the partners and*
– *by bankruptcy of the partnership or of any one of the partners.*

After the dissolution of a partnership the partnership must be wound up.

The Limited Partnership is characterized not only by having general partners, but also partners with limited liability. In many states the limited partnership is governed by the Uniform Limited Partnership Act.

limited partnership

Uniform Limited
Partnership Act

The Uniform Limited Partnership Act states that the limited partner may only be made liable to the extent of her/his contribution to the business and that s/he may not participate in the management of the partnership.

There are also other types of partnerships:

– *Corpnership is a limited partnership with a corporation as a general partner.*

corpnership

– *Silent partnership is a partnership where the names of silent partners are not disclosed.*

silent partnership

Some states allow the formation of special associations which are designed for group practice of certain professions, eg. architects, doctors, lawyers, etc. These professional associations can usually be defined as a mixture between a partnership and a corporation, permitting the members – as shareholders – to participate in the business. Such an association may invest and acquire real property in its own name, since it is a separate legal entity. All share owners must fulfill all qualifications for the exercise of the respective profession, otherwise the association may not be established, and also if the shares are transferred to other people they must possess these qualifications.

professional
associations

1.2.3. Corporations

corporations

A corporation is a legal entity independent of its investors or owners. It may conduct a business, acquire assets and sue people in its own name, but must also pay taxes and have its own bank accounts. It is the corporation that is liable for its debts and business obligations and not the shareholders. The only risk shareholders take is that they might lose all their money invested. Furthermore, the death or withdrawal of a shareholder does not terminate the corporation.

shareholders' risk

In the US corporate law is state law. Theoretically, it would be possible for every single state to have its own corporate law, but in reality in many states corporations are governed by the Uniform Business Corporation Act.

corporate law is state
law

Uniform Business
Corporation Act

Corporations are typically commercial enterprises, but can also be non-commercial enterprises or „corporations not for profit“, as they are also referred to, which can only serve charitable or religious purposes and are subject to special statutory provisions.

For corporations there is only one legal form of organization, although there are two different types of corporations:

(a) public or publicly held corporations

(b) close or closely held corporations

publicy held corporations

A publicly held corporation is a corporation with shares usually held by a large number of shareholders. Corporation statutes do not, however, specify a minimum number of shareholders for a corporation to be considered publicly held. Further indications are the trade of shares on one or more stock exchanges, the supervision by the Securities and Exchange Commission (SEC) on the basis of the Securities and Exchange Act of 1934, the published price quotations of shares and the registration of a public distribution of securities.

Securities and Exchange Commission

closely held corporations

A closely held corporation may only have a specified number of shareholders and may not offer its shares to the public. The transfer of shares is restricted, and it is quite common that all or most of the shareholders participate in the conduct of the business. Further characteristics are that a closely held corporation has never registered a public distribution of securities and is definitely not registered with the SEC.

establishment

A. Establishment

incorporators, founders

One or more persons, the so-called „incorporators" or „founders", whether physical or legal entities, who want to set up a corporation, must conclude the corporate charter which must state:

name

(a) the name of the corporation which must contain the words „corporation" (Corp) or „incorporated" (Inc). The name may not be too similar to the name of any other existing corporation, it must be „distinguishable upon the records of the secretary of state" as § 4.01 of the Revised Model Business Corporation Act states;

objects

(b) the nature and the objects of the corporation (the purposes clause). According to § 3.01 of the Revised Model Business Corporation Act a corporation must have the „purpose of engaging in any lawful business unless a more limited purpose is set forth in the articles of incorporation";

duration

(c) the duration of the corporation which may be, and commonly is, perpetual;

shares

(d) the capital structure, i.e. the number and types of shares and other securities as well as the rights attached to them;

directors

(e) the organization: the number of directors, their names and addresses;

registered office

(f) the registered office;

incorporators

(g) the names and addresses of the incorporators.

The incorporators send the articles of incorporation together with a filing fee to the Secretary of State who checks whether all the fil-

ing requirements have been fulfilled. After having approved the filing the Secretary of State issues a certificate of incorporation and sends it to the incorporators together with a copy of the original document. Some states require additional formalities, e.g. publishing the articles of incorporation in a newspaper. However, the existence of a corporation begins retroactively as of the date and time of the filing of the document after it has been approved by the Secretary of State.

certificate of incorporation

The relevant law for a corporation is the law of incorporation and not the law of the state where the corporation has its registered office. A corporation can incorporate in one state and then transfer its business into any different state, where it is regarded as a foreign corporation. Corporations planning to do business throughout the US will choose a state with the most convenient laws for establishing the company, e.g. Delaware. After a corporation has been set up all the other states must recognize it according to the federal Constitutional requirement of „Full Faith and Credit", which provides that every state of the Union has to honor and recognize decisions rendered by any state authority (e.g. courts) of a sister state. As a „foreign corporation" it must then also comply with requirements of the state in which the corporation is situated or carries out business, in accordance with the respective qualification statutes: an agent must be named for the purpose of serving process, information on the corporation's capital and turnover will have to be filed, etc. The corporation is then also subject to two taxing authorities.

law of incorporation

foreign corporation

full faith and credit

B. Shareholders

shareholders

Each state specifies a model for the management structure of a corporation which is called the „statutory scheme". According to the statute the shareholders may

rights

(a) elect and remove directors;

(b) approve and disapprove of fundamental issues which are not in the regular course of business (mergers, dissolution);

(c) approve and disapprove of changes in the articles of incorporation concerning the shareholders.

(d) file a derivative suit (Since shareholders are barred from exerting direct influence on the board of directors — they may only remove directors in the course of annual shareholders meetings — a remedy was developed providing for an indirect suit filed in the name of the corporation whereby the directors may be held liable for any breach of the fiduciary duty they have vis-à-vis the corporation) or a direct suit (a suit the shareholder initiates because of her/his position as owner of shares and the rights attached thereto).

indirect suit
fiduciary duty of directors
direct suit

Otherwise the shareholders may neither participate nor intervene in the conduct of the business.

shareholders meeting

The shareholders meet at an annual or a special meeting of share-holders where they may exercise their rights. An annual meeting is held, e.g. for the annual election of the directors or any other relevant subject, even if it is not stated on the agenda as contained in the notice. A special meeting is every meeting which is not an annual meeting. It is usually called by the board of directors or by other people who are permitted to do so according to the statute or the bylaws. A special meeting may only deal with those matters which are set forth in the notice.

quorum

In most states the quorum necessary to pass resolutions at shareholders' meetings is the presence of the majority of the outstanding shares. According to the articles of incorporation or the bylaws the quorum may be increased or reduced. The Revised Model Business Corporation Act does not stipulate any minimum, however one-third is a popular figure.

When the quorum necessary is present, the simple majority of the votes in favor is sufficient to pass a resolution binding the corporation. Abstentions are usually treated as negative votes.

board of directors

C. Board of Directors

"All corporate powers shall be exercised by or under the authority of, and the business and affairs of the corporation shall be managed under the direction of, its board of directors, subject to any limitation set forth in the articles of incorporation", § 8.01 (b) of the Revised Model Business Corporation Act.

The board of directors manage and supervise the corporation in all its business and affairs e.g. defining the policy of the corporation and concluding important contracts, etc. The board of directors may appoint officers and managers and delegate the day-to-day decision-making to them.

Most statutes require at least three directors, but some states only require that a board consists of one or two directors. However, every corporation has the possibility to fix the number of directors in its articles of incorporation.

The board of directors hold regular meetings, which are specified in the bylaws of the corporation, as to when and where they are to be held. The directors may also act at a special meeting. Except for certain formal differences, e.g. that notice must be given at least two days before a special meeting, there are no practical distinctions between regular and special meetings.

officers

D. Officers

The officers take care of the actual daily operation of the corporation. Detailed provisions relating to the officers' specific duties appear in the corporate bylaws which may naturally vary from corporation to corporation.

Most statutes require a corporation to have the following officers:

(a) the president is the first executive officer supervising and controlling the business; s/he is subject to the control of the board of directors; `president`

(b) one or more vice-president(s) who is (are) head(s) of a certain department, e.g. personnel, finance or marketing. If the president is absent, a vice-president performs her/his duties; `vice president`

(c) the secretary is, inter alia, responsible for official contacts, and keeps the corporate records and a register of all shareholders; `secretary`

(d) the treasurer takes care of all money matters and is responsible for all funds and securities of the corporation. `treasurer`

These officers may have titles such as chief executive officer (CEO), chief operating officer (COO), general manager or cashier. `CEO, COO, GM`

E. Stock `stock`

In the articles of incorporation the founders determine the amount of authorized capital which the corporation will issue. Usually a corporation authorizes more shares than it actually wants to issue, because if it wants to issue more shares at a later time it need not amend the articles of incorporation before doing so. `authorized capital`

Every shareholder of a corporation has her/his name and address registered in the list of shareholders at the corporation. That is why these shares are referred to as registered shares. US corporate law does not know bearer shares. `registered shares`

A corporation always issues common stock which entitles the owners to vote, inter alia, at the election of directors and to receive the payment of dividends. Other types of securities are the preferred stock which guarantee their holders the payment of dividends before the common shareholders. `common stock` `preferred stock`

F. Duration `duration`

In general, a corporation is not established for a specific time so it could actually continue to do business forever. The death or withdrawal of a shareholder does not terminate the corporation. It may be dissolved by a decision of the shareholders and the board, or by a judicial decree. After the dissolution, the corporation must be wound up. Many statutes state that a corporation continues to exist for a certain period after dissolution so that the corporation can be sued. `dissolution`

An involuntary dissolution occurs when the creditors force the corporation into bankruptcy proceedings, which are instituted by filing an involuntary bankruptcy petition against the corporation. If the corporation challenges these proceedings, a trial will follow, and the court then decides whether the corporation will be dissolved or not. `involuntary dissolution`

1.3. Austria

Austrian corporate law, as well as the corporate law in the UK and the US, recognizes non-corporate and corporate legal forms of business enterprises. Such corporations are:

GmbH

(a) GmbH-Company (Gesellschaft mit beschränkter Haftung, GmbH)

AG

(b) Stock Company (Aktiengesellschaft, AG)

Non-corporate legal forms include:

OHG

(a) General Partnership (Offene Handelsgesellschaft, OHG)

KG

(b) Limited Partnership (Kommanditgesellschaft, KG)

EEG

(c) Registered Partnership (Eingetragene Erwerbsgesellschaft, EEG)

Stille Gesellschaft

(d) Silent Partnership (Stille Gesellschaft)

Einzelkaufmann

(e) Sole Proprietorship (Einzelkaufmann)

GesbR

(f) Civil Law Association (Gesellschaft nach bürgerlichem Recht)

GmbH

1.3.1. Gesellschaft mit beschränkter Haftung (GmbH)

The GmbH-company is governed by the GmbH-Act (Gesetz über Gesellschaften mit beschränkter Haftung) and is just about the most popular legal form for doing business in Austria. It is suited for smaller businesses where shareholders intend to limit their liability and do not plan to transfer shares frequently. Foreign enterprises wishing to set up a subsidiary in Austria usually choose the legal form of a GmbH-company rather than the stock company.

articles of association

Currently, at least two shareholders are needed to form a GmbH by establishing the articles of association in the form of a notarial deed before a notary public. The articles of association must contain:

name, corporate seat

(a) name and corporate seat of the company;

objects

(b) objects of the company;

share capital

(c) the amount of share capital;

initial shareholders' contribution

(d) the initial contribution of each shareholder.

Commercial Register

The registration of the GmbH in the Commercial Register (Firmenbuch) constitutes the legal existence of the company. Once the GmbH-company has been established, it is possible that a shareholder transfers her/his share to the other shareholder, who then is the only shareholder of the GmbH. In such cases, the first shareholder often acts as a trustee of the other shareholder.

A founder or a shareholder can be an individual or a legal person, an Austrian or a foreign citizen or entity.

In the articles of association the founders determine the share capital of the company which may not be less than 500,000 ATS. At least half of the stated share capital must be contributed in cash before registration in the Commercial Register. The rest may be paid in later or at any time immediately upon request of the managing director(s). The contribution of every shareholder determines her/his interest in the company. The minimum contribution of a shareholder must be at least 1,000 ATS.

Contributions in kind are also possible, but at least half of the stated share capital must be contributed in cash. After a formation audit a certified auditor describes the value of every contribution in kind. Assets, as opposed to cash contributions must be paid in full.

contribution in kind
and in cash

The managing board is one of the two obligatory bodies of a GmbH and consists of one or more managing directors who are appointed by the shareholders. The managing directors act for and represent the GmbH-company, e.g. by concluding contracts, preparing annual reports and financial statements, etc. The shareholders themselves may take on the function of the managers, but it is also possible for them to hire third parties to the managing board. The appointment of managers can be revoked by the shareholders. Furthermore, the managing board of a GmbH, as opposed to the stock company, is bound by the decisions of the shareholders.

The second obligatory body of a GmbH-company is the shareholders' meeting, which is the main decision-making body of the company on important matters. It appoints the managing directors and the supervisory board, decides on changes of the articles of association and on the distribution of profits, approves the annual report and releases the managing directors and the supervisory board from their liability.

In general, a supervisory board may be established if the shareholders wish to do so. In some cases a supervisory board must be appointed, e.g. when a GmbH-company has more than 300 employees or runs a specific business (investment or games of chance).

According to Austrian law a GmbH will be dissolved, inter alia,

dissolution

(a) after the passing of the time period for which it was established;

(b) by a shareholders' resolution in the form of a notarial deed;

(c) by decision of an administrative authority or the commercial court.

The shareholders can agree on additional reasons for dissolution of the GmbH- company in the articles of association.

1.3.2. Stock Company (AG)

AG

Regulated in the Stock Company Act 1965 (Aktiengesetz) the stock company is a corporation used for large companies with widespread ownership and frequent transfer of shares. Being a legal entity the stock company is the sole owner of all the assets, can sue and be sued, has its own rights and obligations and is liable for the company's debts.

123

An important advantage of the AG over the GmbH is that it is very flexible and cheap to transfer stock and raise capital for the corporation.

In order to establish a stock company, it is necessary to have at least two founders who determine the articles of association. The articles of association are adopted before a notary public in the course of a founders' meeting and must include

foundation
articles of association
founders' meeting

name; corporate seat   *(a) name and corporate seat of the corporation;*

objects   *(b) objects of the corporation;*

share capital   *(c) amount of share capital;*

shares   *(d) types of shares and their value;*

members   *(e) process of constitution of the managing board and the number of members*

otherwise the stock company cannot be incorporated.

one-stage formation,
successive formation

There are two types of formation of a stock company: the standard or one-stage formation and the successive formation. The main difference between the two is that in the standard formation all shares are subscribed by the founders of the company. In the successive formation not all shares need to be subscribed by the people establishing the stock company, because the rest of the shares is offered for subscription to the public. However, the successive formation is a rather complicated and slow type of formation, and is therefore seldom used.

As with the GmbH-company, the stock company's existence begins with its registration in the Commercial Register.

minimum capital   *In general, the minimum share capital of a stock company is one million ATS, although for some businesses the law requires more capital. For instance investment companies must have at least 10 million ATS and insurance companies at least 100 million ATS. At least 25 percent of the stated share capital of the AG must be paid before registration in the Commercial Register.*

The share capital is divided into shares which must have a face value of 100 ATS, 500 ATS, 1,000 ATS or a multiple of 1,000 ATS each. According to the Stock Company Act, shares may be issued in the form of bearer shares or registered shares. If the articles of association do not provide to the contrary a stock company issues bearer shares.

bearer shares,
registered shares

Shares of a stock company can be transferred easily: bearer shares are simply handed over, whereas registered shares are transferred by endorsement and subsequent registration in the share ledger.

share ledger

executive board   *The executive board is the representative body of a stock company, and consists of one or more members. The members of the executive board act on behalf of the corporation, run the day-to-day business and are responsible for keeping the books. The executive board is appointed by the board of directors for a term of five years; however, reappointment is possible. In addition, it must re-*

port regularly to the board of directors but does not receive instructions from them or the shareholders' meeting. In certain cases, the executive board must obtain the consent of the board of directors before doing anything.

The board of directors, in comparison to the one of the GmbH-company, is a compulsory body of the stock company and is completely independent of the executive board. It consists of at least three members but the articles of association may stipulate a larger number. The members of the board of directors are appointed by the shareholders, although one third of the body consists of staff representatives sent from the works council. The board of directors appoints, supervises and controls the executive board.

board of directors

appointment by shareholders

staff representatives

The shareholders' meeting is also an obligatory body of the AG and is called by the executive board. A shareholders' meeting is held once a year to approve the annual financial statements, the distribution of profits, etc. and whenever the shareholders of 5 percent of the share capital request that a meeting be held. For specific matters, e.g. an amendment to the articles of association or an increase in the stated share capital, a qualified majority of 75 percent of the votes is required, otherwise a simple majority of the votes cast is sufficient to pass a resolution.

1.3.3. General Partnership (OHG)

OHG

The general partnership is a non-corporate legal form of two or more individuals acting under the same business name and formed for the purpose of operating a commercial business. The partners are fully liable and may not limit their liability for the partnerships' debts.

full liability

Although the general partnership is not a legal entity it has its own rights, may incur liabilities and sue or be sued. It is represented by its partners.

According to Austrian law it is not obligatory to establish a partnership agreement, but it is common practice that partners draft an agreement regulating their rights and their duties in order to avoid future misunderstandings.

With a few exceptions, the general partnership must be registered in the Commercial Register.

registration

1.3.4. Limited Partnership (KG)

KG

The limited partnership is an association of two or more individuals or corporations where at least one general partner (Komplementär) is fully liable for the obligations of the partnership, whereas the limited partner (Kommanditist) only has limited liability to the amount of her/his capital contribution. Due to her/his limited liability, the limited partner may not take part in the management of the business and has no signing powers.

general partner

limited partner

This being the major difference from the general partnership, they are otherwise very similar.

A rather popular form of a limited partnership is when the general partner is a GmbH. This is done for limiting the liability of all the partners involved. In such cases the firm name is „GmbH & Co.KG".

EEG

1.3.5. Registered Partnership (EEG)

The general partnership as well as the limited partnership are legal forms which are only available for those businesses exercising a „trade". Therefore, in 1991 the registered partnership was developed for professions which could not establish a commercial partnership for their business purposes, but could only use the form of a civil partnership. The two possible forms of a registered partnership are very similar to the general partnership and the limited partnership:

professions

OEG

(a) General Registered Partnership (Offene Erwerbsgesellschaft, OEG)

KEG

(b) Limited Registered Partnership (Kommanditerwerbsgesellschaft, KEG)

"Free" professions, e.g. lawyers and doctors and businesses in the field of agriculture and forestry are now able to be entered in the Commercial Register, enjoying the advantages of a separate entity which may acquire assets, sue and be sued, have a business name, etc.

Professional registered partnerships will, however, also refuse to let their members hold the requisite licenses or permits to practice or belong to a special group of privileged persons (e.g. spouses or children). Moreover, they are subject to the respective professional regulations which usually provide for limitations as well as for privileges.

Silent partnership

1.3.6. Silent Partnership (Stille Gesellschaft)

In a silent partnership, a person participates in an existing business of another with a contribution in cash or in kind. The silent partner receives a part of the profit, but cannot be held liable for the debts of the business. S/He may not participate in the conduct of the business.

A silent partnership is not entered in the Commercial Register.

1.3.7. Other Business Forms

Other forms of business enterprises are the

sole proprietorship

(a) sole proprietorship which is run by an individual (Einzelkaufmann);

civil law association

(b) civil law association (Gesellschaft bürgerlichen Rechts, GesbR), which until recently was used for partnerships of professionals. It is set up by two or more people wanting to work together (temporary or permanently), and it can be considered a joint venture.

126

2. CROSS BORDER WORK IN CORPORATE LAW

Working with overseas partners in the corporate field may sometimes prove difficult. In order to facilitate communication in this field we have assumed the following scenario: An English company (Miracle Instruments Limited), whose corporate name has been changed to Miracle Computers Limited, would like to establish an Austrian subsidiary in the legal form of a GmbH together with its American affiliate (Miracle Computers Inc.). The Austrian subsidiary shall be called Miracle Gesellschaft mbH. (All names are ficticious.)

The following documents describe the founders and illustrate the necessary steps in connection with the establishment of a subsidiary in Austria:

1. Miracle Instruments, Ltd.:
– *Certificate of Incorporation*
– *Memorandum of Association*
– *Articles of Association*
– *Certificate on Change of Name including Special Resolution*
– *Excerpts from the Minutes of a Meeting of the Board of Directors*
– *Power of Attorney for the Formation of a Subsidiary*

2. Miracle Computers, Inc.:
– *Power of Attorney and Affidavit*
– *Certificate of Incumbency*
– *Certificate of Vice President*

3. Miracle Ges.m.b.H.
– *Gesellschaftsvertrag (articles of association)*
– *Gesellschafterliste (list of shareholders)*
– *Geschäftsführerliste (list of managing directors)*
– *Gesellschafterbeschluß (shareholders' resolution)*
– *Handelsregister- bzw. Firmenbuchantrag (application to the commercial register)*

4.
– *Bausteine für Vollmachten und Gesellschafterbeschlüsse (cut and paste for powers of attorney, proxies and shareholders' resolutions)*
– *Änderung des Betriebsgegenstandes (change of objects)*
– *Änderung des Geschäftsjahres (change of business year)*
– *Allgemeine Stimmrechtsvollmacht (general proxy)*

The documents called "Excerpts from the Minutes of a Meeting of the Board of Directors", "Affidavit", "Certificate of Incumbency" and "Certificate of Vice President" all serve the purpose of evidencing the right of representation of the individuals acting on be-

half of the Anglo-American companies. They are necessary for the incorporation of an Austrian company with Anglo-American parent companies because neither English nor US registers of companies or corporations are able to issue official certificates stating facts about who may represent corporate organisations. The said documents may, however, be used alternatively. Apart from the issue of corporate representation personal representation is of importance in international business. For that purpose the (proof of) identity of the acting individual is evidenced by means of the legalisation process. A notary public legalises the signature of the acting individual. However, in international matters the notary's signature has to be legalised or rather "supra-legalised", too. Pursuant to the Hague Convention of 1961 such "supra-legalisation" is effected by means of the Apostille-procedure.

THE COMPANIES ACT, 1948

English statute regulating companies

COMPANY LIMITED BY SHARES

company limited by shares

MEMORANDUM
and
ARTICLES OF ASSOCIATION
of
MIRACLE INSTRUMENTS, LTD.

foundation document

supplementary document

Incorporated the 8th day of August, 1964.

date of incorporation

CERTIFICATE OF INCORPORATION

certificate of incorporation

I hereby Certify, that Miracle Instruments, Limited is this day Incorporated under the Companies Act, 1948, and the Company is Limited.

Given under my hand at London this 8th day of August, One Thousand Nine Hundred and Sixtyfour.

certification clause

J. L. Wordsworth
Registrar of Companies

registrar

THE COMPANIES ACT, 1948

COMPANY LIMITED BY SHARES

MEMORANDUM OF ASSOCIATION
of
MIRACLE INSTRUMENTS LIMITED

name of the company	*1. The name of the Company is "Miracle Instruments Limited".*
registered office	*2. The registered office of the Company will be situate in England.*
objects clause, to establish a company	*3. The objects for which the Company is established are:*

merchants, to deal with, commodities, to carry on, to transact, to effect business agency business

said

aforesaid

property

(A) To carry on all or any of the business or businesses of manufacturing, importing, exporting, or otherwise dealing in all classes of scientific instruments and computers, and every description of engineering products, electrical and electronic components, all classes of machinery and tools, general merchants and factors and to deal with all commodities used or sold in such business and to carry on, transact and effect all kinds of direct and agency business in relation to raw and other materials, chemicals, fluids, ingredients, commodities, goods, components, accessories, machines, appliances, wares, tools and sundries, necessary or desirable to be used in connection with the said business and any other business which the Company consider may conveniently be carried on in connection with any such business as aforesaid, or be directly or indirectly for the benefit of any part of the Company's property.

to purchase, to sell, to acquire, to rent

in return for consideration

thereof

(B) To purchase, sell, take on lease or in exchange, hire or otherwise acquire, rent, build, construct, equip, execute, carry out, improve, work, develop, administer, maintain, manage or control land, plant, machinery, stock-in-trade, works and conveniences of all kinds, whether for the purpose of the Company or for sale or hire, to or in return for any consideration from any other company or persons, and to contribute to or assist in the carrying out or establishment, construction, maintenance, improvement, management, working, control or superintendence thereof respectively.

to subscribe, to underwrite, to hold, to dispose of shares, stock, securities, to participate in profits, assets, to issue, corporation, body

foreign exchange

(C) To subscribe, underwrite, purchase, or otherwise acquire, and to hold, dispose of, and deal with the shares, stock, securities and evidences of indebtedness or of the right to participate in profits or assets or other similar documents issued by any government, authority, corporation or body, or by any company or body of persons, and any options or rights in respect thereof, and to buy and sell foreign exchange.

130

(D) To purchase or otherwise acquire for any estate or interest any property or assets or any concessions, copyrights, licenses, grants, patents, trademarks or other exclusive or non-exclusive rights of any kind which may appear necessary or convenient for any business of the Company, and to develop and turn to account and deal with the same in such manner as may be thought expedient, and to make experiments and tests and to carry on all kinds of research work.

estate, interest, concessions, copyrights, licenses, grants, patents, trademarks, exclusive

(E) To borrow and raise money and to secure or discharge any debt or obligation of or binding on the Company in such manner as may be thought fit and in particular by mortgages and charges upon the undertaking and all or any of the property and assets (present and future) and the uncalled capital of the Company, or by the creation and issue on such terms and conditions as may be thought expedient of debentures, debenture stock or other securities of any description.

to borrow, to discharge, debt, obligation, binding on, mortgages, charges uncalled capital

debentures

(F) To draw, make, accept, endorse, discount, negotiate, execute and issue, and to buy, sell and deal with bills of exchange, promissory notes, and other negotiable or transferable instruments.

to draw, make, accept, endorse, discount, negotiate, execute, bill of exchange, promissory note, negotiable instrument

(G) To amalgamate or enter into partnership or any joint purse or profit-sharing arrangement with and to co-operate in any way with or assist or subsidise any company, firm or person, and to purchase or otherwise acquire or undertake all or any part of the business, property and liabilities of any person, body or company carrying on any business which this Company is authorised to carry on or possessed of any property suitable for the purposes of the Company.

to amalgamate partnership

(H) To promote or concur in the promotion of any company, the promotion of which shall be considered desirable.

To lend money to and guarantee the performance of the contracts or obligations of any company, firm or person, and the payment and repayment of capital and principal of, and dividends, interest or premiums payable on, any stock, shares and securities of any company, whether having objects similar to those of this Company or not, and to give all kinds of indemnities.

to guarantee performance of contracts principal, dividends, premiums

indemnity

(J) To sell, lease, grant licenses, easements and other rights over, and in any other manner deal with or dispose of, the undertaking, property, assets, rights and effects of the Company or any part thereof for such consideration as may be thought fit, and in particular for stocks, shares or securities of any other company whether fully or partly paid up.

to grant licenses easement

effects

fully/partly paid up

(K) To procure the registration or incorporation of the Company in or under the laws of any place outside England.

to procure, registration under the laws

charitable	*(L) To subscribe or guarantee money for any national, charitable, benevolent, public, general or useful object or for any exhibition, or for any purpose which may be considered likely directly or indirectly to further the objects of the Company or the interests of its members.*

gratuities, employee
officer, director

association, fund, trust

scheme, trustee

(M) To grant pensions or gratuities to any employees or ex-employees and to officers and ex-officers (including Directors or ex-Directors) of the Company or its predecessors in business, or the relations, connections or dependants of any such persons, and to establish and support associations, institutions, clubs, funds and trusts which may be considered calculated to benefit any such persons or otherwise advance the interests of the Company or of its members, and to establish and contribute to any scheme for the purchase by trustees of shares in the Company to be held for the benefit of the Company's employees, and to lend money to the Company's employees to enable them to purchase shares of the Company and to formulate and carry into effect any scheme for sharing the profits of the Company with its employees or any of them.

principal, agent,
contractor

(N) To do all or any of the things and matters aforesaid in any part of the world, and either as principals, agents, contractors, trustees or otherwise, and by or through trustees, agents or otherwise, and either alone or in conjunction with others.

incidental, conducive

(O) To do all such things as may be considered incidental or conducive to the above objects or any of them.

And it is hereby declared that the objects of the Company as specified in each of the foregoing paragraphs of this clause (except only if and sofar as otherwise expressly provided in any paragraph) shall be separate and distinct objects of the Company and shall not be in anywise limited by reference to any other paragraph or the order in which the same occur or the name of the Company.

limited liability

4. The liability of the Members is limited.

share capital

5. The share capital of the Company is Pound Sterling 100,000 divided into 100,000 shares of Pound Sterling 1 each.

WE, the several persons whose names and addresses are subscribed, are desirous of being formed into a Company in pursuance of this Memorandum of Association, and we respectively agree to take the number of Shares in the Capital of the Company set opposite our respective names.

Names, addresses and descriptions of	*Number of Shares taken by each*
subscriber	*Subscribers*
	Subscriber

132

JOHN BLEESE   *Fifty-thousand*
    21, Holland Park Mews
        London WII 3SU
Clerk.

ARTHUR SILLER   *Fifty-thousand*
    8,   Wincott Street
        Kennington,
        London SWII 4NT
Clerk.

DATED the 6th day of August, 1964.
WITNESS to the above Signatures: to witness
                    PEARL McLACHLAN
                        Norfolk Place
                        London W2 1QW
Articled Clerk.

THE COMPANIES ACT, 1948

....

COMPANY LIMITED BY SHARES

articles of association

ARTICLES OF ASSOCIATION
of
MIRACLE INSTRUMENTS LIMITED

PRELIMINARY

regulations

hereinafter, to be
inconsistent with,
provisions, to apply,
clause, construction

1. The regulations contained in Part I (but not Part II) of Table A in the First Schedule to the Companies Act, 1948 (such Part I being hereinafter referred to as "Table A"), shall, except as hereinafter provided and so far as the same are not inconsistent with the provisions of these Articles, apply to the Company, and clause 1 of Table A shall apply to the construction of these Articles.

private company

PRIVATE COMPANY

2. The Company is a Private Company, and accordingly:

transfer of shares

(A) The right to transfer shares in the Company shall be restricted in manner hereinafter appearing.

members/
shareholders

determination

joint(-ly)

(B) The number of members of the Company (not including persons who are in the employment of the Company and persons who, having been formerly in the employment of the Company were while in such employment and have continued after determination of that employment to be members of the Company) is limited to 50; provided that where two or more persons hold one or more shares in the Company jointly they shall for the purposes of this paragraph be treated as a single member.

to go public

(C) No invitation shall be made to the public to subscribe for any shares or debentures of the Company.

CAPITAL

ordinary shares

3. The share capital of the Company is Pound Sterling 100,000, divided into 100,000 Ordinary Shares of Pound Sterling 1 each.

SHARES

unissued shares, to
allot, to grant option

4. All unissued shares shall be at the disposal of the Directors and they may allot, grant options over or otherwise dispose of them to such persons, at such times, and on such terms as they think proper.

LIEN

liens

5. *The liens given by clause 11 of the Table A shall extend to every share in the capital of the Company whether fully paid or not.*

TRANSFER OF SHARES

transfer

6. *Subject to the provisions of clause 24 of Table A any share may at any time be transferred to a person who is already a member of the Company. Save as aforesaid the Directors shall have an absolute right without assigning any reason therefor to refuse to register any transfer of a share (whether fully paid or not).*

save as aforesaid to register the transfer of a share

7. *Two members present in person or by proxy or by representatives under clause 74 of Table A shall be a quorum at any General Meeting. Clause 53 of Table A shall be modified accordingly.*

proxy, representatives, quorum

8. *A poll may be demanded at any General Meeting by the Chairman or by any member present in person or by proxy and entitled to vote. Clause 58 of Table A shall be modified accordingly.*

poll, chairman, entitled to vote

9. *A resolution in writing signed by all the members for the time being entitled to receive notice of and attend and vote at General Meetings shall be as effective as if the same had been passed at a General Meeting of the Company duly convened and held, and may consist of several documents, in the like form, each signed by one or more persons, but a resolution so signed shall not be effective to do anything required by the Act to be done in General Meeting or by Special or Extraordinary Resolution. In the case of a corporation the resolution may be signed on its behalf by a Director thereof or by its duly appointed attorney or duly authorized representative.*

resolution in writing, to receive notice

duly convened and held

special/extraordinary resolution, to sign on behalf

duly appointed attorney

DIRECTORS

to resolve

10. *Unless and until otherwise resolved in accordance with clause 94 of Table A, the Directors shall not be less than two, nor more than four in number. The first Directors shall be appointed in writing by the subscribers of the Memorandum of Association and their number shall be within the limit abovementioned. Clause 75 of Table A shall not apply to the Company.*

11. *A Director shall not be required to hold any shares in the Company by way of qualification. Clause 77 of Table A shall not apply to the Company.*

12. *The ordinary remuneration of the Directors shall from time to time be determined by an Ordinary Resolution of the Company, and shall (unless such Resolution otherwise provides) be divisible among the Directors as they may agree, or, failing agreement, equally, except that any Director who shall hold office for part only of the period in respect of which such remuneration is payable shall be entitled only to rank in such division for a proportion of remuneration related to the period during which he has held office. Clause 76 of Table A shall not apply to the Company.*

remuneration, from time to time, ordinary resolution, divisible

payable, to be entitled to

to incur expenses,
to attend a meeting,
committee

13. The Directors may repay to any Director all such reasonable expenses as he may incur in attending and returning from meetings of the Directors, or of any committee of the Directors, or General Meetings, or otherwise in or about the business of the Company.

BORROWING POWERS

provisio

14. The provisio to clause 79 of Table A shall not apply to the Company.

powers and duties

POWERS AND DUTIES OF DIRECTORS

to enter into a contract

to constitute a quorum

to accrue
place of profit,
auditor

15. No Director shall be disqualified by his position as Director from entering into any contract or arrangement with the Company, and a Director may vote and be taken into account for the purpose of constituting a quorum in respect of any contract or arrangement in which he may be in any way interested, and may retain for his own absolute use or benefit all profits or advantages accruing to him therefrom. A Director may hold any other office or place of profit under the Company other than that of Auditor on such terms as to remuneration and otherwise as the Directors may determine. Sub-clauses (2), (3), (4) and (5) of clause 84 of Table A shall not apply to the Company.

retirement

RETIREMENT OF DIRECTORS

to be vacated

16. The office of a Director shall be vacated in any of the following events, namely:

to be prohibited
by law

(A) If he shall become prohibited by law from acting as Director.

managing director
deputy/assistant

to resign by writing

(B) If (not being a Managing Director or Deputy or Assistant Managing Director holding office as such for a fixed term) he resigns by writing under his hand left at the Registered Office.

receiving order,
to compound with
creditors

(C) If he shall have a receiving order made against him or shall compound with his creditors generally.

(D) If he shall become of unsound mind.

leave

(E) If he shall be absent from meetings of the Directors for six months without leave and the Directors shall resolve that his office be vacated.

Clause 88 of Table A shall not apply to the Company.

rotation

17. The Directors shall not be subject to retirement by rotation and accordingly clauses 89 and 92 of Table A shall not apply to the Company and all other references in Table A to retirement by rotation shall be disregarded.

PROCEEDINGS OF DIRECTORS

18. A resolution in writing signed by all the Directors for the time being in the United Kingdom shall be as effective as a resolution passed at a meeting of the Directors duly convened and held, and may consist of several documents in the like form, each signed by one or more of the Directors. Provided that, where a Director is not himself in the United Kingdom but has appointed an alternate Director, the signature of such alternate Director (if in the United Kingdom) shall be required. Clause 106 of Table A shall not apply to the Company.

alternate director

MANAGING DIRECTORS

managing directors

19. Clauses 107 and 109 inclusive of Table A shall extend to include the posts of Deputy and Assistant Managing Director.

posts

ALTERNATIVE DIRECTORS

20. (A) Any Director may at any time, by writing under his hand and deposited at the Registered Office, appoint any person approved by the Directors to be his alternate Director and may in like manner at any time terminate such appointment.

to terminate an appointment

(B) The appointment of an alternate Director shall ipso facto determine

ipso facto

(i) on the happening of any event which if he were a Director would render him legally disqualified from acting as a Director, or

(ii) if he has a receiving order made against him or compounds with his creditors generally, or

(iii) if he becomes of unsound mind. His appointment shall also determine ipso facto if his appointor ceases for any reason to be a Director.

appointor

(C) An alternate Director shall (subject to his giving to the Company an address within the United Kingdom at which notices may be served upon him) be entitled to receive notices of meetings of the Directors and to attend and vote as a Director at any such meeting at which the Director appointing him is not personally present and generally at such meeting to perform all functions of his appointor as a Director and in the absence of his appointor from the United Kingdom he shall be entitled to sign any resolution in writing of the Directors as hereinbefore provided. An alternate Director shall not (save as aforesaid) have power to act as a Director nor shall he be deemed to be a Director for the purposes of these Articles.

to serve notice upon someone
to perform functions
hereinbefore, save as aforesaid

(D) An alternate Director may be repaid by the Company such expenses as might properly be repaid to him if he were a Director and shall be entitled to receive from the Company such proportion (if any) of the remuneration otherwise payable to his appointor as such appointor may by notice in writing to the Company from time to time direct, but, save as aforesaid, he shall not in respect of such appointment be entitled to receive any remuneration from the Company.

indemnity

secretary

execution and
discharge of duties
according(-ly)

INDEMNITY

21. Subject to the provisions of and so far as may be permitted by the Act every Director, alternate Director, Auditor, Secretary or other officer of the Company shall be entitled to be indemnified by the Company against all costs, charges, losses, expenses and liabilities incurred by him in the execution and discharge of his duties or in relation thereto. Clause 136 of Table A shall be extended accordingly.

Names, addresses and descriptions of Subscribers.

JOHN BLEESE
  21, Holland Park Mews
    LONDON WII 3SU
Clerk.

ARTHUR SILLER
  8, Wincott Street
    Kennington,
    LONDON SWII 4NT
Clerk.

DATED the 6th day of August, 1964.

WITNESS to the above Signatures:

PEARL McLACHLAN,
    Norfolk Place,
    LONDON W2 1QW
Articled Clerk.

MIRACLE INSTRUMENTS, LIMITED

Excerpt from the Minutes of an Extraordinary Shareholders' Meeting held at Clark House, London on 15 March 1983

Upon motion duly made, seconded and unanimously carried it was

RESOLVED

that the name of the Company be changed to

MIRACLE COMPUTERS, LIMITED.

The Secretary was instructed to take the necessary action to have the change of the name registered with the Companies Register with reference to this Resolution.

Chairman of the Meeting

Secretary

I, George Manion, notary public, hereby certify that this is a true excerpt from the Minutes of the Extraordinary Shareholders Meeting of 15 March 1983.

George Manion
Notary Public
London
Seal

MIRACLE INSTRUMENTS, LIMITED

Auszug aus dem Protokoll der außerordentlichen Generalversammlung vom 15. März 1983, abgehalten im Clark House, London

Über ordnungsgemäß eingebrachten und unterstützten (*) Antrag wurde einstimmig der

BESCHLUSS

gefaßt, daß der Firmawortlaut der Gesellschaft auf

MIRACLE COMPUTERS, LIMITED geändert wird.

Der Sekretär (*) wurde mit der Durchführung aller notwendigen Schritte zur Registrierung der Firmawortlautänderung im Firmenregister unter Bezugnahme auf diesen Beschluß beauftragt.

Vorsitzender (der ao Generalversammlung)

Sekretär (*)

Ich, Georg Manion, öffentlicher Notar (*), bestätige hiemit die Richtigkeit dieses Auszuges des Protokolles der außerordentlichen Generalversammlung vom 15. 3. 1983.

George Manion
öffentlicher Notar (*)
London
Amtssiegel (*)

Nachweis über die Firmenänderung	*CERTIFICATE OF INCORPORATION* *ON CHANGE OF NAME*

No. 98765

to certify

I hereby certify that

MIRACLE INSTRUMENTS LIMITED

to be incorporated

having by special resolution changed its name is now incorporated under the name of

MIRACLE COMPUTERS LIMITED

Given under my hand at the Companies Registration Office, London the 7TH JUNE 1990.

authorised officer

James BALDWIN
An Authorised Officer

---

true copy, original, valid evidence

I hereby certify that this is a true copy of the original certificate of incorporation and that this is valid evidence under English Law of the incorporation and true name of the company.

Sylvia PLATH
23RD JUNE 1990
NOTARY PUBLIC
(Seal)

notary public, seal of office

MINUTES OF AN EXTRAORDINARY MEETING OF THE BOARD OF DIRECTORS OF MIRACLE COMPUTERS LIMITED ("THE COMPANY") HELD ON 1 JULY 1990 AT 11:00 A.M. IN LONDON, ENGLAND.

minutes of a board meeting (Protokoll einer Vorstandssitzung)

PRESENT: William Faulkner
                                      F. Scott Fitzgerald
                                      John Steinbeck

presence

A quorum of the Board of Directors being present the meeting was declared open.

quorum, to declare a meeting open

Upon motion duly made, seconded and unanimously carried, the following resolution was made:

motion, to second, to carry unanimously, to make (pass) a resolution

That Mr. Henry James, Secretary and a Director of the Company, is hereby authorised to sign a Power of Attorney on behalf of the Company to be used for the incorporation of Miracle Gesellschaft m.b.H. in Austria as well as the Commercial Register documents and any other documents relative to the incorporation of said company in Austria.

secretary, director, to sign on behalf of, incorporation

relative to

There being no further business to come before the Board, the meeting was adjourned.

business on the agenda, to adjourn a meeting

....

William Faulkner   F. Scott Fitzgerald

_____

                    John Steinbeck

_____

Notarisation:

legalisation

"Sworn and Subscribed before me this 1st day of July 1990"
Katherine Anne Porter, Notary Public, London
My commission expires 11/11/1993

sworn and subscribed

MIRACLE COMPUTERS
LIMITED
London, England

POWER OF ATTORNEY
FOR THE
FORMATION OF A
SUBSIDIARY

I, Henry James, as Secretary and Director of Miracle Computers Limited, having been empowered by a special resolution passed in the course of an extraordinary meeting of the Board of Directors of Miracle Computers Limited on 1st July 1990, hereby declare in full knowledge of the penalty provisions of English and Austrian law that the said company on the date of granting this Power of Attorney was properly organised according to English law and hereby grant to

Franz X.
Solicitor
1010 Vienna

singly and solely power of attorney to establish a company with limited liability under the name "Miracle Gesellschaft m.b.H." or a similar name, to be domiciled in Vienna, Austria, which company shall have a capital of AS 500,000 (Austrian Schillings five hundred thousand) and shall have as objects:

1. rendering of services in the field of computer-assisted data processing and information processing, particularly the computation, processing and transmission of data in Austria and abroad by means of computer-assisted data exchange,

2. the company shall be entitled to engage in all transactions and measures which seem necessary or beneficial for the achievement of the objects of the company, in particular to found branches and subsidiaries in Austria and

MIRACLE COMPUTERS
LIMITED
London, England

VOLLMACHT
ZUR
ERRICHTUNG EINER
TOCHTERGESELLSCHAFT

Ich, Henry James, als Sekretär* und Verwaltungsratsmitglied* der Miracle Computers Limited, bevollmächtigt durch Beschluß der ao Verwaltungsratssitzung der Miracle Computers Limited vom 1. 7. 1990, erkläre hiemit in voller Kenntnis der Strafbestimmungen des englischen und österreichischen Rechts, daß diese Gesellschaft zum Tage der Erteilung dieser Vollmacht nach englischem Recht in aufrechtem Bestand war, und ich erteile hiemit Herrn

Franz X.
Rechtsanwalt
1010 Wien

Einzelvollmacht zur Gründung einer Gesellschaft mit beschränkter Haftung mit der Firma „Miracle Gesellschaft m.b.H" oder einer ähnlichen Firma, mit dem Sitz in Wien, Österreich, mit einem Stammkapital in der Höhe von S 500.000,– (Schilling fünfhunderttausend) und dem folgenden Gesellschaftszweck:

1. Die Erbringung von Leistungen in der automationsunterstützten Datenverarbeitung und Informationstechnik, insbesondere die Ermittlung, Verarbeitung und Übermittlung von Daten im In- und Ausland im Wege des automationsunterstützten Datenverkehrs.

2. Die Gesellschaft ist zu allen Geschäften und Maßnahmen berechtigt, die zur Erreichung des Gesellschaftszweckes notwendig oder nützlich erscheinen, insbesondere zur Errichtung von Zweigniederlassungen und Tochtergesellschaften

abroad and to acquire interests in other enterprises.

To acquire for Miracle Computers Limited a participation in the total share capital of AS 250,000 (Austrian Schillings two hundred and fifty thousand) to be fully paid in, to provide for and determine all other provisions of the articles of association and related documents as well as amendments thereto and to sign the required notarial deed, to appoint one or more business managers and to take all steps necessary to make and receive declarations, to sign documents, applications and writings in all required formality, including notarial deeds, as may be necessary for the establishment and registration of the Company.

The holder of this Power of Attorney is further authorised for and on behalf of Miracle Computers Limited to exercise its voting rights in all general meetings of the shareholders of the Company and, in general, to represent Miracle Computers Limited with full authority and subject to no limitation in all matters which may concern the new company.

The holder of this Power of Attorney shall also be entitled to assign the rights conferred upon him by means of this instrument to a person of his choice.

Henry James
Secretary
For and on behalf of
MIRACLE COMPUTERS LTD.
London, 2 July 1990
I, Franz X., solicitor, Vienna, hereby accept this appointment.

Vienna, 7 July 1990

im In- und Ausland sowie zur Beteiligung an anderen Unternehmen.

Er ist weiters berechtigt und beauftragt, für Miracle Computers Limited einen Geschäftsanteil in der Höhe von S 250.000,– (Schilling zweihundertfünfzigtausend), welcher zur Gänze einbezahlt wird, zu übernehmen, alle sonstigen Bestimmungen des Gesellschaftsvertrages und allfälliger Nachträge festzulegen, Notariatsakte zu errichten, einen oder mehrere Geschäftsführer zu bestellen und alle notwendigen Schritte zur Abgabe und Entgegennahme von Erklärungen zu setzen, Urkunden, Anträge und Schriftsätze in jeder vorgeschriebenen Form, wie sie für die Errichtung und Registrierung der Gesellschaft notwendig ist, zu zeichnen.

Der Vollmachtsnehmer ist außerdem berechtigt, namens der Miracle Computers Limited das Stimmrecht in allen Generalversammlungen der Gesellschaft auszuüben und allgemein Miracle Computers Limited ohne jedwede Einschränkung in allen Angelegenheiten, die die neue Gesellschaft betreffen, gültig zu vertreten.

Der Vollmachtsnehmer ist weiters berechtigt, die ihm aufgrund dieses Dokuments übertragenen Rechte an eine Person seiner Wahl zu übertragen.

Henry James
Sekretär*
Namens und auftrags der
MIRACLE COMPUTERS LTD
London, am 2. Juli 1990
Ich, Franz X., Rechtsanwalt in Wien, nehme diese Bestellung hiemit an.

Wien, am 7. Juli 1990

affidavit

power of attorney

AFFIDAVIT
and
POWER OF ATTORNEY

the undersigned

acting secretary

president

to declare under oath

corporation, duly
formed and existing,
under the laws of

to be empowered, to
represent, inclusive
but not limited to,
proxy, to exercise vo-
ting rights, wholly-
owned subsidiary

duly authorized

Messrs.

singly and solely

registered office
stated share capital
objects

to subscribe to a share
... in the amount of

to be fully paid up

We, the undersigned,

a) Peter Williams, as acting Secretary and

b) Norman Tailer, as President

of MIRACLE COMPUTERS, INC., Washington D.C., USA hereby declare under oath the following:

1) MIRACLE COMPUTERS, INC., Washington D.C. is a corpora- tion duly formed and existing under the laws of the state of Dela- ware and we, Peter Williams as the Secretary of this corporation and Norman Tailer as the President of this corporation are fully familiar with all its incorporation and other documents relating to the existence of the corporation and the persons entitled and empowered to validly represent this corporation inclusive but not limited to the granting of unlimited powers of attorney and proxies for this corporation with respect to the exercise of all voting rights in this corporation's wholly-owned subsidiaries.

2) We hereby confirm that the two persons signing this affidavit and power of attorney are duly authorized to grant such power of attorney and proxies and especially to grant such to our attorneys in Vienna, Austria

Messrs.
Franz X. & Peter Y.
Attorneys-at-Law
A-1010 Vienna

3) We hereby grant to Messrs. X. & Y. singly and solely (individu- ally) power of attorney to establish a corporation according to Austrian corporation law with the name "MIRACLE GESELL- SCHAFT M.B.H." or a similar name, with its registered office in Vienna, Austria, with a stated share capital of AS 500,000 (Aus- trian Schillings five hundred thousand) and the following objects:

1. Rendering of services in the field of computer-assisted data processing and information processing, particularly the computa- tion, processing and transmission of data in Austria and abroad by means of computer-assisted data exchange;

2. the company shall be entitled to engage in all transactions and measures which seem necessary or beneficial for the achievement of the objects of the company, in particular to found branches and subsidiaries in Austria and abroad and to acquire interests in other enterprises;

and to subscribe to a share of the stated capital in the amount of AS 250,000 (Austrian Schillings two hundred and fifty thousand) for and on behalf of MIRACLE COMPUTERS, INC., which shall be fully paid up.

144

Furthermore, the said Gentlemen shall be empowered to provide for and determine for and on behalf of MIRACLE COMPUTERS, INC. all other terms and provisions of the Articles of Association, By-Laws and other necessary documents and amendments thereto in whatever form necessary. They shall be entitled to appoint managing directors and remove them from office.

They shall be entitled to take all steps necessary to make and receive declarations, to sign documents, applications and writings in all required formality, including but not limited to notarial deeds, as may be necessary for the establishment and registration of the company.

They shall also be entitled to convene shareholders' meetings, to exercise the voting rights of MIRACLE COMPUTERS, INC. at such meetings and to do whatever they think feasible and beneficial for the sake of MIRACLE Gesellschaft m.b.H.

said, for and on behalf of, terms and provisions, articles of association, by-laws, amendments, to appoint s.o., to remove s.b. from office

to make and receive declarations, applications, required formality, deeds

to convene a meeting, to exercise voting rights

....

Peter Williams   Norman Tailer
Secretary   President
Washington, D.C., this 6th day of July 1990
(notarization of signatures)

notarization of signatures

CERTIFICATE OF INCUMBENCY

I, Peter Williams, do hereby CERTIFY that I am the duly elected, qualified and acting SECRETARY of MIRACLE COMPUTERS, INC., a Delaware corporation, and I do hereby further certify that Norman Tailer, as of this date, is the duly elected, qualified and acting President of MIRACLE COMPUTERS, INC. and that the signature appearing below is the genuine signature of said officer.

Norman Tailer

IN WITNESS WHEREOF, I have hereunto set my hand this 10th day of July, 1990.

Peter Williams
Secretary)

THE CORPORATE SEAL

of
MIRACLE COMPUTERS, INC.
DELAWARE

ZEUGNIS DER AMTSINHABUNG

Ich, Peter Williams, BEZEUGE hiemit, daß ich der ordnungsgemäß gewählte, befugte und geschäftsführende SEKRETÄR* der MIRACLE COMPUTERS, INC., einer Gesellschaft des Staates Delaware, bin; und ich bestätige weiters, daß Herr Norman Tailer heute der ordnungsgemäß gewählte, befugte und geschäftsführende Präsident* der MIRACLE COMPUTERS, INC ist, und daß die unten angesetzte Unterschrift die echte Unterschrift dieses Amtsinhabers* ist.

Norman Tailer

URKUND DESSEN habe ich heute, am 10. 7. 1990, dieses Dokument unterfertigt

Peter Williams
(Sekretär)*

DAS (OFFIZIELLE) FIRMEN-SIEGEL*

der
MIRACLE COMPUTERS, INC.
DELAWARE

CERTIFICATE OF VICE PRESIDENT

I, JACK UPDIKE, do hereby certify that I am a duly elected, qualified and acting Vice President of MIRACLE COMPUTERS, INC. (the "Company"), a corporation duly organized and existing by virtue of the laws of the State of Delaware, USA, and hereby certify the following:

1) That Mr. Peter Williams is the duly elected, qualified and acting Secretary of the Company; and

2) That Mr. Norman Tailer is the duly elected, qualified and acting President of the Company; and

3) That Mr. Peter Williams and Mr. Norman Tailer have the power to sign any incorporation documents on behalf of the Company to be used to incorporate MIRACLE GESELLSCHAFT M.B.H. in Austria, and in particular to sign:

(i) powers of attorney

(ii) Commercial Registry documents

IN WITNESS WHEREOF, I have signed this Certificate in Washington, D.C., on this 2nd day of July, 1990.

MIRACLE COMPUTERS, INC.

By: ....

    Jack Updike, Vice President

"Sworn and Subscribed before me this 2nd day of July, 1990"

Charlie Smith, Notary Public

My commission expires on 11/11/1992

Notarial seal

BESTÄTIGUNG DES VIZE-PRÄSIDENTEN

Ich, JACK UPDIKE, bestätige hiemit, daß ich ein ordnungsgemäß gewählter, befugter und geschäftsführender Vizepräsident der MIRACLE COMPUTERS INC (die „Gesellschaft"), einer nach den Gesetzen des Bundesstaates Delaware, USA, ordnungsgemäß errichteten und sich im aufrechten Bestand befindlichen Gesellschaft bin, und bestätige hiemit weiters wie folgt:

1. Herr Peter Williams ist der ordnungsgemäß gewählte, befugte und geschäftsführende Sekretär* der Gesellschaft.

2. Herr Norman Tailer ist der ordnungsgemäß gewählte, befugte und geschäftsführende Präsident* der Gesellschaft.

3. Die Herren Peter Williams und Norman Tailer sind berechtigt, gemeinsam namens der Gesellschaft Gründungsdokumente, welche für die Eintragung der MIRACLE GESELLSCHAFT MBH in Österreich benötigt werden, zu zeichnen, insbesondere:

(i) Vollmachten

(ii) Handelsregister-/Firmenbuchunterlagen

URKUND DESSEN habe ich heute, am 2.7.1990 in Washington, DC diese Bestätigung unterfertigt.

MIRACLE COMPUTERS, INC.

Durch ....

    Jack Updike, Vizepräsident*

„Vor mir unterschrieben und durch Eid bekräftigt am 2. Juli 1990."

Charlie Smith, öffentl Notar*

Meine Amtsbefugnis läuft am 11. 11. 1992 aus.

Amtssiegel

GESELLSCHAFTSVERTRAG

ARTICLES OF ASSOCIATION

I. Firma und Sitz der Gesellschaft

I. Name and registered domicile of the company

1. Die Gesellschaft führt die Firma
Miracle Gesellschaft mbH

1. The company shall be named Miracle Gesellschaft m.b.H.

2. Die Gesellschaft hat ihren Sitz in Wien.

2. The company shall have its registered domicile in Vienna.

II. Gegenstand des Unternehmens

II. Objects

1. Gegenstand des Unternehmens ist die Erbringung von Dienstleistungen in der automationsunterstützen Datenverarbeitung und Informationstechnik, insbesondere die Ermittlung, Verarbeitung und Übermittlung von Daten im In- und Ausland im Wege des automationsunterstützten Datenverkehrs.

1. Objects of the business shall be the rendering of services in the field of computer-assisted data processing and information processing, particularly the computation, processing and transmission of data in Austria and abroad by means of computer assisted data exchange.

2. Die Gesellschaft ist zu allen Geschäften und Maßnahmen berechtigt, die zur Erreichung des Gesellschaftszweckes notwendig oder nützlich erscheinen, insbesondere zur Errichtung von Zweigniederlassungen und Tochtergesellschaften im In- und Ausland sowie zur Beteiligung an anderen Unternehmen.

2. The company shall be entitled to engage in all transactions and measures which seem necessary or beneficial for the achievement of the objects of the company, in particular to found branches and subsidiaries in Austria and abroad and to acquire interests in other enterprises.

III. Stammkapital und Stammeinlagen

III. Stated capital and capital contributions

1. Das Stammkapital beträgt S 500.000,– (Schilling fünfhunderttausend).

1. The company's stated capital shall amount to AS 500,000,– (Austrian Schillings five hundred thousand).

2. Hievon übernehmen die nachstehenden Gesellschaften die folgenden sofort voll und bar einzuzahlenden Stammeinlagen:

2. The following shareholders shall subscribe to the stated capital, which shall be fully paid up immediately as follows:

1. Miracle Computers, Ltd
S 250.000,– (Schilling zweihundertundfünfzigtausend),

*1. Miracle Computers, Ltd.
AS 250,000,– (Austrian Schillings two hundred and fifty thousand),*

2. Miracle Computers, Inc
S 250.000,– (Schilling zweihundertundfünfzigtausend).

*2. Miracle Computers, Inc.
AS 250,000,– (Austrian Schillings two hundred and fifty thousand).*

IV. Geschäftsführer

IV. Managing directors

1. Die Gesellschaft hat einen oder mehrere Geschäftsführer, welche von den

1. The company shall have one or several managing directors which shall be

Gesellschaftern bestellt und abberufen werden.

2. Die Gesellschaft wird, wenn nur ein Geschäftsführer bestellt ist, durch diesen, wenn zwei oder mehrere Geschäftsführer bestellt sind, durch je zwei Geschäftsführer oder durch einen Geschäftsführer gemeinsam mit einem Prokuristen vertreten.

3. Die Gesellschafter haben für die Geschäftsführung eine Geschäftsordnung zu beschließen.

V. Generalversammlung

1. Die Beschlüsse der Gesellschafter werden in der Generalversammlung gefaßt.

2. Die schriftliche Beschlußfassung gemäß Paragraph 34 des Gesetzes über Gesellschaften mit beschränkter Haftung ist zulässig.

3. Die Generalversammlungen finden am Ort des Sitzes der Gesellschaft statt. Eine Generalversammlung hat wenigstens einmal jährlich zur Beschlußfassung über den Jahresabschluß innerhalb von 8 (acht) Monaten nach Ablauf des Geschäftsjahres stattzufinden.

4. Das Stimmrecht richtet sich nach der übernommenen Stammeinlage.

5. Die Beschlüsse werden, soweit nicht zwingende Gesetzesbestimmungen oder der Gesellschaftsvertrag etwas anderes bestimmen, mit einfacher Mehrheit der abgegebenen Stimmen gefaßt.

VI. Geschäftsjahr

1. Das Geschäftsjahr ist das Kalenderjahr.

2. Das erste Geschäftsjahr der Gesellschaft endet mit Ablauf des Kalenderjahres, in welchem die Gesellschaft im Handelsregister/Firmenbuch eingetragen worden ist.

appointed and removed by its shareholders.

2. If there is only one managing director, the company shall be represented by him, if there are two or several managing directors, the company shall be represented by joint signatures of two managing directors or joint signatures of a managing director together with a procurist. *

3. The shareholders shall pass internal rules for the managing directors.

V. General shareholders' meeting

I. Resolutions of the shareholders shall be passed at the general shareholders' meeting.

2. The passing of written resolutions pursuant to Section 34 of the Austrian GmbH-Company Statute shall be admissible.

3. The general shareholders' meetings shall be held at the company's corporate seat. A general shareholders' meeting shall be convened at least once a year to resolve the annual closing of accounts within 8 (eight) months after the end of a business year.

4. The voting right shall be determined in accordance with the shares in the stated capital subscribed to.

5. Resolutions shall be passed by a simple majority of votes cast unless mandatory statutory provisions or the Articles of Association provide otherwise.

VI. Business year

1. The business year shall be the calender year.

2. The first business year shall end with the end of the calendar year in which the company was registered with the Commercial Register(*)/Register of Companies(*).

VII. Jahresabschluß

Die Geschäftsführer haben den Jahresabschluß (Bilanz und Gewinn- und Verlustrechnung) innerhalb von 5 (fünf) Monaten aufzustellen, unverzüglich den Gesellschaftern zuzusenden und spätestens innerhalb von 8 (acht) Monaten nach Ende des Geschäftsjahres der Generalversammlung zur Beschlußfassung vorzulegen. Diese Fristen können von der Generalversammlung nach den gesetzlichen Bestimmungen verlängert werden.

2. Die Generalversammlung beschließt über die Prüfung und Genehmigung des Jahresabschlusses, über die Verwendung des Reingewinnes, die Entlastung der Geschäftsführung und wählt einen oder mehrere Abschlußprüfer für das laufende Geschäftsjahr.

VII. Annual closing of accounts

The managing directors shall draft the annual closing of the accounts (balance sheets and profit and loss account) within 5 (five) months, mail it to the shareholders without delay and shall present the said closing to the general shareholders meeting for resolution within 8 (eight) months after the end of each business year at the latest. These deadlines may be extended by the general shareholders meeting in accordance with the statutory provisions.

2. At the general shareholders' meeting, decisions shall be made on the audit and approval of the annual closing of the accounts, on the use of the net profits, on the giving of a release to the managing directors, and elections shall take place for one or several auditors for the current business year.

VIII. Übertragung und Teilung von Anteilen

1. Die Übertragung, Belastung und Teilung von Geschäftsanteilen bedarf der Zustimmung der Generalversammlung.

2. Die Übertragung und Teilung von Geschäftsanteilen an zur Gänze im Eigentum stehenden Tochtergesellschaften der Gesellschafter ist unbeschränkt zulässig.

VIII. Transfer and division of company shares

1. The transfer, encumbrance, and division of company shares shall be subject to approval at the general shareholders' meeting.

2. The transfer and division of company shares to wholly-owned subsidiaries of the shareholders shall be admissible without restrictions.

IX. Dauer

Die Gesellschaft wird auf unbestimmte Zeit errichtet.

IX. Duration

The company shall exist for an unlimited period of time.

X. Gründungskosten

Alle mit der Errichtung und Registrierung der Gesellschaft verbundenen Kosten, Gebühren, Steuern und Abgaben aller Art sind bis zu einem Höchstbetrag von S 80.000,– (Schilling achtzigtausend) von der Gesellschaft zu tragen.

X. Foundation costs

All costs, duties, taxes and levies incurred in connection with the establishing and registration of the company shall be borne by the company up to the amount of AS 80,000,– (Austrian Schillings eighty thousand).

XI. Mitteilungen

Alle in diesem Vertrag und nach dem Gesetz der Gesellschaften mit beschränkter Haftung vorgesehenen Mitteilungen und Erklärungen gelten bis zum Beweis des Gegenteils als rechtzeitig und ordnungsgemäß abgegeben, wenn sie am letzten Tag der Frist mit eingeschriebenem Brief an die zuletzt der Gesellschaft bekanntgegebene Adresse abgeschickt wurden.

XII. Ausfertigungen

Ausfertigungen dieses Notariatsaktes können in beliebiger Anzahl an die Gesellschafter, Geschäftsführer sowie dereinstigen Liquidatoren wie auch an die Gesellschaft selbst, jeweils auf Kosten des Verlangenden, hinausgegeben werden.

* * *

XI. Notifications

All notifications and declarations provided for in this contract as well as pursuant to the GmbH-Company Statute shall be deemed timely and properly effected until proven to the contrary if they have been sent by registered mail on the last day of any term to the address last notified to the company.

XII. Counterparts

Counterparts of this notarial deed may be handed out to the shareholders, the managing directors, any eventual liquidators as well as to the company itself in any number at the expense of the person demanding such counterpart.

* * *

GESELLSCHAFTERLISTE der MIRACLE GESELLSCHAFT MBH		
Gesellschafter	übernommene Stammeinlage	hierauf einbezahlt
MIRACLE COMPUTERS LTD London	S 250.000,–	S 250.000,–
MIRACLE COMPUTERS, INC Washington D.C.	S 250.000,–	S 250.000,–

LIST OF SHAREHOLDERS of MIRACLE GESELLSCHAFT M.B.H.		
Shareholder	*share capital subscribed to*	*paid-up*
MIRACLE COMPUTERS LTD. London	*AS 250,000*	*AS 250,000*
MIRACLE COMPUTERS, INC. Washington DC	*AS 250,000*	*AS 250,000*

GESCHÄFTSFÜHRERLISTE

Name, Beruf, Wohnsitz und gewöhnlicher Aufenthalt des Geschäftsführers

---

Karl Müller, Angestellter, *31. 7. 1947
Domgasse 8
1010 Wien
Peter Williams, *15. 1. 1958
Angestellter
164 M Street
Washington, D.C., USA

LIST OF MANAGING DIRECTORS

Name, occupation, domicile and residence of the managing director

---

Karl Müller, employee, born July 31, 1947
Domgasse 8
A-1010 Vienna
Peter Williams, born January 15, 1958
employee
164 M Street
Washington, DC, USA

GESELLSCHAFTER-BESCHLUSS
der
MIRACLE GESELLSCHAFT MBH

Die Gesellschafter der MIRACLE GE-SELLSCHAFT MBH in Gründung, MI-RACLE COMPUTERS, LTD, London und MIRACLE COMPUTERS, INC, Washington, DC bestellen hiemit einstimmig die Herren

Peter Williams,
Angestellter,
Washington, D.C.
USA
und
Karl Müller,
Angestellter,
Wien
Österreich
zu Geschäftsführern mit kollektiver Vertretungsbefugnis.
Die Erteilung der Einzelprokura an Herrn
Matthäus Fischer,
Angestellter,
Bad Fischau
Österreich
wird zur Kenntnis genommen.

Wien, am 9. Juli 1990
(Franz X.)

für die Gesellschafter

SHAREHOLDERS' RESOLUTION
of
MIRACLE GESELLSCHAFT M.B.H.

The Shareholders of MIRACLE GE-SELLSCHAFT M.B.H., incorporation pending, MIRACLE COMPUTERS, LTD., London and MIRACLE COMPUTERS, INC., Washington, D.C. hereby unanimously appoint Messrs.

Peter Williams
employee
Washington, DC
USA
and
Karl Müller
employee
Vienna
Austria
managing directors with joint powers of representations.
The appointment of
Matthäus Fischer
employee
Bad Fischau
Austria
as "Prokurist" has been noted. (Anm.: Das Konzept der Prokura kann nur unter Bezugnahme auf die einschlägigen gesetzl Bestimmungen erläutert werden.)*

Vienna, July 9, 1990
(Franz X.)

on behalf of the shareholders

154

An das Handelsgericht Wien Handelsregister/Firmenbuch Riemergasse 7 1010 Wien	*To the* *Commercial Court of Vienna* *Commercial Register/Register of* *Companies* *Riemergasse 7* *A-1010 Vienna*

Die Geschäftsführer der
MIRACLE GESELLSCHAFT MBH
vertreten durch: Dr. Franz X.
Rechtsanwalt
1010 Wien

ANTRAG
auf
Registrierung einer
Gesellschaft mit
beschränkter Haftung

The managing directors of
MIRACLE GESELLSCHAFT M.B.H.
represented by: *Dr. Franz X.*
Solicitor
A-1010 Vienna

APPLICATION
for
Registration of a
GmbH-Company

Mit Notariatsakt vom 9. Juli 1990 (Beilage ./A) wurde der Gesellschaftsvertrag der MIRACLE GESELLSCHAFT MBH errichtet. Mit Gesellschafterbeschluß vom selben Tage (Beilage ./B) wurden Herr Peter Williams und Herr Karl Müller zu Geschäftsführern mit kollektiver Vertretungsbefugnis bestellt. Weiters wurde Herrn Matthäus Fischer Einzelprokura erteilt.

Die Geschäftsführer geben hiemit gemäß Paragraph 10 GesmbH-Gesetz die verbindliche Erklärung ab, daß die übernommenen Stammeinlagen zur Gänze bar einbezahlt wurden und sie in ihrer Verfügung darüber nicht, namentlich nicht durch Gegenforderungen, beschränkt sind.

Herr Peter Williams wird als Geschäftsführer die wie immer hergestellte Firma der Gesellschaft zeichnen wie folgt:

By means of a notarial deed dated July 9, 1990 (Exhibit A) the Articles of Association of MIRACLE GESELLSCHAFT M.B.H. were concluded. By means of a shareholders' resolution of the same date (Exhibit B) Mr. Peter Williams and Mr. Karl Müller were appointed managing directors with joint power of representation. In addition, Mr. Matthäus Fischer was granted power of procuration*.

The managing directors hereby declare pursuant to Section 10 of the Austrian GmbH-Company Statute that the share capital subscribed to has been fully paid up in cash and that there are no limitations whatsoever, expressly no counterclaims, on their right to dispose of the said funds.

As managing director Mr. Peter Williams shall sign the name of the Company regardless of the way it has been reproduced as follows:

MIRACLE GESELLSCHAFT MBH
(Musterfirmenzeichnung)

MIRACLE GESELLSCHAFT M.B.H.
(Specimen Signature)

Herr Karl Müller wird als Geschäftsführer die wie immer hergestellte Firma der Gesellschaft zeichnen wie folgt:

As managing director Mr. Karl Müller shall sign the name of the Company regardless of the way it has been reproduced as follows:

MIRACLE GESELLSCHAFT MBH
(Musterfirmenzeichnung)

*MIRACLE GESELLSCHAFT M.B.H
(Specimen Signature)*

Herr Matthäus Fischer wird als Einzelprokurist die wie immer hergestellte Firma der Gesellschaft zeichnen wie folgt:

Mr. Matthäus Fischer, in his capacity of "procurist"* shall sign the name of the Company regardless of the way it has been reproduced as follows:

MIRACLE GESELLSCHAFT MBH
(Musterfirmenzeichnung)

*MIRACLE GESELLSCHAFT M.B.H.
(Specimen Signature)*

Weiters legen wir vor eine Bankbestätigung (Beilage ./C), Firmenwortlautgutachten der Wiener Handelskammer (Beilage ./D) sowie die Unbedenklichkeitsbescheinigung des Finanzamtes für Gebühren und Verkehrsteuern (Beilage ./E) und stellen sohin den

In addition we are submitting a bank statement confirming the deposit of the stated capital (Exhibit C), an opinion on the admissibility of the Company's name issued by the Viennese Chamber of Commerce (Exhibit D) as well as a waiver of objections issued by the competent revenue authorities (Exhibit E) and are thus submitting this

ANTRAG

auf Registrierung der Gesellschaft im Firmenbuch Wien sowie auf Veranlassung aller erforderlichen Veröffentlichungen.

Geschäftsadresse: Wien I, Domgasse 18

Wien, am 30. 7. 1990 P. Williams
                                  K. Müller

APPLICATION

for the registration of the Company in the Register of Companies of Vienna and for causing all necessary steps for publication.

Company's address: Domgasse 18, A-1010 Vienna

*Vienna, 7/30/90 P. Williams
                              K. Müller*

BAUSTEINE FÜR VOLLMACH-TEN UND GESELLSCHAFTER-BESCHLÜSSE

CUT AND PASTE FOR POWERS OF ATTORNEY AND SHAREHOLDERS' RESOLUTIONS

Die folgenden Bausteine können für die wichtigsten gesellschaftsrechtlichen Vorgänge, an denen ausländische Gesellschafter einer österreichischen Gesellschaft beteiligt sind, kombiniert werden.

VOLLMACHT (a)
STIMMRECHTSVOLLMACHT (b)

(a) POWER OF ATTORNEY
(b) PROXY

Als (alleinige) Gesellschafterin der MIRACLE GESELLSCHAFT MBH, registriert zu 7 HRB 58.251a im Handelsregister Wien, bevollmächtigen und beauftragen wir, MIRACLE COMPUTERS LTD, London, England, Herrn

As (sole) shareholder(s) of MIRACLE GESELLSCHAFT M.B.H., registered under 7 HRB 58.251a in the Commercial Register of Vienna, we, MIRACLE COMPUTERS LTD., London, England, hereby appoint and instruct

Dr. Franz X., Rechtsanwalt
Wien I

*Mr. Franz X., solicitor
A-1010 Vienna*

für uns am ... oder zu einem späteren Zeitpunkt eine (außerordentliche) Generalversammlung einzuberufen, für uns dabei das Stimmrecht auszuüben und dabei insbesondere folgende Beschlüsse zu fassen:

to convene a(n) (extraordinary) shareholders's meeting on ... or at a later point in time and to exercise my (our) voting right(s) and in particular to pass the following resolutions:

(c) Herr Peter Williams wird als Geschäftsführer abberufen,

(c) Mr. Peter Williams shall be removed from office as managing director;

(d) für seine Tätigkeit wird ihm die Entlastung erteilt, (und)

(d) his actions shall be formally approved of; (and)

(e) Herr Karl Müller vertritt nunmehr die Gesellschaft alleine.

(e) in future Mr. Karl Müller shall solely represent the Company.

(f) Frau Elisabeth Starkl, Angestellte, 1080 Wien, wird zur weiteren Geschäftsführerin bestellt.

(f) Mrs. Elisabeth Starkl, employee, 1080 Vienna, shall be appointed managing director;

(g) sie vertritt die Gesellschaft allein

(g) she shall solely represent the Company;

(h) sie vertritt die Gesellschaft gemeinsam mit einem zweiten Geschäftsführer

(h) she shall represent the Company together with a second managing director;

(i) oder zusammen mit einem Kollektivprokuristen

(i) or together with a "procurist" with joint powers of representation.*

(j) Frau Katharina Bauer, Angestellte, 1130 Wien, wird zur Prokuristin mit kollektiver Vertretungsbefugnis bestellt;

(j) Mrs. Katharina Bauer, employee, 1130 Vienna, shall be appointed "procurist" with joint powers of representation;*

157

(k) sie vertritt die Gesellschaft gemeinsam mit einem zweiten Kollektivprokuristen

(l) sie vertritt die Gesellschaft gemeinsam mit einem Geschäftsführer

(k) she shall represent the Company together with a second "procurist"* with joint powers of representation;

(l) she shall represent the Company together with a managing director.

(m) Das Geschäftsjahr der Gesellschaft wird geändert, so daß dieses nunmehr mit dem 1. November eines Jahres beginnt und an dem 31. Oktober des folgenden Jahres endet.

(n) Die bezughabende Bestimmung des Gesellschaftsvertrages wird entsprechend geändert und lautet wie folgt:
[. . .]

(m) The business year of the Company shall be changed so that it shall commence on November 1st of each year and terminate on October 31st of the following year.

(n) The relevant provision of the Articles of Association shall be amended accordingly and shall read as follows:
[. . .]

(o) Der Betriebsgegenstand der Gesellschaft wird um ... erweitert.
[. . .]

(o) The objects of the Company shall be extended to include . . .
[. . .]

(p) Das Stammkapital der Gesellschaft wird um S ... erhöht, und die Gesellschafter werden im Verhältnis ihrer bisherigen Beteiligung (oder: wie folgt) zur Übernahme der Kapitalerhöhung zugelassen.
[. . .]

(p) The Company's stated capital shall be increased in the amount of AS . . . and the shareholders shall be entitled to subscribe to such increase pro rata their share (or: in the following amounts) held prior to the capital increase.
[. . .]

(q) Das Stammkapital der Gesellschaft wird um S ... herabgesetzt
[. . .]

(r) Die Gesellschaft wird aufgelöst. Der (die) bisherige(n) Gesellschafter/Herr . . . wird (werden) zu(m) Liquidator(en) bestellt. Er (sie) vertritt (vertreten) die Gesellschaft allein (gemeinsam). Die Gesellschaft trägt den Firmenzusatz „in Liquidation".

(s) Herr ... wird für das Geschäftsjahr 1993 zum Buchprüfer der Gesellschaft bestellt.

(q) The stated capital of the Company shall be reduced by AS . . .
[. . .]

(r) The Company shall be dissolved (wound-up). The current managing director(s) Mr. . . . shall be appointed liquidator(s) with sole/joint powers to represent the Company. Henceforth, the term "in liquidation" shall be added to the Company's name.

(s) Mr. ... shall be appointed auditor for the business year of 1993.

Muster eines Certificate of Incorporation
Bundesstaat Arizona/USA

OFFICE OF THE

CORPORATION COMMISSION

To all to Whom these Presents shall Come, Greeting:

    I, the Executive Secretary of the Arizona Corporation Commission, DO HEREBY CERTIFY that

             *** X GROUP, INC. ***

a Domestic Corporation organized under the laws of the State of Arizona, did incorporate on
         JULY 5, 1970.

    I FURTHER CERTIFY that this corporation has filed all affidavits and annual reports and paid all annual filing fees required to date and, therefore, is in good standing in this state.

IN WITNESS WHEREOF, I have hereunto set my hand and affixed the official seal of the Arizona Corporation Commission. Done at Phoenix, the Capital, this

12TH day of _____APRIL_____,

19 88 ____, A.D.

_____
           Executive Secretary

By_____

INC: 0048 Rev. 1/85

3. ENGLISH TRUSTS

Owen McIntyre B.A. LL.B.
Faculty of Law University of Manchester.

INTRODUCTION

[I]f we were asked what is the greatest and most dis-
tinctive achievement performed by Englishmen in the
field of jurisprudence I cannot think that we should
have any better answer to give than this, namely the
development from century to century of the trust idea.

[Maitland]

legal title, equitable
title, settlor

to hold on trust
beneficiary, trustee
common law

express private trust

legal relationship
assets
for the benefit of

estate

in the name of
on behalf of

to be accountable

imposed by law

express trusts
to transfer property
on trust for so.
private trusts
public or charitable
trusts

discretionary or
non-discretionary
trusts

A trust is a legal device which permits a division of the ownership
or "title" of property into legal title and equitable title. Typically,
the original owner of the property, the "settlor", creates a trust by
conveying the property to trustees with the intention that it be held
on trust for named beneficiaries. The trustees control the property
and become the owners at common law but all benefits arising
from the property, e.g. interest earned on money or rental income
from land, pass to the named beneficiary. Such an arrangement is
an example of an express private trust. Article 2 of the Hague
Trust Convention defines the term "trust" as

"the legal relationships created – inter vivos or on death – by a
person, the settlor, when assets have been placed under the con-
trol of a trustee for the benefit of a beneficiary or for a specified
purpose." *Article 2 goes on to state that a trust has the following*
characteristics:

"(a) the assets constitute a separate fund and are not a part of
the trustee's own estate;

(b)   title to the trust assets stands in the name of the trustee or
in the name of another person on behalf of the trustee;

(c)   the trustee has the power and the duty, in respect of which
he is accountable, to manage, employ or dispose of the as-
sets in accordance with the terms of the trust and the spe-
cial duties imposed upon him by law."

There are four basic classes of trust:

(i) Express trusts, where a person actively executes a deed trans-
ferring property to trustees on trust for a named beneficiary.
These can be further classified into (a) private trusts, which bene-
fit private individuals, and (b) public or charitable trusts, which
benefit certain public purposes. Express private trusts can be fur-
ther divided between discretionary and non-discretionary trusts. A
discretionary trust allows trustees to decide how property is to be
divided between several beneficiaries, whereas a non-discretion-
ary trust does not.

(ii) Implied trusts, where a trust arises as a result of what the law infers as having been a person's intention.

implied trusts

(iii) Constructive trusts, which arise where there is no intention, express or implied, to create a trust but the law imposes a trust and requires that property be held, not beneficially, but on trust for beneficiaries. For example, where trust property is bought from trustees in breach of trust, other than in good faith, the buyer is forced to hold the property on trust for the original beneficiaries.

constructive trusts
in breach of trust
in good faith

(iv) Statutory trusts, which arise in particular situations specifically provided for under a statute. For example, section 33 of the Law of Property Act 1925 provides that the administrators of an intestate estate hold the property on a trust for sale.

statutory trusts
administrators
intestate estate

*Control over the trust property is typically given to trustees because the settlor, or the law, does not regard the beneficiary, the intended recipient of the gift, as being the most apppropriate person to exercise that control. The beneficiary may lack capacity due to age or mental illness, or, there may be several beneficiaries holding an interest in a single item of property who can not all hold formal legal title. However, trusts have a very wide variety of social uses. The French lawyer Pierre Lepaulle had the utility and flexibility of the trust instrument in mind when he said that **"The trust is the guardian angel of the Anglo-Saxon, accompanying him everywhere, impassively, from the cradle to the grave."***

Among the most common uses of the trust are:

*(i) Family settlements. Trusts are commonly used to pass on familial property and are often a very tax advantageous method of doing so. They may be made by will or **inter vivos** , i.e. between living people.*

family settlements
inter vivos

(ii) Share ownership. Instead of being owned outright by shareholders, the legal estate in shares may be held by a nominee in trust for the shareholders. This often may occur where the trustee manages an investment portfolio, e.g. in the case of unit trusts.

share ownership
nominee
unit trusts

(iii) Unincorporated bodies. It is usual for unincorporated bodies, such as charities, trade unions, clubs and societies, to be constituted as trusts. Trust status enables such bodies to hold property. The property is actually held for the purposes of the body by trustees who are normally individuals sympathetic to the purposes of the body.

unincorporated bodies
trust status

(iv) Marital property or the property of cohabitees. Trusts often arise from informal family arrangements, e.g. where one cohabitee contributes money towards the purchase of a home conveyed into the name of the other cohabitee alone, a resulting trust arises so that both parties share equitable title.

marital property,
cohabitees
to share equitable title

At this point it might be useful to make some general observations about trusts. Firstly, the settlors, trustees and beneficiaries need not be different people. A settlor can create a trust by declaring himself trustee of his own property, on behalf of one or more ben-

eficiaries, including himself – <u>Paul v. Constance [1977]</u>. Secondly, the property settled can include an existing equitable interest. In other words, a beneficiary under a trust may constitute a further

subtrusts
tax avoidance
irrevocable arrange-
ment

trust of his equitable interest, creating a subtrust. Subtrusts are widely used in settlements which aim to avoid tax. Thirdly, the intention to create a trust must be irrevocable as a trust is an irrevocable arrangement. However, the intention must be to create a trust rather than some other transaction, such as an outright gift. Finally, if a trust is charitable (public trust) there may be no easily discernible benificiaries, yet such trusts are valid and will be enforced by the Attorney-General.

FORMALITIES

legal instrument

As a legal instrument the trust is not overburdened with strict requirements as to form, thereby allowing it to remain flexible. The

formal requirements

type of property and
interest

formal requirements for the creation of a valid trust depend on (a) the type of property, and (b) the type of interest. As land was traditionally regarded as very valuable and as land transactions are often very complicated, trusts concerning land usually involve more formalities. Creation or "declaration" of trusts relating to

personalty

documentary evidence
to prevent fraud

personalty do not generally require writing. Due to the intangible nature of equitable interests documentary evidence is usually required in order to prevent fraud. Also, documents enable the trustees to find where equitable interests lie and so to carry out the trust. Therefore, dispositions or transfers of equitable interests

extinguishment or
termination

will require writing. The extinguishment or termination of trusts, by merger of the beneficial and legal interests, generally do not require writing.

CERTAINTIES

Although trusts are not subject to excessive formal written requirements, all trusts, to be valid, must satisfy three essential conditions. They must be certain as to the intention to create a trust, certain as to the property that is to be the subject-matter of the trust, and, certain as to the objects of the trust. These require-

three certainties

*ments are commonly referred to as the **"three certainties"**.*

certainty of intention

Establishing certainty of intention to create a trust will not generally present a problem. As a settlor may establish a trust without any writing whatsoever, (unless there are formal statutory requirements), or even without words, the intention of a settlor to create a trust may be inferred from his conduct. However, problems may

precatory words

arise where precatory words, i.e. words which are wishful as opposed to imperative, have been used. Precatory words may still give rise to a binding trust if intention to create a trust can be inferred from the wording generally. The intention of the settlor therefore depends on the construction of the settlors words in each case.

162

Regarding certainty of subject-matter, the trust must be clear as to the exact amount and particular items of the settlor's property which are to be settled. Also, there should be certainty as to the amount of each beneficial interest if more than one beneficiary is named. However, in the case of uncertainty as to the size of each beneficial interest, the Courts will try to validate the trust and will often apply the maxim *"equality is equity"* where no guidance on sharing has been given.

certainty of subject-matter, amount and items of property

amount of beneficial interests

equality is equity

There must be certainty as to the objects or beneficiaries for two reasons: (i) the trustees must be aware who the beneficiaries are in order to be able to carry out their duties, and (ii) if the trustees fail to carry out their duties or exercise their discretion improperly, it must be possible to ascertain who has *locus standi* to take an action in court. If the gift is made to specified beneficiaries no problem arises. However, if the gift is made in favour of a class of people, different rules apply depending on whether the trust is fixed, i.e. non-discretionary, or discretionary.

certainty of objects or beneficiaries

locus standi

In the case of a fixed trust, the class of people must be ascertainable, i.e. it must be possible to list all the beneficiaries, as the property is to be divided among all the beneficiaries in fixed proportions. If unspecified, the property would be distributed in equal shares on the basis of the *"equality is equity"* maxim. In order for a discretionary trust to be valid it is only necessary to ascertain whether an individual is a member of the class. The courts have applied the *"individual ascertainability test"* in relation to discretionary trusts because a requirement of equal distribution might make a nonsense of the settlor's intention.

discretionary trusts

individual ascertainability test

A trust instrument may contain a power to cure uncertainty. A fatal element of uncertainty may be removed by giving the power to decide a particular matter to particular people, usually the trustees or community leaders. In *Re Tucks Settlement Trusts [1978]* the question of whether or not a beneficiary worshipped *"according to the Jewish faith"* was to be determined by *"the Chief Rabbi in London of either the Portuguese or Anglo-German community"*. This term removed any uncertainty and allowed the trust to succeed. However, such a power to adjudicate can only be given in relation to matters of fact, not of law, as this would be an attempt to oust the jurisdiction of the courts and so contrary to public policy and therefore invalid.

power to cure uncertainty

power to adjudicate

TRUSTEES

trustees

Normally trustees will be appointed by the trust document which ought also to provide for the appointment of additional or replacement trustees. Where nobody is able or willing to act as trustee, for example where the nominees have predeceased the testator, absence of trustees will not invalidate the trust. If the trust is *inter vivos* the settlor will become trustee, if by will the personal

appointment

nominees, testator

representatives of the testator will hold on trust. If the trust instrument expressly gives someone the power to appoint he will do so. Otherwise, the court will appoint. An express trust cannot compel a person to become a trustee though one may be compelled by operation of law, for example, under a constructive trust. Once the office is accepted it is usually lifelong and cannot later be renounced. Also, retirement from the office is difficult. If a nominee does not disclaim the office as soon as possible a presumption of acceptance may be inferred. Anyone with the legal capacity to hold legal title to property may be appointed a trustee. A corporation may be appointed if its constitution so authorises. Indeed, a trust corporation can provide longevity, financial stability and a high level of expertise though the administration fees may be considered high. The courts have always had an inherent power to appoint trustees whenever it is expedient that an appointment should be made but where it is impracticable without the courts' assistance. This power has been given a statutory basis by section 41 of the Trustees Act 1925. Applications may be made to the court by a beneficiary or trustee and the court may also act where there are allegations of misconduct. Where nobody has the power to appoint or where nobody is able or willing to exercise such a power, the courts may be the only means of replacing elderly or infirm trustees who have become incapable of acting – Re Phelp's WT [1885]. However, certain principles govern the court's selection. For example, it will not make an appointment which favours interests of certain beneficiaries above others or appoint against the known wishes of the settlor. A trustee may only retire from the trust if a power is contained in the trust instrument, if all the beneficiaries consent, or, if the court agrees to discharge him. Also, he may retire under the provisions of section 39 of the Trustees Act 1925 if he leaves at least two trustees or a trust corporation, if the remaining trustees consent, and, if anyone empowered to appoint consents. The courts will only remove a trustee forcefully in exceptional circumstances. On the death of a trustee, the office and trust estate devolve on the surviving trustees. When the sole surviving trustee dies, the trust property devolves on the personal representatives of the testator and is held by them on the terms of the trust. The personal representatives only act until new trustees are appointed and they will often have the power to appoint.

The powers and duties conferred upon trustees vary according to the terms and character of the trust. Where the trust instrument does not provide detailed measures, statutory provisions will apply. Generally, trustees will be under a duty to:

(i) protect the trust assets through investment. General principles apply to the investment of trust assets. There is a duty to act fairly as between the beneficiaries when investing. For example, while producing income for income beneficiaries (life beneficiaries), the

Margin glossary:
- acceptance of office
- misconduct
- forceful removal
- to devolve on so
- personal representatives
- trustees' duties
- investment of trust assets
- income beneficiaries

trustees must preserve the capital for capital beneficiaries (remaindermen). Also, there are limitations of the making of risky investments, including a duty to diversify. The Trustee Investment Act 1961 contains detailed rules regarding trustees' duties and powers of investment which will apply where the trust instrument does not give adequate guidance. However, today it is usual to give trustees very wide powers of investment and further authority to amend these powers if necessary. Also, it is usual to expressly exclude the 1961 Act. This allows the trustees to react quickly to investment opportunities.

(ii) ensure proper payment of tax, keep accounts and supply copies to beneficfiaries.

(iii) consider the sale of trust property where appropriate. The power of sale is usually given, expressly or impliedly, by the trust instrument, or, if absent, often permitted by statute or by order of the court.

(iv) provide for infant beneficiaries.

(v) exercise the power to appoint.

These powers and duties apply only to express trusts. As constructive trusts arise by operation of law and the constructive trustee may not even be aware of the fact that he holds on trust until the issue has been determined by a court, he is under no comparable duties. His only duty is to hold the property or proceeds on behalf of the beneficiaries.

*As trustees are concerned not only with the beneficiaries' wishes but also with those expressed by the settlor on the creation of the trust, no general principle permits the beneficiaries to control trustees in the exercise of their discretions. However, where the beneficiaries collectively are absolutely entitled to the entirety of the trust, where they are all **sui juris**, i.e. of the age of majority, and, where they agree unanimously, they may terminate the trust. This is known as the rule in Saunders v Vautier [1841]. If they wish to set up a new trust, as settlors, they can resettle the property on any terms. Effectively, this is the extent of the beneficiaries' power over the trustees. Trustees are not compelled to disclose the reasons behind the exercise of a discretion and, generally, they need not disclose any confidential documents to the beneficiaries. However, one exception to this rule is that beneficiaries are at all times entitled to examine trust accounts.*

FIDUCIARY NATURE OF TRUSTEESHIP

The law imposes a fiduciary duty on trustees which is owed to the trust, and therefore, to the beneficiaries. Generally, where a fiduciary relationship exists, the fiduciary must not have any personal interest in the way his duties are performed. Lord Herschell described the nature of a trustee's duty in Bray v Ford [1896]:

capital beneficiaries
remaindermen
duty to diversify

proper tax payment
keeping of accounts

power of sale

infant beneficiaries
power to appoint

beneficiaries' control
of trustees

entirety of the trust
age of majority

beneficiaries' power
over trustees

fiduciary duty

court of equity	*It is an inflexible rule of a court of equity that a person in a fiduciary position ... is not, unless otherwise expressly provided, entitled to make a profit; he is not allowed to put himself in a position where his interest and duty conflict. It does not appear to me that this rule is, as has been said, founded upon principles of*
morality	*morality. I regard it rather as based on the consideration that human nature being what it is, there is a danger, in such circumstances, of the person holding a fiduciary position being swayed by interest rather than duty, and thus prejudicing those whom he is*
to be bound to protect so.	*bound to protect. It has, therefore, been deemed expedient to lay down this positive rule. But, I am satisfied that this may be departed from in many cases, without any breach of morality, without any wrong being inflicted, and without any consciousness of*
wrongdoing	*wrongdoing.*
strict application of fiduciary duty	*Therefore, the fiduciary duty is to be strictly applied, regardless of the fact that the trustee has acted honestly or was unaware of the wrongdoing. Factual applications of the trustee's fiduciary duty include:(i) the general rule that a trustee may not be paid for his*
no payment	*efforts unless payment is authorised by the trust instrument, by statute, or by the court. A solicitor-trustee may charge a fee for work done on behalf of the trust but under the rule in <u>Cradock v Piper [1850]</u> he may recover his professional costs only.*
no profit, by virtue of	*(ii) the rule that a trustee may not profit by virtue of his position as a trustee. This principle extends to any profits earned by virtue of a fiduciary position and the profits received are held by the fiduciary on a constructive trust for the beneficiaries. In <u>Re Macadam [1946]</u>, trustees who used their positions as shareholders to have themselves appointed to directorships of a company were held liable to account to the trust for all fees received as directors.*
no competition	*(iii) the rule that a trustee may not set himself up in competition with a business belonging to the trust. If he does so he will be held liable to the trust to account for profits – <u>Re Thompson [1930]</u>. The court may also grant an injunction preventing the trustee from competing with the trust or may remove the trustee altogether.*
no purchase of trust property voidable, behest	*(iv) the rule that a trustee may not purchase trust property for himself. Where a trustee does purchase trust property, the transaction is voidable at the behest of any interested beneficiary, no matter how fair, open and honest it may have been. In <u>Tito v Waddell [1977]</u>, Megarry VC described this rule, often referred to as the*
self-dealing rule	***"self-dealing rule"**, as a disability on the trustee rather than a duty.*

TERMINOLOGIE ZUM GESELL-SCHAFTSRECHT

CORPORATE LAW TERMINOLOGY

abberufen	*dismiss, remove from office*
Abberufung	*removal from office, dismissal*
abgegebene Stimmen	*votes cast*
abhalten (Versammlung)	*hold (a meeting)*
Abschlußprüfung	*audit*
Abstimmung	*vote, poll*
Abtretung von Geschäftsanteilen/Aktien	*assignment/transfer of shares*
Abtretungspreis	*purchase price*
Abtretungsvertrag	*assignment deed, contract of assignment, share purchase agreement/deed*
abwickeln (eine Gesellschaft)	*to wind up a company/partnership*
Abwicklung	*winding-up*
Agio	*premium*
Aktien	*shares (UK and US), stock (US)*
Aktien begeben	*issue shares*
Aktien zeichnen	*subscribe for shares*
Aktien zur Einziehung	*redeemable shares*
Aktienarten	*types of shares*
Aktienausgabe	*issue of shares*
Aktienbörse	*stock exchange*
Aktienbuch	*book of shares, share ledger*
Aktiengattung	*class of shares*
Aktiengesellschaft	*joint-stock corporation (US)/company (UK)*
Aktiengesetz	*Stock Company Act*, Stock Corporation Act**
Aktienkapital	*share capital*
Aktienkaufvertrag	*share purchase agreement*
Aktienkurs	*share price*
Aktienplazierung	*placement of an issue*
Aktienurkunde	*share certificate*
Aktienzuteilung	*allotment of shares*
Aktionär	*shareholder*
Aktionärsbeschluß	*shareholders' resolution*
Allfälliges	*miscellaneous*
amtierend	*incumbent*
Amtsenthebung	*removal from office*
amtsinhabend	*incumbent*
an der Börse notiert	*publicly quoted/listed*
an die Börse gehen	*go public*
Anbot	*bid*
Anlagegeschäft	*investment business*
Anlageschutz	*investment protection*
Anleger	*investor*
(optimistischer)	*(bull)*
(pessimistischer)	*(bear)*
Anteil am Kapital übernehmen/zeichnen	*subscribe to/for capital*

167

Antrag	*motion*
Antrag ablehnen	*reject/deny a motion*
Antrag genehmigen	*carry/approve a motion*
Antrag stellen	*move for*
Antrag unterstützen	*second a motion*
Apostille (Haager Konvention)	*appostille*
Art der Verständigung	*means of communication*
auf die Tagesordnung setzen	*put on the agenda*
Aufgeld	*premium*
Auflösung einer Gesellschaft	*dissolution/winding-up of a company/ partnership*
Auflösungsbeschluß	*resolution to wind up*
Aufsichtsrat	*supervisory board**
Aufsichtsratsvorsitzender	*chairman of the supervisory board**
Ausfertigung(en)	*counterpart(s)*
Ausgabekurs	*issuing price*
(über Nennwert)	*(at a premium, above par)*
(unter Nennwert)	*(at a discount, below par)*
ausgegebene Aktien	*outstanding shares*
ausgegebenes Kapital	*issued capital*
ausgewiesenes Grundkapital	*stated capital*
Ausgleich (A) (insolvenzrechtlich)	*assignment for the benefit of one's creditors**
außerbörslicher Handel	*off board trading, off the floor trading*
außerordentliche General-/Hauptversammlung	*extraordinary/special shareholders meeting; extraordinary general meeting (EGM) (UK)*
Baisse	*bear market*
Bareinlage	*contribution in cash, cash contribution, money capital*
beantragen	*move for*
Beginn des Geschäftsjahres	*commencement of the business year*
beglaubigte Unterschrift	*legalized/notarized signature*
beglaubigter Firmenbuchauszug	*certified excerpt from the commercial register**
Beglaubigung	*certification, legalization**
Beirat	*advisory board/council**
Belastung von Geschäftsanteilen	*encumbrance of shares*
beschließen	*resolve, pass a resolution*
Beschluß	*resolution*
Beschluß der Aktionärsversammlung	*resolution of shareholders' meeting*
Beschluß der Generalversammlung	*resolution of general shareholders' meeting*
Beschluß der Hauptversammlung	*resolution of general shareholders' meeting*
Beschluß fassen	*pass a resolution, resolve*
Beschluß über die Abberufung eines Geschäftsführers	*resolution to recall/to discharge a managing director, resolution to remove a managing director from office*
Beschluß über die Abwicklung der Gesellschaft	*resolution to wind up the company*

168

Beschluß über die Auflösung der Gesellschaft	*resolution on the dissolution of the company*
Beschluß über die Bestellung eines Geschäftsführers	*resolution to appoint a managing director**
Beschluß über die Entlastung eines Geschäftsführers	*resolution to grant official approval for actions as managing director**
Beschluß über die Gewinnverteilung	*resolution on distribution of profits*
Beschluß über die Kapitalerhöhung	*resolution on capital increase*
Beschluß über die Kapitalherabsetzung	*resolution on capital reduction*
Beschluß über die Liquidation fassen	*pass a resolution to liquidate*
beschlußfähig sein	*to constitute a quorum*
beschlußfähige Mehrheit	*quorum*
Bestätigung über die Amtsinhabung	*certificate of incumbency**
Bestellung	*appointment*
Beteiligungsgesellschaft	*affiliated company/corporation*
Beteiligungsgesellschaft, an der eine Beteiligung von max. 50% besteht	*associated/affiliated company/corporation*
Betriebsgegenstand	*objects (of the company)*
Betriebsgegenstandsklausel	*objects clause*
Betriebsrat	*works council*
Bilanz	*balance sheets*
Bilanzstichtag	*balance sheet date*
Börse	*stock exchange*
Börsenaufsicht	*stock exchange supervision*
Börsenaufsichtsbehörde (US)	*Securities and Exchange Commission (SEC)*
Börsenaufsichtsgesetz (US)	*Securities and Exchange Act*
Börseneinführung	*admission to official listing, quotation*
börsenfähige Aktien	*marketable shares*
Börsengesetz (A)	*Stock Exchange Act**
Börsenhandel	*stock exchange trading*
Börsenkurs	*quotation, price*
Börsenmakler	*stock exchange broker*
Börsenparkett	*floor*
Börsenprospekt	*prospectus*
Börsenumsatzsteuer	*Stock Exchange Turnover Tax**
Buchführung	*book-keeping*
Buchhaltung	*book-keeping, accounting*
Buchprüfer	*chartered accountant (CA) (UK), certified public accountant (C.P.A.) (US), auditor*
Buchprüfung	*audit*
Buchsachverständiger	*auditor*
bürgerlich-rechtliche Gesellschaft	*partnership as regulated by the German and Austrian Civil Code**
Dauer der Gesellschaft	*duration of company/partnership*
Dirimierungsrecht	*casting vote*
Disagio	*discount*
Dividende	*dividend*
Effektenbörse	*stock/securities exchange*
eidesstättige/eidesstattliche Erklärung	*affidavit**

Eigenkapital	equity capital
einberufen (Versammlung)	call/convene a meeting
einfache Mehrheit	simple majority*
einfacher Beschluß	ordinary resolution
eingefordertes Kapital	called-up capital
Eingetragene Erwerbsgesellschaft (EEG) (A)	registered partnership*
eingetragenes Kapital	registered capital
Einheitsgründung	one-stage formation
Einpersonenfirma	one-person firm
Eintragung (einer Gesellschaft)	incorporation, registration
Eintragungsgebühren	filing fees
Eintragungsvorschriften	filing requirements
Einzelkaufmann	sole proprietor (US), sole trader (UK)
Einzelrechtsnachfolge	singular succession*
Einzelunternehmen	sole proprietorship (US)
Einzelunternehmer	sole proprietor (US), sole trader (UK)
Einzelvertretungsbefugnis	individual/single/sole right to represent the company, sole right of representation, individual power of representation
Einziehung von Aktien	cancellation/redemption of shares
Emission	issue, issuance
Emissionsbedingungen	conditions of issue
emittieren	to issue
Ende des Geschäftsjahres	end/termination of the business year
Errichtung einer Gesellschaft	creation/formation/foundation/ establishment of a company/corporation
Erwerb von mehr als 50% einer Gesellschaft	buyout, takeover
Erwerb von mehr als 50% einer Gesellschaft durch die Geschäftsführung/ leitenden Angestellten	management buyout
feindliche Übernahme	hostile takeover
Firma (der Gesellschaft)	name of the company/corporation/ partnership
Firmenbuch	commercial register*
Firmenbuchantrag	application to the commercial register*
Firmenbuchantrag auf Eintragung einer Gesellschaft	application for registration/incorporation*
Firmenbuchauszug	excerpt from the commercial register*
Firmensitz	registered office*, principal place of business*
Formalitäten	formalities
freiwillige Auflösung	voluntary dissolution
freiwillige Liquidation	voluntary liquidation
freiwilliger Konkursantrag	(voluntary) petition for bankruptcy
Fremdkapital	loan capital
Fusion	merger, amalgamation
geheime Wahl	(secret) ballot
Geldeinlage	money capital
genehmigtes Kapital	authorized capital
Generaldirektor	president*, chief executive officer*

170

Generaldirektorstellvertreter	*vice president, chief operating officer**
Generalversammlung	*general shareholders' meeting*
außerordentliche	*extraordinary/special general meeting*
ordentliche	*ordinary/annual general meeting*
gerichtlich bestellter Liquidator	*court-appointed liquidator*
gerichtliche Auflösung	*judicial dissolution*
Gesamtrechtsnachfolge	*universal succession**
Geschäftsanschrift	*registered/business address*
Geschäftsanteil übernehmen	*subscribe for a share interest**
Geschäftsanteile	*shares, stake, share interests*
Geschäftsanteile/Aktien abtreten	*assign shares/share interests**
Geschäftsbücher	*books and records*
Geschäftsfrau	*businesswoman*
Geschäftsführer	*managing director**
Geschäftsführerliste	*list of managing directors**
Geschäftsführung	*management (board), board of managers, managing board**
Geschäftsjahr	*business year*
Geschäftsmann	*businessman*
Geschäftsordnung	*internal rules (governing conduct of management, supervisory board, etc.)*
Gesellschaft	*company, corporation, partnership, joint-stock corporation (US), company (UK)**
Gesellschaft abwickeln	*wind up a company*
Gesellschaft bürgerlichen Rechts	*civil law association**
Gesellschaft eintragen (lassen)	*incorporate/register a company/corporation*
Gesellschaft gründen	*set-up/found a company/corporation*
Gesellschaft liquidieren	*liquidate a company*
Gesellschaft mit beschränkter Haftung	*corporation*, GmbH-company*
Gesellschafter	*shareholder, partner*
Gesellschafter einer Kapitalgesellschaft	*shareholder*
Gesellschafter einer Personengesellschaft	*partner*
Gesellschafterbeschluß	*shareholders' resolution*
Gesellschaftsgründung	*setting-up/establishment of a company/corporation/partnership*
Gesellschaftsvertrag	*articles of association, partnership agreement*
Gesellschaftsvertrag für Personengesellschaft	*partnership agreement*
Gewinn	*profit(s)*
Gewinn nach Steuern	*profit after tax*
Gewinn vor Steuern	*profit before tax*
Gewinn- und Verlustrechnung	*income statement (US), profit and loss account (UK)*
Gewinnverteilung	*distribution of profits*
Gläubigermehrheit	*plurality of creditors*
Glücksspiele	*games of chance*
Gratisaktien	*bonus shares*
Gründer	*incorporator(s), founder(s)*
Grundkapital	*stated capital, nominal capital, capital stock*
Gründung	*formation, setting-up*
Gründungsurkunden	*foundation documents*

Haftung	*liability*
Handelsgesellschaft	*trading partnership*
Hauptversammlung	*shareholders meeting, general meeting*
Hausse	*bull market*
Holdinggesellschaft	*holding company*
Illiquidität	*illiquidity*
in Konkurs gehen	*become bankrupt, go bankrupt*
Indossament	*endorsement*
Inhaberaktien	*bearer shares*
Insolvenz	*insolvency*
Jahreabschluß	*year-end financial statement, annual financial statements, financial statements, annual accounts, annual closing of accounts*
Jahreshauptversammlung	*annual general meeting (AGM) (UK), annual shareholders meeting*
junge Aktien	*new shares*
Kalenderjahr	*calendar year*
Kapital	*capital*
Kapitalgesellschaft	*company (UK), corporation (US)*
Kapitalgesellschaft ohne Gewinnerzielungsabsicht	*corporation not for profit*
Kassier	*treasurer*
Klage	*court action*
Kollektivvertretungsbefugnis	*joint power/collective right of representation*
Kommandit-Erwerbsgesellschaft (KEG) (A)	*limited partnership for professionals and other individuals not eligible for partnerships regulated by the Commercial Code**
Kommanditgesellschaft (KG)	*limited partnership*
Kommanditist	*limited partner*
Komplementär	*general partner*
Konferenz	*meeting, conference*
Konkurs	*bankruptcy*
Konkursantrag mangels Kostendeckung abweisen	*to discharge a petition for bankruptcy for want of assets to cover costs of bankruptcy proceedings*
Konkursantrag stellen	*file for bankruptcy*
Konten	*accounts*
Körperschaft	*corporate body*
Kosten	*cost(s)*
Kupon	*coupon*
Kurs	*price, quotation*
Kursmakler	*official exchange broker*
leitender Angestellter	*officer, executive*
Liquidation	*liquidation*
Liquidationserlös aufteilen	*distribute assets upon liquidation*

172

Liquidator	*liquidator*
Liquidator bestellen	*appoint a liquidator*
Liquidität	*liquidity*
Löschung einer Gesellschaft	*cancellation/deletion of a company/ partnership*
mangelnde Liquidität	*illiquidity*
Masseverwalter	*receiver*, estate administrator, trustee in bankruptcy*
Masseverwalter bestellen	*appoint a receiver**
Masseverwaltung	*receivership**
Mehrheit	*majority*
(einfache)	*(simple*)*
(qualifizierte)	*(qualified*)*
Mitglied des Aufsichtsrates	*member of the supervisory board**
Mitglied des Vorstandes	*member of the executive/management board**
Musterfirmazeichnung	*sample signatures*, specimen (of) signatures**
Muttergesellschaft	*parent company*
Nachzugsaktien	*deferred shares (UK/US), deferred stock (US)*
Namensaktien	*registered shares*
Nennwert	*nominal/par/face value*
nicht ausgegebenes Kapital	*unissued capital*
nicht eingefordertes Kapital	*uncalled capital*
nicht eingetragen	*unincorporated*
Nominalwert	*face/nominal/par value*
Notariatsakt	*notarial deed**
notarielle Beglaubigung	*notarization*
Notierung	*listing, quotation*
Offene Erwerbsgesellschaft (OEG) (A)	*general partnership for professionals and other individuals not eligible for partnerships regulated by the Commercial Code**
Offene Handelsgesellschaft (OHG)	*general partnership**
öffentliche Versorgungsunternehmen	*public utilities*
offizielles Börseneinführungspapier	*prospectus*
optimistischer Anleger	*bull*
ordentliche General-/Hauptversammlung	*general/ordinary shareholders meeting*
Organe	*(executive) bodies (of a company)*
Paragraph-10-Erklärung der Geschäftsführer (A)	*statement of managing directors pursuant to Section 10 of the Austrian GmbHG**
Personalvertreter	*staff representative*
Personenhandelsgesellschaft	*partnership*
pessimistischer Anleger	*bear*
Prokurist	*„procurist"* (an officer of the company whose powers to represent and act on behalf of the company are defined by the Austrian/German Commercial Code), authorized agent*

Protokoll	*minutes (of a meeting)*
Protokoll führen	*to keep minutes, to put on record*
qualifizierte Mehrheit	*qualified majority**
qualifizierter Beschluß	*special resolution*
Quorum	*quorum*
Rechnungsprüfer	*auditor*
Rechtsbehelf	*remedy*
Registerbeamter	*registrar*
Registerführer	*registrar*
Registrierungsgebühr	*registration fee*
Reingewinn	*net profit*
Rohgewinn	*gross profit*
Rückführung einer an der Börse gehandelten Gesellschaft in eine Nicht-Publikums-gesellschaft	*going private*
Sacheinlage	*contribution in kind, real capital*
Sachverständiger	*expert*
Satzung	*articles of association, corporate charter*
Schadenersatz	*(compensation for) damages*
schriftlich beschließen	*resolve in writing*
schriftlicher Beschluß	*written resolution*
Sitz	*principal place of business*, registered office**
Sitzung	*meeting, session*
Sitzungsprotokoll	*minutes of a meeting*
Sozietät (freie Berufe)	*non-trading partnership, professional partnership, professional association*
Stammaktien	*common stock (US), ordinary shares (UK)*
Stammeinlage	*initial contribution*
Stammkapital	*nominal capital, stated capital, capital stock*
stellvertretender Vorsitzender	*deputy chairman*
stille Gesellschaft	*silent partnership**
stiller Gesellschafter	*silent/dormant partner*
stillschweigende Vereinbarung	*tacit agreement*
Stimmabgabe durch Bevollmächtigten	*vote by proxy*
stimmberechtigte Aktien	*voting shares*
Stimme abgeben	*cast a vote*
Stimmenmehrheit	*majority of votes*
Stimmenthaltung	*abstention*
Stimmrecht	*voting right, right to vote*
Stimmrecht ausüben	*exercise one's voting right*
Stimmrechtsbevollmächtigter	*proxy*
stimmrechtslose Aktien	*non-voting shares*
Stimmrechtsvollmacht	*proxy*
Stimmzettel	*ballot*
Stufengründung	*successive formation*
Tagesordnung	*agenda*
Tagesordnungspunkt	*item on the agenda*

Teilung von Geschäftsanteilen	*division of shares*
teilweise einbezahltes Stammkapital	*partly-paid capital*
Telefonhandel	*inter-office trading*
Tochtergesellschaft	*subsidiary (company)*
Treuhänder	*trustee**
über Nennwert	*above par, at a premium*
Übernahme	*subscription*
Überschuldung	*over-indebtedness, over-leverage*
Übertragung von Geschäftsanteilen/Aktien	*transfer of share interests/shares*
Überzeichnung	*over-subscription*
Umlaufbeschluß	*written shareholders' resolution*
Umstrukturierung	*(corporate) reorganization/restructuring*
Umwandlung	*transformation, restructuring*
Umwandlungsbeschluß	*resolution to change the legal form of a business enterprise*
Umwandlungsgesetz (A)	*Transformation Statute**
Unbedenklichkeitsbescheinigung (A)	*declaration of non-objection issued by tax authorities upon payment of capital transfer tax on share capital**
unter Nennwert	*at a discount, below par*
Unternehmen	*business enterprise/undertaking*
Unternehmenserwerb	*acquisition of a business enterprise*
Unternehmenskauf	*purchase of a business enterprise*
Unternehmer	*entrepreneur*
Unterschrift	*signature*
Urkunde über die Eintragung einer Kapitalgesellschaft	*certificate of incorporation (UK/US)*
Verband	*association*
Verein	*association*, club**
Vereinigung	*association, federation*
verfügen über	*dispose of*
Verfügung über Geschäftsanteile/Aktien	*disposition of shares*
Vergleich (D) (insolvenzrechtlich)	*assignment for the benefit of one's creditors**
Verhinderung	*incapacity*
Verlust	*loss(es)*
Versammlung	*meeting*
Verschmelzung	*merger, amalgamation*
Verständigung	*notification*
Vertretung	*representation*
Vertretungsbefugnis	*power/right of representation, authority/power to bind the company*
Vollmacht	*power of attorney*
Vorkaufsrecht	*right of first refusal*
Vorkaufsrecht ausüben	*to exercise the right of first refusal*
Vorschlag	*proposal*
Vorschlag ablehnen	*reject a proposal*
Vorschlag annehmen	*accept a proposal*
Vorsitz haben	*chair, preside over*
Vorstand	*management board*, executive board**

Vorstandsmitglied	*member of the management/ executive board*
Vorstandsvorsitzender	*chairman of the management/ executive board, (CEO*) (US: Chief Executive Officer)*
Vorzugsaktien	*preference shares (UK/US), preferred stock (US)*
Wahl	*ballot, vote, election, poll*
Wahl durch Handzeichen	*vote by show of hands*
Wahlhelfer	*election agent*
Wandelschuldverschreibungen	*convertible bonds/debentures*
Warenbörse	*commodity exchange*
Weisungen an die Geschäftsführung	*directives to the managing directors**
Wirtschaftsprüfer	*chartered accountant (UK), certified public accountant (C.P.A.) (US)*
Wirtschaftsunternehmen	*commercial enterprise*
wohltätiger oder religiöser Zweck	*charitable or religious purpose*
Zeichnung von Aktien	*subscription for shares*
Zeichnungsberechtigung	*power/right to sign on behalf of the company*
zur Gänze einbezahlt	*fully paid-up*
Zustellbevollmächtigter	*service of process agent**
Zwangsliquidation	*compulsory liquidation*
Zwangsverwaltung	*receivership**
Zweigniederlassung	*branch (office)*
Zwischenschein	*interim certificate*

CORPORATE LAW TERMINOLOGY

TERMINOLOGIE ZUM GESELL-SCHAFTSRECHT

above par	über Nennwert
abstain	sich (der Stimme) enthalten
abstention	(Stimm-)Enthaltung
accept a proposal	einen Vorschlag annehmen
accounts	Konten, Geschäftsbücher
acquisition (of a business enterprise)	Unternehmenserwerb
adjudicated bankrupt	gerichtlich festgestellter Bankrotteur
advisory board	Beirat* (A/D)
advisory council	Beirat* (A/D)
affidavit	eidesstattliche/eidesstättige Erklärung
affiliated company	Beteiligungsgesellschaft
agenda	Tagesordnung
allotment of shares	Aktienzuteilung
amalgamation	Fusion, Verschmelzung
annual accounts	Jahresabschluß
annual closing of accounts	Jahresabschluß
annual financial statements	Jahresabschluß
annual general meeting (AGM) (UK)	Jahreshauptversammlung
annual shareholders meeting	Jahreshauptversammlung, jährliche Generalversammlung
application for registration/incorporation	Firmenbuchantrag auf Eintragung einer Gesellschaft
appoint a liquidator	einen Liquidator bestellen
appoint a receiver/trustee (in bankruptcy)	einen (Masse-)Verwalter bestellen
appoint so. to the board of directors	jmd. zum Mitglied des Verwaltungsrates bestellen
appostille	Apostille (Haager Konvention)
articles of association (UK)	ergänzendes Satzungsdokument einer UK-Kapitalgesellschaft, mit welchem insbesondere das Innenverhältnis näher geregelt wird
articles of incorporation (US)	Gundsatzdokument einer US-Kapital-gesellschaft, mit welchem insbesondere das Außenverhältnis geregelt wird
articles of partnership (US)	Gründungsdokument einer US-Personen-gesellschaft
assign shares	Geschäftsanteile/Aktien abtreten
assignment contract	Abtretungsvertrag
*assignment for the benefit of one's creditors**	Ausgleich (A), Vergleich (D)
assignment of shares	Abtretung von Geschäftsanteilen/Aktien
associated company	Beteiligungsgesellschaft, an der eine Beteiligung von max. 50% besteht; (vertraglich) verbundene Gesellschaft
association	Vereinigung, Verband, Verein
at a discount	unter Nennwert
at a premium	über Nennwert

audit	(Abschluß)-Prüfung
auditor	Buchsachverständiger, Rechnungsprüfer, Abschlußprüfer, Wirtschaftsprüfer
authority to bind the company	Vertretungsbefugnis
authorized capital	genehmigtes Kapital
B.O.D. (board of directors)	Verwaltungsrat*
(siehe Kommentar zu board of directors)	
balance sheet date	Bilanzstichtag
balance sheets	Bilanz
ballot	Stimmzettel
bankruptcy	Konkurs
be appointed general manager	zum Geschäftsführer* bestellt werden (A/D)
bear	pessimistischer Anleger
bearer shares	Inhaberaktien
bearish	pessimistisch (Börse)
become bankrupt	in Konkurs gehen
below par	unter Nennwert
bid	Anbot
blue chip	konservatives, risikoarmes Papier
blue sky laws (US)	US-bundesstaatliche Gesetze, die den Wertpapierhandel regeln
board of directors (B.O.D.)	Verwaltungsrat* einer US/UK-Kapital-gesellschaft *(Auf die unterschiedliche Struktur und die unterschiedlichen Funktionen der einzelnen Organe im Vergleich zu den dt. und österr. Organen einer Kapitalgesellschaft wird hingewiesen.)*
bodies (of a company)	Organe
bonus shares	Gratisaktien
book of shares	Aktienbuch
book-keeping	Buchführung, Buchhaltung
books	(Geschäfts-)Bücher
branch (office)	Zweigniederlassung
bull	optimistischer Anleger
bullish	optimistisch (Börse)
business enterprise	Unternehmen
business undertaking	Unternehmen
business year	Geschäftsjahr
businessperson	Geschäftsmann/-frau
buyout	Erwerb von mehr als 50%
bylaws (US) auch: by(e)-laws	ergänzendes Satzungsdokument einer US Kapitalgesellschaft, mit welchem insbesondere das Innenverhältnis geregelt wird
call a meeting	eine Sitzung/Versammlung/Konferenz einberufen
called-up capital	eingefordertes Kapital
cancellation of shares	Einziehung von Aktien
capital	Stammkapital, Grundkapital
capital stock	Stammkapital, Grundkapital

178

cash contribution	Bareinlage
cast a vote	eine Stimme abgeben
casting vote	Dirimierungsrecht
CEO (chief executive officer) (US)	Generaldirektor* (zumeist auch Vorsitzender des Board of Directors)
certificate of incorporation	Urkunde über die Eintragung einer Kapitalgesellschaft (US/UK)
certificate of vice president	Urkunde des Verwaltungsratsvorsitzenden-stellvertreters (mit der z.B. die Vertretungs-befugnis von für die Gesellschaft Auf-tretenden belegt wird (Hilfsdokument, notwendig zur Registrierung in A/D, da sonst die Vertretungsbefugnis von Organenvon US/UK Gesellschaften nicht nachgewiesen werden kann.)
certified excerpt from the commercial register*	beglaubigter Firmenbuchauszug*
certified public accountant (C.P.A.) (US)	eingetragener Wirtschafts-/Buchprüfer
CFO (chief financial officer) (US)	höchster Funktionär für Finanzangelegen-heiten, üblicherweise im Rang eines Senior Vice President
chair	den Vorsitz haben
chairman of the board of directors	Verwaltungsratsvorsitzender*
chairman of the supervisory board	Aufsichtsratsvorsitzender*
charitable or religious purpose	wohltätiger oder religiöser Zweck
chartered accountant (UK)	eingetragener Wirtschafts-/Buchprüfer
chief executive officer (CEO) (US)	Generaldirektor* (zumeist auch Vorsitzen-der des Board of Directors)
chief financial officer (CFO) (US)	höchster Funktionär für Finanzangelegen-heiten, üblicherweise im Rang eines Senior Vice President
chief operating officer (COO) (US)	zweithöchster Funktionär einer US-Kapital-gesellschaft nach dem Generaldirektor
civil law association*	Übersetzung für: Gesellschaft bürgerlichen Rechts (A/D)
class of shares	Aktiengattung
closely held corporation (US)	Kapitalgesellschaft, deren Anteile nicht öffentlich gehandelt werden
commencement of business year	Beginn des Geschäftsjahres
commercial enterprise	Wirtschaftsunternehmen, Handelsunter-nehmen
commercial register	Firmenbuch* (A), Handelsregister* (D) (Anm.: ein Pendant zum A/D Firmen-buch/Handelsregister existiert in UK/US nicht; vgl. lediglich companies register)
common stock (US)	Stammaktien
Companies Act (UK)	UK-Gesetz über die Kapitalgesellschaft
Companies Register (UK)	UK-Register für Kapitalgesellschaften
Companies Registration Office (UK)	UK-Register für Kapitalgesellschaften
company	Gesellschaft (i.w.S.) (UK & US) Kapitalgesellschaft (i.e.S.) (UK)
company limited by shares (Ltd.)	Kapitalgesellschaft (UK)

company seal	offizielles Firmensiegel (US/UK) (Anm.: zusammen mit Unterschrift ähnlich A/D vollständige Firma)
compensation for damages	Schadenersatz
compulsory liquidation	zwangsweise Liquidation
conditions of issue	Emissionsbedingungen
conduit entity	Bezeichnung einer Personen(handels)-gesellschaft im Hinblick darauf, daß diese selbst kein (Ertrags-)Steuersubjekt ist, sondern der Geschäftserfolg den Gesellschaftern zugerechnet wird und diese dann der Besteuerung unterliegen
contribution in cash	Bareinlage
contribution in kind	Sacheinlage
control of the B.O.D.	Kontrolle des Verwaltungsrats
convene a meeting	eine Sitzung/Versammlung/Konferenz einberufen
convertible bond	Wandelschuldverschreibung, Wandelanleihe
convertible debenture	Wandelschuldverschreibung
COO (chief operating officer) (US)	zweithöchster Funktionär einer US-Kapitalgesellschaft nach dem Generaldirektor
Corp. (corporation) (US)	Firmenzusatz für US-Kapitalgesellschaft
corpnership (US)	vergleichbar mit A/D GmbH & Co. KG
corporate body	Körperschaft
corporate charter	Satzung, Gesellschaftsvertrag
corporate legal form	Rechtsform einer Kapitalgesellschaft
corporation	Kapitalgesellschaft (US)
corporation not for profit	Kapitalgesellschaftsform ohne Gewinn-erzielungsabsicht
counterpart(s)	Ausfertigung(en)
coupon	Kupon
court action	Klage, Gerichtsverfahren
court-appointed liquidator	gerichtlich bestellter Liquidator
creation of a company/corporation	Errichtung einer Gesellschaft
deferred shares (UK/US)	Nachzugsaktien
deferred stock (US)	Nachzugsaktien
deny a motion	einen Antrag ablehnen
deputy chairman	Vorsitzender-Stellvertreter, stellvertretender Vorsitzender
derivative action (US)	aus der Treuepflicht des Verwaltungsrates gegenüber der Gesellschaft abgeleitetes indirektes Klagsrecht der Gesellschafter gegen den Verwaltungsrat im Namen der Gesellschaft*
derivative suit (US)	aus der Treuepflicht des Verwaltungsrates gegenüber der Gesellschaft abgeleitetes indirektes Klagsrecht der Gesellschafter gegen den Verwaltungsrat im Namen der Gesellschaft*

directives to management	Weisungen an die Geschäftsführung
discharge a petition for bankruptcy for want of assets to cover the costs of bankruptcy proceedings	einen Konkursantrag mangels Kostendeckung abweisen
discount	Disagio
dismiss a director/an executive	ein Verwaltungsratsmitglied/einen Funktionär* abberufen, entlassen
disposition of shares	Verfügung über Geschäftsanteile/Aktien
distribute assets upon liquidation	Liquidationserlös aufteilen
distribution of profit	Gewinnverteilung
dividend	Dividende
division of shares	Teilung von Geschäftsanteilen
election	Wahl
election agent	Wahlhelfer
encumbrance of shares	Belastung von Geschäftsanteilen
endorsement	Indossament, Unterstützung
entrepreneur	Unternehmer
equity capital	Eigenkapital
establishment of a company/corporation	Gesellschaftsgründung
executive	Funktionär*, leitender Angestellter* (vom Verwaltungsrat [B.O.D.] ernannt, insbes. president, vice president, secretary)
exercise one's voting right	sein Stimmrecht ausüben
expert	Sachverständiger
extraordinary general meeting (EGM) (UK)	außerordentliche General-/ Hauptversammlung
extraordinary shareholders meeting	außerordentliche General-/ Hauptversammlung
face value	Nominalwert
fiduciary duty	Treuepflicht*
file for bankruptcy	Konkursantrag stellen
filing fees	Registrierungsgebühren, Eintragungsgebühren
filing requirements	Registrierungsvorschriften
Financial Act (UK)	UK-Gesetz über Investitionen und Investitions-/Anlageschutz
financial statements	Jahresabschluß
formalities	Formelles, Formalitäten
formation of a company/corporation	Errichtung einer Gesellschaft
found a company/corporation	eine Gesellschaft gründen
foundation documents	Gründungsurkunden
foundation of a company/corporation	Errichtung einer Gesellschaft
founder(s)	Gründer
franchise tax	jährliche Registergebühr (US/UK)
Full Faith and Credit (US)	US-Verfassungsprinzip, gemäß welchem jeder Bundesstaat hoheitliche Entscheidungen aus einem Schwesternstaat anerkennen muß
fully-paid capital	zur Gänze einbezahltes Kapital

games of chance	Glücksspiele
general partner	Komplementär
general partnership	(UK/US) vergleichbar OHG in A/D*
general shareholders meeting	ordentliche General-/Hauptversammlung
going private	Rückführung einer an der Börse gehandelten Gesellschaft in eine Nicht-Publikumsgesellschaft
going public	an die Börse gehen
gross profit	Rohgewinn
hold a meeting	eine Sitzung/Versammlung/Konferenz abhalten
holding company	Holding(-gesellschaft)
hostile takeover	feindliche Übernahme
illiquidity	mangelnde Liquidität
Inc. (incorporated) (US)	(US) Firmenzusatz für Kapitalgesellschaft
incapacity	Verhinderung
income statement (US)	Gewinn- und Verlustrechnung
incorporate a company/corporation	eine Gesellschaft eintragen (lassen)
incorporation	Eintragung (einer Gesellschaft)
incorporator (US)	Gründer
incumbent	amtsinhabend, amtierend
individual power of representation	Einzelvertretungsbefugnis
individual proprietor	Einzelkaufmann/-unternehmer
initial contribution	Stammeinlage
insolvency	Insolvenz
Insolvency Act (UK)	UK-Gesetz über die Insolvenz
inspection	Buchprüfung, Einsichtnahme in die Bücher
interim certificate	Zwischenschein
internal rules	Geschäftsordnung*
investment business	Investitionen, Anlagegeschäft
investment protection	Anlageschutz
issuance	Emission
issue	Emission
issue shares	Aktien begeben
issued capital	ausgegebenes Kapital
item on the agenda	Tagesordnungspunkt
joint activity	gemeinsame Vorgangsweise, gemeinsames Vorgehen
joint power of representation	Kollektivvertretungsbefugnis
judicial dissolution	gerichtliche Auflösung
legalization	Beglaubigung
liability of B.O.D. to the shareholders	Haftung des Verwaltungsrates gegenüber den Aktionären
limited liability company (US)	in den USA gebräuchlicher Begriff für eine Personengesellschaft, die gesellschaftsrechtlich eine Hybridform darstellt.

182

	Während steuerrechtlich die für Personengesellschaften anwendbaren Regeln gelten, genießen die Gesellschafter den Schutz der Haftungsbegrenzung einer Kapitalgesellschaft. weiters: irreführende Übersetzung für Gesellschaft mit beschränkter Haftung (A/D)
limited partner	Kommanditist
limited partnership	(UK/US) vergleichbar KG in A/D*
Limited Partnership Act 1907 (UK)	UK-Gesetz über die Personen(handels)-gesellschaft
liquidate a company	eine Gesellschaft liquidieren
liquidation	Liquidation
liquidity	Liquidität
listing	Notierung
LLC (Limited Liability Company) (US)	in den USA gebräuchlicher Begriff für eine Personengesellschaft, die gesellschaftsrechtlich eine Hybridform darstellt. Während steuerrechtlich die für Personengesellschaften anwendbaren Regeln gelten, genießen die Gesellschafter den Schutz der Haftungsbegrenzung einer Kapitalgesellschaft.
loan capital	Fremdkapital
loss	Verlust
Ltd.	Firmenzusatz für eine nicht notierte Kapitalgesellschaft (UK)
majority	Mehrheit
management buyout	Erwerb von mehr als 50% einer Gesellschaft durch die Geschäftsführung/ leitenden Angestellten
managing board	Geschäftsführung
*managing director**	Geschäftsführer* (A/D)
means of communication	Art der Verständigung
meeting	Sitzung, Versammlung, Konferenz
member of the B.O.D./S.B.	Mitglied des Verwaltungsrates/ Aufsichtsrates*
memorandum of association (UK)	Grundsatzdokument einer UK Kapitalgesellschaft – Außenverhältnis
merger	Fusion, Verschmelzung
minutes	Protokoll
minutes of a board meeting	Protokoll einer Verwaltungsratssitzung
minutes of a shareholders meeting	Protokoll einer General-/ Hauptversammlung
miscellaneous	Allfälliges
money capital	Geldeinlage, Bareinlage
motion	Antrag
move for	beantragen
name of the company/corporation	Firma (der Gesellschaft)
net profit	Reingewinn

new shares	junge Aktien
nominal capital	Stammkapital, Grundkapital
nominal value	Nennwert, Nominalwert
non-commercial enterprise	nicht auf Gewinn orientiertes Unternehmen
non-trading partnership	Sozietät (freie Berufe) (UK)
non-voting shares	stimmrechtslose Aktien
notarial deed*	Übersetzung für: Notariatsakt (A/D)
notarization	notarielle Beglaubigung
notification	Verständigung
NYSE (New York Stock Exchange)	New Yorker Börse
objects (of the company)	Betriebsgegenstand
objects clause	Betriebsgegenstandsklausel
officer	Funktionär*, leitender Angestellter
one-person firm	Einmannfirma
one-stage formation	Einheitsgründung
operating officer	geschäftsführender Funktionär*
ordinary partnership (UK)	vgl. GesBR, OHG nach A/D-Recht
ordinary resolution	einfacher Beschluß
ordinary shareholders meeting	ordentliche General-/Hauptversammlung
ordinary shares	Stammaktien
outside board member	unternehmensfremdes Verwaltungsratsmitglied*
outstanding shares	ausgegebene Aktien
over-subscription	Überzeichnung
overleverage	Überschuldung
overseas company (UK)	ausländische Gesellschaft
par value	Nennwert
parent company	Mutter(-gesellschaft)
partly-paid capital	teilweise einbezahltes Stammkapital
partner	Gesellschafter einer Personengesellschaft
partnership	Personen(handels)gesellschaft
Partnership Act 1890 (UK)	UK-Gesetz über die Personen(handels)gesellschaft
partnership agreement	Gesellschaftsvertrag für Personengesellschaft
pass a resolution	einen Beschluß fassen
pass a resolution to liquidate	einen Beschluß über die Liquidation fassen
perpetual	zeitlich unbeschränkt, auf Dauer
petition for bankruptcy	freiwilliger Konkursantrag
place of incorporation (UK/US) („incorporated in Delaware", i.e. organized under the laws of Delaware)	Registrierungsort (Anm.: aufgrund des Inkorporationsstatutes entscheidend für das anzuwendende Recht)
placement of an issue	Aktienausgabe, Aktienplazierung
Plc. (public limited company) (UK)	UK-Firmenzusatz für Publikums-Aktiengesellschaft*
plurality of creditors	Gläubigermehrheit
poll	geheime Wahl
power of representation	Vertretungsbefugnis
power to bind the company	Vertretungsbefugnis

power to sign on behalf of the company	Zeichnungsberechtigung
preference shares (UK/US)	Vorzugsaktien
preferred stock (US)	Vorzugsaktien
premium	Agio
preside over	vorsitzen
president	Präsident, Generaldirektor
principal place of business	Sitz*
private company limited by shares (Ltd.) (UK)	vergleichbar mit Gesellschaft mit beschränkter Haftung in A/D*
private limited company (Ltd.) (UK)	vergleichbar mit Gesellschaft mit beschränkter Haftung in A/D*
process agent	Zustellbevollmächtigter
professional association (US)	Sozietät (freie Berufe)
professional partnership (US)	Sozietät, EEG (A) (freie Berufe)
profit after tax	Gewinn nach Steuern
profit and loss account (UK)	Gewinn- und Verlustrechnung
profit and loss statement	Gewinn- und Verlustrechnung
profit before tax	Gewinn vor Steuern
profit(s)	Gewinn
proposal	Vorschlag
prospectus	offizielles Börseneinführungspapier, Prospekt
proxy	Stimmrechtsvollmacht, Stimmrechtsbevollmächtigter
public limited company (plc.) (UK)	vergleichbar mit einer Publikums-Aktiengesellschaft in A/D*
public utilities	öffentliche Versorgungsunternehmen
publicly quoted	an der Börse notiert
publicly-held corporation (US)	vergleichbar mit einer Publikums-Aktiengesellschaft in A/D*
put on the agenda	auf die Tagesordnung setzen, in die Tagesordnung aufnehmen
qualified majority*	qualifizierte Mehrheit
quorum	beschlußfähige Mehrheit
quotation	Notierung
rate	Kurs
rating	Kurs
real capital	Sacheinlage
receivership*	Zwangsverwaltung, Masseverwaltung
reconstruction	Umwandlung, Umstrukturierung
redeemable shares	Aktien zur Einziehung
redemption of shares	Einziehung von Aktien
register a company/corporation	eine Gesellschaft eintragen (lassen)
register of companies	Firmenregister (UK)
registered capital	eingetragenes Kapital
registered office	Firmensitz*, Sitz*, Geschäftsadresse*
registered partnership*	Übersetzung für: Eingetragene Erwerbsgesellschaft (EEG) (A)
registered shares	Namensaktien

registrar	Registerführer
registration (of a company/corporation)	Eintragung (einer Gesellschaft)
reject a proposal	einen Vorschlag ablehnen
remedies for breach of fiduciary duty	Rechtsbehelfe bei Verletzung der Treuepflicht
removal from office	Abberufung, Amtsenthebung
reorganization pursuant to chapter 11 of the Bankruptcy Act (US)	Zwangsumstrukturierung* nach US-Konkursrecht
representation	Vertretung
resolution	Beschluß
resolution on distribution of profits	Beschluß über die Gewinnverteilung
resolution to appoint an officer	Beschluß über die Bestellung eines Funktionärs
resolution to discharge/remove an officer	Beschluß über die Abberufung eines Funktionärs
resolution to grant official approval for actions	Beschluß über die Entlastung
resolution to wind up the company	Beschluß über die Auflösung der Gesellschaft
resolve	beschließen
resolve in writing	schriftlich beschließen
responsibility of B.O.D.	Verantwortung des Verwaltungsrats*
retire by rotation	Funktionsbeendigung nach dem Rotationsprinzip
Revised Model Business Corporation Act (US)	einheitliches US-Gesetz über die Kapitalgesellschaften
right to vote	Stimmrecht
S-Corporation (US)	eine bestimmte Art der Kapitalgesellschaft, die nach US-Bundeseinkommen-/-körperschaft-steuerrecht als Personengesellschaft behandelt wird
second a motion	einen Antrag unterstützen* (Anm.: im anglo-amerikanischen Sitzungswesen muß jeder Antrag zumindest von einer zusätzlichen Stimme unterstützt werden)
secretary	„Gesellschaftssekretär"*, Funktionär/ Angestellter einer Kapitalgesellschaft, der u.a. die Zeichungs- und Vertretungsbefugnis der für die Gesellschaft Auftretenden bestätigt
Securities and Exchange Act (US)	US-Börsenaufsichtsgesetz
Securities and Exchange Commission (SEC) (US)	US-Börsenaufsichtsbehörde
set-up a company/corporation	eine Gesellschaft gründen
setting-up of a company/corporation	Gesellschaftsgründung
share capital	Stammkapital, Grundkapital, Aktienkapital
share certificate	Aktienurkunde
share ledger	Aktienbuch
share purchase agreement	Aktienkaufvertrag
shareholders	Gesellschafter, Aktionäre
shareholders meeting	Generalversammlung, Hauptversammlung
shares	Aktien (UK und US)
signatures	Unterschriften

silent partner	stiller Gesellschafter
silent partnership*	Übersetzung für: Stille Gesellschaft (A)
simple majority*	einfache Mehrheit
sole proprietor (US)	Einzelkaufmann/-unternehmer
sole proprietorship (US)	Einzelunternehmen
sole trader (UK)	Einzelkaufmann/-unternehmer
special resolution	qualifizierter Beschluß
special shareholders meeting	außerordentliche General-/ Hauptversammlung
staff representative	Personalvertreter
stated capital	ausgewiesenes Grundkapital
statutory company (UK)	UK-Kapitalgesellschaft, die per Gesetz geschaffen wird; wird für öffentliche Verwaltungsaufgaben genutzt
stock (US)	Aktien
stock company*	Übersetzung für: Aktiengesellschaft (A/D)
stock corporation	Kapitalgesellschaft (US)
stock exchange	(Aktien-)Börse
subscribe to capital	einen Anteil am Kapital übernehmen/ zeichnen
subscribe to shares	Aktien zeichnen, einen Anteil am Kapital übernehmen
subscriber	Zeichnender, Übernehmer
subscription	Übernahme, Zeichnung
subsidiary (company)	Tochtergesellschaft
successive formation	Stufengründung
supervisory board (S.B.)	Aufsichtsrat*
tacit agreement	stillschweigendes Übereinkommen
termination of business year	Ende des Geschäftsjahres
trading company incorporated by royal charter (UK)	UK-Handelsgesellschaft per königlicher Ermächtigung
trading partnership	Handelsgesellschaft
transfer of shares	Übertragung von Geschäftsanteilen/Aktien
treasurer	für Finanz- und Rechnungsfragen zuständiger Funktionär
trustee (in bankruptcy)	Treuhänder*, Masserverwalter*
uncalled capital	nicht eingefordertes Kapital
Uniform Business Corporation Act (US)	einheitliches US-Gesetz über die Kapitalgesellschaft
Uniform Partnership Act (UPA) (US)	einheitliches US-Gesetz über die Personen(handels)gesellschaft
unincorporated	nicht eingetragen
unissued capital	nicht ausgegebenes Kapital
unlimited company (UK)	UK-Kapitalgesellschaft mit unbeschränkter Haftung
vice president	Vizepräsident*, Generaldirektorstell- vertreter*
voluntary dissolution	freiwillige Auflösung
voluntary liquidation	freiwillige Liquidation

vote by proxy	Stimmabgabe durch Bevollmächtigten
vote by show of hands	Wahl durch Handzeichen
voting right	Stimmrecht
voting shares	stimmberechtigte Aktien
wholly-paid capital	zur Gänze einbezahltes Kapital
wind up a company	eine Gesellschaft abwickeln
winding-up	Abwicklung
works council	Betriebsrat
year-end financial statement	Jahresabschluß

IV. INSURANCE

In the case of all types of insurance a person (the insured) contracts with the insurer (an insurance company) for a policy of insurance that indemnifies her/him upon the occurrence of an event or against a specific risk, e.g. loss of property, life or health, or in the event of an accident. Except in the case of life insurance, the risk covered is an event with some element of uncertainty, an event which may or may not occur.

Versicherungsnehmer
Versicherer,
V.-gesellschaft
V.-polizze
Verlust, Unfall
Lebensversicherung

Insurance coverage is granted against conclusion of an insurance contract and payment of the insurance premium, which may consist of recurring payments or of a lump-sum payment.

Deckung, V.-vertrag
V.-prämie

An insurance contract is characterized by the concept of risk-distribution: many people bearing the same or similar risks pay a pre-determined amount (premium) into a certain fund that is administered by an insurer or an underwriter. Out of this fund the insured receives compensation for an economic loss according to the insurance policy. Each member of the group contributes a small part toward the compensation which is given to the person who suffered the loss. Through the principle of risk-distribution the economic risk of loss is shared.

Risikostreuung

The premium is measured according to the probability or likelihood of losses for a period and also includes administrative costs. The more insurance policies are issued the easier it is for the insurer to predict the amount of losses and to keep the premiums low. The assessment of a premium involves mathematics and statistics.

Wahrscheinlichkeit

Bemessung der
Prämie

Insurers are organized as stock insurance companies (GB: joint-stock insurance companies, proprietary offices) which operate for the benefit of their shareholders, as mutual insurance companies (GB: mutual insurance associations, mutual offices) which are non-profit organizations set up for the mutual interest of their members, or as individual underwriters such as Lloyds, the most famous of all insurers, which is an organized market for insurance.

V.-Akiengesellschaften

V.-Vereine auf
Gegenseitigkeit

nicht gewinnorientiert

Apart from these private or quasi-private insurers, states often act as insurers as well. In particular, in continental Europe national insurance networks in the field of social security are common practice. Social security may provide for health insurance, old-age pensions, unemployment insurance and the like. Apart from these types of insurance, which lie in the public interest, the state may also cover certain risks relating to exports by means of an export credit insurance. Finally, it must be noted that insurers themselves need to be protected, which is achieved by reinsurance.

Sozialversicherung,
Krankenv., Rentenv.,
Arbeitslosenv.

Exportkreditv.
Rückversicherung

A person seeking insurance, also called a proposer, contacts an insurance salesperson, agent or broker, and negotiates the individual package. Insurable interests may be manifold and the insurance contract concluded will either be standardized or made to

V.-werber
V.-vertreter,
V.-makler
versicherbares
Interesse

vorläufige Deckungs-
zusage bis zur Aus-
stellung der Polizze

*measure. Upon acceptance of the proposal by the insurer a binder
(GB: cover note) may be issued pending the issue of the actual insurance policy.*

V.-arten

1. TYPES OF INSURANCE

Lebensv., private
Krankenv., Unfallv.,
Haftpflichtv., KFZ-V.,
Feuerv., Transportv.,
Hausratsv., Diebstahlv.,
Reisev., Reisegepäckv.,
Produkthaftpflichtv.,
Glasbruchv., Betriebs-
anlagenv., Betriebsunter-
brechungsv., Hagelv.

*There are many types of insurance: life insurance (GB: life assu-
rance), private health insurance, personal accident insurance,
personal liability insurance, automobile insurance (GB: motor in-
surance), fire insurance, marine and inland marine insurance, domestic (household) insurance, burglary insurance, travel insu-
rance, luggage insurance, product liability insurance, and all
sorts of commercial insurance, e.g. glass insurance, engineering
insurance, business interruption insurance, hail insurance, etc.*

*In the following, life, fire, casualty and marine insurance are dealt
with in detail.*

Lebensv.

1.1. LIFE INSURANCE (GB: LIFE ASSURANCE)

*A life insurance obliges the insurer to make a payment of a sum
upon the death of a person whose life is insured. It is possible that
many different people are involved in a policy of a life insurance:*

Polizzeninhaber

Begünstigter

*(i) the person who concludes the insurance policy and pays the
premiums (the owner of the policy); (ii) the person whose life is
insured; (iii) the person who receives the payments (the beneficiary). But it is also possible that only one person is involved in
case her/his estate becomes beneficiary of the life insurance.*

There are several types of life insurance:

Versicherung auf den
Todes- u. Erlebensfall

(a) ***Endowment Life Insurance***
   *The insurer must pay a fixed sum either at the end of a spe-
   cific period, which the insured has survived, or in the event of
   death if the insured should die within the same period. If the
   insured survives the period s/he receives a lump sum or annuities.*

Todesfallv.

(b) ***Whole Life Insurance*** *provides for payment of proceeds upon
   the death of the insured. The premiums can be paid in various
   ways: either all premiums are paid at once in a lump sum, or
   they are paid throughout the life of the insured or only for a
   specified number of years. The insured may cancel the life insurance after it has been in force for at least two or three*

Rückkaufwert

   *years. Then s/he is paid the "cash surrender value" of the
   policy. This not only gives her/him the possibility of insurance, but also of investment.*

(c) ***Term Life Insurance*** *provides coverage of the insured only
   for a term specified in the insurance policy (one month, one
   year, five years). Proceeds are paid only if s/he dies within the
   agreed term. If the insured survives the specified term the insurer keeps all the premiums paid. Contrary to whole life in-*

surance, in term life insurance there is no possibility of receiving a "cash surrender value" from the insurer. This type of life insurance only offers protection and no aspect of investment, which allows the insurer to ask for lower premiums than those for a whole life insurance.

1.2. FIRE INSURANCE

Feuerv.

Fire insurance covers any damage or loss caused by fire, except in the case when the insured commits arson.

Brandstiftung begehen

Without referring to the specific insurance policy, US courts distinguish between losses caused by a "hostile" fire and a "friendly" fire. Generally, a fire insurance only covers losses caused by a "hostile" fire. A "friendly" fire is considered to be a fire set at a place which is intended for a fire: stove or fireplace. A fire which occurs outside such a place is a "hostile" fire.

A fire insurance policy also includes coverage for losses through water, wind, rain, earthquake, explosion and lightning.

1.3. CASUALTY INSURANCE

V. gegen Schäden

Casualty insurance covers burglary and theft, property damage, accident and health, collision and legal liability. Fire and casualty insurance together cover most damage to and losses of realty and personal property.

1.4. MARINE INSURANCE

Seev.

Marine Insurance is an all-risk insurance providing coverage for the ship (hull insurance) and cargo against perils of the seas, pirates, fire, seizures and war perils. Insurance may be concluded for a single voyage or for a specific time. Marine insurance does not include losses and damage to transportation on inland waterways, but it may be extended thereto.

2. PREMIUMS

Prämien

In order to receive coverage from an insurance policy for damage or losses suffered it is necessary to pay premiums. These premiums are fixed at the beginning of a period by trying to calculate the overall amount of losses during the same. They also include the administration costs and a profit for the insurance.

*The **net premium** is the amount of money the insured must pay so that the insurance can cover all the losses during a period. The methods of calculation differ depending on the type of insurance, e.g. for life insurance data is collected to find out the average age at which men or women of a certain class die. For automobile or fire insurance the "manual rating method" is used to predict losses during the period of insurance. They set up tables based on* *experience in order to predict the dollar amount of losses that will occur per $ 100 of building value. This way the insurer fixes the rate of insurance.*

*In addition to the net premium the insurance adds administering costs, e.g. agent's commissions, executive salaries and office expenses arriving at the **total (gross) premium**. These costs are loaded onto the net premium. They also include a contingency surplus in case the insurance must cover more losses than predicted.*

Sicherheitsaufschlag

3. DOCTRINE OF INSURABLE INTEREST

The doctrine of insurable interest provides that an insured person should not make any net profit from the event insured against, but should only receive coverage for the actual loss. This already being stated in the Act of Parliament in 1746, the doctrine of insurable interest is especially applied to marine insurance because before the above mentioned Act came into force many ships and cargoes insured were fraudulently lost or destroyed due to the fact that insurance companies did not require any further proof of interest than the policy.

in Betrugsabsicht

Section 281 of the California Insurance Code, for instance, defines insurable interest as "Every interest in property, or any relation thereto, or liability in respect thereof, of such a nature that a contemplated peril might directly damnify the insured."

Today, without an insurable interest an insurance contract cannot be enforced. Some statutes require an insurable interest at the time of the loss, others at the time of inception of the policy and at the time of loss.

Beginn

4. PROCEDURE FOR CLAIMING COVERAGE

Insurance policies generally require the insured to comply with certain conditions when it comes to a loss against which s/he is insured. Otherwise it is possible that the insurer refuses any payment.

unverzügliche Bekanntgabe

*First of all, the insured must give notice immediately after the occurrence of any loss (**notice of loss**). Immediacy of notice is necessary because it is easier to examine the scene where the loss occurred while the evidence is fresh and has not been touched or removed. Considering all the circumstances, courts often see this requirement fulfilled when the insured gives notice within a reasonable time. The courts already have excused a delay of fifty days.*

innerhalb eines angemessenen Zeitraumes

*Besides the notice of loss the insured must also file a **proof of loss** giving detailed information about the loss. According to the policy, the insurer may request more information if the submitted proof of loss is not sufficient. Then the insured, within her/his ability, has the possibility of providing more information, otherwise the insurer may defend any payment.*

192

Insurance policies and sometimes even statutes stipulate that any action must be filed within a specified period after the date of the loss. It may happen that courts allow an action to be filed after the specific period has passed because e.g. the insurance company had delayed the payment of proceeds or the insured was not able to file the action (e.g. incapacity).

5. REINSURANCE

An insurer may want to reduce or even eliminate some or all of the liability which it has underwritten in an insurance contract. The insurer will want to do so if the risks under the existing policies are a threat to the solvency of the insurer. This is why the insurer itself will take out a liability insurance (reinsurance) with another insurance company (reinsurer), thus the insurer becoming an insured. This is a different form of insurance than the one where the original insured concludes several policies against the same risk with different insurers. Actually, any insurance company issuing normal insurance policies may also act as a reinsurer, although usually there are insurance companies which specialize in the business of reinsurance.

Depending on the reinsurance contract, the reinsurer will indemnify the insurer either for the whole value of the loss incurred or only for a specified part or percentage of any liability. Some statutes, however, provide that the insurer may not reinsure the full amount of any liability, but must always bear some part of the risk.

The contract of reinsurance may provide for rights of the original insured against the reinsurer. If this is the case the original insured has the choice of bringing an action against the insurer, the reinsurer or both, according to the terms of the contract of reinsurance. Should the reinsurance contract not provide for any rights of the originally insured against the reinsurer then s/he may only claim proceeds from the insurer.

Rückv.

Haftung reduzieren

Zahlungsunfähigkeit des Versicherers

Rückversicherer

Co-operative Insurance

Domestic Combined Policy

Contents Insurance

We (the Co-operative Insurance Society Limited) agree with you (the Policyholder named in the Schedule) that, subject to the General Exclusions and Conditions of this Policy, we will provide the insurance set out in the Policy Sections and Endorsements specified as operative in the Schedule in respect of events occurring during the Period of Insurance shown in the Schedule and any further period for which we may accept a renewal premium.

We will provide indemnity in respect of such events, subject to the Claims Settlement Provisions in the case of loss of or damage to property.

Claims under this Policy will be met from our Share Capital, General Business Fund and General Reserve only.

Signed on our behalf.

Ala   D. Sneddon

Chief General Manager

Important: If the words REPLACEMENT POLICY appear after the Period of Insurance stated in the Schedule, this Policy is not valid unless it is accompanied by a Confirmation of Renewal document issued by us for the same Period of Insurance. You should keep the Confirmation of Renewal document with this Policy as evidence of validity.

Schedule

	Policy Number
Policyholder	
	Agency Number

Period of Insurance	from	to	
Sections Operative		Risk Address and other Policy Details	

Endorsements Operative	Date Policy Issued	Cancelled Policy No.	Net First Premium or Return (RTN)

Definition of Terms

Each of the following words and expressions is given a specific meaning which applies wherever it appears in **bold type** in this Policy.

Contents: means household goods, personal effects, **Money** and fixtures and fittings (not the landlord's) owned by or the legal responsibility of the **Family** or any domestic servant residing with the **Family**, but not

(a) **Money** in excess of £150

(b) property more specifically insured

(c) securities, certificates and documents other than **Money**, animals, boats, aircraft, mechanically propelled vehicles (other than domestic gardening equipment), caravans, trailers, and their accessories while attached to them

(d) any part of the **Home**, including ceilings, wallpaper, tiles and the like.

No curio, stamp or coin or medal collection, picture or other work of art will be treated as being of greater value than 5% of the **Sum Insured on Contents** and, where loss or damage is caused by malicious persons or thieves, this limitation will apply also to any watch or article of precious metal, jewellery or fur.

The total value of watches and articles of precious metal, jewellery or fur together will be treated as not exceeding one-third of the **Sum Insured on Contents**.

Films, photographs, tapes, cassettes, records, discs and the like are insured up to their value as unused material or, where purchased pre-recorded, for an amount not exceeding the maker's latest list price.

Credit Card: means any credit card, charge card, debit card, cheque guarantee card or cash dispenser card issued in the United Kingdom, the Isle of Man or the Channel Islands to the **Family**.

Excess: means the amount of the claim which is to be borne by you. We will deduct that amount from the amount payable in respect of the claim after the application of any relevant monetary limits specified in this Policy.

Excluded Events: means

(a) mechanical or electrical failure

(b) loss or damage caused by

  (i) wear and tear, atmospheric, climatic or weather conditions, the action of light, or any gradually operating cause

  (ii) vermin, insects or fungus

  (iii) any process of installing, erecting, dismantling, repairing, altering or adjusting

  (iv) delay, confiscation or detention by Customs or other officials.

Family: means you or any member of your family permanently residing with you.

Freezer: means any domestic deep freezer or fridge/freezer in the **Home**.

Home: means the private dwelling and its domestic garages, greenhouses and outbuildings, all at the Risk Address specified in the Schedule.

Insured Peril: means

1) Fire, smoke, explosion, lightning or earthquake, excluding smoke damage due to any gradually operating cause.

2) Riot, civil commotion, labour and political disturbances.

3) Malicious persons, excluding loss or damage caused by any person lawfully on the premises at the Risk Address specified in the Schedule.

4) Storm or flood.

5) Escape of water from any fixed domestic water or heating system (excluding damage to the system itself resulting from such escape of water) or any washing or dishwashing machine or fish tank.

6) Leakage of oil from any fixed domestic heating system.

7) Falling trees or branches.

8) Theft or attempted theft, excluding theft by you or your spouse.

9) Impact with the **Home** by aircraft or aerial devices, trains, road vehicles or animals.

10) Breakage of aerials, their fixtures or masts.

11) Subsidence or heave of the site, or landslip.

Money: means current coin and banknotes, postal orders, current postage stamps, National Savings stamps and certificates, premium bonds, travellers' cheques, luncheon vouchers, gift vouchers, trading stamps and travel tickets.

Sports: means angling, archery, badminton, billiards, bowls, cricket, golf, hockey, lacrosse, pool, snooker, squash, table tennis and tennis.

Sum Insured on Contents: means the sum specified as such in the Schedule or in the latest subsequent Confirmation of Renewal document or Endorsement Schedule. This sum will be deemed to be adjusted monthly in accordance with the percentage change in the Consumer Durables Section of the General Index of Retail Prices.

Unfurnished: means insufficiently furnished for full habitation.

Claims Settlement Provisions

A. Claims for loss of or damage to property (other than property which is the subject of a claim under subsection G of the Contents Section) will be settled on the following basis by payment or, at our option, by repair or replacement, subject to any relevant monetary limit specified in this Policy: —

1. If the **Contents** are insured under

   (i) Standard Cover, the cost of repair or of replacement as new if an article is totally lost or destroyed, less an allowance for any depreciation and wear and tear

   (ii) Standard Plus Cover, the cost of repair or of replacement as new if an article is totally lost or destroyed. An allowance for any depreciation and wear and tear will be made only in respect of
   (a) clothing and household linen
   (b) property insured under the Contents Section if at the time of the loss or damage the **Sum Insured on Contents** is less than the cost of replacing all the **Contents** of the **Home** as new without deduction for depreciation and wear and tear, except for clothing and household linen.

2. Except in the circumstances described in 3 an **Excess** of £25 will apply to each claim unless the claim is made under the Contents Section and the **Home** is situated in a London Postal District or in the local government district of Glasgow, Manchester, Liverpool, Knowsley, Sefton (except postcodes PR8 and PR9) or Wirral (except postcodes L47, L48, L60 and L61), when an **Excess** of £50 will apply.

   If a claim is made under more than one subsection of the Contents Section for loss or damage caused at the same time by the same event, only one **Excess** will apply.

3. No **Excess** will apply to a claim for loss or damage caused in the **Home** by **Insured Peril** 8 if the intruder gained entry

   (i) by violent and forcible means through a door or window protected by a properly set intruder alarm system in full working order, or

   (ii) by violent and forcible means through
   (a) a door, other than a patio door, locked by a mortice deadlock meeting at least British Standard 3621, or by a rim automatic deadlock, or
   (b) a patio door locked by a key-operated lock designed to prevent the door from being lifted off its track, or
   (c) a window locked by a key-operated lock or bolt
   provided that the key had been withdrawn from the lock or bolt if the **Home** was without an occupant at the time, or

   (iii) by violence or threat of violence against the **Family**, or by deception, or

   (iv) by violent and forcible means otherwise than through a door or a window designed to be opened.

B. For the purpose of any claim settlement, repair or replacement as near as is reasonably practicable will be sufficient even though the former appearance or condition of the property may not be precisely restored.

C. We will not be liable for the replacement of or work on

   (a) any undamaged items or remaining parts solely because they form part of a set, suite, group or collection of articles of a similar nature, colour, pattern or design

   (b) an undamaged carpet or floor covering not in the room or area in which the damage occurred, solely because the undamaged carpet or floor covering matches the damaged carpet or floor covering in colour, pattern or design.

D. We will not be liable to make a payment under more than one Section of this Policy in respect of loss of or damage to the same property caused by the same event.

Contents Section

What IS Insured	What is NOT Insured
A. Contents in the Home Loss of or damage to the **Contents** in the **Home** caused by an **Insured Peril**. We will not pay more than the **Sum insured on Contents** in respect of any one event, less the **Excess**, if applicable, specified in the Claims Settlement Provisions.	**A.** (a) Loss or damage excluded from **Insured Peril** 1, 3, 5 or 8. (b) Loss or damage caused by **Insured Peril** 8 while the **Home** or any part of it is lent, let or sub-let or is used for the accommodation of paying guests or if it is a flat which is not self-contained, unless such loss or damage involves entry to or exit from the **Home** by violent and forcible means.

B. Contents outside the Home
1) Loss of or damage to the **Contents** caused by an **Insured Peril** and occurring while the **Contents** are temporarily
 	
  (i) stored in a furniture depository or other building pending removal to your new permanent residence
 	
  (ii) removed from the **Home** into any bank, safe deposit, occupied private dwelling or any building where the **Family** is residing, employed or carrying on business
 	
  (iii) removed from the **Home** to anywhere else.
 	
2) Loss of or damage to the **Contents** in transit between any two of the following places: —
the **Home**; any furniture depository or other building in which the **Contents** are stored pending removal to your new permanent residence; your new permanent residence.
 	
We will not pay more than the **Sum Insured on Contents** in respect of any one event, less the **Excess** specified in the Claims Settlement Provisions.
	B.
	1) Loss or damage excluded from **Insured Peril** 1, 3, 5 or 8.
	
	  (i) Loss or damage caused by **Insured Peril** 8 unless involving entry to or exit from the building by violent and forcible means.
	
	  (ii) Loss of or damage to **Money** if caused by **Insured Peril** 8 unless involving entry to or exit from the building by violent and forcible means.
	
	  (iii) (a) Loss or damage caused by **Insured Peril** 8 unless involving entry to or exit from a building by violent and forcible means.
	    (b) Loss of or damage to property not in a building or caravan if caused by **Insured Peril** 4.
	
	2) (a) Loss of or damage to **Money**, watches, articles of precious metal, jewellery, furs or stamp, coin or medal collections.
	  (b) Cracking, scratching or breakage of china, glass, earthenware or other articles of a brittle nature unless packed for removal by expert packers.

C. Loss of Rent If the **Home** is made uninhabitable by an **Insured Peril** 1) rent which continues to be payable by you 2) the reasonable additional cost of comparable alternative accommodation incurred by you in respect of the period necessary for reinstatement. We will not pay more than 15% of the **Sum Insured on Contents** in respect of any one event.	**C.**
D. Audio and Video Equipment Accidental damage to television sets, radios, video cassette recorders or any other recording, video or audio equipment, home computer or video game equipment owned by or the legal responsibility of the **Family** if the damage occurs in the **Home** or in any other occupied private dwelling to which the equipment is temporarily removed.	**D.** (a) **Excluded Events**. (b) Damage to records, discs, cassettes, tapes or styli. (c) Damage to any item (other than a portable television set or a remote control unit) designed to be portable.
E. Mirrors and Fixed Glass in Furniture Accidental breakage in the **Home** of mirrors, plate glass tops to and fixed glass in furniture and fish tanks, and ceramic in hobs.	**E.** Breakage of lighting fixtures and fittings.

Contents Section

What IS Insured	What is NOT Insured

F. Tenant's Indemnity

If you are a tenant of the **Home** and not the owner or leaseholder

1) (i) damage to the **Home** caused by **Insured Peril** 4, 5, 6, 8 or 10
(ii) accidental damage to underground pipes, drains and cables (including their inspection covers) serving the **Home**
if you are liable for such damage under the tenancy agreement

2) (i) accidental breakage of glass and sanitary fittings fixed to and forming part of the **Home**
(ii) damage in the **Home** to interior decorations and landlord's fixtures and fittings that are not otherwise insured, if caused by an **Insured Peril** whether or not you are liable for such breakage or damage under the tenancy agreement.

We will not pay more than 15% of the **Sum Insured on Contents** in respect of any one event, less the **Excess**, if applicable, specified in the Claims Settlement Provisions.

F.

1) Damage occurring during any period in excess of 30 consecutive days in which the **Home** is **Unfurnished**.

2) Breakage or damage occurring during any period in excess of 30 consecutive days in which the **Home** is **Unfurnished**.

G. Family and Occupier's Liability

All sums which the **Family** becomes legally liable to pay in respect of accidents resulting in bodily injury to or disease contracted by any person or loss of or damage to property.

We will not pay more than £1,000,000 (in addition to costs and expenses incurred with our consent) in respect of all accidents arising from any one event except in respect of bodily injury to or disease contracted by a person in the employment of the **Family** where such injury or disease arises out of and in the course of such employment.

G.

(a) Bodily injury to or disease contracted by the **Family**.
(b) Loss of or damage to property owned by or in the care of the **Family**.
(c) Bodily injury, disease, loss or damage caused by or arising from
(i) the ownership or occupation of any land or building other than the occupation of the premises at the Risk Address specified in the Schedule
(ii) the profession, trade, occupation, business or employment of the **Family**
(iii) animals (other than domestic animals), the use of lifts (other than chair lifts in the **Home**), caravans, boats, aircraft, model aircraft, mechanically propelled vehicles (other than domestic gardening equipment) and horses for hunting, racing or steeple-chasing, unless the bodily injury, disease, loss or damage is sustained by a person in the employment of the **Family** and arises out of and in the course of such employment.
(d) Liability which arises only because of an agreement.

H. Fatal Injury in the Home

If you or your spouse suffer accidental bodily injury in the **Home** caused by **Insured Peril** 1, 8 or 9 wo will pay £6,000 if within 12 months that injury alone causes death.

H.

Each of the following Sections is operative only if specified as operative in the Schedule

Freezer Section

What IS Insured	What is NOT Insured
1) Accidental damage to the **Freezer**.	1) The cost of repairing or replacing the **Freezer** or any part of it as the result of **Excluded Events**.
2) Loss of or damage to food in the **Freezer** caused by failure of the **Freezer** or the power supply, and the reasonable cost of temporarily hiring alternative freezer space in order to avoid or diminish such loss or damage.	2) Loss or damage occasioned by the deliberate act of the electricity supply authority or its employees.
We will not pay more than £1,000 in respect of any one event, less the **Excess** specified in the Claims Settlement Provisions.	

Personal Money Section

What IS Insured	What is NOT Insured
1) Loss of **Money** belonging to the **Family** and not kept or used for business purposes.	(a) **Excluded Events**, depreciation in value or shortages due to errors or omissions in receipts, payments or accountancy.
2) All sums which the **Family** becomes liable to pay to the issuing organisation as a result of the fraudulent use by any unauthorised person (not being the **Family**) of any **Credit Card**.	(b) Any loss not reported to the police within 24 hours of its discovery by the **Family**.
We will not pay more than £500 in respect of any one event, less the **Excess**, if applicable, specified in the Claims Settlement Provisions.	(c) Payment of any amount under 2) unless the holder of the **Credit Card** has complied with all the terms and conditions subject to which it was issued.

Pedal Cycle Section

What IS Insured	What is NOT Insured
Loss of or damage to any pedal cycle owned by the **Family**.	(a) **Excluded Events**.
We will not pay more than £1,000 for any one pedal cycle in respect of any one event, less the **Excess**, if applicable, specified in the Claims Settlement Provisions.	(b) Theft of accessories unless stolen with the pedal cycle.

Sports Equipment Section

What IS Insured	What is NOT Insured
Loss of or damage to **Sports** equipment owned by the **Family**.	(a) **Excluded Events**.
We will not pay more than £1,000 per person in respect of any one event, less the **Excess**, if applicable, specified in the Claims Settlement Provisions.	(b) Breakage of rackets and their strings, cricket bats and hockey and lacrosse sticks.

General Exclusions

1. **Geographical Limits:** This Policy does not insure any damage, breakage, loss, injury or liability arising outside Great Britain, Northern Ireland, the Isle of Man or the Channel Islands but these geographical limits will not apply under the Personal Money Section, the Pedal Cycle Section and the Sports Equipment Section during the first 60 days of any period in which property insured under such Sections is outside such limits.

2. **Sonic Bangs:** This Policy does not insure loss, destruction or damage occasioned by pressure waves caused by aircraft or other aerial devices travelling at sonic or supersonic speeds.

3. **War Risks:** This Policy does not insure any consequence whether direct or indirect of war, invasion, act of foreign enemy, hostilities (whether war be declared or not), civil war, rebellion, revolution, insurrection or military or usurped power.

4. **Nuclear Risks:** This Policy does not insure
   (a) loss or destruction of or damage to any property whatsoever or any loss or expense whatsoever resulting or arising therefrom or any consequential loss
   (b) any legal liability of whatsoever nature
   directly or indirectly caused by or contributed to by or arising from the radioactive, toxic, explosive or other hazardous properties of any explosive nuclear assembly or nuclear component thereof or ionising radiations or contamination by radioactivity from any nuclear fuel or from any nuclear waste from the combustion of nuclear fuel.

Conditions

1. **Observance of Terms:** Anyone claiming indemnity or benefit under this Policy must comply with its terms as far as they can apply.

2. **Precautions:** You must take all reasonable precautions to reduce or remove the risk of damage, loss or injury.

3. **Notification:** You must report any damage or loss to us in writing as soon as reasonably possible and notify the police immediately of any damage or loss by theft, riot or malicious persons. You must send any claim by a third party or notice of any proceedings to us immediately. No expense in making good damage may be incurred without our written consent except for emergency repairs to prevent further loss or damage.

4. **Conduct of Claim:** You must at your own expense provide us with such proofs, evidence, certificates and assistance as we may reasonably ask for in connection with any claim. No property may be abandoned to us. We will be entitled to the full conduct and control of the defence or settlement of any claim from a third party and no admission of liability may be made without our written consent.

5. **Other Insurance:** If any other insurance covers the same damage, loss or liability we will pay only our rateable proportion of any claim.

6. **Cancellation:** We may cancel this Policy by sending at least 7 days' notice to your last known address. You will then be entitled to a proportionate return of premium. You too may cancel the Policy. Any refund of premium will be calculated from the date we receive your written notice of cancellation and will be the full premium less premium at our short period rates for the period the Policy has been in force.

Endorsements

Each of the following endorsements is operative only when the endorsement number appears in the Schedule under the heading "Endorsements Operative".

DC.30 - Unoccupancy: This Policy does not insure loss or damage occurring during any period in the months of December, January, February and March in which the **Home** is left without an occupant for more than 48 consecutive hours if the loss or damage is caused by
(a) **Insured Peril** 1 unless at that time the gas and electricity supplies were turned off at the mains
(b) **Insured Peril** 6 unless at that time the water supply was turned off at the stopcock and the water and heating systems drained.

DC.31 - Intruder Alarm: This Policy does not insure loss or damage occurring in the **Home** if caused by **Insured Peril** 8 unless the intruder alarm system installed in the **Home** is
(a) tested and put into operation on each and every occasion that the **Home** is left without an occupant, and
(b) inspected and maintained under the terms of the agreement with the installing company.

TERMINOLOGIE ZUM VERSICHE-RUNGSRECHT

INSURANCE LAW TERMINOLOGY

Ableben	*death*
Ablebensversicherung	*whole-life insurance*
Altersgrenze	*age limit*
Anspruch	*claim*
Anspruch begleichen	*to settle a claim*
Anspruch erheben	*to make a claim, to assert a claim, to claim*
Anspruch geltend machen	*to assert a claim*
anteilige Rückerstattung der Prämie	*proportionate return of premium*
Antrag	*proposal, application*
Arbeitslosenversicherung	*unemployment insurance*
Arbeitsunfähigkeit	*inability to work, disability, incapacity*
ärztlicher Befund	*medical report*
Aufruhr	*riot*
Begleichung eines Anspruchs	*settlement of a claim*
Begünstigter	*beneficiary*
Berufshaftpflicht	*professional liability insurance*
Beschädigung	*damage*
Betriebsunfallversicherung	*industrial injuries insurance*
Betriebsunterbrechung	*business interruption*
Betriebsunterbrechungsversicherung	*business interruption insurance*
Beweis	*evidence*
Bezugsberechtigter	*beneficiary*
bis zum Betrag von ... versichert sein	*to be insured for an amount not exceeding ...*
böswillige Beschädigung	*malicious damage*
Brandstiftung	*arson*
Dauer	*term of insurance, period of coverage*
Deckung	*cover (UK), coverage (US)*
Deckung erlangen	*to obtain cover/coverage*
Deckungszusage	*binder (US), cover note (UK)*
Diebstahl	*theft*
Diebstahlversicherung	*insurance against theft, burglary insurance*
Einbruchsversicherung	*burglary insurance, Insurance against theft*
Er- und Ablebensversicherung	*endowment life insurance*
Erdbeben	*earthquake*
Erkrankung	*illness*
Erlebensfall	*pure endowment*
Erlebensversicherung	*pure endowment insurance*
Ersatz	*replacement*

Ersatzpolizze	*renewal policy*
Erstversicherer	*original insurer, primary insurer*
Erstversicherter	*original insured*
Erstversicherung	*direct/original/primary insurance*
Explosion	*explosion*
Feuer	*fire*
Gefahr(en)	*peril(s)*
gerichtliche Geltendmachung eines Anspruchs	*assertion of a claim in court*
Gesundheit	*health*
Glasbruch	*breakage of glass*
Haftpflichtversicherung	*liability insurance*
Haftung	*liability*
Haftungsausschluß	*disclaimer/exclusion of liability*
Haftungsbeschränkung	*limit/limitation of liability*
Haftungssumme	*liability coverage*
Havarie	*average*
Höhe des Schadenersatzes	*level of damages/coverage*
Indexierung	*stable-value clause, index clause, stable-value provision*
Instandsetzung	*repair*
KFZ-Haftpflicht	*automobile liability insurance*
Kosten	*cost(s)*
Krankenversicherung	*health insurance*
Krankheit	*disease*
kündigen	*to give notice of termination/ cancellation*
Kündigung	*cancellation, termination*
Kündigung mittels eingeschriebenem Brief	*cancellation/termination by registered mail/letter*
Kündigungsfrist	*notice of termination*
Lebenserwartung	*life expectancy*
Lebensversicherung	*life insurance (US), (life) assurance (UK)*
Leibrente	*life annuity*
Makler	*(insurance) broker*
medizinische Betreuung	*medical treatment*
Mitteilung an die Versicherung	*notification of insurer*
Neuwert	*reinstatement value, value as new*
Pensionsversicherung	*old-age pension insurance*
Personenschaden	*injury (to persons)*
polizeiliche Meldung	*notification of the police*
Polizze	*policy*

Polizzeninhaber	*policyholder*
Prämie	*premium*
Privatversicherung	*private insurance*
radioaktive Strahlung	*nuclear radiation*
Rechtsschutzversicherung	*legal expense(s) insurance*
Reisegepäckversicherung	*baggage insurance, luggage insurance*
Reiseversicherung	*travel insurance, voyage insurance*
Risiken	*risks, perils, contingencies*
Rückerstattung der Prämie	*return of premium*
Rückkaufwert	*cash surrender value*
Rückversicherer	*reinsurer*
Rückversicherung	*reinsurance*
Sachschaden	*property damage*
Schaden	*damage*
Schaden geltend machen	*to claim*
Schaden wiedergutmachen	*to compensate*
Schadenersatz	*damages*
Schadenersatzlimit	*limitation of damages*
Schadensabteilung	*claims department*
Schadensereignis	*(damaging) event*
Schadensfall	*claim*
Schadenssumme	*amount of damages*
Schmerzengeld	*(compensation for) pain and suffering*
Schutz	*protection, coverage*
schutzfähige Objekte	*insurable objects*
Selbstbehalt	*deductible, retention*
Sozialversicherung	*social security*
technische Risiken	*engineering contingencies*
Todesfall	*event of death*
Überversicherung	*overinsurance*
Unfall	*accident*
unzureichende Deckung	*incomplete/inadequate/insufficient cover/ coverage*
Verdienstentgang	*loss of wages*
Verlängerungspolizze	*renewal policy*
Verlängerungsprämie	*renewal premium*
Verletzung	*injury*
Verlust	*loss*
Vermögensschaden	*property damage*
Verschleiß (gewöhnlicher)	*(normal) wear and tear*
versicherbares Interesse	*insurable interest*
Versicherer	*insurer*
versichert sein gegen	*to be insured against*
Versicherter	*insured, insured person*
versicherter Wert	*insured value, covered value*

Versicherung	*insurance, assurance (UK), underwriting*
Versicherung auf den Todesfall	*whole-life insurance*
Versicherungs-Aktiengesellschaft	*joint-stock insurance company*
Versicherungsarten	*types of insurances*
Versicherungsbetrug	*insurance fraud*
Versicherungsfall	*insured event*
Versicherungsleistung	*performance under a policy*
Versicherungsnehmer	*insured, insured person, client*
Versicherungsrecht	*insurance law*
Versicherungssumme	*insured sum, insured amount*
Versicherungsverein auf Gegenseitigkeit	*mutual insurance association*
Versicherungswerber	*proposer*
Vinkulierung	*restriction/exclusion of transferability*
Vollkaskoversicherung	*collision damage waiver*
vollständige Wiederherstellung	*complete reinstatement*
Voraussetzungen	*preconditions, prerequisites*
Vorkehrungen	*precautions*
vorläufige Deckungszusage	*provisional cover note*
vorsätzliche Schadenszufügung	*intentional/wilful/deliberate causing of loss/infliction of injury*
Wasserschaden	*damage caused by water*
Wertanpassung	*inflation provision*
Wiederherstellung	*reinstatement*
Zedent	*ceding insurer*
Zeitwert	*current value*
Zusatzleistung	*additional/supplementary benefits*
Zusatzversicherung	*additional/supplementary/collateral insurance*

INSURANCE LAW TERMINOLOGY

TERMINOLOGIE ZUM VERSICHERUNGSRECHT

accident	Unfall
accidental breakage of glass	Glasbruch
accidental damage	Schaden durch Unfall
admit liability	Haftung zusagen, übernehmen
agent	(Versicherungs)Makler, -agent
aggregate limit	Schadenersatzlimit
amount insured	Versicherungssumme
amount of loss	Schadenssumme
annuity contracts	private Pensionsversicherung
appointed agent	beauftragter Makler (einer ausländischen Gesellschaft im Inland)
arson	Brandstiftung
automobile insurance (US)	Kraftfahrzeugversicherung
average	Havarie
beneficiary	Begünstigter, Bezugsberechtigter
benefit	Leistung
binder (US)	vorläufige Deckungszusage
bodily injury to a person	Verletzung einer Person
broker	(Versicherungs)Makler
burglary insurance	Diebstahlversicherung, Einbruchversicherung
business interruption insurance	Betriebsunterbrechungsversicherung
cancellation	Kündigung
cash surrender value	Rückkaufwert
ceding insurer	Erstversicherer, Zedent
claim	Anspruch, Schaden, Schadensfall
claim	Anspruch erheben, Schaden geltend machen
claimant	Anspruchswerber
claims department	Schadensabteilung
client's present position	derzeitiger Zustand des Kunden/ Versicherungsnehmers
collision damage waiver	Vollkaskoversicherung
conditions (of a policy)	Versicherungsbedingungen
contract of indemnity	Schadensversicherungsvertrag
costs of medical treatment	Kosten der medizinischen Betreuung
cover (UK)	Deckung
cover note (UK)	vorläufige Deckungszusage
coverage (US)	Deckung
damage	Schaden
damages	Schadenersatz
deductible	Selbstbehalt

disease contracted by a person	Krankheit einer Person
domestic insurance	Haushaltsversicherung
earthquake fire	durch Erdbeben ausgelöstes Feuer
endowment insurance	Versicherung auf den Todes- und Erlebensfall
engineering contingencies	technische Risiken
event	Versicherungsfall
evidence	Beweis
excluded events	von der Deckung ausgeschlossene Vorfälle
exclusion	Haftungsausschluß
explosion	Explosion
fire	Feuer
franchise	Selbstbehalt
fringe benefits	Zusatzleistungen im Dienstverhältnis
health insurance	Krankenversicherung
inadequate sums insured	unzureichende Versicherungssummen
incomplete cover/coverage	unzureichende Deckung
industrial injuries insurance (UK)	Betriebsunfallversicherung
inflation provision	Wertanpassung, Indexierung
injuries	Verletzungen
insurance company	Versicherung(sgesellschaft)
insurance plans	Zusatzversicherungen, Pensionspläne
insurance premium	Versicherungsprämie
insured	Versicherungsnehmer
insured for an amount not exceeding ...	bis zum Betrag von ... versichert
insured up to the value of	bis zu einem bestimmten Wert versichert
insurer	Versicherer
joint-stock insurance company (UK)	Versicherungs-Aktiengesellschaft
legal expenses insurance	Rechtsschutversicherung
level of damages	Höhe des Schadenersatzes
liability	Haftung
liability at law	gesetzliche Haftung
liability insurance	Haftpflichtversicherung
life annuity	Leibrente
life assurance (UK)	Lebensversicherung
life expectancy	Lebenserwartung
life insurance (US)	Lebensversicherung
limit of liability	Haftungsbeschränkung
limitation of liability	Haftungsbeschränkung
loss	Verlust
loss of wages	Verdienstentgang
make a claim against	Anspruch erheben, Schaden geltend machen gegenüber

make good on damage	Schaden wiedergutmachen
malicious damage	vorsätzliche Schadenszufügung, böswillige Beschädigung
marine insurance	UK: Seeversicherung, US: allgemeine Transportversicherung
MEDICAID (US)	US-Sozialversicherungsplan für sozial Schwache
medical costs	Kosten der medizinschen Betreuung
medical report	ärztlicher Befund
MEDICARE (US)	US-Sozialversicherungsplan für alte Menschen
motor vehicle insurance (UK)	Kraftfahrzeugversicherung
mutual insurance association (UK)	Versicherungsverein auf Gegenseitigkeit
mutual insurance company (US)	Versicherungsverein auf Gegenseitigkeit
mutual office (UK)	Versicherungsverein auf Gegenseitigkeit
National Health Service (NHS) (UK)	UK-Gesundheitswesen
National Insurance (UK)	UK-Sozialversicherung
notify the policy within 24 hours of the discovery	die Polizei innerhalb von 24 Stunden nach Entdeckung verständigen
obtain cover/coverage	Deckung erlangen
old-age, survivors and disability insurance (US)	Alters-, Hinterbliebenen- und Invaliditätsversicherung
overinsurance	Überversicherung
payment taking into account pain and suffering	Schmerzengeld
perils	Risiken, Gefahren
period of insurance	Versicherungsdauer
period of notice of termination/ cancellation	Kündigungsfrist
policy	Versicherungspolizze
policyholder	Polizzeninhaber
potential liability claim	möglicher (Eventual-) Anspruch
precautions	Vorkehrungen
private health insurance	private (Zusatz-) Krankenversicherung
professional liability insurance	Berufshaftpflichtversicherung
proof	Beweis
proportionate return of premium	anteilige Prämienrückerstattung (im Kündigungsfall)
proposal	Antrag
proposer	Versicherungswerber
proprietary office (UK)	Versicherungs-Aktiengesellschaft
protect oneself against	sich schützen vor/gegen
protection	(Versicherungs)Schutz
provide indemnity	Versicherungsschutz bieten
provide insurance	Versicherungsschutz bieten

re-insurance	Rückversicherung
reinstatement basis of settlement	Versicherung, die die Kosten der vollständigen Wiederherstellung/ Instandsetzung deckt
renewal premium	Verlängerungsprämie
replacement as new	Neuwertversicherung
replacement policy	Ersatzpolizze, Verlängerungspolizze
report to the insurance company in writing	der Versicherung schriftlich Mitteilung machen
settlement of claims	Begleichung der Ansprüche
shortfall in cover/coverage	unzureichende Deckung
social security	Sozialversicherung
stock insurance company (US)	Versicherungs-Aktiengesellschaft
subterranean fire	unterirdisches Feuer
suffer damage	Schaden/Verlust erleiden
sum insured	Versicherungssumme
survivorship annuity	Hinterbliebenenversicherung(-rente)
take precautions	Vorkehrungen treffen
termination	Kündigung
travel insurance	Reiseversicherung
types of insurances	Versicherungsarten
underinsurance	Unterversicherung
underwriter	spezielle Form des Versicherers
unemployment insurance	Arbeitslosenversicherung
voluntary schemes	freiwillige Pensionspläne
wear and tear	Verschleiß
whole life insurance/assurance	Todesfallversicherung
without prejudice	unpräjudiziell
workmen's compensation insurance (US)	Betriebsunfallversicherung

V. ARBITRATION

The following definition was taken from R. Coulson, Business Arbitration – What you need to know, 3rd, 1986, 8.

"Arbitration is the submission of a disagreement to one or more impartial persons. Usually, the parties agree to abide by the arbitrator's decision. Because the decision is binding, arbitration differs from mediation or conciliation, where the third party brings the parties together to discuss settlement. It also differs from fact-finding, where an impartial person studies the situation and makes a report. In most instances, arbitrators' decisions are private and only of interest to the parties involved. Few arbitration awards come to the attention of the courts."

Übergabe einer Meinungsverschiedenheit; unparteiisch; sich unterwerfen Vermittlung; Streitbeilegung/Schlichtung; Vergleich; Schiedsbegutachtung Gutachten nicht-öffentl, Einschaltung der Gerichte

In terms of international trade, arbitration has become increasingly important. Parties involved in international transactions tend to opt for arbitration for a number of reasons:

int Handelsbeziehungen

First, by choosing arbitration, the parties have a neutral forum, thus avoiding the case being heard before a court located in the sphere of one of the parties. Second, arbitrators are very often experts in their respective fields, which may be very beneficial for the dispute and the parties involved. Arbitration proceedings tend to be informal, straightforward and rather short compared to regular court proceedings. In most cases, an arbitration award would settle a dispute for good, with judicial review or appeals being the exception.

neutraler Boden Fall; vor ein Gericht kommen Sachverständige

Rechtsstreit Schiedsverfahren formlos ord Gerichtsverfahren; Schiedsspruch; endgültig ord Rechtsweg, Berufung

All these advantages have made arbitration popular and have led to an institutionalization of arbitration panels and other bodies throughout the world. In the United States, the American Arbitration Association (AAA), with its headquarters in New York, is the most important of all institutions offering services related to alternative dispute resolution. In Europe, several national chambers of commerce have established bodies providing for settlement by arbitration.

Schiedsgerichte

alternative Streitbeilegung Handelskammern

Probably the most famous of these is the ICC Court of Arbitration headquartered in Paris. When the parties to an agreement want to opt for arbitration as the means for settling all disputes arising from or in connection with a contract, they may resort to one of the standard clauses recommended by the large courts of arbitration. The ICC standard arbitration clause reads as follows:

mit dem Sitz, sich für S. entscheiden, zur Streitbeilegung

Standardklauseln, ICC Standard: „Alle sich aus dem gegenwärtigen Vertrag ergebenden Streitigkeiten werden nach der Vergleichs- und Schiedsgerichtsordnung der Internat Handelskam-

All disputes arising in connection with the present contract shall be finally settled under the Rules of Conciliation and Arbitration of the International Chamber of Commerce by one or more arbitrators appointed in accordance with the said Rules.

mer von einem oder mehreren gemäß dieser Schiedsordnung bestellten Schiedsrichtern endgültig entschieden"

The AAA standard clause for insertion in general commercial contracts reads as follows:

*Any controversy or claim arising out of or relating to this contract, or the breach thereof, shall be settled by arbitration in accordance with the Commercial Arbitration Rules of the American Arbitration Association, and judgement upon the award rendered by the Arbitrator(s) may be entered in any court having jurisdiction thereof. (Cited from Coulson, Business Arbitration, **see supra, 17**).*

Musterschiedsspruch

Following is a sample arbitration award as typically rendered by the American Arbitration Association presented with annotations.

durchsetzen

klagen aufgrund des Schiedsspruches
Mitgliedschaft bei int Abkommen, die Schiedssprüche anerkennen
mangelnde inl Gerichtsbarkeit, Unzuständigkeit, öffentl Interesse (ordre public*)

The question of whether or not an arbitration award may be enforced directly against the party who lost the arbitration case or whether the winning party first has to sue on the grounds of the arbitration award depends on the forum of enforcement, particularly on the individual country's membership to an international convention granting full recognition to such arbitration awards. Concerning an individual case, a court may still refuse to enforce an award for lack of jurisdiction, incompetence or for public policy considerations.

AMERICAN ARBITRATION ASSOCIATION
ADMINISTRATOR

Verwaltungsbeamter

COMMERCIAL ARBITRATION TRIBUNAL

Handelsschiedsgericht
in der Schiedssache
ABC gegen (versus)
XY

in the Matter of the Arbitration between   *

*

ABC International., Ltd.   *

                AWARD   *

VS   *OF*   *   Schiedsspruch

          ARBITRATORS   *

XY Ges.m.b.H.   *

  *

CASE NUMBER: 12-A-222-23456-87   *   Fallnummer

WE, THE UNDERSIGNED ARBITRATORS, having been designated in accordance with the Arbitration Agreement entered into by the above-named Parties and dated March 4, 1987, and having been duly sworn, and having duly heard the proofs and allegations of the Parties, do hereby, AWARD as follows:

Schiedsrichter
Schiedsvereinbarung
Parteien, vereidigt
Beweise u Vorbringen

1. Within thirty (30) days from the date of transmittal of this Award to the Parties, XY Ges.m.b.H., hereinafter referred to as RESPONDENT, shall pay to ABC International, Ltd., hereinafter referred to as the CLAIMANT, the sum of ONE HUNDRED AND FIFTY THOUSAND DOLLARS ($ 150,000.00) together with interest thereon at the rate of ten percent (10%) per annum, commencing with the date of July 1, 1989, to the date of payment.

nachstehend bezeichnet als Beklagter
Kläger

Zinsen

Zahlungstag

2. The compensation of the ARBITRATORS totalling FOUR THOUSAND FIVE HUNDRED DOLLARS ($ 4,500.000), shall be borne three fourths by RESPONDENT and one fourth by CLAIMANT. Therefore, RESPONDENT shall pay to CLAIMANT the sum of ONE THOUSAND ONE HUNDRED AND SEVENTY FIVE DOLLARS ($ 1,175.00), representing that portion of the ARBITRATORS' compensation previously advanced by CLAIMANT to the ASSOCIATION.

Kostenersatz

3. The administrative fee and expenses of the American Arbitration Association totalling TWO THOUSAND FIVE HUNDRED AND NINETY DOLLARS ($ 2,590.00), shall be borne one fourth by CLAIMANT, and three fourths by RESPONDENT. Therefore, RESPONDENT shall pay ONE THOUSAND SIX HUNDRED AND TWO DOLLARS AND FIFTY CENTS ($ 1,602.50), representing that portion of the administrative fee and expenses previously advanced by CLAIMANT to the Association, and RESPONDENT shall pay to the American Arbitration Association the sum of THREE HUNDRED AND FORTY DOLLARS ($ 340.00), representing the balance of the administrative fee and expenses still due said Association.

Verwaltungskosten
und Auslagen

Differenz
noch der Vereinigung
geschuldet

213

endgültige Bereini-
gung aller Ansprüche

4. This Award is in full settlement of all Claims submitted to this Arbitration.

....

(name, date, arbitrator)

....

(name, date, arbitrator)

....

(name, date, arbitrator)

symbol Siegel

State of New York   )

)   ss:

County of New York)

Berufung auf den
Schiedsrichtereid

I, CHARLES F. KING, do hereby affirm upon my oath as Arbitrator that I am the individual described in and who executed this instrument, which is my Award.

....

(Dated)   (Signature of Arbitrator)

State of Florida   )

)   ss:

County of Collier   )

I, PETER O'CONNOR, do hereby affirm upon my oath as ARBITRATOR that I am the individual described in and who executed this instrument, which is my Award.

....

(Dated)   (Signature of Arbitrator)

(… third arbitrator … see above)

ARBITRATION TERMINOLOGY

TERMINOLOGIE ZUR SCHIEDS-GERICHTSBARKEIT

abide by an award	sich einem Schiedspruch unterwerfen
adjourn a meeting	eine Sitzung vertagen
adjournment	Vertagung
adversaries	Gegner
advisory opinion	Gutachten, gutächterliche Stellungnahme
Alternative Dispute Resolution (ADR)	Alternative Streitbeilegung/ Streitschlichtung/ Konfliktlösung
analyse the issues	Rechtsfragen analysieren
answer to the request	Klagebeantwortung erstatten
appeal	Anfechtung
appeal	anfechten
apply for postponement/adjournment	Erstreckung/Vertagung beantragen
arbitration	Schiedsgerichtsbarkeit
arbitration award	Schiedsspruch
arbitration clause	Schiedsklausel
arbitration proceedings	Schiedsverfahren
arbitrator	Schiedsrichter
arbitrator exceeding authority	Kompetenzüberschreitung durch Schiedsrichter
arbitrator misconduct	Fehlverhalten der Schiedsrichter
ask for confirmation	um Bestätigung ersuchen
authenticity of documents	Echtheit der Urkunden
award	Schiedsspruch
awards that contravene public policy	Schiedssprüche, denen das öffentliche Interesse entgegensteht (ähnl* ordre public)
bar subsequent objections	spätere Einwendungen ausschließen
bias	Parteilichkeit
binding commitment on both parties	bindende Unterwerfung beider Parteien
claim	Anspruch, Forderung
claimant	Kläger, Anspruchswerber
closing statement(s)	Schlußvortrag, abschließendes Vorbringen
commencement of proceedings	Einleitung, Beginn des Verfahrens
compliance with an award	Erfüllung eines Schiedsspruches
comply with an award	einen Schiedsspruch erfüllen
compromise	Kompromiß, Vergleich
conciliation	Streitbeilegung
conflict(s)	Streit(punkte), Differenzen, Meinungs- verschiedenheiten
constitute grounds for the vacation of an award	einen Grund für die Aufhebung eines Schiedsspruches darstellen
contested facts	bestrittene Fakten/Tatsachen
controversy	Differenzen
corruption	Bestechlichkeit

costs	(Verfahrens-)Kosten
counterclaim	Gegenforderung, Widerklage
court of arbitration	Schiedsgericht
cross-examination	Kreuzverhör
cross-examine	ins Kreuzverhör nehmen
damages	Schadenersatz
defending party	Antragsgegner
demand for arbitration	Aufforderungsschreiben, Anspruchs-schreiben, Schiedsklage
demand postponement/adjournement	Erstreckung/Vertagung verlangen
deposit to cover costs	Kostenvorschuß
depositions	Vorbringen
direct testimony	Zeugenaussage über Selbsterlebtes (im Gegensatz zu „hearsay")
disagreements	Meinungsverschiedenheiten
discovery procedures	dem eigentlichen Beweisverfahren vorgelagertes Verfahren zur Erkundung von Beweisen, Verpflichtung zur Herausgabe aller geforderten Dokumente (anglo-amerikanisches Institut)
discussion of remedies	Erörterung des Rechtsbehelfs
dispute settlement	Streitbeilegung
dispute(s)	Streit, Streitpunkte
document	Urkunde
documentary evidence	Urkundenbeweis
due process	(US Verfassungsrecht) ähnl* rechtliches Gehör
enforce an arbitration award	einen Schiedsspruch vollstrecken
enforceability	Vollstreckbarkeit
enforceable	vollstreckbar, durchsetzbar
enforcement	Durchsetzung, Vollstreckung
enter judgement upon award	ein Gerichtsurteil im Sinne des Schiedsspruchs erlassen
erroneous evidence	falsches Beweismittel
escrow fund	Treuhandkonto, Treuhanderlag
establish an escrow fund	ein Treuhandkonto einrichten
establish authenticity of documents	die Echtheit der Urkunden feststellen
evidence	Beweismittel, Beweisverfahren
expert	Sachverständiger
expert testimony	Ausage des Sachverständigen
expert witness	Sachverständiger als Zeuge
fact-finding	Schiedsbegutachtung
facts	Fakten, Tatsachen
failure to meet statutory requirements	Nichteinhaltung gesetzlicher Bestimmungen
file a claim	Anspruch geltend machen, klagen
file a report	einen Bericht erstatten
formalities	Formales
formula for compromise	Kompromißformel

216

fraud	Betrug
fulfil(l) an award	einen Schiedsspruch erfüllen
fulfilment of an award	Erfüllung eines Schiedsspruches
grounds for overturning an award	Gründe für die Aufhebung eines Schiedsspruchs
hearing	Hearing, Verhandlung
hearsay evidence	„Hörensagen", Zeugenaussage über nicht selbst Erlebtes; nach anglo-amerikanischem Prozeßrecht idR unzulässig, im Schiedsgerichtsverfahren uU zulässig
hold on/in escrow	treuhändig halten
identify authenticity of documents	die Echtheit der Urkunden angeben/ zugestehen/identifizieren
initiating papers	verfahrenseinleitende Dokumente
initiation of proceedings	Einleitung, Beginn des Verfahrens
interrogate	befragen, verhören
interrogation	Befragung, Verhör
investigations	Untersuchungen
irrelevant evidence	verfahrensirrelevantes/unbeachtliches Beweismittel
issue a subpoena	verbindlich laden (quasi-gerichtliche Handlung, uU durchsetzbar)
issue(s)	Rechtsfrage(n)
judgement	Gerichtsurteil
judgement confirming award	Gerichtsurteil, welches auf der Basis des Schiedsspruchs ergeht (ieS auch Exekutionsbewilligung)
judicial review	Anfechtung, Überprüfung eines Schiedsspruchs durch die ordentlichen Gerichte
keep records	aufzeichnen, protokollieren
lack of impartiality	mangelnde Unpartcilichkeit
leading questions	Fragen, welche die Antwort suggerieren
make an award	einen Schiedsspruch erlassen
make depositions	vorbringen
make presentations to a panel	vor den Schiedsrichtern vorbringen
making of an award	Erlassung eines Schiedsspruches
mandatory conciliation	verpflichtendes Vergleichsverfahren
mediation	Vermittlung (-sverfahren)
mediation rules	Verfahrensregeln für die Streitschlichtung
mediators	Vermittler
memorandum	Memorandum, schriftliche Aufzeichnung, Aktennotiz, Bericht
mini-trial	Kurzverfahren (institutionalisiert)
minutes of a meeting	Sitzungsprotokoll

modification of award	(Ab-)Änderung des Schiedsspruchs selbst (durch das Gericht AA; in Österreich und Deutschland nicht möglich)
modify an award	einen Schiedsspruch abändern
money award	zugesprochener Geldbetrag
motion for a judgement	Antrag (uU Klage) auf Gerichtsurteil
motion for vacatur/vacation of award	Antrag auf Aussetzung eines Schiedsspruchs
move for a judgement	ein Gerichtsurteil beantragen
move for postponement/adjournement	Erstreckung/Vertagung beantragen
moving party	Antragsteller
negotiations	(Vergleichs-) Verhandlungen
non-compliance	Nichterfüllung
non-reviewable awards	unanfechtbarer Schiedsspruch (kein Rechtsmittel)
notification	Verständigung, Benachrichtigung, Bekanntgabe
notification of arbitration	Verständigung über Schiedsverfahren
notification of arbitrators	Verständigung der Schiedsrichter
notification of respondent	Verständigung des Gegners
object to	Einspruch erheben
objections	Einwendungen, Einspruch
on-site inspection	Lokalaugenschein
on-site visit	Lokalaugenschein
opening statements	einleitendes Vorbringen
optional conciliation	freiwilliges Vergleichsverfahren
out-of-court settlement	außergerichtlicher Vergleich
overturn an award	einen Schiedsspruch aufheben
panel	Schiedsrichterkollegium (vermehrt um Parteien)
parties	Parteien
perform an award	einen Schiedsspruch erfüllen
performance	Erfüllung, Leistung
performance pursuant to an award	Erfüllung eines Schiedsspruches
performance pursuant to the terms of an award	Erfüllung gemäß Schiedsspruch
place of arbitration	(Tagungs-)Ort des Schiedsverfahrens/ Schiedsgerichtes
pleadings	Vorbringen
postpone a decision	Entscheidung vorbehalten
postpone a hearing/meeting	Sitzung vertagen(erstrecken)
postponement	Erstreckung, Vertagung
prehearing conferences	Vorbesprechungen
present the issues	Rechtsfragen darstellen, vorbringen
presentations	Vorbringen
proceedings	Verfahren
professional mediators	ausgebildete Vermittler
put on record	protokollieren, zu Protokoll nehmen

rebut	Klagebeantwortung erstatten
record	aufzeichnen
recording agency	protokollführende Einrichtung (bei internationalen Schiedsgerichten oft institutionalisiert)
recording agent	Protokollbeamter, Protokollführer
records	Aufzeichnungen, Protokolle
records of transaction	Geschäftsunterlagen
referee	Schiedsrichter (bei Kollegium der Vorsitzende)
relevant evidence	verfahrensrelevantes Beweismittel
render an award	einen Schiedsspruch erlassen, zusprechen
rent-a-judge (US)	„Mietrichter"
reply	Klagebeantwortung
reply	Klagebeantwortung erstatten
report	Bericht
request for arbitration	Einleitung des Schiedsverfahrens
request for conciliation	Antrag auf Einleitung des Vergleichs- verfahrens
request postponement/adjournement	Erstreckung/Vertagung verlangen
resolve an issue	eine Rechtsfrage lösen
resort to arbitration	auf Schiedsgerichtsbarkeit ausweichen
respondent	Beklagter, Anspruchsgegner
rules governing proceedings	anwendbare Verfahrensregeln
serve the request for arbitration on the other party	Klage an die andere Partei zustellen
service	Zustellung
settle for	sich vergleichen
settlement	Vergleich, iwS Einigung
specific performance	Erfüllung gemäß Vertrag (Anm.: Im anglo- amerikanischen Recht tritt bei Vertrags- bruch idR nur Schadenersatzpflicht, nicht jedoch die Pflicht zur Erfüllung gemäß Vertrag ein)
submission agreement	Unterwerfungsvereinbarung, Schiedsvereinbarung
submit a report	einen Bericht überreichen, einreichen
submit to arbitration	sich der Schiedsgerichtsbarkeit unterwerfen
subpoena	verbindliche Ladung
terms of settlement	Vergleichsbedingungen
testify	Zeugenschaft ablegen, als Zeuge aussagen
testimony	Zeugenaussage
transcripts	Mitschrift, Aufzeichnungen
tribunal administrator	Verfahrensadministrator
umpire	Schiedsrichter (bei Kollegium der Vorsitzende)
uncontested facts	unbestrittene Fakten/Tatsachen

vacate an award	einen Schiedsspruch aussetzen, aufheben
vacation of an award	Aufhebung eines Schiedsspruches
vacatur of an award	Aussetzung eines Schiedsspruches
venue of arbitration	(Tagungs-)Ort des Schiedsverfahrens/ Schiedsgerichtes
waive objections	auf Einspruch verzichten
witness	Zeuge

TERMINOLOGIE ZUR SCHIEDS-GERICHTSBARKEIT

ARBITRATION TERMINOLOGY

Abänderung eines Schiedsspruchs	*modification of an award*
Ad hoc-Schiedsgericht	*mini-trial (US)*
anfechten	*to appeal*
Anfechtung	*appeal*
Anspruch	*claim*
Anspruch geltend machen	*to claim, to file a claim, to assert a claim*
Anspruchsgegner	*respondent*
Anspruchsschreiben	*letter of demand*
Anspruchswerber	*claimant*
Antrag	*motion, application, request*
Antrag auf Aussetzung eines Schiedsspruchs	*motion for vacatur/vacation of an award*
Antrag auf Bestellung eines Sachverständigen	*request for appointment of an expert*
Antrag auf Einleitung des Verfahrens	*demand for arbitration, request of arbitration*
Antrag stellen	*to move for, to apply for, to request*
Antragsgegner	*defending party, defendant*
Antragsteller	*moving party*
Anzahl von Schiedsrichtern	*number of arbitrators*
auf Einspruch verzichten	*to waive an objection*
auf Einwendungen verzichten	*to waive objections*
Aufforderungsschreiben	*demand for arbitration*
Aufhebung eines Schiedsspruchs	*vacation of an award*
Aufhebungsgründe	*grounds for overturning an award*
aufzeichnen	*to keep records, to put on record, to record*
Aufzeichnungen	*records*
Aussage	*testimony*
aussagen	*to testify*
außergerichtlicher Vergleich	*out-of-court settlement*
Aussetzung eines Schiedsspruchs	*vacatur of an award*
Beklagter	*respondent*
Bericht	*report*
Bericht erstatten	*to report, to file a report, to submit a report*
Bestätigung des Schiedsspruchs	*confirmation of an award*
Bestechlichkeit	*corruption*
Bestellung eines Schiedsgerichts	*appointment of a court of arbitration*
Bestellung von Schiedsrichtern	*appointment of arbitrators*
bestrittene Tatsachen	*contested facts*
Betrug	*fraud*
Beweismittel	*evidence*
Beweisverfahren	*evidence (procedure)*
bilaterale Vollstreckbarkeitsabkommen	*bilateral law enforcement treaties*
Durchsetzbarkeit	*enforceability*
Durchsetzung	*enforcement*

Echtheit von Urkunden	*authenticity of documents*
Echtheit von Urkunden feststellen	*to establish authenticity of documents*
Einigung auf Schiedsrichter	*agreement on arbitrators*
Einleitung des Verfahrens	*initiation of proceedings, commencement of proceedings*
Einspruch	*objection*
Einspruch erheben	*to object to*
Einwendungen	*objections*
Einwendungen ausschließen	*to bar objections*
Einwendungen zulassen	*to sustain objections*
Entscheidung	*decision, award*
Entscheidung vorbehalten	*to postpone a decision*
Erfüllung eines Schiedsspruchs	*compliance with/ fulfilment of/ performance pursuant to an award*
Erfüllung gemäß Schiedsspruch	*performance pursuant to the terms of an award*
Erlassen eines Schiedsspruchs	*making/rendering of an award*
Ernennung von Schiedsrichtern	*appointment of arbitrators*
Erstreckung	*postponement, adjournment*
Erstreckung beantragen	*to move for an adjournment, to request an adjournment*
Erstreckung verlangen	*to demand an adjournment*
Fehlverhalten	*(arbitrators') misconduct*
freiwilliges Schiedsverfahren	*optional conciliation*
freiwilliges Vergleichsverfahren	*optional conciliation*
Gegner	*adversary*
gerichtliche Überprüfung eines Schiedsspruchs	*judicial review of an award*
Gerichtsurteil	*judgement*
Gerichtsurteil basierend auf Schiedsspruch	*judgement confirming award*
Gerichtsurteil beantragen	*to move for a judgement*
Gutachten	*opinion, expert opinion, advisory opinion*
internationale Vollstreckbarkeitsabkommen	*international/multilateral law enforcement treaties/conventions*
Klage	*request for arbitration, demand for arbitration*
Klagebeantwortung	*answer to the request*
Kläger	*claimant*
Kompetenzüberschreitung	*arbitrator(s) exceeding authority*
Kompromiß	*compromise*
Kompromiß finden	*to reach a compromise, to compromise*
Kompromißformel	*formula for compromise*
Kosten	*costs*
Kostenvorschuß	*advance/deposit to cover costs*
Kurzverfahren	*mini-trial (US)*
laden	*to subpoena so., to summon so., to issue a subpoena*
Ladung	*subpoena, summons*
Lokalaugenschein	*on-site visit, on-site inspection*

Nichterfüllung	*non-performance, non-compliance*
Ort des Schiedsgerichts	*place/venue of arbitration*
Partei	*party*
Parteilichkeit	*bias, lack of impartiality*
Protokoll	*minutes, records*
Protokoll führen	*to keep minutes/records, to put on record, to record*
protokollieren	*to record*
Rechtsfrage	*issue*
Rechtsfrage analysieren	*to analyse an issue*
Rechtsfrage darstellen	*to present an issue*
Rechtsfrage lösen	*to resolve an issue*
Sachverständigen bestellen	*to appoint an expert*
Sachverständigenaussage	*expert testimony*
Sachverständigengutachten	*expert opinion*
Sachverständiger	*expert*
Schadenersatz	*damages*
Schiedsgericht	*court of arbitration*
Schiedsgericht bestellen	*to appoint a court of arbitration*
Schiedsgericht vereinbaren	*to agree on arbitration*
Schiedsgerichtsbarkeit	*arbitration*
Schiedsgerichtsverfahren	*arbitration proceedings*
Schiedsgutachten	*fact-finding (*), mini-trial (*) (US)*
Schiedsgutachter	*referee (*)*
Schiedsklage dem Beklagten zustellen	*to serve the demand for arbitration upon respondent*
Schiedsklausel	*arbitration clause*
Schiedsrichter	*arbitrator (allg.); referee (v.a. Schiedsgutachter); umpire (Vorsitzender eines Schiedsrichterkollegiums)*
Schiedsrichterkollegium	*panel, board of arbitrators*
Schiedsspruch	*arbitration award, arbitral award*
Schiedsspruch anfechten	*to appeal an award*
Schiedsspruch aufheben	*to vacate an award, to overturn an award*
Schiedsspruch aussetzen	*to vacate an award*
Schiedsspruch erlassen	*to make an award, to render an award*
Schiedsspruch vollstrecken	*to enforce an award*
Schlußvortrag	*closing statement, final statement*
sich der Schiedsgerichtsbarkeit unterwerfen	*to submit to arbitration*
sich einem Schiedsspruch unterwerfen	*to submit to an award*
Sitz des Schiedsgerichts	*place/venue of arbitration*
Sitzung/Verhandlung erstrecken	*to adjourn/to postpone a meeting/hearing*
Sprache des Schiedsgerichts	*language of arbitration*
Streit	*dispute, conflict, controversy, disagreement*
Streitbeilegung	*conciliation*
Streitpunkte	*conflicts, issues*
Streitschlichtung	*dispute resolution, conciliation*

223

Tagungsort des Schiedsgerichts	*place/venue of arbitration*
Tatsachen	*facts*
Treuhand	*escrow (trust*)*
Treuhanderlag	*escrow fund*
treuhändig	*to hold in escrow*
Treuhandkonto	*escrow account*
um Bestätigung des Schiedsspruchs ersuchen	*to ask for confirmation of the award*
unanfechtbarer Schiedsspruch	*non-reviewable award*
unbestrittene Tatsachen	*uncontested facts*
Untersuchung	*investigations*
Untersuchung durchführen	*to investigate*
Unterwerfung unter einen Schiedsspruch	*submission to an award*
Urkunde	*document, (exhibit)*
Vereinbarung über Schiedsgerichtsbarkeit	*arbitration agreement*
Verfahren	*proceedings, procedure*
Verfahren einleiten	*to initiate proceedings, to commence proceedings*
Verfahrensregeln	*rules governing proceedings*
Vergleich	*settlement*
vergleichen (sich)	*to settle (for), to reach a settlement/ compromise*
Vergleichsbedingungen	*terms of settlement*
Vergleichsverhandlungen	*settlement talks, negotiations*
Verhandlung	*hearing, (meeting)*
Verhandlungen	*negotiations*
Vermittler	*mediator*
Vermittlung	*mediation*
Verständigung	*notification*
vollstreckbar	*enforceable*
Vollstreckbarkeit	*enforceability*
Vollstreckbarkeitsabkommen	*law enforcement treaty*
Vollstreckung	*enforcement*
Vorbringen	*deposition, pleadings*
vorbringen	*to take depositions, to plead, to present*
Zeuge	*witness*
Zeugenaussage	*testimony (by witness)*
Zusammensetzung eines Schiedsgerichts	*the board of arbitrators shall consist of ...*
Zustelladresse	*address for service*
Zustellbevollmächtigter	*process agent*
zustellen	*to serve*
Zustellung	*service*
zwingendes Schiedsverfahren	*mandatory conciliation*
zwingends Vergleichsverfahren	*mandatory conciliation*

VI. TAX LAW

Mag. Regina Reiter, KPMG Austria
Beeideter Wirtschaftsprüfer und Steuerberater, CPA (USA)

1. UNITED STATES

1.1. Business Taxation

1.1.1. Domestic Corporations

A company's taxable status depends on whether it is incorporated. A corporation is a taxable entity, taxed on net profits at the corporate level. No deduction is permitted for corporate profits distributed as dividends to shareholders. Dividends are taxable to the shareholders as income, subject to certain dividends-received deductions allowable to corporate shareholders. A partnership or a sole proprietorship is not a taxable entity; items of income and loss are passed through and taxed directly to the owners.

taxable status
taxable entity
deduction, corporate profits
dividends
income
deductions, allowable

Corporate taxable income generally is taxed twice in the United States: first to the corporation and then, if and when the corporate earnings are distributed, to its shareholders.

taxable income

Gross Income

gross income

A domestic corporation is taxed on its worldwide income. Gross income for U.S. tax purposes is broadly defined as income from whatever source derived. Gross income is not, however, equivalent to gross receipts; gross receipts must be reduced by the cost of goods sold to arrive at gross income. Gross income can be reflected under several accounting methods, including the accrual method and, where appropriate, the cash receipts and disbursements method. Other methods are available for special situations (e.g. percentage of completion for long-term construction contracts). The method of accounting used for tax purposes generally may differ from that used for financial reporting purposes.

source
gross receipts

accounting methods
accrual method
cash receipts and disbursements method

Deductions

deductions

Once gross income is determined, allowable deductions are subtracted to arrive at taxable income. Generally, all ordinary and necessary expenses of earning income are deductible.

deductible

Depreciation is calculated by ACRS (Accelerated Cost Recovery System). In lieu of these accelerated cost recovery deductions, taxpayers may irrevocably elect to claim straight-line ACRS deductions over the regular recovery period.

depreciation, ACRS
tax payer

A deduction is available for state, local, and foreign taxes paid or accrued during the year incurred in carrying on a trade or business, including real property taxes, personal property taxes, and income taxes. If the foreign tax credit is claimed for the year, a deduction for foreign income taxes may not be claimed.

tax credit

interest	*Interest paid or accrued generally is deductible except for certain types of interest to which special rules are applied.*
dividends-received deduction	**Dividends-Received Deduction.** *A corporation generally is permitted to deduct 80 percent of the dividends received from a 20-percent-owned domestic corporation. In certain cases this deduction is increased to 100 percent or decreased to 70 percent.*
charitable deduction	**Charitable Deduction.** *A domestic corporation generally may deduct up to 10 percent of its taxable income, with adjustments, for charitable contributions to qualified U.S. charities. Excess charitable deductions can be carried over for five years.*

tax rates	***Tax Rates***
surtax	*Taxable income (gross income less deductions) of a corporation is taxed at rates from 15 percent to 35 percent. A surtax of 5 percent is imposed on certain amounts of income.*
allowable credits	*The tax is then reduced by allowable credits, such as the foreign tax credit and the research credit.*
corporate income taxes	*Most of the states also impose corporate income taxes.*

1.1.2. Foreign Corporations

The income of foreign corporations is segregated into two categories, each of which is taxed separately:

– **Business Income:** *income related (i.e., effectively connected) to a business carried on in the United States.*

source investment passive income	– **Nonbusiness Income:** *certain types of U.S. source investment and other passive income that are not effectively connected with a U.S. business.*
graduated rates	*Worldwide income effectively connected with the conduct of a trade or business in the United States is taxed on a net basis at the regular graduated rates. U.S. source nonbusiness income is taxed on a gross basis at a flat 30-percent rate (unless reduced or eliminated by statute or income tax treaty).*
branch profits tax	*Foreign corporations that operate businesses in the United States may pay, in addition to the regular corporate income tax, a branch profits tax equal to 30 percent of their effectively connected earnings (after regular tax) that are not reinvested in the United States. The application of this tax may be modified or eliminated by treaty.*

nonbusiness income	***Nonbusiness Income***
	Only certain types of nonbusiness income from U.S. sources are subject to U.S. tax. The principal types of this income are:
FDAP	– *Fixed or determinable annual or periodical income (FDAP);*
	– *Certain original issue discount on debt obligations when payments of principal or interest are received or when the obligations are sold;*

- *Certain gains from the disposal of timber, coal, or domestic iron ore; and*
- *Certain gains from the sale of patents and other intangible property to the extent the proceeds are contingent on the future productivity, use, or disposition of the property.*

Business Income

business income

***Trade or Business.** The trade or business concept is an amorphous one, generally described as depending on the facts and circumstances of a particular case. A degree of activity in the United States that is regular and continuous, as opposed to one that is sporadic, is generally needed for a finding of trade or business status. Income tax treaties, however, generally exempt from taxation income arising from a U.S. trade or business unless the income is attributable to a U.S. permanent establishment (e.g., a U.S. branch).*

regular and continous degree of activity

attributable

Moreover, the taxpayer's primary purpose for engaging in the activity must be for income or profit. An element also usually considered necessary to a finding of trade or business status is an income-producing transaction, such as a sale. The mere purchase of goods in the United States for sale elsewhere will not ordinarily be viewed as the conduct of a U.S. trade or business. If both the purchase and sale occur in the United States, however, a trade or business would probably be deemed to exist, even if the goods are destined for export.

Deductions

deductions

A foreign corporation generally is entitled to the same types of deductions that are allowable to a domestic corporation. However, in computing taxable income, a foreign corporation is allowed deductions only to the extent that they are connected to income effectively connected with the conduct of a trade or business in the United States.

Credits and deductions are allowable to a corporation only if it files a U.S. corporation income tax return.

tax return

1.1.3. Dispositions of U.S. Real Property Interests

The Foreign Investment in Real Property Tax Act of 1980 (-FIRPTA) treats a foreign person's gain or loss from the disposition of a U.S. real property interest as if such gain or loss were effectively connected with a trade or business. Both nonrecognition relief and treaty relief are limited, and significant withholding requirements are imposed to assist tax collection.

disposition of real property interest

nonrecognition relief
treaty relief
withholding requirements

A U.S. real property interest (USRPI) generally includes any interest in real property located in the United States or in the U.S. Virgin Islands and any interest (other than solely as a creditor) in a domestic corporation that is or was a U.S. real property holding corporation (USRPHC).

1.1.4. Taxation of Foreign Currency Transactions

foreign currency

functional currency

The Tax Reform Act of 1986 provided a comprehensive set of rules for the U.S. tax treatment of transactions involving foreign currency. The act generally adopted the financial accounting concept of functional currency and requires all federal income tax determinations to be made in a taxpayer's functional currency. U.S. corporations and U.S. branches operating in the United States generally have the U.S. dollar as their functional currency. A taxpayer or a qualified business unit with a foreign functional currency must translate its income subject to U.S. tax into U.S. dollars at appropriate exchange rates.

nonfunctional currency

Foreign currency gains and losses attributable to certain transactions in a nonfunctional currency are calculated separately from any gains or losses on the underlying transactions and generally are taxable as ordinary income or losses.

1.1.5. Affiliated Groups

consolidated federal
income tax return

Certain affiliated corporations may elect to file a single, consolidated federal income tax return for all members of the affiliated group instead of filing separate income tax returns for each member. Filing one return for all members of the group is simply a tax computation mechanism and does not convert the group into a single corporation. Each member of the group is jointly and severally liable for the entire tax of the consolidated group.

joint and several
liability

The basic advantages of filing a consolidated return are:

– The ability to apply a member's losses against the income of other members;

– The full exclusion of dividends from member corporations from taxable income; and

– Deferral of tax on income from intercompany transactions.

1.1.6. Relief from Losses

net operating losses
to carry back/forward

Net operating losses of the current year generally may be carried back 3 years and carried forward 15 years. A net operating loss is defined as the excess of the deductions permitted for a taxable year over the gross income of the taxpayer for that year. The net operating loss for the taxable year is carried first to the earliest year to which such loss may be carried and then to each succeeding year, and applied to the extent taxable income exists for each of those years.

carryover

Limits are placed on the use of net operating loss carryovers of corporations after ownership changes resulting from taxable purchases of the corporation's stock and from certain tax-free reorganizations.

Limits are also imposed on the use of net operating losses generated by dual resident corporations.

1.1.7. Tax Credits

tax credits

Domestic and foreign corporations are allowed certain credits, within limits, against their U.S. tax. These credits, unlike deductions, reduce the U.S. tax dollar for dollar. The major credits are:

- *The foreign tax credit, which is allowable within limits for foreign income taxes paid on foreign source income subject to U.S. tax;*

foreign tax credit

- *The targeted jobs credit, which is allowed to employers for certain wages paid to newly hired members of certain disadvantaged groups; and*

targeted jobs credit

- *The research credit, which is allowable for qualifying U.S. research and experimentation expenditures.*

research credit

1.1.8. Additional Taxes

Alternative Minimum Tax

alternative minimum tax

A special 20-percent alternative minimum tax (AMT) on a corporation's alternative minimum taxable income (AMTI), less an exemption amount, is imposed to the extent the tax so calculated exceeds the corporation's regular tax.

AMT
AMTI

Environmental Tax

environmental tax

An environmental tax is imposed on a corporation at 0.12 percent on the excess of its modified AMTI in excess of $ 2,000,000. The tax is one of several sources of funding for the Superfund, used to clean up hazardous wastes that have been released into the environment. The tax applies whether or not the corporation has AMT liability. As a result of the Superfund tax, all large corporations will effectively be forced to compute and maintain AMT records, whether or not they are subject to AMT.

Superfund tax

Accumulated Earnings Tax

accumulated earnings tax, penalty tax

The accumulated earnings tax is a penalty tax imposed on corporations that accumulate earnings with a purpose to avoid taxes on shareholders. It is imposed on the accumulated taxable income at a rate of 39.6 percent of the accumulated taxable income. Accumulated taxable income is defined as taxable income of the corporation with special adjustments and reduced by the current earnings that are retained for the reasonable needs of the business.

accumulated taxable income

Personal Holding Company Tax

personal holding company tax

An additional tax of 39.6 percent is imposed on the undistributed personal holding company income of a personal holding company. This type of company is a domestic or foreign corporation of which more than 50 percent of the value is owned by five or fewer individuals and of which more than 60 percent of the adjusted ordinary gross income is personal holding company income.

229

1.1.9. Allocation of Income and Expenses
Among Related Persons

Internal Revenue Code
arm's-length dealings
IRS (Internal Revenue
System)

Section 482 of the Internal Revenue Code requires arm's-length dealings between related parties. IRS may reallocate gross income, deductions, credits, or allowances among two or more related organizations, trades, or businesses, whether or not organized in the United States, if it determines that such adjustments are necessary to correctly reflect income. Section 482 is applied to transactions between domestic parent corporations and their foreign subsidiaries and to transactions between U.S. subsidiaries and their foreign parents. In addition to general guidance, the tax regulations issued under section 482 contain detailed rules for the appropriate pricing of loans, leases, licenses, services, and sales of goods.

payroll taxes

employment taxes

1.1.10. Payroll Taxes

The federal government imposes several employment taxes on employers. Employers are required to deduct and withhold from the salaries and wages of their employees amounts representing the income taxes of their employees. The appropriate amount to be withheld is determined by reference to tables setting forth the number of pay periods per year, the number of withholding exemptions claimed by the employees, and the amount of wages paid. These amounts are periodically deposited with the federal government. Social Security taxes and unemployment insurance taxes are also imposed on employers. State and local governments also require that their income taxes be withheld from wages.

1.1.11. Special Corporations

Set forth below are a number of special corporations which qualify for certain tax rules and advantages:

FSCs

Foreign Sales Corporations (FSCs)

Domestic corporations with an active business of exporting their products to foreign countries may find it advantageous to form a FSC for their export activity. A FSC is a foreign corporation that generally derives substantially all of its income from exporting U.S. goods. The benefit of a FSC is that a portion of its income is exempt from U.S. tax when earned.

DISCs

Domestic International Sales Corporations (DISCs)

deferral

As an alternative to an FSC, a small exporter may use a DISC, which permits a deferral of tax on substantially all DISC income. This deferral is available with respect to annual gross export receipts up to $ 10 million. These DISCs are called interest-charge DISCs because the DISC shareholders are required to pay an interest charge, annually, on their tax that has been deferred due to the deferral of the DISC income.

S Corporations

An S corporation is a domestic corporation that elects to be taxed generally as if it were a partnership. The income, deductions, and credits flow through and are treated as such to the shareholders. An S corporation must have 35 or fewer shareholders, all of whom generally must be U.S. citizens or resident alien individuals.

S Corporations

1.2. Indirect Taxation

indirect taxation

1.2.1. Federal Excise Taxes

federal excise taxes

The federal government imposes excise taxes on the manufacture or sale of numerous goods and services in the United States. The producer, seller, or importer of these products generally must collect and remit the applicable taxes to the federal government. These taxes fall into several categories, e.g. gasoline, tires and tubes, coal, air transportation, foreign insurers, luxury tax etc.

1.2.2. State and Local Indirect Taxes

indirect taxes

Property Taxes

Real estate and personal property taxes are imposed by state and local governments. Property is periodically assessed by the relevant government, and the tax is based on the assessed valuation and the applicable tax rate.

real estate taxes, personal property taxes

Sales and Use Taxes

sales taxes, use taxes

Sales taxes are imposed by most states and by some local governments on goods sold at the ultimate consumer level. These taxes are based on a percentage of the selling price, collected by the seller and remitted by the seller to the appropriate state government. Use taxes are imposed on property purchased outside the taxing state and brought into the taxing state for use inside the taxing states.

taxing state

Motor Vehicle Taxes

motor vehicle taxes

States levy taxes on the licensing of motor vehicles inside their borders. These taxes are imposed annually.

Other Taxes

State and local governments collect a number of other taxes, including taxes on special commodities (alcohol, tobacco, motor fuel), fees for business and professional licenses, and taxes on special types of businesses, such as banking or insurance.

1.3. Taxation of Individuals

residents

1.3.1. Taxable Income of Residents

subject to income tax

Foreign citizens who are U.S. resident aliens generally are taxed in the same manner as U.S. citizens; that is, their worldwide income is subject to U.S. income tax.

gross income

Gross Income

The gross income of citizens and resident aliens generally comprises income from all sources, including wages and salaries, interest, dividends, business profits, income from partnerships, annuities, premiums, and gains from the sale of property. Certain items are excluded from gross income, including gifts, proceeds from life insurance policies, inheritances, certain scholarships, and qualifying state or municipal bond interest.

deductions

Deductions

tax base

Deductions are provided for a variety of expenses, both to provide a tax base that more accurately depicts an individual's disposable income and to encourage expenditures that further certain legislatively determined social and economic goals. Deductions are divided into two categories – those allowed in computing adjusted gross income and those called itemized deductions.

tax rate schedules

Tax Rate Schedules

After all deductions and personal exemptions are taken to determine taxable income, the appropriate tax rate schedule is applied to compute tax liability. The four tax rate schedules are for:

– Married individuals (and surviving spouses) filing joint returns;

– Heads of households;

– Single persons; and

– Married persons filing separate returns.

tax burden

Use of the appropriate rate schedule is important because the tax burden on any given taxable income amount increases from the first to the last schedule listed. A joint return by a married couple offers the lowest tax rate and is permitted even if only one spouse had any income.

graduated marginal rates

The tax rates are graduated marginal rates ranging from 15 percent to 39,6 percent.

nonresident aliens

1.3.2. Taxable Income of Nonresident Aliens

segregated income

Segregrated Income

Nonresident aliens are taxable on their U.S. source fixed and determinable income that is not effectively connected with a U.S. trade or business at a flat rate of 30 percent (or lower treaty rate).

Additionally, nonresident alien individuals are taxed at graduated rates on their effectively connected income and generally are allowed deductions only to the extent they are connected to this effectively connected business income. Certain deductions are allowed in all cases.

Nonresident Alien's Capital Gains Excluding Real Estate   capital gains

If a nonresident alien is physically present in the United States for 183 days or more during a taxable year, U.S. source gains from the sale or exchange during the year of capital assets, excluding U.S. real property interests, in excess of capital losses allocable to U.S. sources are taxable at a 30-percent rate, provided that such gains or losses are not U.S. effectively connected business income.

1.3.3. Estate and Gift Taxes   estate and gift taxes

The United States has a unified gift and estate tax system that applies to taxable gifts of property made by an individual during life and taxable bequests made at death.

One system of estate and gift taxation applies to U.S. citizens and foreign citizens domiciled in the United States. A separate system applies to foreign citizens who are not domiciled in the United States.

233

2. UNITED KINGDOM

2.1. Business Taxation

2.1.1. Corporations

partial imputation system

The corporation tax system in force in the UK is a partial imputation system, the basic principles of which are as follows.

single rate

– A company pays corporation tax at a single rate (currently 33 percent) on all its profits, whether income or capital gains, and whether distributed or undistributed.

small companies rate

marginal relief

– A reduced "small companies' rate" (currently 25 percent) is payable where total profits are £ 250,000 or less, and marginal relief is available where profits are up to £ 1,250,000. These limits are reduced where there are other associated companies (including overseas companies).

– Income tax is not deducted from dividends (except for deductions from payments to non-residents). Interest, royalties and other annual payments may, however, be subject to deduction of income tax at source at the basic rate.

advance corporation tax

– A company paying a dividend is required to account to the Inland Revenue for advance corporation tax (ACT) thereon at a certain rate. The dividend plus the related ACT is referred to as a "franked payment".

to set off against

– ACT in respect of dividends paid during an accounting period (irrespective of the year for which they are declared) may be set off against the company's corporation tax liability for that accounting period, and may also be carried back to other periods beginning within the previous six years, or carried forward without time limit.

– A dividend on which ACT has been paid generally carries a tax credit equal to the amount of the ACT. The receipt of such a payment gives rise to no further tax liability on a UK resident company (and may reduce its own ACT liability). For basic-rate taxpayers the income tax charge is at 20 percent on the aggregate of the dividend and the tax credit (rather than the usual basic rate of 25 percent) and this liability is covered by the tax credit. Individuals taxable at the higher (40 percent) rate have to pay an additional 20 percent (i.e., 40 percent less 20 percent).

chargeable periods

Chargeable periods

Corporation tax is charged on profits arising in a financial year (1 April to the following 31 March) at the rate applicable to that year. Companies are assessed by reference to accounting periods, which are normally the same as those for which they make up their statutory accounts.

Residence

The term "resident" in relation to a company is not defined by statute but its meaning has evolved from a number of court decisions. Broadly, a company is resident where its central management and control (as opposed to day-to-day administration) is exercised. A company which is incorporated in the UK is also regarded as UK resident, irrespective of where it is controlled.

A company which is resident in the UK is chargeable to corporation tax in respect of all its profits (both income and capital gains) wherever arising, whether or not remitted to the UK.

corporation tax

A company not resident here, but which carries on a trade in this country through a branch, is chargeable to corporation tax in respect of:

– trading income directly or indirectly attributable to the branch. (Where applicable this will be the business profits attributable to the UK "permanent establishment" under a double tax treaty);

trading income

– income from property or rights used or held by the branch;

income from property

– capital gains arising on the disposal of assets in the UK which are used for the purpose of the trade, or acquired or held for the purposes of the branch.

capital gains

A company not resident in the UK may be chargeable to income tax on its other UK source income – ie., income not attributable to a UK branch.

It may be possible to establish a local office in the UK without creating a taxable branch. Such a "representative office" would deal with a limited range of activities, such as advertising and promotion, or the purchase of goods and services. It would not be able to negotiate and conclude sales contracts.

2.1.2. Taxation of non-corporate entities

non-corporate entities

Unincorporated associations, such as members' clubs, are subject to corporation tax in the same way as companies.

unincorporated associations

By contrast, profits made by partnerships of individuals are subject to income tax and capital gains tax, as appropriate. The amounts concerned are apportioned among the partners and the tax liability determined according to their individual circumstances. In the case of trading or professional profits, however, the tax thus found to be due is collected by means of a global assessment on the partnership and the partners have joint and several liability for the sum concerned.

to apportion

trading profits, professional profits, global assessment

Special rules apply to partnerships which have companies among their members; broadly, the effect is that company partners are charged corporation tax on their share of any profits.

2.1.3. Taxation of profits and gains

The computation of profits for tax purposes is based on the results shown by the audited annual accounts, adjusted in accordance with the tax legislation. Some of the more important adjustments are considered below.

audited annual
accounts
adjustments

tax relief for expenses

— ***Expenses*** *Tax relief is not available to a trading company for expenses which are not wholly and exclusively incurred for the purposes of its trade; in the case of an investment or holding company, relief is given for managment expenses properly incurred. Capital expenses are not deductible in computing trading profits (but allowances may be available).*

capital expenses

business entertainment
expenditure

— ***Business entertainment*** *Expenditure on business entertainment ist not allowable.*

pre-trading expenditure

— ***Pre-trading expenditure*** *No relief is available for revenue expenditure incurred by a trading company more than seven years before it commenced trading.*

depreciation charge

The depreciation charge appearing in a company's accounts is not allowed for tax purposes. Instead reliefs known as "capital allowances" are given for expenditure on a wide range of assets.

deduction for interest

Deduction for interest. In the case of a trading company, short interest (ie, broadly, interest on debts intended to be outstanding for less than a year) and interest payable to a bank carrying on business in the UK are deductible as trading expenses.

trading expenses

Certain types of interest other than that paid to a bank in the UK are not deductible as a trading expense and are treated either as a charge on income or in the same way as dividends.

2.1.4. Groups and consortia

UK companies within the same group (consisting of a parent and its 51 percent subsidiaries) may elect not to pay ACT in respect of intra-group dividends. Any income received in this way is referred to as "group income" and, while not taxable, may not be set off against franked payments in the same way as franked investment income to reduce the recipient's own ACT liability. Group companies may similarly elect not to deduct income tax at source from annual payments.

group income

group relief

Trading losses, excess management expenses of an investment company, and excess charges on income may be transferred from one company to another, by way of "group relief", where both are members of a group (consisting of a parent and its 75 percent subsidiaries).

losses

2.1.5. Losses

A company which sustains a trading loss (as adjusted for tax purposes) may carry it forward without time limit, to set against profits of the same trade in future periods. Alternatively, it may be set against other income (for example, investment income) and capital gains of the same accounting period or, subject to certain limitations, against income and gains of the preceding three years, taking later periods first.

As a result of anti-avoidance legislation, trading losses carried forward may not always be available for relief against profits after a substantial change in ownership of the company's share capital.

anti-avoidance legislation

Trading losses carried forward may not be set against future capital gains. Capital losses may be set against capital gains realised in the same or a subsequent accounting period, but may not be carried back or set against trading profits.

2.1.6. Capital gains

Chargeable gains are calculated by deducting the cost of the asset, together with any enhancement expenditure or incidental costs of disposal, from the gross proceeds of sale. Special rules apply to assets acquired before March 31, 1982.

to deduct the cost from the gross proceeds of sale

Relief for inflationary gains is given in the form of an "indexation allowance", which is calculated by applying the movement in the Retail Prices Index during the period of ownership (excluding any part of that period before March 31, 1982) to the cost or March 1982 value, whichever is the higher. If a "global" election has been made for the use of the March 1982 value in the calculation of the gain itself, the indexation allowance is computed on the same basis.

relief for inflationary gains, indexation allowance

2.1.7. Relief for foreign taxes

A company resident in the UK may claim credit for foreign tax which it has suffered on income from any overseas source, against the UK corporation tax payable on that income. In the case of dividends received by a UK company holding at least 10 percent of the voting power in the overseas company, it will also be entitled to a credit for the "underlying" tax – ie, the relevant proportion of the tax paid by the overseas company on the profits out of which the dividend is declared. Credit may also be claimed for foreign tax paid on capital gains against the UK corporation tax payable on those gains.

credit for foreign tax

2.1.8. Transfer pricing

The Inland Revenue has the power to adjust, for taxation purposes, the prices at which transactions are carried out between a UK resident company and its non-resident associated companies, to ensure that the taxable profit reflects those transactions on the basis of arm's length prices. A company is "associated" with another for this purpose where one controls the other, or both are under common control. The power to make adjustments applies

Inland Revenue

not only to purchases and sales of goods, but to rental and hire payments, transfers of other assets, and the giving of any business facility.

withholding taxes

2.1.9. Withholding taxes

Income tax at the basic rate must be withheld from payments such as royalties, annual interest (except where paid to a bank in the UK) and, where the recipient is not a UK resident, payments of rent. In certain circumstances the terms of a relevant double taxation treaty may reduce or extinguish the liability to basic tax rate, in which case a repayment claim may be made or, with prior clearance from the UK Inspector of Foreign Dividends, relief may be given at source. There is no withholding tax on management fees.

double taxation treaty

2.2. Indirect Taxation

indirect taxes

The principal indirect taxes affecting businesses in the UK are import duties, value added tax (VAT), excise duties, vehicle excise duty and stamp duty.

VAT

Value added tax (VAT)

VAT is charged on a wide range of goods and services when supplied in the UK and also on the importation of taxable goods from outside the EC. It is a general consumer expenditure tax of which the basic principle is to charge tax at each stage in the production of goods and services, with each supplier receiving credit for the tax he has paid so that the total tax is actually borne by the final consumer. The standard rate of VAT is 17.5 percent. The exceptions to VAT take the form of either zero rated or exempt supplies.

2.3. Taxation of individuals

2.3.1. Taxable Income

Residence and domicile

Three principal factors are relevant in determining an individual's liability to UK tax: residence, ordinary residence and domicile.

resident

Broadly, an individual is deemed to be resident in the UK for a tax year (6 April to 5 April following) if:

– s/he is physically present in the UK for 183 days or more in the year; or

– s/he visits the UK year after year and the annual visits average 91 days or more a year for at least four consecutive years.

Ordinary residence means, broadly, habitual residence, and depends as much on intention as on physical presence.

238

A person's place of domicile is, in very general terms, the place that he or she regards as his/her permanent homeland – ie, the place to which, wherever his/her present residence may be, s/he intends eventually to return.

place of domicile

Generally, UK-resident individuals are liable to tax on all income or gains regardless of the location of the source. Individuals who are UK-resident but not UK-domiciled are, in most cases, liable to UK tax on income or gains derived from an overseas source only to the extent that the income or gain is remitted to the UK. Non-residents are generally liable to UK tax only in respect of UK source income; in the case of income from employment they are only liable to UK tax to the extent that the earnings are for duties carried out in the UK. Interest and penalties can be imposed for late payment of tax or non-declaration of income or gains.

Married persons are treated separately for tax purposes.

Individuals may be liable to inheritance tax on certain gifts made during their lifetime and on the value of their estate on death.

inheritance tax

There are three rates of income tax:

income tax rates

Lower rate: *20 percent on taxable income up to a certain amount*

Basic rate: *25 percent on taxable income between certain amounts*

Higher rate: *40 percent on taxable income over a certain amount*

The tax rates do not vary between UK-resident and non-resident individuals or between one source of income and another.

Capital gains are charged to tax as the top slice of an individual's income.

All individuals are entitled to a personal allowance for income tax purposes, the amount of which may be related to the age of the individual. This is deductible from income in computing the taxable amount.

Taxable income includes earnings from employment, income from self employment, income from real property, interest and dividends, pensions and annuities.

Deductions

Generally expenses are deductible against the different types of income provided they were incurred wholly and exclusively for the purposes of the specific income.

2.3.2. Taxation of capital gains

capital gains tax (CGT)

chargeable gains on disposals of assets

An individual who is UK-domiciled and UK-resident or ordinarily resident for a tax year is liable to capital gains tax (CGT) in respect of chargeable gains on disposals of assets during the year wherever situated.

An individual who is UK-resident or ordinarily resident but not UK-domiciled is liable to CGT on gains arising in the UK, but gains arising from the disposal of assets situated abroad are liable to CGT only to the extent that those gains are remitted here.

An individual who is neither UK-resident nor ordinarily resident but who exercises a trade, profession or vocation in the UK through a branch or agency is liable to capital gains tax in respect of chargeable gains arising on the disposal of assets situated in the UK and used or held for the purpose of the trade, profession or vocation.

2.3.3. Inheritance tax

The liability to tax

Inheritance tax is, in broad terms, a tax on certain gifts made by an individual during his/her lifetime and on the value of his/her estate on death. Individuals domiciled in the UK are liable on assets wherever situated, but individuals not domiciled in the UK are liable to inheritance tax only in respect of assets situated in the UK.

Transfers between husband and wife are generally exempt. A number of other exemptions and reliefs are available which limit and reduce the impact of the tax.

3. AUSTRIA

3.1. Business Taxation

3.1.1. Corporations

Stock companies and GmbH-companies are subject to corporate income tax (Körperschaftsteuer). Partnerships as such are not taxable entities for corporate income tax purposes; partners are liable to personal income tax on their share of the partnership's profit.

AG und GmbH
Körperschaftsteuer

Einkommensteuer

Corporations resident in Austria are subject to corporate income tax on their world-wide income (unlimited tax liability). Non-resident companies are only taxable with their income from sources in Austria (limited tax liability), including business income derived through a permanent establishment or a permanent representative (as defined in the respective double taxation agreements), income from agriculture and forestry, income from immovable property located in Austria and certain other types of income on which tax is withheld at source.

unbeschränkte Steuerpflicht

beschränkte Steuerpflicht

Corporations are considered resident in Austria if they have their legal seats in Austria or if the effective management is carried out in Austria.

Sitz

All the proceeds drawn by a corporation fall into the category "business income" and the total taxable income is taxed at a uniform rate of 34 percent. Resident legal entities have to pay a minimum corporate income tax of ATS 50.000 per annum. This payment may be credited against the corporate income tax liability of the assessment period or of subsequent years.

Non-resident corporations are subject to corporate income tax on their Austrian income either by way of annual assessment (e.g., if they have a permanent establishment or immovable property located in Austria) or by way of deduction at source.

In the case of an Austrian branch of a foreign corporation, the profit attributable to the branch is subject to corporate income tax at the standard rate. Reasonable portions of head office expenses may be deducted from the profit of the branch.

The taxable income is determined on the basis of the results shown in the annual financial statements with adjustments to comply with specific fiscal provisions.

All assets have to be valued as of the end of the fiscal year. Valuation is based on purchase or production cost, less depreciation, if applicable, or lower market value.

Tangible fixed assets are subject to depreciation on cost with only the straight-line method being accepted for tax purposes.

Intangible fixed assets must be capitalized only if acquired for consideration, and are to be amortized over their useful lives. For tax purposes, however, goodwill acquired is considered an asset amortizable over a useful life of 15 years. Self-developed intangible assets must not be capitalized.

Capital gains are treated as ordinary income and taxed at standard rates.

Inventories are valued at the lower of cost or market with cost usually determined following the weighted average or first-in-first-out (FIFO) method.

Accruals and allowances on receivables are only tax deductible if they can be substantiated on a case by case basis with the proviso that there is an adequate degree of certainty and that the liability or loss was actually incurred. General accruals or allowances taken on a lump-sum basis at flat rates are no longer deductible.

Special rules are applied to the calculation of accruals for severance payments and pension accruals.

Special tax incentives exist for investments (investment allowance).

Disallowed expenses are improper payments (such as bribe money), charitable donations, gifts to non-employees, entertainment expenses, expenses incurred in connection with non-taxable income, 50 percent of the emoluments to the members of the supervisory board and corporate income tax itself, including prior year items.

Gesellschaftereinlagen
Sanierungsgewinne

Contributions of the shareholders and gains from the cancellation of debts by creditors meant to restore the financial position of the corporation (Gesellschaftereinlagen, Sanierungsgewinne) are tax-exempt income.

3.1.2. Relief from Losses

Losses may be carried forward indefinitely provided that proper books and records are maintained. This applies both to Austrian enterprises and, under certain circumstances, also to Austrian branches of foreign enterprises. A carry back of losses is not permissible in Austria.

3.1.3. Affiliated Groups of Companies
(fiscal unit – "Organschaft")

Organschaft

A business enterprise may control another completely, viz. financially, economically and organizationally, so that the dependent enterprise has no freedom of decision and, in fact, constitutes merely an operating division of the controlling enterprise. If both the controlling parent corporation and the controlled subsidiary are resident corporations and, moreover, have entered into an agreement under which the controlled enterprise commits to transfer its entire profits to the controlling enterprise and the controlling enterprise commits to assume the entire losses of the controlled enterprise, the profit (loss) of such controlled enterprise as computed for corporate income tax purposes shall be attributed to the controlling enterprise.

242

3.1.4. Participation Privilege ("Schachtelbegünstigung")

National participation privilege:

Under this privilege any dividends received by Austrian (resident) companies from Austrian (resident) companies remain exempt from corporate income tax with the recipient. Capital gains realized on the sale of holdings in Austrian (resident) companies remain fully taxable at standard rate.

International participation privilege:

Special rules are applied to the tax exemption of dividends paid by foreign (non-resident) companies to resident companies as well as to capital gains yielded from foreign companies.

3.1.5. Withholding Tax on Dividends and Interest

The withholding tax amounts to 25 percent and is applicable to certain capital yields derived in Austria from domestic capital (e.g. dividends, capital yields from securities representing money claims, interest income from cash deposits with banks).

Corporate recipients residing in Austria have to gross up the (exceptionally taxable) dividend or interest received. In case the income tax was withheld, this tax withheld is treated as a tax prepayment and credited against the assessed (corporate) income tax liability. Non-resident recipients of investment income subject to Austrian withholding tax are usually entitled to credit at least part of this withholding tax against their foreign tax liability subject to the provisions of the respective double tax treaty. For non-residents, the withholding tax is a final levy for Austrian taxation purposes, unless the income is received by an Austrian permanent establishment of the non-resident.

3.2. Indirect Taxation

The principal indirect taxes affecting business in Austria are value added tax (VAT), import duties, real estate transfer tax, capital transfer tax, stock exchange turnover tax, insurance tax, stamp tax on bills of exchange, dues.

Value added tax (VAT)

In principle, value added tax (VAT) is neither an expense nor an income item to most businesses. Subject to exceptions input tax paid to suppliers is recoverable from the fiscal authorities and tax collected from customers is payable to such authorities.

The standard rate is 20 percent.

VAT covers any entrepreneur (sole traders, partnerships, companies etc) who independently carries out supplies and renders services within the domestic territory for a consideration within the scope of this enterprise regardless of nationality or residence.

The taxable transactions comprise the supply of goods, the performance of services (transport, repair and maintenance, professional services, advertising, etc), the importation of goods from a non-EU territory into Austria (VAT is chargeable on imports irrespective of whether the importer is a taxable person or not), withdrawal of goods for non-business purposes if the goods gave rise to a refund of input VAT and use of services for non-business purposes.

*Exempted are, **inter alia**, most of banking and insurance services, leases of land and buildings to entrepreneurs (however, an option for taxation combined with input tax refund is available) and small entrepreneurs with a turnover not exceeding ATS 300,000 in the assessment period.*

*Zero-rated are, **inter alia,***

– supply of goods into non-EU territories (export)

– contract improvements for foreign principals if the goods are subsequently transported to non-EU territories

– transportation of goods in transports across the border and in international railroad freight traffic

– transportation of persons by ships and aircraft in transports across the border

– supply of goods to an entrepreneur located within the EU territory if he is entitled to claim input VAT for refund.

*Special rules apply to **Intra-Community Trade**.*

Real Estate Transfer Tax

A real estate transfer tax at a rate of 3.5 percent on the consideration is due if title to real property situated in Austria is transferred. This rate also applies, however, to twice the assessed value, if within the course of reorganizations, such as mergers etc., title to real estate is transferred. The tax is also due if all shares in a company which owns real estate are joined in one owner.

Capital Transfer Tax

The capital transfer tax is generally imposed at a rate of 1 percent on certain capital contributions, e.g. the initial acquisition of shares in an Austrian company, certain contractual or voluntary contributions in cash or in kind.

3.3. Taxation of individuals

3.3.1. Taxable Income of Residents

unbeschränkte
Steuerpflicht

Individuals residing in Austria are, in prinicple, subject to Austrian income tax based on their world-wide income (unlimited tax liability; unbeschränkte Steuerpflicht), whereas non-residents are subject to Austrian income tax only on certain categories of income from Austrian sources (limited tax liability; beschränkte Steuerpflicht).

A resident individual is one whose domicile or customary place of abode is in Austria. The existence of either factor is sufficient to establish the residence of an individual.

Residents are subject to income tax on their world-wide income drawn from the following seven sources:

– Agriculture and forestry
– Trade or business, including gains on the sale of a business or partnership share
– Independent personal services; typically professional activities
– Employment; e.g. wages and salaries, social security pensions
– Investment of capital; e.g. dividends, interest, profit shares of dormant partners
– Rentals and royalties
– Other income specified in the individual Income Tax Act; e.g. certain recurring income; gains on so-called speculative transactions, gains on sale of holdings of more than 10 percent in stock companies and GmbH-companies.

Income which does not fall within one of the seven categories is not taxable; e.g. capital gains in the private sphere. There exist tax exemptions for certain kinds of income e.g. various fringe benefits up to certain limits, certain overtime payments (to a very restricted extent), and others.

Resident taxpayers are taxed on their world-wide income from the above seven categories of income unless certain foreign income is exempt under tax treaties.

Net income from agriculture and forestry, from trade or business, and from independent occupations is called profit; it is determined by deducting business expenses (Betriebsausgaben) from gross income. The accrual method is mandatory if turnover exceeds ATS 5 million (in the case of grocery retailing and general merchandise stores ATS 8 million). Losses incurred in these categories may be carried forward as set out above, provided that proper books and records are maintained.

Net income from the other categories is determined by deducting from gross income any expenses that are incurred to acquire, safeguard and maintain this income (income-related expenses; Werbungskosten).

The taxable income can be reduced by the following items if certain criteria are met:

Special personal expenses not related to income of a particular source (Sonderausgaben). They include premiums to voluntary health, accident and life insurances; payments incurred to finance private house building and improvement; purchase of newly issued shares or profit-sharing certificates.

außergewöhnliche
Belastungen

Extraordinary expenses (außergewöhnliche Belastungen) neces-sarily incurred by a taxpayer due to extraordinary circumstances may be deducted from taxable income.

Taxable income is taxed at graduated marginal rates ranging from 10 percent to 50 percent.

Certain deductions from the income tax due are available to resident taxpayers.

3.3.2. Taxable Income of Non-Residents

Non-residents are subject to income tax on the following categories of income only derived from Austrian sources:

- *Domestic agriculture and forestry*
- *Trade or business carried out through a permanent establishment or a permanent representative in Austria*
- *Independent personal services performed or used in Austria*
- *Employment if the activities are performed or used in Austria*
- *Capital yields such as dividends and other earnings from Austrian stock companies and private GmbH-companies, similar earnings from participation rights, earnings from a dormant partnership, interest on loans secured by mortgages on real estate located in Austria*
- *Rentals and royalties if the real estate is located, or the patents etc are utilized in Austria*
- *Speculative transactions referring to Austrian real estate*
- *Gain on the sale of interests (at least 10 percent) held in Austrian stock companies and private GmbH-companies.*

Where income tax is assessed, income or business related expenses are only deductible to the extent that they are economically related to the respective Austrian source income. Losses from one category of income may only be offset against profits from another if both categories are subject to tax through assessment rather

Sonderausgaben

than withholding. Special personal expenses (Sonderausgaben) are only deductible if incurred in relation to circumstances which are positioned in Austria.

3.3.3. Capital Gains

For business enterprises, a gain on the sale of business assets is generally included in taxable income and taxed at ordinary rates. Where sales of fixed assets result in capital gains, tax may be deferred by offsetting gains against the cost of other fixed assets acquired within a certain period following the date of sale (rollover relief).

However, a gain on the sale by an individual of his/her entire business or an independent division thereof, or a partnership interest, is taxed only at half of the standard income tax rate if the enterprise or the partnership interest has been held for at least 7 years.

In Austria, individuals are generally not taxed on gains from the sale or other disposition of non-business property, except in certain cases.

3.3.4. Inheritance and Gift Tax

*Inheritance and gift tax (**Erbschafts- und Schenkungssteuer**) is imposed on gratuitous transfer of property by reason of death or of gifts during lifetime.*

Erbschafts- und
Schenkungssteuer

The tax rates range from 2 percent to 60 percent, depending on the relationship of the deceased/donor to the beneficiary.

TAX LAW TERMINOLOGY

TERMINOLOGIE ZUM STEUER-RECHT

abatement of tax	Steuernachlaß
Accelerated Cost Recovery System (ACRS) (US)	Möglichkeit einer beschleunigten vorzeitigen Abschreibung über das wirtschaftliche Erfordernis
accounting methods	Rechnungslegungsmethoden
accruals	Rückstellungen
accrual method	periodengerechte Abgrenzung
accrue	auflaufen, anfallen, rückstellen
accumulated earnings tax (US)	Zusatzsteuer auf nicht ausgeschüttete Gewinne
ACRS (Accelerated Cost Recovery System) (US)	Möglichkeit einer beschleunigten vorzeitigen Abschreibung über das wirtschaftliche Erfordernis
ACT (advance corporation tax) (UK)	spezielle Form der Kapitalertragssteuer
adjustments	Anpassungen
Advance Corporation Tax (ACT) (UK)	spezielle Form der Kapitalertragssteuer
affiliated group (US)	Konzern
allowable credits	anrechenbare Steuern
allowable deductions	steuerliche Abzugsposten
allowances	Steuerfreibeträge, Abzugsposten
alternative minimum tax (AMT) (US)	alternative Mindestkörperschaftssteuer
alternative minimum taxable income (AMTI) (US)	Bemessungsgrundlage der alternativen Mindestkörperschaftssteuer
amortise	amortisieren, tilgen, abschreiben
annual assessment	jährliche Veranlagung
annual financial statement	Jahresabschluß
annuity	Rente, Rate
anti-avoidance legislation	Gesetzgebung gegen Steuervermeidung
arm's length prices	Preise im Rahmen des Fremdvergleichs
arm's-length dealings (US)	Fremdvergleich
assess	(steuerlich) veranlagen
assessed valuation (US)	steuerliche Vermögensbewertung
assessment	steuerliche Veranlagung
assessment notice	Steuerbescheid
assets	Vermögen(swerte), Aktiva
at source	an der Quelle
audited annual accounts	geprüfter Jahresabschluß
basic rate	Normalsteuersatz
benefit(s)	Steuervorteil(e), Steuerentlastung, Steuererleichterung, Steuervergütung
Board of Customs and Excise (UK)	oberste brit. Finanzbehörde für Zölle/Verbrauchssteuern
Board of Inland Revenue (UK)	oberste brit. Finanzbehörde für direkte Steuern
branch profits tax	Betriebsstättensteuer

business expenses	Betriebsausgaben (A)
business income (US)	unternehmerisches Einkommen*
capital allowances (UK)	steuerliche Abzugsposten*
capital gains tax (CGT) (UK)	Kapitalgewinnsteuer
capital transfer tax	Kapitalverkehrsteuer
capitalise	aktivieren
carry over	vortragen
carryback (US)	Rücktrag
carryover	Vortrag
cash receipts and disbursement method	Einnahmen- und Ausgabenmethode
CGT (capital gains tax) (UK)	Kapitalgewinnsteuer
Chancellor of the Exchequer (UK)	brit. Finanzminister
chargeable to	zurechenbar zu
charitable deduction	abzugsfähige Spende
consideration	Gegenleistung
consolidated	konsolidiert
consortia	Konsortien
consumer expenditure tax	Verbrauchsteuer
consumption tax (US)	Verbrauchsteuer (US)
contributions of shareholders	Übersetzung für: Gesellschaftereinlagen/ -zuschüsse (A/D)
coporate income tax	Körperschaftsteuer
corporate earnings	Unternehmensgewinn*
corporate profits	Unternehmensgewinn*
corporation tax	Körperschaftsteuer
current assets	Umlaufvermögen
customary place of abode	gewöhnlicher Aufenthaltsort
customs duty	Zoll(abgabe)
death duty	Erbschaftssteuer
deductible	steuerlich abzugsfähig
deduction	Absetzung, Abzug
deduction at source	Quellenabzug, Quellenbesteuerung
deferral of tax	Verlagerung der Steuerpflicht
Department of the Treasury (US)	US-Finanzministerium
depreciation	Abschreibung
depreciation charge	Abschreibungsaufwand
direct tax	direkte Steuer
disallowed	nicht abzugsfähig
DISC (domestic international sales corporation) (US)	steuerbegünstigtes Exportunternehmen
dividends-received deduction (US)	Dividendenzuflüsse steuerbefreit von der Bundeseinkommensteuer
domestic international sales corporations (DISCs) (US)	steuerbegünstigte Ausfuhrtochter- gesellschaft
domicile	Wohnsitz (mehr als residence)
dormant partner	stiller Gesellschafter
double tax treaty	Doppelbesteuerungsabkommen
double taxation treaty	Doppelbesteuerungsabkommen
due date	Fälligkeitstermin
duty	Abgabe

250

emoluments	Vergütungen
employment taxes (US)	lohn- und gehaltsbezogene Abgaben
entertainment expenses	Bewirtungskosten
environmental tax (US)	Umweltschutzsteuer
estate	Nachlaß, Verlassenschaft
estate duty (UK)	Erbschaftssteuer (UK bis 1975)
exchange rate	Wechselkurs
excise duty	Verbrauchssteuer
excise tax (US)	Verbrauch- und Aufwandsteuern
expenditure	Ausgaben
expenses	Spesen
extraordinary expenses	außergewöhnliche Belastungen (A)
FDAP (fixed or determinable annual or periodical income)	steuerpflichtige sonstige Einkünfte*
federal excise tax (US)	Bundes-Verbrauch- und Aufwandsteuern
FICA (Federal Insurance Contribution Act) tax (US)	Bundes-Sozialversicherungsbeitrag (US)
file one's tax return	Steuererklärung abgeben/einreichen
FIRPTA (Foreign Investment in Real Property Tax Act of 1980) (US)	US-Gesetz über ausländische Investitionen in Immobilien
first-in-first-out (FIFO) method	Fifo-Methode
fiscal provisions	steuerliche Bestimmungen
fiscal unit	Übersetzung für: Organschaft (A)
fixed assets	Anlagevermögen
flat rate	Einheitssatz
for financial reporting purposes	zu Berichtszwecken in Abschlüssen
foreign currency	Fremdwährung
Foreign Investment in Real Property Tax Act (FIRPTA) (US)	US-Gesetz über ausländische Investitionen in Immobilien
foreign sales corporations (FSCs) (US)	Exportgesellschaft
foreign tax credit	Anrechnung ausländischer Steuern
foreign taxes	ausländische Steuern
franked investment income	körperschaftsteuerfreie Kapitalerträge
franked payment	nach Steuerabzug geleistete Zahlungen
free of tax	steuerfrei
FSC (foreign sales corporation) (US)	Exportgesellschaft
functional currency	maßgebende Währung
FUTA (Federal Unemployment Tax Act) tax (US)	Bundesgesetz über Arbeitslosen- versicherungsbeitrag (US)
gains from the cancellation of debts by creditors meant to restore the financial position of the corporation	Übersetzung für: Sanierungsgewinne (A/D)
gift and estate tax	Schenkungs- und Erbschaftsteuer (US)
gift tax	Schenkungssteuer
global assessment	Veranlagung der Welteinkünfte*
goodwill	Firmenwert
graduated marginal rates	abgestufte Grenzsteuersätze
graduated rates	abgestufte Steuersätze
gratuitous transfer	unentgeltliche Übertragung

251

gross income	Bruttoeinkommen, Bruttogewinn (US)
gross receipts	Bruttoeinnahmen
gross up	Hochrechnung
group	Konzern
group companies	Konzerngesellschaften
group relief	Konzernbegünstigung
H.M. Customs (UK)	Zollbehörde Ihrer Majestät
immovable property	unbewegliches Vermögen
import duties	Einfuhrzölle
import duty	Einfuhrzoll, Importzoll
income	Einkommen
income tax	Einkommensteuer
income-related expenses	Werbungskosten (A)
indexation allowance	Scheingewinnentsteuerung*
indirect tax	indirekte Steuer
indirect taxation	indirekte Besteuerung
inflationary gains	Scheingewinne
inheritance tax	Erbschaftsteuer
Inland Revenue (UK)	brit. Finanzverwaltung
input tax	Vorsteuer
input tax refund	Vorsteuerrückvergütung
input VAT	Vorsteuer
insurance tax	Versicherungsteuer
intangible fixed assets	immaterielles Anlagevermögen
interest	Zinsen
interest charge	Zinsaufwand
Internal Revenue Code (US)	einheitliches Steuergesetz der USA
Internal Revenue Service (IRS) (US)	US-Bundessteuerbehörde
investment allowance	Investitionsfreibetrag
IRC (Internal Revenue Code) (US)	einheitliches Steuergesetz der USA
IRS (Internal Revenue Service) (US)	US-Bundessteuerbehörde
land tax	Grundsteuer (US)
legal seat*	Übersetzung für: Sitz
levy	Gebühr
levy tax	Steuer erheben/einheben
lifetime transfer	Schenkung zu Lebzeiten
local taxes	kommunale Steuern
lower market value	niedrigerer Marktwert
lump-sum basis	Pauschalbasis
maintain books and records	Bücher und sonstige Aufzeichnungen führen
marginal relief	ermäßigter Steuersatz für geringe Einkommen
methods of valuation	Bewertungsmethoden, Bewertungsregeln
motor vehicle licence duty (UK)	KFZ-Steuer (UK)
motor vehicle tax	KFZ-Steuer
moving-average basis	Gleitendes Durchschnittspreisverfahren

National Insurance Contributions (NIC) (UK)	Sozialversicherungsbeiträge (UK)
net operating loss	Verlust aus laufender Geschäftstätigkeit
net profit	Jahresgewinn
net trading loss (UK)	Nettobetriebsverlust
non-declaration	Nichtangabe
nonfunctional currency	Fremdwährung*
nonrecognition relief	Nichtzutreffen einer Steuerermäßigung
offshore company	in einem Steuerparadies eingetragene Gesellschaft
offshore location	Steuerparadies (nicht der Steuerpflicht im Mutterland unterliegend)
ordinary residence	gewöhnlicher Wohnsitz
participation privilege	Übersetzung für: Schachtelbegünstigung (A)
pass through	zurechnen, durchrechnen
PAYE (pay as you earn) (UK)	direkter Abzug aller Steuern und Abgaben vor Auszahlung des Lohns
payroll tax (US)	lohn- und gehaltsbezogene Steuern
pension contributions	Pensionsbeiträge
pension schemes	Pensionspläne
personal holding company	personenbezogene Holding
personal holding company tax (US)	Steuer für personenbezogene Holdings
personal income tax	Einkommensteuer
personal property tax	Vermögensteuer*
poll tax (UK)	„Kopfsteuer" (UK)
pre-trading expenditure	Aufwendungen vor Betriebseröffnung
profits	Gewinn(e)
progressive tax	progressive Steuer
property tax	Vermögensteuer
property tax (US)	Grundsteuer*
proportional tax	proportionale Steuer
qualify for allowances	einen Steuerfreibetrag haben
real estate transfer tax	Übersetzung für: Grundverkehrsteuer (A)
real property tax	Grundsteuer
receivables	Forderungen
recurring income	wiederkehrende Bezüge
reduced rate	ermäßigter Steuersatz
regressive tax	regressive Steuer
remit	erlassen (Steuer)
research credit	Freibetrag für Forschungsaufwendungen
residence	Wohnsitz, Sitz
Retail Prices Index (UK)	Index der Einzelhandelspreise
retain	einbehalten, nicht ausschütten, nicht verteilen
revenue	Staatseinnahmen, Staatseinkünfte
rollover relief	Übertragungsrücklage

sales tax (US)	Umsatzsteuer auf Warenverkäufe einzelstaatlich geregelt
self-developed intangible assets	selbsterstellte immaterielle Wirtschafts-güter
separate taxation	getrennte Veranlagung, Individual-veranlagung
severance payment	Abfertigungszahlung
Social Security taxes	Sozialversicherungssteuern
special personal expenses	Sonderausgaben (A)
special personal expenses not related to income of a particular source	Sonderausgaben (A)
stamp duty	Stempelgebühren
state taxes (US)	US-bundesstaatliche Steuern
statutory accounts	landesrechtliche Buchführung, Jahresabschluß
straight-line ACRS deductions	lineare Abschreibung über das wirtschaftliche Erfordernis
straight-line method	lineare Abschreibungsmethode
substantiate	nachweisen, begründen
surtax	Zusatzsteuer
tangible fixed assets	Sachanlagevermögen
targeted jobs credit	Steuerermäßigung für Arbeitsplätze/ Stellenbesetzung
tariffs	Zölle
tax	Steuer
tax	besteuern
tax advantages	Steuervorteile
tax advisor	Steuerberater
tax avoidance	Steuervermeidung, Steuerumgehung
tax benefits	Steuervorteile
tax bracket	Steuerklasse
tax burden	Steuerlast
tax charge	Steuerlast, Steuervorschreibung
tax collection	Steuereinziehung
tax consultant	Steuerberater
tax counsel	Steuerberater
tax credit	Steuergutschrift, Steueranrechnung
tax cut	Steuersenkung
tax deductible	abzugsfähig
tax evasion	Steuerhinterziehung
tax exempt	von Besteuerung ausgenommen
tax exempt amount	Freibetrag
tax fraud	Steuerbetrug
tax free	steuerfrei
tax haven	Steuerparadies, Steueroase
tax law	Steuerrecht
tax legislation	Steuergesetzgebung
tax losses	steuerlich wirksame Verluste
tax mitigation	Steuervermeidung
tax on land	Grundsteuer
tax prepayment	Steuervorauszahlung

tax privilege	Steuerbegünstigung
tax purposes	Steuerzwecke
tax rate	Steuersatz
tax rate schedules	Steuersatztabelle
Tax Reform Act (US)	US-Steuerreformgesetz von 1986
tax refund	Steuerrückzahlung, Steuerrückerstattung
tax regulations	Steuerbestimmungen
tax relief	Steuererleichterung, Steuervergünstigung
tax return	Steuererklärung
tax shelter	Besteuerungsausnahmen; Niedrigsteuer-land
tax treatment	steuerrechtliche Behandlung
taxable	steuerpflichtig, zu versteuern
taxable entity	Steuersubjekt
taxable income	zu versteuerndes Einkommen
taxable status	Art der Steuerpflicht
taxation	Besteuerung, Steuern
taxpayer	Steuerzahler
top rate	Höchststeuersatz
trading expenses	Betriebsausgaben
translate	umrechnen (Währungen)
Treasury (UK)	brit. Finanzministerium
treaty relief	Begünstigung durch Doppelbesteuerungs-abkommen
U.S. real property holding corporation (USRPHC)	US-Grundstücksverwaltungsgesellschaft
unemployment insurance tax	Arbeitslosenversicherungssteuer
use taxes	Verbrauchssteuern
useful life	Nutzungsdauer
value added tax (VAT)	Mehrwertsteuer, Umsatzsteuer
VAT (value added tax)	Mehrwertsteuer, Umsatzsteuer
vehicle excise duty (UK)	KFZ-Steuer
weighted average	gewogener Mittelwert
withholding exemptions	Quellensteuerbefreiung
withholding requirements	Quellensteuerbestimmungen
withholding tax	Quellensteuer
write-down of export receivables	Teilwertabschreibung von Exportforderungen
writing-down allowances	Abschreibungsfreibeträge
zero rated (UK)	von der Mehrwertsteuer echt befreit

TERMINOLOGIE ZUM STEUER-RECHT

TAX LAW TERMINOLOGY

Abfertigungszahlung	*severance payment*
Abgabe	*duty, levy*
abgestufte Grenzsteuersätze	*graduated marginal rates*
abgestufte Steuersätze	*graduated rates*
abschreiben	*amortise*
Abschreibung	*depreciation, amortization, write down*
Abschreibungsaufwand	*depreciation charge*
Abschreibungsfreibeträge	*writing-down allowances*
Absetzung	*deduction*
Abzug	*deduction*
abzugsfähig	*tax deductible*
abzugsfähige Spende	*charitable deduction*
Abzugsposten	*allowances*
Aktiva	*assets*
aktivieren	*capitalise*
amortisieren	*amortise*
an der Quelle	*at source*
anfallen	*accrue*
Anlagevermögen	*fixed assets*
Anpassungen	*adjustments*
anrechenbare Steuern	*allowable credits*
Anrechnung ausländischer Steuern	*foreign tax credit*
Arbeitslosenversicherungssteuer	*unemployment insurance tax*
Art der Steuerpflicht	*taxable status*
auflaufen	*accrue*
Aufwendungen vor Betriebseröffnung	*pre-trading expenditure*
Ausgaben	*expenditure*
ausgenommen (von der Besteuerung)	*tax exempt*
ausländische Steuern	*foreign taxes*
außergewöhnliche Belastungen	*extraordinary expenses*
begründen	*substantiate*
Begünstigung durch Doppelbesteuerungsabkommen	*treaty relief*
Berufung	*appeal*
Berufung gegen Steuerbescheid	*appeal of assessment notice*
Berufung gegen Steuervorschreibung	*appeal of tax assessment*
Berufungsfrist	*deadline for appeal*
Berufungsinstanz	*appellate instance/division*
beschränkte Steuerpflicht	*limited tax liability*
besteuern	*tax*
Besteuerung	*taxation*
Besteuerungsausnahmen	*tax shelter*
Betriebsausgaben	*business expenses, trading expenses*
Betriebsstättensteuer	*branch profits tax*

256

bewegliches Vermögen	*moveable assets, chattel(s)*
Bewertung	*valuation*
Bewertungsmethoden	*methods of valuation*
Bewertungsregeln	*methods of valuation*
Bewirtungskosten	*entertainment expenses*
Börsenumsatzsteuer	*stock exchange turnover tax**
Bruttoeinkommen	*gross income*
Bruttoeinnahmen	*gross receipts*
Bruttogewinn	*gross income*
Bücher und sonstige Aufzeichnungen führen	*maintain books and records*
direkte Steuer	*direct tax*
direkter Abzug aller Steuern und Abgaben vor Auszahlung des Lohns	*PAYE (pay as you earn) (UK)*
Doppelbesteuerungsabkommen	*double taxation treaty*
durchrechnen	*pass through*
einbehalten (Gewinne)	*retain (profits)*
Einfuhrzölle	*import duties*
Einheitssatz	*flat rate*
Einheitswert	*assessed value (value assessed by tax authority that serves as basis for tax assessment)*
Einheitswertbescheid	*assessment notice*
Einkommen	*income*
Einkommensteuer	*personal income tax*
Einkünfte	*income, earnings*
Einnahmen- und Ausgabenmethode	*cash receipts and disbursement method*
Erbschaftssteuer	*inheritance tax*
erlassen (Steuer)	*remit*
ermäßigter Steuersatz	*reduced tax rate*
Fälligkeitstermin	*due date*
Fälligkeitstermin für Steuervorauszahlung	*due date for payment of tax advance*
Fälligkeitstermin für Abgabe der Steuererklärung	*due date for filing one's tax return*
Fälligkeitstermin für Entrichtung der Steuer	*due date for payment of tax*
Finanzamt	*tax office*
Finanzamt für Gebühren und Verkehrsteuern	*tax office for charges and transaction taxes**
Finanzamt für Körperschaften	*tax office for corporations*
Finanzbeamter	*taxman, tax officer*
Finanzbehörde	*finance authority*
Finanzminister	*Minister of Finance**
Firmenwert	*goodwill*
Forderungen	*accounts receivable, receivables*
Freibetrag	*tax exempt amount, allowance*

Freibetrag für Forschungsaufwendungen	*research credit*
Fremdvergleich	*arm's-length dealings (US)*
Fremdwährung	*foreign currency*
Gebühr	*levy, charge*
Gegenleistung	*consideration*
geprüfter Jahresabschluß	*audited annual accounts*
Gesellschaftereinlagen	*contributions of shareholders*
Gesellschafterzuschüsse	*contributions of shareholders*
Gesellschaftssteuer	*company tax* (type of capital transfer tax levied on the payment of the stated capital and any increase thereof)*
Gesetzgebung gegen Steuervermeidung	*anti-avoidance legislation*
getrennte Veranlagung	*separate taxation*
Gewerbesteuer	*(municipal) trade tax**
Gewinn nach Steuern	*profit after tax*
Gewinn vor Steuern	*profit before tax*
Gewinn(e)	*profit(s), earnings*
Gewinnbesteuerung	*tax on earnings*
Gewinnvortrag	*profit carried forward*
gewogener Mittelwert	*weighted average*
gewöhnlicher Aufenthaltsort	*customary place of abode*
gewöhnlicher Wohnsitz	*ordinary residence*
Gleitendes Durchschnittspreisverfahren	*moving-average basis*
Grunderwerbsteuer	*land acquisition tax, land transfer tax**
Grundsteuer	*real property tax, tax on land, land tax*
Grundverkehrsteuer	*real estate transfer tax*
Hälftesatz	*tax rate reduced by 50%*
Hochrechnung	*gross up*
Höchststeuersatz	*top tax rate*
immaterielles Anlagevermögen	*intangible fixed assets*
Importzoll	*import duty*
in einem Steuerparadies eingetragene Gesellschaft	*offshore company*
Index der Einzelhandelspreise	*Retail Prices Index (UK)*
indirekte Besteuerung	*indirect taxation*
indirekte Steuer	*indirect tax*
Individualveranlagung	*separate taxation*
Investitionsfreibetrag	*investment allowance*
Jahresabschluß	*(annual) financial statement*
Jahresgewinn	*net profit*
jährliche Veranlagung	*annual assessment*
Kapitalertragsteuer	*tax on income from capital, investment income tax**
Kapitalverkehrsteuer	*capital transfer tax*

KFZ-Steuer	*motor vehicle tax, motor vehicle licence duty (UK)*
kommunale Steuern	*local taxes*
konsolidiert	*consolidated*
Konsortien	*consortia*
Konzern	*group, affiliated group (US)*
Konzernbegünstigung	*group relief*
Konzerngesellschaften	*group companies*
Körperschaftsteuer	*corporation/corporate income tax*
körperschaftsteuerfreie Kapitalerträge	*franked investment income*
landesrechtliche Buchführung	*statutory accounts*
lineare Abschreibungsmethode	*straight-line method*
lohn- und gehaltsbezogene Abgaben	*employment taxes (US)*
lohn- und gehaltsbezogene Steuer	*payroll tax (US)*
Lohnsteuer	*income tax on wages & salaries*
maßgebende Währung	*functional currency*
Mehrwertsteuer	*value added tax (VAT)*
nach Steuerabzug geleistete Zahlungen	*franked payment*
Nachlaß	*estate*
nachweisen	*substantiate*
Nettobetriebsverlust	*net trading loss (UK)*
nicht abzugsfähig	*disallowed*
Nichtangabe	*non-declaration*
Nichtzutreffen einer Steuerermäßigung	*nonrecognition relief*
niedrigerer Marktwert	*lower market value*
Niedrigsteuerland	*tax shelter*
Normalsteuersatz	*basic tax rate, regular tax rate*
Nullsatz	*zero tax rate*
Nutzungsdauer	*useful life*
Organschaft	*fiscal unit*
Pauschalbasis	*lump-sum basis*
Pensionsbeiträge	*pension contributions*
Pensionspläne	*pension schemes*
periodengerechte Abgrenzung	*accrual method*
Preise im Rahmen des Fremdvergleichs	*arm's length prices*
progressive Steuer	*progressive tax*
proportionale Steuer	*proportional tax*
Quellenabzug	*deduction at source*
Quellenbesteuerung	*deduction at source*
Quellensteuer	*withholding tax*
Quellensteuerbefreiung	*withholding exemptions*
Quellensteuerbestimmungen	*withholding requirements*

Rate	*annuity*
Rechnungslegung	*accounting*
Rechnungslegungsmethoden	*accounting methods*
regressive Steuer	*regressive tax*
Rente	*annuity*
rückstellen	*accrue*
Rückstellungen	*accruals*
Rücktrag	*carryback (US)*
Sachanlagevermögen	*tangible fixed assets*
Sanierungsgewinne	*gains from the cancellation of debts by creditors meant to restore the financial position of the corporation*
Schachtelbegünstigung	*participation privilege*
Scheingewinne	*inflationary gains*
Schenkung	*donation*
Schenkung zu Lebzeiten	*lifetime transfer*
Schenkungs- und Erbschaftsteuer	*gift and estate tax*
Schenkungssteuer	*gift tax*
selbsterstellte immaterielle Wirtschaftsgüter	*self-developed intangible assets*
Sitz	*registered office, legal seat, seat, residence*
Sonderausgaben	*special personal expenses (not related to income of a particular source)*
Sozialversicherungsbeiträge	*Social Security contributions*
Sozialversicherungssteuern	*Social Security taxes*
Spesen	*expenses*
Staatseinkünfte	*revenue*
Stempelgebühren	*stamp duties*
Steuer	*tax*
Steuer einheben	*levy tax*
Steueranrechnung	*tax credit*
Steueranreiz	*tax incentive*
Steuerbegünstigung	*tax privilege*
Steuerberater	*tax advisor, tax consultant, tax counsel*
Steuerbescheid	*assessment notice*
Steuerbestimmungen	*tax regulations*
Steuerbetrug	*tax fraud*
Steuereinziehung	*tax collection*
Steuerentlastung	*tax benefits*
Steuererhöhung	*tax increase*
Steuererklärung	*tax return*
Steuererklärung einreichen	*file one's tax return*
Steuererleichterung	*tax relief, tax benefit*
Steuerfahndung	*tax search*
Steuerflucht	*tax evasion*
steuerfrei	*free of tax, tax free, tax exempt*
Steuerfreibetrag haben	*qualify for allowances*
Steuerfreibeträge	*allowances*
Steuergesetzgebung	*tax legislation*
Steuergutschrift	*tax credit*

Steuerhinterziehung	*tax evasion*
Steuerklasse	*tax bracket*
Steuerlast	*tax burden, tax charge*
steuerlich abzugsfähig	*deductible*
steuerlich wirksame Verluste	*tax losses*
steuerliche Abzugsposten	*allowable deductions,*
	capital allowances (UK)
steuerliche Bestimmungen	*fiscal provisions*
steuerliche Veranlagung	*assessment*
steuerliche Vermögensbewertung	*assessed valuation (US)*
Steuernachlaß	*abatement of tax*
Steuerparadies	*tax haven, offshore location*
Steuerpflicht	*tax liability*
steuerpflichtig	*taxable, subject to tax*
Steuerrecht	*tax law*
steuerrechtliche Behandlung	*tax treatment*
Steuerreform	*tax reform*
Steuerrückerstattung	*tax refund*
Steuerrückzahlung	*tax refund*
Steuersatz	*tax rate*
Steuersatztabelle	*tax rate schedule*
Steuersenkung	*tax cut, tax reduction*
Steuersubjekt	*taxable entity*
Steuerumgehung	*tax avoidance*
Steuervergünstigung	*tax relief*
Steuervermeidung	*tax avoidance, tax mitigation*
Steuervorauszahlung	*tax prepayment, tax advance*
Steuervorschreibung	*tax charge, tax assessment*
Steuervorteile	*tax advantages, tax benefits*
Steuerzahler	*taxpayer*
Steuerzwecke	*tax purposes*
stiller Gesellschafter	*dormant partner*
Substanzverringerung	*depletion*
Teilwertabschreibung von Exportforderungen	*write-down of export receivables*
tilgen	*amortise*
Übertragungsrücklage	*rollover relief*
Umlaufvermögen	*current assets*
umrechnen (Währungen)	*translate*
Umsatzsteuer	*value added tax (VAT),*
	sales tax (US)
Umweltschutzsteuer	*environmental tax*
unbewegliches Vermögen	*immovable property*
unentgeltliche Übertragung	*gratuitous transfer*
veranlagen	*assess*
Veranlagung	*assessment*
Verbrauchssteuer	*consumer expenditure tax, use tax,*
	excise duty, consumption tax
Vergütungen	*emoluments*

Verlagerung der Steuerpflicht	*deferral of tax*
Verlassenschaft	*estate*
Verlust	*loss(es)*
Verlust aus laufender Geschäftstätigkeit	*net operating loss*
Verlustvortrag	*loss carried forward*
Vermögensteuer	*(personal) property tax*
Vermögenswerte	*assets*
Versicherungsteuer	*insurance tax*
Verwaltungsgerichtshof	*Supreme Court of Administration**
von der Mehrwertsteuer echt befreit	*zero rated (UK)*
Vorsteuer	*input tax/VAT*
Vorsteuerrückvergütung	*input tax/VAT refund*
Vortrag	*carryover*
vortragen	*carry over*
Wechselkurs	*exchange rate*
Werbungskosten	*income-related expenses*
wiederkehrende Bezüge	*recurring income*
Wohnsitz	*domicile, residence*
Wohnsitzfinanzamt	*local tax office (of residence)*
Zinsaufwand	*interest charge*
Zinsen	*interest*
Zoll	*customs duty, tariff*
Zollabkommen	*tariff agreement/treaty*
Zollamt	*customs office*
Zollbehörde	*customs office*
zollfrei	*duty-free*
Zollfreizone	*duty free zone*
zu Berichtszwecken in Abschlüssen	*for financial reporting purposes*
zu versteuerndes Einkommen	*taxable income*
zurechenbar zu	*chargeable to*
zurechnen	*pass through*
Zusatzsteuer	*surtax*
zuständiges Finanzamt	*competent tax office*

VII. ACCOUNTING

Dr. Robert Reiter, KPMG Austria
Beeideter Wirtschaftsprüfer und Steuerberater, CPA (USA)

1. UNITED STATES

1.1. Financial Statements

The financial statements of the reporting entity should present fairly in all material aspects the financial position as of a specific date, and the results of its operations and its cash flow for the period then ended.

The basic concepts as determined by the Generally Accepted Accounting Principles (GAAP) are:

– Historical cost accounting

– Accrual accounting versus cash accounting

– Going concern

– Consistency and comparability

The financial statements should include the balance sheets (assets, liabilities and equity), statement of income and retained earnings, statement of cash flow and statement of changes in stockholders' equity. Notes to the financial statements are an integral part and disclose additional specific details as well as significant accounting policies.

For the format some flexibility is allowed, however, specific rules prescribe the presentation of certain items such as extraordinary items in the income statement.

> financial statements, reporting entity, financial position, results of operations, cash flow
>
> Generally Accepted Accounting Principles (GAAP) historical cost accounting, accrual accounting vs. cash accounting, going concern
>
> consistency and comparability balance sheets, statement of income and retained earnings, statement of cash flow, statement of changes in stockholders' equity

1.2. Accounting Standards

The generally accepted accounting principles (GAAP) are derived primarily from the following sources:

– Financial Accounting Standards Board (FASB) as the best known organization of the Financial Accounting Foundation (FAF). The FASB has 7 full-time members not necessarily being Certified Public Accountants or having positions in industry or private firms. FASB issues statements covering financial accounting and reporting standards for activities and transactions dealing with most of all problem areas and issues for all public and nonpublic enterprises except state and local governmental entities. Such statements are abbreviated as SFAS (Statements of Financial Accounting Standards) and numbered, such as SFAS 1 "Disclosure of Foreign Currency Information" or SFAS 109 "Accounting for Income Taxes".

– Governmental Accounting Standards Board (GASB) establishes financial accounting and reporting standards for state and local governmental entities.

> Certified Public Accountant

263

Additionally, other organizations are also providing accounting standards:

– American Institute of Certified Public Accountants (AICPA) through its Accounting Standards Executive Committee (Statements of Position on specific accounting areas)

10 K Report

– Securities and Exchange Commission (SEC) for the format and contents of and requirements for financial statements of publicly held companies. Especially the 10 K Report to be filed by any company listed provides all necessary information in detail and is sent by the reporting entity to any person requesting this report.

1.3. Balance Sheet

1.3.1. Intangible Assets

intangible assets to recorded at cost, capitalization

Intangible assets acquired from third parties should be recorded at cost. Specific rules apply to the capitalization of developed computer software and other developed specific identifiable intangible assets under the expectation of future benefits.

amortization
estimated life
straight-line method

The amortization of the capitalized cost should be based on the estimated life not exceeding 40 years using the straight-line method. Another method may be used if more appropriate.

1.3.2. Property, Plant and Equipment

fixed assets, capital assets, to expense as incurred
depreciation
salvage value
declining balance method, sum of the years's digits method, unit of production or hours of use method

Fixed assets representing capital assets are recorded at cost. Expenditures for repairs and maintenance are expensed as incurred.

Depreciation is calculated over the estimated useful life considering the expected salvage value. The methods most commonly used are the straight-line method, declining balance, sum of the year's digits and unit of production or hours of use.

Capitalization of interest is possible under specific circumstances.

1.3.3. Investments

investments, current assets, non current assets, marketable securities

Investments should be presented either as current assets or as non current assets. For marketable equity securities cost versus marketable value may be compared on an aggregate basis and the lower amount should be recorded. Securities other than marketable

write down to market
valuation allowance

securities may be carried at cost except a write down to market is required. Write downs should be shown as valuation allowance. For non current marketable equity securities this valuation allowance is not reflected in the income statement, but is included in the equity section.

In the notes a disclosure of the net realized gains or losses, change in the valuation allowance, any hypothecation or pledging and gross unrealized gains or losses is mandatory.

1.3.4. Capital Leases

Lease transactions must be scrutinized whether the criteria of a capital lease or a financial lease are met. Depending on the point of view of the lessee or lessor the sales type leases, leveraged leases, other direct financing leases must be recorded as capital lease or operating lease taking into consideration the transfer of the ownership, the content of a bargain purchase option, the lease term of at least 75 percent of the property's economic useful life and the present value of the minimum lease of at least 90 percent of the fair value of the leased property.

capital lease, financial lease

operating lease

Detailed rules are included in various SFAS (most important SFAS 13) concerning the recording in balance sheet and income statement and disclosing of various data in the notes.

1.3.5. Accounts Receivable

Accounts receivable are recorded when the related sale of goods or performance of services are realized. An allowance for doubtful accounts considering the collectibility must be deducted. In case of factored receivables the clauses of a possible recourse are the decision factor for the accounting treatment.

accounts receivable
doubtful accounts
collectibility

In the notes additional disclosures, such as current and not current, related party amounts, receivables pledged as collateral for loans, allowance for doubtful accounts, proceeds from transfers of receivables sold with recourse are mandatory.

1.3.6. Inventories and Work in Progress

Inventories should be stated at the lower of cost or market. Various cost methods (LIFO, FIFO, average cost method, specific identification method) may be used. There exists a floor principle, i.e. if the market value is lower than the net realizable value reduced by an approximately normal profit margin, the reduced net realizable value is to be recorded.

inventories, lower of cost or market, cost methods, floor principle

For long-term contracts the percentage of completion method as well as the completed contract method are acceptable.

In the notes the cost method inter alia must be disclosed.

1.3.7. Capital and Reserves

The stockholders' equity includes the capital stock less stock reacquired by the company, paid-in capital and retained earnings. Depending on the specific situation the stock may have to be divided into common stock and all classes of preferred stock having different rights and privileges.

equity, capital stock, stock reacquired by the company, paid-in capital, retained earnings, common stock, preferred stock

In the notes the stockholders' equity must be disclosed in detail including a reconciliation of all changes.

reconciliation of changes

265

1.3.8. Liabilities

current liabilities

accounts payable

Current liabilities include liabilities payable within one year of the balance sheet date or whose payment is expected to require the use of current assets. Liabilities should be divided into accounts payable and significant items of accrued and other liabilities.

Long-term debts as liabilities due more than one year from the balance sheet date must be disclosed very detailedly in the notes.

1.3.9. Provisions

loss provisions

No general provision for the entrepreneur's risk is allowed. Loss provisions may be recorded for identifiable transactions. Specific provisions can be recorded for estimated liabilities and contingent losses if it is probable that an asset will be impaired or a liability will be incurred and the amount can be reasonably estimated.

Such provisions may include litigation, claims, assessments, warranties, severance indemnities and other employee benefits such as postretirement benefits for health care or life insurance.

For the accounting treatment of pensions there are detailed regulations in various SFASs. The basic accounting treatment is the expensing and funding of the pension cost during the active working period of the entitled working force taking into account future increase of compensation.

For defined contribution pension plans the contribution called for the period is the pension expense. For defined benefit pension plans the pension expense consists mainly of the service cost, interest cost, return on plan assets and amortization of prior service cost.

A pension accrual is recorded if the pension expense exceeds the cumulative contributions to the pension plan. Special rules exist for the accounting of gains and losses arising from pension settlements or significant reduction in or elimination of pension obligations.

For pension accruals details of the pension plan, net pension cost for the period, reconciliation of the funded status of the plan with the amounts reported in the financial statements and the interest rates used for the returns of pension plan assets, the rate of compensation increase and vested benefits must be disclosed.

Certain commitments, such as guarantees or unused letters of credit, should be disclosed as contingent liabilities even if the possibility of a loss is remote.

1.3.10. Related Party Transactions

related party

All material transactions with related parties should be disclosed. A related party is defined as any party with which the reporting entity deals and one party controls or can significantly influence the management or operating policies of the other.

disclosure

No specific accounting principles are to be observed for related party transactions, however, for disclosure purposes comprehen-

sive information will be necessary and therefore efficient accounting provides the required information using different accounts avoiding any additional efforts.

1.4. Income Statement

1.4.1. Revenue Recognition

Revenue is recognized when realized and earned. A realization requires the exchange of goods, services, merchandise or other assets for cash or claims to cash. An earning is provided when the entity is entitled to payment having substantially accomplished its obligation.

For long-term contracts the percentage of completion method and the completed contract method are accepted.

revenue recognition

realization

earning

1.4.2. Research and Development

Research and development costs should be expensed as incurred. Under specific circumstances costs for computer software may be capitalized.

R & D

1.4.3. Extraordinary Items

Extraordinary items are events or transactions that are distinguished by their unusual nature and by infrequency of their occurrence, taking into account the environment in which the entity operates.

Extraordinary items must be recorded net of tax and reported as a separate item in the income statement.

extraordinary items

1.4.4. Discontinued Operations

The effect of discontinued operations which represent a major business line must be recorded net of tax and reported as a separate item in the income statement.

discontinued operations

1.4.5. Prior Period Adjustments

Adjustments resulting from errors in the financial statements of prior periods, such as the mistake in the application of accounting principles, should be charged or credited net of tax to the opening balance of retained earnings.

prior period adjustments, errors in financial statements of prior periods

1.4.6. Changes in Accounting Principles

Under specific circumstances it is appropriate to change from an acceptable accounting principle to another, such as the change in the method of inventory or depreciation method. The cumulative effect of this change should be reported as a separate item in the income statement following the extraordinary items.

changes in accounting principles

1.4.7. Income Taxes

tax effect

In the income statement the related tax effect of all events or transactions recorded must be accounted for. The income tax expense

current tax

deferred tax

consists of the current tax as liable to the tax authorities and the deferred tax relating to temporary differences. Non-deductible amounts of provisions such as warranty based on the accrual

tax deductibility

principle give rise for a deferred tax asset as tax deductibility will be given in the period of cash disbursement. Depreciation in the financial statements exceeding the allowable depreciation for tax

deferred tax liability

purposes will lead to a deferred tax liability.

liability method

The deferred tax asset or liability should be calculated under the liability method considering the prudence principle for a deferred tax asset by establishing an appropriate allowance.

A reconciliation of the income tax as reported with the computed income tax on reported income using the statutory tax rate is requested.

1.4.8. Earnings per Share

earnings per share

The earnings per share as the amount of earnings attributable to each share of the common stock must be reported. Earnings per share are mostly presented as primary earnings per share and fully diluted earnings per share considering stock options, warrants and their equivalents.

Earnings per share must be disclosed on the following bases:

– Income from continuing operations

– Income before extraordinary items

– Cumulative effect of a change in accounting principles

– Net income

1.4.9. Foreign Currency Translation

foreign currency
translation

The foreign currency translation relates to transactions in foreign currencies and to the translation of foreign currency financial statements for consolidation and other purposes. A major criterion is the determination of the functional currency as the currency of the primary economic environment in which the entity operates; normally this is the currency of the environment in which an entity primarily generates and expends cash. There are several criteria for the determination of the functional currency, such as cash flow, sales prices, sales market, expenses, financing, intercompany transactions.

Depending on the determination of the functional currency either the current rate method or the remeasurement method will apply

translation for
consolidation purposes

hedging costs

to the translation for consolidation purposes.

Costs of hedging for a specific transaction should be amortized over the term of the forward contract. The costs include the difference between the spot rate and the negotiated future rate at the date of entering into the forward contract. At balance sheet date, the actual gain or loss must be recorded additionally.

A disclosure of the aggregate transaction gain or loss and additional other information is necessary.

1.4.10. Segmental Information

For public companies a comprehensive reporting is provided about segmental information. Segmental information relates to different industries and foreign corporations within the reporting entity. A reportable segment is defined as a segment that accounts for 10 percent or more of the combined segment revenue, operating profit or loss, or identifiable asset.

segmental information

reportable segment

Additionally, information by geographical areas for operations, export sales and major customer revenue should be disclosed.

1.4.11. Subsequent Events

Subsequent events are events occurring after the date of the financial statements but before their issuance.

subsequent events

Events that provide evidence of conditions not existing at the balance sheet date must be disclosed if material, such as catastrophic losses. Events that provide conditions existing at the balance sheet date should cause an adjustment in the financial statements.

2. UNITED KINGDOM

2.1. Financial Statements

The financial statements of the reporting entity should give a true and fair view.

The basic concepts are:

going concern

– Going concern

prudence

– Prudence

accrual accounting

– Accrual accounting

consistency

– Consistency

separate determination and valuation

– Separate determination and valuation of individual assets and liabilities

historical cost

The basic concept is also to use the historical cost, however, alternative accounting rules are allowed:

intangible fixed assets

– Intangible fixed assets may be recorded at their current cost

tangible fixed assets

– Tangible fixed assets may be recorded at their market value or current cost

non current investments

– Non current investments may be recorded at market value (estimate of the director's or formal valuation)

current investments

– Current investments may be recorded at their current cost

stocks

– Stocks may be recorded at their current cost

Current cost is the lower of an asset's net current replacement cost or recoverable amount.

Companies have the option to use the pure historical cost convention, the current cost or the historical cost convention modified for the revaluation of certain assets.

director's report, balance sheet, profit and loss account, statement of source and application of funds

The financial statements should include a director's report, a balance sheet, a profit and loss account, a statement of source and application of funds. Notes to the financial statements disclose the accounting policies used and other specific details.

According to the Fourth EC Directive the format of the profit and loss statement and the balance sheet is prescribed in every detail. A company may choose between 2 formats for the profit and loss statement and 4 formats for the balance sheet.

2.2. Accounting Standards

The generally accepted accounting standards are derived primarily from the following sources:

– Companies Act 1985 (several amendments in line with the Fourth EC Directive) setting forth format for the balance sheet and profit and loss account, valuation rules and detailed disclosure requirements.

– Statements of Standard Accounting Practice (SSAPs) issued by the independent Accounting Standards Board

- *Statements of Recommended Practice (SORPs)*
- *Continuing Obligation by the United Kingdom's Stock Exchange*

2.3. Balance Sheet
2.3.1. Intangible Assets

Intangible assets acquired from third parties should be recorded at cost. Under specific circumstances assets created by the company and development costs may be capitalized. Goodwill purchased may be capitalized. All intangible assets except goodwill may be revalued, any surplus or deficit should be charged or credited to the revaluation reserve.

intangible assets

goodwill

to revalue
revaluation reserve

The amortization of the capitalized amounts should be based on the estimated life.

estimated life

2.3.2. Property, Plant and Equipment

Fixed assets representing capital assets are recorded at cost. Expenditures for repairs and maintenance are expensed as incurred. Fixed assets may be revalued, any surplus or deficit to be determined for individual assets should be charged or credited to the revaluation reserve.

fixed assets

Gains or losses are calculated using the carrying value optionally including any remaining amount of the revaluation reserve.

Depreciation is calculated over the estimated useful life considering already the expected residual value. The methods most commonly used are straight-line method, sum of the year's digits, and unit of production or hours of use.

depreciation

Capitalization of interest is possible.

capitalization of
interest

2.3.3. Investments

Investments should be presented either as current or non current assets. Current asset investments are stated at the lower of cost or market. Non current asset investments are stated at cost. Under the revaluation method current assets can be recorded at current cost, non current assets at market value as described above. Any surplus or deficit should be charged or credited to the revaluation reserve.

investments

surplus, deficit

Gains and losses are calculated using the carrying value optionally including any remaining amount of the revaluation reserve.

The accounting standards prescribe a lot of detailed information especially for investments exceeding 10 percent and even more information for investments exceeding 20 percent for disclosure.

2.3.4. Capital Leases

capital lease,
operating lease

Lease transactions must be scrutinized whether the criteria of a capital lease or an operating lease are met. Depending on the point of view of the lessee or lessor the lease transactions must be recorded as capital lease or operating lease taking into consideration the transfer of all risks and rewards of the ownership, the present value of the minimum lease payments equals 90 percent of the fair value of the leased asset.

Detailed rules are included in some SSAPs concerning the recording in balance sheet and profit and loss account and disclosing of various data in the notes.

2.3.5. Accounts Receivable

accounts receivable

prudence principle
factored receivables
recourse clause

Accounts receivable are recorded when the related sale of goods or performance of services is realized taking into account the prudence principle. An allowance for doubtful accounts considering the collectibility must be deducted. In case of factored receivables the economic substance of the recourse clause is the decisive factor for the accounting treatment.

split of the receivables
due

In the notes an analysis including a split of the receivables due within one year of the balance sheet date and after one year, trade receivables, other receivables and accrued income, prepayments and related parties (group companies and undertakings in which the reporting entity has a participating interest) has to be disclosed.

inventories

2.3.6. Inventories and Work in Progress

Inventories should be stated at the lower of cost or net realizable value. Various cost methods (LIFO, FIFO, average cost method, specific identification method) may be used. If the alternative accounting rules are used, stocks are stated at their current cost.

stocks

For long-term contracts in practice the percentage of completion method as well as the completed contract method are acceptable.

In the notes an analysis of the inventories (raw materials, consumables, work in progress, finished goods, goods for resale and payments on account) and the cost method used must be disclosed.

2.3.7. Capital and Reserves

called-up share capital
paid-in capital,
realized reserves

unrealized reserves

The stockholders' equity includes the called-up share capital, paid-in capital and the realized reserves transferred from the profit and loss account. The revaluation reserve is considered as an unrealized reserve. Specific restrictions exist for the use of the paid-in capital.

272

In the notes details of the issued capital, the paid-in capital, the authorized capital and other detailed information must be disclosed.

2.3.8. Liabilities

Liabilities due within one year from the balance sheet date must be disclosed separately from the liabilities due after one year and liabilities due after five years. Additionally, a split including debenture loans, bank loans and overdrafts, payments received on accounts, trade creditors, bills of exchange, amounts owed to group companies and undertakings in which the reporting entity has a participating interest, other creditors and deferred income must be provided. Additionally, details of security provided and the total amount of secured liabilities must be disclosed.

liabilities due

2.3.9. Provisions

No general provision for the entrepreneur's risk is allowed. Loss provisions should be recorded considering the probability and reasonable estimate of the amount.

loss provisions

Such provisions may include litigation, claims, assessments, warranties, severance indemnities and other employee benefits.

For the accounting treatment of pensions there are detailed regulations in SSAP 24. The basic accounting treatment is the expensing and accruing of the pension cost during the active working period of the entitled working force.

For defined contribution pension plans the contribution called for the period is the pension expense. For defined benefit pension plans the pension expense is derived from an actuarial calculation considering current and future pensionable earnings.

A pension accrual is recorded if the pension expense exceeds the cumulative contributions to the pension plan. For pension accruals details of the pension plan and information, different for defined contribution pension plans and defined benefit pension plans, must be disclosed.

2.3.10. Related Party Transactions

All balance sheet items with amounts owed to or by group companies and undertakings in which the reporting entity has a participating interest must be disclosed.

amounts owed to or by group companies or undertakings

No specific accounting principles are to be observed for related party transactions, however, for disclosure purposes efficient accounting provides the required information using different accounts and avoiding any additional efforts.

related party transactions

2.4. Profit and Loss Account

2.4.1. Revenue Recognition

ultimate cash
realization

Revenue is recognized when realized. A realization requires the exchange of goods, services, merchandise or other assets for cash or other assets whose ultimate cash realization can be assessed with reasonable certainty.

For long-term contracts the percentage of completion method and the completed contract method are accepted.

R & D

2.4.2. Research and Development

Research and development costs should be expensed as incurred. Under specific circumstances development costs may be capitalized.

2.4.3. Extraordinary Items

events outside the
ordinary activities

Extraordinary items are defined as items that derive from events or transactions that fall outside the ordinary activities of the reporting entity and that are therefore expected not to recur frequently or regularly. Extraordinary items do neither include exceptional items nor prior years' items.

The effect of extraordinary items including the tax effect must be disclosed.

2.4.4. Discontinued Operations

discontinued operations

The effect of discontinued operations which represent a material and separately identifiable component of the business operations must be disclosed.

2.4.5. Prior Period Adjustments

errors of prior period
financial statements

Adjustments resulting from errors in the financial statements of prior periods, such as a mistake in the application of accounting principles, should be treated by adjustments of the prior period profit and loss account and balance sheet. The note relating to the reserves should be reconciled.

2.4.6. Changes in Accounting Principles

Changes in accounting principles are treated in the same manner as prior period adjustments.

2.4.7. Income Taxes

current tax and
deferred tax

In the profit and loss account the related tax effect of all events or transactions recorded must be accounted for. The income tax expense consists of the current tax as liable to the tax authorities and the deferred tax relating to timing differences. Non-deductible

274

amounts of provisions based on the accrual principle give rise for a deferred tax asset as the tax deductibility will be given in the period of cash disbursement. Interest recorded as realized but not yet received as cash will lead to a deferred tax liability. The deferred tax asset and liability should be calculated on a partial provision basis under the liability method but recorded only to the extent that it is probable that a tax liability or asset will materialize. In the notes details of the tax expense must be disclosed.

period of cash disbursement

deferred tax liability

2.4.8. Earnings per Share

Earnings per share as the amount of earnings attributable to the shares eligible for dividends in the period will be reported as basic earning per share. Additionally, calculation of fully diluted earnings per share includes the effect of shares not yet eligible for a dividend and the effect of conversion rights.

conversion rights

2.4.9. Foreign Currency Translation

The foreign currency translation relates to transactions in foreign currencies and to the translation of foreign currency financial statements for consolidation and other purposes.

transactions in foreign currency

Transactions denominated in foreign currency should be translated using the exchange rate at the date of the transaction. At balance sheet date assets and liabilities denominated in foreign currencies should be translated using the exchange rate in effect on the balance sheet date.

to be denominated

Financial statements in foreign currency for consolidation should be translated using the closing rate. The temporal method is to be used under specific circumstances.

closing rate, temporal method

2.4.10. Segmental Information

Segmental reporting is required. The disclosure must comprehend definition of reported segment (business and geographical), specific data as turnover, results, net assets and information relating to associated entities. An omission is possible under specific circumstances.

segmental reporting

2.4.11. Subsequent Events

Subsequent events are events occurring after the date of the financial statements but before the approval by the board of directors.

approval by B.O.D.

Events that provide evidence of conditions not existing at the balance sheet date should be disclosed if material. Events that provide conditions existing at the balance sheet date are defined as adjusting events and the effects should be included in the financial statements.

adjusting events

3. AUSTRIA

3.1. Financial Statements

The financial statements of the reporting entity should give a true and fair view of the company's assets, liabilities, financial position and profit and loss in conformity with generally accepted accounting principles. Due to the mandatory strict use and observation of the accounting standards in Austria the true and fair view is mostly impaired. The basic concepts are:

– Historical cost accounting

– Going concern

– Prudence

– Accrual accounting

– Consistency

– Separate determination and valuation of individual assets and liabilities

The financial statements should include a director's report, a balance sheet, an income statement and notes which disclose the accounting policies used and other specific details.

According to the Fourth EC Directive the format of the income statement and the balance sheet is prescribed in all details. A company may choose between 2 formats for the income statement, whereas the format for the balance sheet is prescribed. The presentation should include the figures for 2 years.

3.2. Accounting Standards

The generally accepted accounting standards are derived primarily from the following sources:

HGB
– Commercial Code (amended in line with the Fourth EC Directive) setting forth format for the balance sheet and income statement, valuation rules and detailed disclosure requirements.

Kammer der
Wirtschaftstreuhänder
– Uncodified standard practices by the Austrian Institute of the Chamber of Accountants generally observed as Accounting Practices.

Steuerrecht
– Tax law according to the principle of relevance of tax law regulations over Commercial Code regulations to achieve tax deductibility, which ends in a reverse relevance.

3.3. Balance Sheet

3.3.1. Intangible Assets

start-up cost
Intangible assets acquired from third parties should be recorded at cost. Under specific circumstances start-up cost may be capitalized. Goodwill purchased may be capitalized.

The amortization of the capitalized amounts should be based on the estimated life.

3.3.2. Property, Plant and Equipment

Fixed assets representing capital assets are recorded at cost. Expenditures for repairs and maintenance are expensed as incurred.

Depreciation is calculated over the estimated useful life. The method most commonly used is the straight-line method as accepted for fiscal purposes, but also the methods sum of the year's digits, declining balance method and unit of production or hours of use are acceptable.

Capitalization of interest is possible.

3.3.3. Investments

Investments should be presented either as current or non current assets. Current asset investments are stated at the lower of cost or market. A lower value is possible to avoid a devaluation in the near future.

Non current asset investments are stated at cost, however, a write down is mandatory if the decline in the value is considered permanent.

The accounting standards prescribe a lot of detailed information especially for investments exceeding 10 percent and even more information for investments exceeding 20 percent for disclosure.

3.3.4. Capital Leases

Lease transactions must be scrutinized as to whether the criteria of a capital lease or an operating lease are met. In practice the criteria of the tax regulations are used for accounting purposes. Depending on the point of view of the lessee or lessor the lease transactions must be recorded as capital lease or operating lease taking into consideration the transfer of all risks and rewards of the ownership. The present value of the minimum lease payments equals 90 percent of the fair value of the leased asset, the minimum lease term that cannot be cancelled is 75 percent of the estimated useful life of the leased asset.

In the notes the leasing expense for the next year and the next five years must be disclosed.

3.3.5. Accounts Receivable

Accounts receivable are recorded when the related sale of goods or performance of services is realized taking into account the prudence principle. An allowance for doubtful accounts considering the collectibility must be deducted. In case of factored receivables the economic substance of the recourse clause is the decisive factor for the accounting treatment.

In the notes an analysis including a split of the receivables due within one year of the balance sheet date and after one year, trade receivables, other receivables and accrued income, prepayments and related parties (group companies and undertakings in which the reporting entity has a participating interest) has to be disclosed.

3.3.6. Inventories and Work in Progress

Inventories should be stated at the lower of cost or net realizable value. Various cost methods (LIFO, FIFO, average cost method, specific identification method) may be used, but according to the principle of relevance of tax law regulations the average cost method is most common.

For long-term contracts the completed contract method and in practical terms a modified very conservative percentage of completion method are acceptable.

In the notes an analysis of the inventories (raw materials, consumables, work in progress, finished goods, goods for resale and payments on account) and the used cost method must be disclosed.

3.3.7. Capital and Reserves

The stockholders' equity includes the called-up share capital, paid-in capital as capital reserves and the reserves transferred from the profit and loss account. Specific restrictions exist for the use of the paid-in capital.

In the notes details of the issued capital, the paid-in capital, the authorized capital and other detailed information must be disclosed.

3.3.8. Liabilities

Liabilities due within one year from the balance sheet date must be disclosed separately from the liabilities due after one year and liabilities due after five years. Additionally, a split including debenture loans, bank loans and overdrafts, payments received on accounts, trade creditors, bills of exchange, amounts owed to group companies and undertakings in which the reporting entity has a participating interest, other creditors and deferred income must be provided. Additionally, details of security given and the total amount of secured liabilities must be disclosed.

3.3.9. Provisions

No general provision for the entrepreneur's risk is allowed. Loss provisions should be recorded considering the probability and reasonable estimate of the amount.

Such provisions may include litigation, claims, assessments, warranties, severance indemnities and other employee benefits.

The basic accounting treatment is the expensing and accruing of the pension cost during the active working period of the entitled working force.

278

For the accounting treatment of defined benefit pension plans the actuarial calculations as provided for tax purposes are mostly used. As tax regulations accept only an interest rate of 6 percent and current salary level, an additional actuarial calculation for accounting purposes is necessary. If the amounts of the two actuarial calculations differ materially, the higher amount must be recorded.

For defined contribution pension plans the contribution called for the period is the pension expense.

A pension accrual is recorded if the pension expense exceeds the cumulative contributions to the pension plan. For pension accruals the method used must be disclosed.

3.3.10. Related Party Transactions

All balance sheet items with amounts owed to or by group companies and undertakings in which the reporting entity has a participating interest must be disclosed.

No specific accounting principles are to be observed for related party transactions, however, for disclosure purposes efficient accounting provides the required information using different accounts and avoiding any additional efforts.

3.4. Income Statement

3.4.1. Revenue Recognition

Revenue is recognized when realized. A realization requires the exchange of goods, services, merchandise or other assets for cash or other assets whose ultimate cash realization can be assessed with reasonable certainty.

For long-term contracts the completed contract method and a modified conservative percentage of completion method are accepted.

3.4.2. Research and Development

Research and development costs should be expensed as incurred. In the director's report the activity in the areas of research and development should be discussed.

3.4.3. Extraordinary Items

Extraordinary items are defined as items that derive from events or transactions that fall outside the ordinary activities of the reporting entity and that are therefore expected not to recur frequently or regularly. Extraordinary items do neither include exceptional items nor prior years' items.

Extraordinary items must be recorded as a separate item in the income statement and further details have to be disclosed in the notes.

3.4.4. Discontinued Operations

The effect of discontinued operations which represent a material and separately identifiable component of the business operations must be reported as extraordinary item and details have to be disclosed in the notes.

3.4.5. Prior Period Adjustments

Adjustments resulting from errors in the financial statements of prior periods, such as the mistake in the application of accounting principles, are included in the current financial statements without a correction of prior year's financial statements. Reclassifications in the presentation only should also adjust the figures of the preceding year.

3.4.6. Changes in Accounting Principles

Changes in accounting principles are treated in the same manner as prior period adjustments, but the effect should be disclosed in the notes.

3.4.7. Income Taxes

In the income statement the related tax effect of all events or transactions recorded must be accounted for. The income tax expense consists of the current tax as liable to the tax authorities and any deferred tax liability, if any, relating to temporary differences. Deferred tax assets such as not deductible amounts of provisions based on the accrual principle giving theoretically rise for a deferred tax asset should not be recorded, however, a deferred tax liability must be accounted for.

An envisaged amendment to the Austrian Commercial Code to be implemented with effect 1 January 1996 will provide for treatment of deferred tax assets similarly to the liability method with additional details to be disclosed in the notes.

In the notes details of the tax expense as influenced by establishing untaxed reserves must be disclosed.

3.4.8. Earnings per Share

No calculation or disclosure requirements exist.

3.4.9. Foreign Currency Translation

The foreign currency translation relates to transactions in foreign currencies and to the translation of foreign currency financial statements for consolidation and other purposes.

Transactions denominated in foreign currency should be translated using the exchange rate at the date of the transaction. At balance sheet date assets and liabilities denominated in foreign cur-

rencies should be translated using the exchange rate in effect on the balance sheet date, observing the principle of conservatism avoiding the recording of unrealized gains.

Financial statements in foreign currency for consolidation should be translated using the method best appropriate and on a consistent basis. The modified historical rate method is used predominantly.

3.4.10. Segmental Information

Segmental reporting is required. The disclosure must comprehend definition of reported segment (business and geographical), specific data as turnover, results, net assets and information relating to associated entities. An omission is possible under specific circumstances.

3.4.11. Subsequent Events

Subsequent events are events occurring after the date of the financial statements but before the preparation of the financial statements.

Events that provide evidence of conditions not existing at the balance sheet date should be disclosed if material. The effects of events that provide conditions existing at the balance sheet date should be included in the financial statements.

ACCOUNTING TERMINOLOGY

TERMINOLOGIE ZUM RECHNUNGS-WESEN

10 K Report (US)
Börsenberichterstattung der an der New Yorker Börse notierten Kapital-gesellschaften

accounting
Rechnungswesen, Rechnungslegung

accounting treatment
buchmäßige Behandlung

accounts payable
Verbindlichkeiten

accounts receivable
Forderungen, Außenstände

accrual accounting
Buchhaltung auf Basis Aufwand und Erträge

actuarial calculation
versicherungsmathematische Berechnung

adjusting events
Vorgänge, die noch im Jahreabschluß berücksichtigt werden müssen

aggregate basis
Gruppenbewertung

amortization
Abschreibung, Aufwandsverteilung, Tilgung (in Verbindung mit intangible/deferred assets)

annual financial statement
Jahresabschluß

assets
Aktiva

authorized capital
satzungsmäßiges Kapital

average cost method
Bewertung zu Durchschnittspreisen

balance sheet date
Bilanzstichtag

balance sheets
Bilanz

bargain purchase option
Kaufoption zu einem wirtschaftlich nicht ausschlaggebenden Wert

CA (Chartered Accountant) (UK)
Wirtschaftstreuhänder UK

called-up share capital
eingefordertes Aktienkapial

capital assets
Vermögensgegenstände

capital lease
Finanzierungs-Leasing

capital reserve
Kapitalrücklage

capital stock
Grundkapital

capitalization
Aktivierung

capitalization of interest
Aktivierung von Fremdkapitalzinsen

carrying value
Buchwert

cash accounting
Buchhaltung auf Basis Einnahmen und Ausgaben

cash disbursements
Ausgaben

cash flow
Cashflow

Certified Public Accountant (CPA) (US)
Wirtschaftstreuhänder US

Chamber of Accountants
Kammer der Wirtschaftstreuhänder (A)

chartered accountant (CA) (UK)
Wirtschaftstreuhänder UK

classes of stock
Aktiengattungen

closing rate method
Fremdwährungsumrechnung zu Stichtagskursen

collectibility	Einbringlichkeit
Commercial Code	Handelsgesetz
common stock (US)	Stammaktien
completed contract method	Grundsatz der Gewinnrealisierung bei Beendigung der Transaktion
consistency	Prinzip der Kontinuität
consistency and comparability	Prinzip der Kontinuität und Vergleichbarkeit
contingent liabilities	drohende Verluste
contingent losses	voraussichtliche Ausfälle
cost methods	Kalkulationsverfahren für die Bewertung
CPA (Certified Public Accountant) (US)	Wirtschaftstreuhänder (US)
cumulative effect of a change in accounting principles	kumulativer Effekt einer erlaubten Änderung einer Bilanzierungsmethode
current assets	Umlaufvermögen
current cost	Wiederbeschaffungskosten, Zeitwert
current cost convention	Anwendung von Wiederbeschaffungskosten
current liabilities	kurzfristige Verbindlichkeiten
current rate method	Methode des Stichtagskurses
current tax liabilities	Steuerverbindlichkeiten geschuldet nach ertragssteuerrechtlichen Vorschriften
declining balance method	degressive Abschreibung
deferred tax assets	Posten der aktiven Steuerabgrenzung
deferred tax liabilities	Posten der passiven Steuerabgrenzung
deficit	Verlust, Fehlbetrag
depreciation	Abschreibung (in Verbindung mit tangible assets)
direct financing lease	Direktfinanzierungs-Leasing
director's report (UK)	Geschäftsbericht, Lagebericht
director's valuation	Bewertung durch das Management
disclosure requirements	Ausweispflichten, Angabepflichten
discontinued operations	eingestellter Betrieb
doubtful accounts	zweifelhafte Forderungen
earning	Einnahme, Gewinn, Erlös
earnings per share	Gewinn je Aktie
economic useful life	wirtschaftliche Nutzungsdauer
entity	Unternehmen, Organisation, Einheit
equity	Eigenkapital
estimated liabilities	geschätzte Verbindlichkeiten/ Rückstellungen
estimated useful life	geschätzte Nutzungsdauer
expenditures	Aufwendungen
expense	als Aufwand verbuchen
extraordinary items	außerordentliche Posten
factored receivables	an einen Faktor verkaufte Forderungen
fair value	Zeitwert
FIFO (First In First Out)	FIFO-Methode
financial accounting	Finanzbuchhaltung

financial lease	Finanzierungs-Leasing
financial position	wirtschaftliche Lage, Bild der Vermögens-, Ertrags- und Finanzlage
financial statement (US)	Jahresabschluß
fixed assets	(Sach)Anlage
floor principle	Mindestbewertungsansatz
foreign currency translation	Umrechnung von Fremdwährungen
formal valuation	dokumentierte Bewertung
forward contract	Terminkontrakt
fully diluted earnings per share	Gewinn je Aktie unter Berücksichtigung möglicher Wandelrechte und Kapitalveränderungen
functional currency	wirtschaftlich maßgebende Währung
GAAP (Generally Accepted Accounting Principles) (US)	US-Grundsätze ordnungsgemäßer Rechnungslegung
general provision	allgemeine Rückstellung
Generally Accepted Accounting Principles (GAAP) (US)	US-Grundsätze ordnungsgemäßer Rechnungslegung
generally accepted accounting standards (UK)	Grundsätze ordnungsgemäßer Rechnungslegung UK
going concern	Going Concern, Unternehmensfortführung
hedging	Kurssicherungsgeschäft
historical cost	historische Anschaffungs- oder Herstellungskosten
historical cost accounting	Kostenrechnung zu historischen Kosten
historical cost convention	Anwendung historischer Kosten
historical rate method	Umrechnung zu Anschaffungskosten
hypothecation (US)	Verpfändung
identifiable transactions	einzeln identifizierbare Transaktionen
impair	beeinträchtigen
income before extraordinary items	Gewinn vor außerordentlichen Posten
income from continuing operations	Ergebnis aus laufender und fortzuführender Geschäftstätigkeit
intangible assets	immaterielle Anlagen
interest cost	Zinsaufwand
inventories	Vorräte
investments	Investitionen, Beteiligungen, Wertpapiere
issued capital	gezeichnetes Kapital
item	Posten
lease term	Leasingdauer
lessee	Leasingnehmer
lessor	Leasinggeber
leveraged lease	besondere Art des Finanzierungs-Leasings
liabilities	Schulden, Verbindlichkeiten
LIFO (Last In First Out)	LIFO-Methode
long-term debts	langfristige Verbindlichkeiten
loss provision	Verlustrückstellung

marketable securities	marktgängige Wertpapiere
marketable value	Marktwert, Zeitwert, Börsenpreis
negotiated future rate	vereinbarter zukünftiger Devisenkurs
net current replacement cost	Wiederbeschaffungskosten
net deficit	nicht durch Eigenkapital gedeckter Fehlbetrag
net income	Reingewinn
net of tax	nach Berücksichtigung des Steuereffektes
net realizable value	Nettorealisationswert
net realized gains or losses	realisierte Gewinne oder Verluste
non-current assets	Anlagevermögen
notes to the financial statement	Anhang des Jahresabschlusses
operating lease	Operating-Leasing
paid-in capital	Kapitalrücklage
pension accrual	Pensionsrückstellung
percentage of completion method	zeitanteilige Gewinnrealisierung
pledging	Verpfändung
preferred stock (US)	Vorzugsaktien
primary earnings per share	Gewinn je Aktie ohne Berücksichtigung möglicher Wandelrechte
principle of conservatism	Vorsichtsprinzip
prior period adjustments	Anpassung betreffend Vorgänge aus Vorperioden
prior service cost	Aufwendungen für Vordienstzeiten
profit and loss account (UK)	Gewinn- und Verlustrechnung
profit margin	Gewinnspanne, Deckungsbeitrag
provision	Rückstellung; Wertberichtigung
prudence	(kaufmännische) Vorsicht
prudence principle	Vorsichtsprinzip
reconciliation	Abstimmung, Überleitung
record	ausweisen
record at cost	zum Anschaffungs- oder Herstellungswert ausweisen
recourse	Regreß
recoverable amount	erzielbarer Verkaufserlös
related party	Konzernunternehmen
remeasurement method	nachträgliche Umrechnung
reportable segment	ausweispflichtige(r) Sparte/Tätigkeitsbereich
residual value	Restwert
retained earnings	einbehaltene Gewinne, Bilanzgewinne und Gewinnrücklagen
return on plan assets	Erträge auf Sondervermögen zur Deckung der Pensionsrückstellung
revaluation method	Neubewertungsmethode
revaluation reserve	Neubewertungsrücklage
revalue	neubewerten
revenue	Umsatzerlös
revenue recognition	Erlösrealisierung

sales type lease	besondere Art des Finanzierungs-Leasing
salvage value	Restwert, Schrottwert
SEC (Securities and Exchange Commission) (US)	US-Börsenaufsichtsbehörde
Securities and Exchange Commission (SEC) (US)	US-Börsenaufsichtsbehörde
segmental information	Informationen zu Tätigkeitsbereichen/ Sparten
segmental reporting	Berichterstattung zu Tätigkeitsbereichen/ Sparten
separate determination and valuation of individual assets and liabilities	Einzelbewertung
service cost	anteiliger Aufwand für laufende Periode der Tätigkeit
significant items of accrued and other liabilities	wesentliche Posten von sonstigen Verbindlichkeiten
specific identification method	Einzelbewertungsmethode
spot rate	Kassakurs
start-up cost	Kosten der Ingangsetzung, Anlaufkosten
statement of cash flow	Cashflow-Darstellung
statement of changes in stockholders' equity	Darstellung der Veränderung des Eigenkapitals
statement of income (US)	Gewinn- und Verlustrechnung (US)
statement of retained earnings (US)	Darstellung der Veränderung des Bilanzgewinns und Gewinnrücklagen
statement of source and application of funds (UK)	Kapitalflußrechnung
stock reacquired by the company	eigene Aktien
straight-line method	lineare Abschreibungsmethode
subsequent events	Vorgänge nach dem Schluß des Geschäftsjahres
sum of the year's digits method	digitale Abschreibung
surplus	Überschuß
tangible assets	Sachanlagevermögen
tax deductibility	steuerliche Abzugsfähigkeit
temporal method	Methode zur Umrechnung von Fremdwährungsposten
trade creditors	Verbindlichkeiten aus Lieferungen und Leistungen
unit of production or hours of use method	lcistungsbczogcne Abschrcibung
unrealized gains or losses	nicht realisierte Gewinne oder Verluste
useful life	Nutzungsdauer
valuation allowance (US)	Wertberichtigung auf einen Wertpapier- bestand
valuation rules	Bewertungsvorschriften
vested benefits	unverfallbarer Anspruch
write down	Abschreibung, Abwertung
write down to market	auf den Zeitwert/Marktwert abwerten

TERMINOLOGIE ZUM RECHNUNGS-WESEN

ACCOUNTING TERMINOLOGY

Abschreibung	*depreciation* (bei *tangible assets*), *amortization* (bei *intangible/deferred assets*), *write down*
Abstimmung	*reconciliation*
Abwertung	*write down*
Aktiengattungen	*classes of stock*
Aktiva	*assets*
Aktivierung	*capitalization*
Aktivierung von Fremdkapitalzinsen	*capitalization of interest*
allgemeine Rückstellung	*general provision*
als Aufwand verbuchen	*expense*
Angabepflichten	*disclosure requirements*
Anhang des Jahresabschlusses	*notes to the financial statement*
Anlage	*fixed asset*
Anlagevermögen	*non-current assets*
Anlaufkosten	*start-up cost*
Anpassung betreffend Vorgänge aus Vorperioden	*prior period adjustments*
anteiliger Aufwand für laufende Periode der Tätigkeit	*service cost*
Anwendung historischer Kosten	*historical cost convention*
Anwendung von Wiederbeschaffungskosten	*current cost convention*
auf den Zeitwert/Marktwert abwerten	*write down to market*
Aufwandsverteilung	*amortization*
Aufwendungen	*expenditures*
Aufwendungen für Vordienstzeiten	*prior service cost*
Ausgaben	*cash disbursements*
Außenstände	*accounts receivable*
außerordentliche Posten	*extraordinary items*
ausweisen	*record*
Ausweispflichten	*disclosure requirements*
ausweispflichtige(r) Sparte/Tätigkeitsbereich	*reportable segment*
beeinträchtigen	*impair*
Berichterstattung zu Tätigkeitsbereichen/ Sparten	*segmental reporting*
Bewertung durch das Management	*director's valuation*
Bewertung zu Durchschnittspreisen	*average cost method*
Bewertungsvorschriften	*valuation rules*
Bilanz	*balance sheets*
Bilanzstichtag	*balance sheet date*
Bild der Vermögens-, Ertrags- und Finanzlage	*financial position*
Buchhaltung auf Basis Aufwand und Erträge	*accrual accounting*
Buchhaltung auf Basis Einnahmen und Ausgaben	*cash accounting*
buchmäßige Behandlung	*accounting treatment*
Buchwert	*carrying value*

Cashflow	*cash flow*
Cashflow-Darstellung	*statement of cash flow*
Darstellung der Veränderung des Bilanzgewinns und Gewinnrücklagen	*statement of retained earnings (US)*
Darstellung der Veränderung des Eigenkapitals	*statement of changes in stockholders' equity*
Deckungsbeitrag	*profit margin*
degressive Abschreibung	*declining balance method*
digitale Abschreibung	*sum of the year's digits method*
Direktfinanzierungs-Leasing	*direct financing lease*
dokumentierte Bewertung	*formal valuation*
drohende Verluste	*contingent liabilities*
eigene Aktien	*stock reacquired by the company*
Eigenkapital	*equity*
einbehaltene Gewinne	*retained earnings*
Einbringlichkeit	*collectibility*
eingefordertes Aktienkapial	*called-up share capital*
eingestellter Betrieb	*discontinued operations*
Einnahme	*earning*
Einzelbewertung	*separate determination and valuation of individual assets and liabilities*
Einzelbewertungsmethode	*specific identification method*
einzeln identifizierbare Transaktionen	*identifiable transactions*
Ergebnis aus laufender und fortzuführender Geschäftstätigkeit	*income from continuing operations*
Erlös	*earnings*
Erlösrealisierung	*revenue recognition*
Erträge auf Sondervermögen zur Deckung der Pensionsrückstellung	*return on plan assets*
erzielbarer Verkaufserlös	*recoverable amount*
Fehlbetrag	*deficit*
Finanzbuchhaltung	*financial accounting*
Finanzierungs-Leasing	*capital lease, financial lease*
Forderungen	*accounts receivable, receivables*
Forderungen, an einen Faktor verkauft	*factored receivables*
Fremdwährungsumrechnung zu Stichtagskursen	*closing rate method*
Geschäftsbericht	*director's report (UK)*
geschätzte Nutzungsdauer	*estimated useful life*
geschätzte Rückstellungen	*estimated liabilities*
geschätzte Verbindlichkeiten	*estimated liabilities*
Gewinn	*profit, earnings*
Gewinn je Aktie	*earnings per share*
Gewinn je Aktie ohne Berücksichtigung möglicher Wandelrechte	*primary earnings per share*
Gewinn je Aktie unter Berücksichtigung möglicher Wandelrechte und Kapitalveränderungen	*fully diluted earnings per share*
Gewinn vor außerordentlichen Posten	*income before extraordinary items*

Gewinn- und Verlustrechnung	*profit and loss account (UK), statement of income, income statement (US)*
Gewinnspanne	*profit margin*
gezeichnetes Kapital	*issued capital*
Grundkapital	*capital stock*
Grundsatz der Gewinnrealisierung bei Beendigung der Transaktion	*completed contract method*
Grundsätze ordnungsgemäßer Rechnungslegung	*generally accepted accounting standards (UK), Generally Accepted Accounting Principles (GAAP) (US)*
Gruppenbewertung	*aggregate basis*
Handelsgesetz	*Commercial Code*
historische Anschaffungs- oder Herstellungskosten	*historical cost*
immaterielle Anlagen	*intangible assets*
Informationen zu Tätigkeitsbereichen/Sparten	*segmental information*
Investitionen	*investments*
Jahresabschluß	*annual financial statement (UK), financial statement (US)*
Kalkulationsverfahren für die Bewertung	*cost methods*
Kammer der Wirtschaftstreuhänder	*Chamber of Accountants*
Kapitalflußrechnung	*statement of source and application of funds (UK)*
Kapitalrücklage	*capital reserve, paid-in capital*
Kassakurs	*spot rate*
Kaufoption zu einem wirtschaftlich nicht ausschlaggebenden Wert	*bargain purchase option*
Konzernunternehmen	*group company, related party*
Kosten der Ingangsetzung	*start-up cost*
Kostenrechnung zu historischen Kosten	*historical cost accounting*
kumulativer Effekt einer erlaubten Änderung einer Bilanzierungsmethode	*cumulative effect of a change in accounting principles*
Kurssicherungsgeschäft	*hedging*
kurzfristige Verbindlichkeiten	*current liabilities*
Lagebericht	*director's report (UK)*
langfristige Verbindlichkeiten	*long-term debts*
Leasingdauer	*lease term*
Leasinggeber	*lessor*
Leasingnehmer	*lessee*
leistungsbezogene Abschreibung	*unit of production or hours of use method*
lineare Abschreibungsmethode	*straight-line method*
marktgängige Wertpapiere	*marketable securities*
Marktwert	*marketable value*
Methode des Stichtagskurses	*current rate method*
Methode zur Umrechnung von Fremd- währungsposten	*temporal method*
Mindestbewertungsansatz	*floor principle*

nach Berücksichtigung des Steuereffektes	*net of tax*
nachträgliche Umrechnung	*remeasurement method*
Nettorealisationswert	*net realizable value*
neubewerten	*revalue*
Neubewertungsmethode	*revaluation method*
Neubewertungsrücklage	*revaluation reserve*
nicht durch Eigenkapital gedeckter Fehlbetrag	*net deficit*
nicht realisierte Gewinne oder Verluste	*unrealized gains or losses*
Nutzungsdauer	*useful life*
Operating-Leasing	*operating lease*
Pensionsrückstellung	*pension accrual*
Posten	*item*
Posten der aktiven Steuerabgrenzung	*deferred tax assets*
Posten der passiven Steuerabgrenzung	*deferred tax liabilities*
Prinzip der Kontinuität	*consistency*
Prinzip der Kontinuität und Vergleichbarkeit	*consistency and comparability*
realisierte Gewinne oder Verluste	*net realized gains or losses*
Rechnungslegung	*accounting*
Rechnungswesen	*accounting*
Regreß	*recourse*
Reingewinn	*net income*
Restwert	*residual value*
Rückstellung	*provision*
Sachanlage	*fixed asset*
Sachanlagevermögen	*tangible assets*
satzungsmäßiges Kapital	*authorized capital*
Schrottwert	*salvage value*
Schulden	*liabilities*
Stammaktien	*ordinary shares (UK), common stock (US)*
steuerliche Abzugsfähigkeit	*tax deductibility*
Steuerverbindlichkeiten geschuldet nach ertragssteuerrechtlichen Vorschriften	*current tax liabilities*
Terminkontrakt	*forward contract*
Tilgung	*amortization*
Überleitung	*reconciliation*
Überschuß	*surplus*
Umlaufvermögen	*current assets*
Umrechnung von Fremdwährungen	*foreign currency translation*
Umrechnung zu Anschaffungskosten	*historical rate method*
Umsatzerlös	*revenue*
Unternehmensfortführung	*going concern*
unverfallbarer Anspruch	*vested benefits*
Verbindlichkeiten	*liabilities, accounts payable*
Verbindlichkeiten aus Lieferungen und Leistungen	*trade creditors*

vereinbarter zukünftiger Devisenkurs	*negotiated future rate*
Verlust	*deficit*
Verlustrückstellung	*loss provision*
Vermögensgegenstände	*capital assets*
Verpfändung	*pledging, hypothecation*
versicherungsmathematische Berechnung	*actuarial calculation*
voraussichtliche Ausfälle	*contingent losses*
Vorgänge nach dem Schluß des Geschäftsjahres	*subsequent events*
Vorgänge, die noch im Jahreabschluß berücksichtigt werden müssen	*adjusting events*
Vorräte	*inventories*
Vorsicht	*prudence*
Vorsichtsprinzip	*principle of conservatism, prudence principle*
Vorzugsaktien	*preference shares (UK), preferred stock (US)*
Wertberichtigung	*provision*
Wertberichtigung auf einen Wertpapierbestand	*valuation allowance (US)*
wesentliche Posten von sonstigen Verbindlichkeiten	*significant items of accrued and other liabilities*
Wiederbeschaffungskosten	*current cost, net current replacement cost*
wirtschaftlich maßgebende Währung	*functional currency*
wirtschaftliche Lage	*financial position*
wirtschaftliche Nutzungsdauer	*economic useful life*
Wirtschaftstreuhänder	*Certified Public Accountant (CPA) (US), chartered accountant (CA) (UK)*
zeitanteilige Gewinnrealisierung	*percentage of completion method*
Zeitwert	*fair value, marketable value, current cost*
Zinsaufwand	*interest cost*
zum Anschaffungs- oder Herstellungswert ausweisen	*record at cost*
zweifelhafte Forderungen	*doubtful accounts*

AUSTRIA	UNITED STATES (US)	UNITED KINGDOM (UK)
BILANZ	**BALANCE SHEET**	**BALANCE SHEET CLASSIFICATION**
Aktivseite	**Assets**	**Assets**
A. Anlagevermögen	A. Fixed assets	A. Fixed assets
I. Immaterielle Vermögensgegenstände	I. Intangible assets	I. Intangible assets
1. Konzessionen, gewerbliche Schutzrechte und Vorteile sowie daraus abgeleitete Lizenzen	1. Concessions, trademarks and similar rights, licences	1. Concessions, patents, licences, trade marks and similar rights and assets
2. Geschäfts(Firmen-)wert	2. Goodwill	2. Goodwill
3. Geleistete Anzahlungen	3. Prepayments	3. Payments on account
II. Sachanlagen	II. Property, plant and equipment	II. Tangible assets
1. Bebaute Grundstücke und Bauten auf fremdem Grund	1. Land with buildings and buildings on non-owned land	1. Land and buildings
2. Unbebaute Grundstücke	2. Land without buildings	2. Land without buildings
3. Maschinen und maschinelle Anlagen	3. Machinery and equipment	3. Plant and machinery
4. Werkzeuge, Betriebs- und Geschäftsausstattung	4. Tools, furniture and fixtures	4. Fixtures, fittings, tools and equipment
5. Geleistete Anzahlungen und Anlagen in Bau	5. Prepayments and construction in progress	5. Payments on account and assets in course of construction
III. Finanzanlagen	III. Financial assets	III. Investments
1. Beteiligungen, davon Anteile an verbundenen Unternehmen	1. Investments, thereof group	1. Shares in group undertakings
2. Ausleihungen	2. (long term) borrowings	2. Loans
3. Wertpapiere (Wertrechte) des Anlagevermögens	3. Securities	3. Securities
4. Geleistete Anzahlungen	4. Prepayments	4. Payments on account

AUSTRIA	UNITED STATES (US)	UNITED KINGDOM (UK)
B. Umlaufvermögen	B. Current assets	B. Current assets
I. Vorräte	I. Inventory	I. Stocks
1. Roh-, Hilfs- und Betriebsstoffe	1. Raw materials and supplies	1. Raw materials and consumables
2. Unfertige Erzeugnisse	2. Semi-finished goods	2. Work in progress
3. Fertige Erzeugnisse und Waren	3. Finished goods and merchandise	3. Finished goods and goods for resale
4. Noch nicht abrechenbare Leistungen	4. Services rendered, not yet chargeable	4. Services rendered, not yet chargeable
5. Geleistete Anzahlungen	5. Prepayments	5. Payments on account
II. Forderungen und sonstige Vermögensgegenstände	II. Receivables and other assets	II. Debtors
1. Forderungen aus Lieferungen und Leistungen	1. Accounts receivable-trade	1. Trade debtors
2. Forderungen gegen verbundene Unternehmen	2. Accounts receivable-group	2. Amounts owed by group undertakings
3. Forderungen gegen Unternehmen, mit denen ein Beteiligungsverhältnis besteht	3. Accounts receivable-affiliates	3. Amounts owed by undertakings in which the company has a participating interest
4. Sonstige Forderungen und Vermögensgegenstände	4. Other receivables and assets	4. Other debtors
III. Wertpapiere und Anteile	III. Securities and interests	III. Investments
1. Eigene Anteile	1. Treasury stock	1. Own shares
2. Anteile an verbundenen Unternehmen	2. Interests in group (companies)	2. Shares in group undertakings
3. Sonstige Wertpapiere und Anteile	3. Other securities and interests	3. Other investments
IV. Kassenbestand, Schecks, Guthaben bei Kreditinstituten	IV. Cash on hand and in banks, checks	IV. Cash at bank and in hand
C. Rechnungsabgrenzungsposten	C. Prepaid expenses and deferred charges	C. Prepayments and accrued income

294

AUSTRIA	UNITED STATES (US)	UNITED KINGDOM (UK)
Passivseite	**Liabilities and Shareholders' Equity**	**Liabilities**
A. Eigenkapital	A. Owners' equity	A. Capital and reserves
I. Nennkapital (Grund-, Stammkapital)	I. Share capital, registered capital	I. Called up share capital
II. Kapitalrücklagen	II. Additional paid-in capital	II. Share premium account
1. Gebundene	1. Appropriated	1. Appropriated reserves
2. Nicht gebundene	2. Unappropriated	2. Unappropriated reserves
III. Gewinnrücklagen	III. Reserves from retained earnings	III. Other reserves
1. Gesetzliche Rücklage	1. Statutory reserve	1. Statutory reserve
2. Satzungsmäßige Rücklagen	2. Reserve under by-laws	2. Reserves under the article of association
3. Andere (freie) Rücklagen	3. Other reserves (voluntary reserve)	3. Other (free) reserves
IV. Bilanzgewinn/Bilanzverlust	IV. Retained earnings	IV. Profit and loss account
B. Unversteuerte Rücklagen	B. Untaxed reserves	B. Untaxed reserves
1. Bewertungsreserve auf Grund von Sonderabschreibungen	1. Valuation reserve due to special depreciations	1. Reserves from additional capital allowances
2. Sonstige unversteuerte Rücklagen	2. Other untaxed reserves	2. Other untaxed reserves
C. Rückstellungen	C. Accruals and provisions	C. Provisions
1. Rückstellungen für Abfertigungen	1. Accrual for severance payment	1. Provision for termination payments
2. Rückstellung für Pensionen	2. Accrual for pension	2. Provision for pensions
3. Steuerrückstellungen	3. Accruals for taxes	3. Taxation including deferred taxation
4. Sonstige Rückstellungen	4. Other accruals	4. Other provisions

AUSTRIA	UNITED STATES (US)	UNITED KINGDOM (UK)
D. Verbindlichkeiten	D. Liabilities	D. Creditors
1. Anleihen	1. Bonds	1. Debenture loans
2. Verbindlichkeiten gegenüber Kreditinstituten	2. Bank loans and overdraft	2. Bank loans and overdrafts
3. Erhaltene Anzahlungen auf Bestellungen	3. Prepayments received	3. Payments received on account
4. Verbindlichkeiten aus Lieferungen und Leistungen	4. Accounts payable-trade	4. Trade creditors
5. Verbindlichkeiten aus der Annahme gezogener Wechsel und der Ausstellung eigener Wechsel	5. Notes and drafts payable	5. Bills of exchange payable
6. Verbindlichkeiten gegenüber verbundenen Unternehmen	6. Accounts payable-group	6. Amounts owed to group undertakings
7. Verbindlichkeiten gegenüber Unternehmen, mit denen ein Beteiligungsverhältnis besteht	7. Accounts payable-affiliates	7. Amounts owed to undertakings in which the company has a participating interest
8. Sonstige Verbindlichkeiten	8. Other liabilities	8. Other creditors
E. Rechnungsabgrenzungsposten	E. Deferred income and credits	E. Accruals and deferred income

AUSTRIA	UNITED STATES (US)	UNITED KINGDOM (UK)
GEWINN- UND VERLUSTRECHNUNG	**INCOME STATEMENT**	**PROFIT AND LOSS ACCOUNT**
Gliederung	**Classification (format and items listed)**	**Classification**
Gesamtkostenverfahren	**Expenditure (total cost) format**	**Expenditure format**

AUSTRIA	UNITED STATES (US)	UNITED KINGDOM (UK)
1. Umsatzerlöse	1. Net sales, turnover	1. Turnover
2. Erhöhung/Verminderung des Bestandes an fertigen und unfertigen Erzeugnissen sowie an noch nicht abrechenbaren Leistungen	2. Increase or decrease in inventory	2. Change in stocks of finished goods and in work in progress
3. Im Anlagevermögen berücksichtigte Eigenleistungen	3. Own work capitalized	3. Own work capitalized
4. Sonstige betriebliche Erträge	4. Other operating income	4. Other operating income
a) Erträge aus dem Abgang vom und der Zuschreibung zum Anlagevermögen mit Ausnahme der Finanzanlagen	a) Income from retirement and write-up excluding financial assets	a) Income from retirement and write-up excluding financial assets
b) Erträge aus der Auflösung von Rückstellungen	b) Income from reversal of accruals and provisions	b) Income from reversal of accruals and provisions
c) Übrige	c) Sundry	c) Other
5. Materialaufwand und Aufwendungen für bezogene Leistungen	5. Costs of materials and services	5. Cost of materials and services
6. Personalaufwand	6. Personnel expenses	6. Staff costs
a) Löhne	a) Wages	a) Wages
b) Gehälter	b) Salaries	b) Salaries
c) Aufwendungen für Abfertigungen und Pensionen	c) Expenses for severance payments and pensions	c) Expenses for termination payments and pensions
d) Aufwendungen für gesetzlich vorgeschriebene Sozialabgaben sowie vom Entgelt abhängige Abgaben	d) Expenses for statutory social security and payroll related contributions	d) Social security costs and payroll related taxes

AUSTRIA	UNITED STATES (US)	UNITED KINGDOM (UK)
e) Sonstige Sozialaufwendungen	e) Other social benefits	e) Other social benefits
7. Abschreibungen auf immaterielle Vermögensgegenstände und Sachanlagen sowie auf Aufwendungen für das Ingangsetzen, Erweitern und Umstellen eines Betriebes	7. Amortization of intangible assets and depreciation of fixed assets and capitalized start-up, expansion and restructuring costs	7. Amortization of intangible assets and depreciation of fixed assets and capitalized start-up, expansion and restructuring costs
8. Sonstige betriebliche Aufwendungen	8. Other operating expenses	8. Other operating charges
a) Steuern, soweit sie nicht unter Z 21 fallen	a) Taxes not included in line 21	a) Taxes, not included in line 21
b) Übrige	b) Sundry	b) Other
9. Zwischensumme aus Z 1. bis 8.	9. Subtotal (line 1 to 8)	9. Subtotal (line 1 to 8)
10. Erträge aus Beteiligungen	10. Income from investments	10. Income from participating interests
11. Zinsenerträge, Wertpapiererträge und ähnliche Erträge, davon aus verbundenen Unternehmen	11. Income from interest, securities and similar, thereof group	11. Income from interest, securities and similar, thereof group undertaking
12. Erträge aus dem Abgang von und der Zuschreibung zu Finanzanlagen	12. Income from retirement and write-up of financial assets	12. Income from retirement and write-up of financial assets
13. Aufwendungen aus Beteiligungen	13. Investment related expenses	13. Investment related expenses
14. Abschreibungen auf sonstige Finanzanlagen und auf Wertpapiere des Umlaufvermögens	14. Depreciation of other financial assets, and other current assets' securities	14. Depreciation of other financial assets and other current assets' securities
15. Zinsen und ähnliche Aufwendungen, davon betreffend verbundene Unternehmen	15. Interest and similar expenses, thereof group	15. Interest payable and similar charges, of which in group undertakings
16. Zwischensumme aus Z 10. bis 15.	16. Subtotal (line 10 to 15)	16. Intermediary amount 10 to 15
17. Ergebnis der gewöhnlichen Geschäftstätigkeit	17. Ordinary business result	17. Profit or loss on ordinary activities
18. Außerordentliche Erträge	18. Extraordinary income	18. Extraordinary income

AUSTRIA	UNITED STATES (US)	UNITED KINGDOM (UK)
19. Außerordentliche Aufwendungen	19. Extraordinary expenses	19. Extraordinary charges
20. Außerordentliches Ergebnis	20. Extraordinary result	20. Extraordinary profit or loss
21. Steuern vom Einkommen und vom Ertrag	21. Income taxes	21. Taxes on income
22. Jahresüberschuß/ Jahresfehlbetrag	22. Annual income/loss before changes in reserves	22. Profit or loss for the year
23. Auflösung unversteuerter Rücklagen	23. Reversal of untaxed reserves	23. Reversal of untaxed reserves
24. Auflösung von Kapitalrücklagen	24. Reversal of additional paid-in capital	24. Reversal of share premium account
25. Auflösung von Gewinnrücklagen	25. Reversal of reserves from retained earnings	25. Reversal of other reserves
26. Zuweisung zu unversteuerten Rücklagen	26. Allocation to untaxed reserves	26. Allocation to untaxed reserves
27. Zuweisung zu Gewinnrücklagen	27. Allocation to reserves from retained earnings	27. Allocation to other-reserves
28. Gewinnvortrag/ Verlustvortrag aus dem Vorjahr	28. Profit/Loss brought forward	28. Profit/Loss brought forward
29. Bilanzgewinn/Bilanzverlust	29. Retained earnings	29. Profit or loss

AUSTRIA	UNITED STATES (US)	UNITED KINGDOM (UK)
Umsatzkostenverfahren	**Operational (cost of sales) format**	**Operational format**
1. Umsatzerlöse	1. Net sales	1. Turnover
2. Herstellungskosten der zur Erzielung der Umsatzerlöse erbrachten Leistungen	2. Costs of goods sold	2. Cost of sales
3. Bruttoergebnis vom Umsatz	3. Gross profit	3. Gross profit or loss
4. Sonstige betriebliche Erträge	4. Other operating income	4. Other operating income
a) Erträge aus dem Abgang vom und der Zuschreibung zum Anlagevermögen mit Ausnahme der Finanzanlagen	a) Income from retirement and write-up excluding financial assets	a) Income from retirement and write-up excluding financial assets
b) Erträge aus der Auflösung von Rückstellungen	b) Income from reversal of accruals and provisions	b) Income from release of accruals
c) Übrige	c) Sundry	c) Other
5. Vertriebskosten	5. Selling expenses	5. Distribution costs
6. Verwaltungskosten	6. Administrative expenses	6. Administrative expenses
7. Sonstige betriebliche Aufwendungen	7. Other operational expenses	7. Other operating expenses
8. Zwischensumme aus Z 1. bis 7.	8. Subtotal (line 1 to 7)	8. Subtotal (line 1 to 7)
9. Erträge aus Beteiligungen	9. Income from investments	9. Income from participating interests
10. Zinsenerträge, Wertpapiererträge und ähnliche Erträge, davon aus verbundenen Unternehmen	10. Income from interest, securities and similar, thereof group	10. Income from interest, securities and similar, thereof group undertakings
11. Erträge aus dem Abgang von und der Zuschreibung zu Finanzanlagen	11. Income from retirement and write-up of financial assets	11. Income from retirement and write-up of financial assets
12. Aufwendungen aus Beteiligungen	12. Investment related expenses	12. Investment related expenses
13. Abschreibungen auf sonstige Finanzanlagen und auf Wertpapiere des Umlaufvermögens	13. Depreciation of other financial assets and other current assets' securities	13. Depreciation of other financial assets and other current assets' securities

300

AUSTRIA	UNITED STATES (US)	UNITED KINGDOM (UK)
14. Zinsen und ähnliche Aufwendungen, davon betreffend verbundene Unternehmen	14. Interest and similar expenses, thereof group	14. Interest payable and similar charges, of which in group undertakings
15. Zwischensumme aus Z 9. bis 14.	15. Subtotal (line 9 to 14)	15. Subtotal (line 9 to 14)
16. Ergebnis der gewöhnlichen Geschäftstätigkeit	16. Ordinary business result	16. Profit or loss on ordinary activities
17. Außerordentliche Erträge	17. Extraordinary income	17. Extraordinary income
18. Außerordentliche Aufwendungen	18. Extraordinary expenses	18. Extraordinary charges
19. Außerordentliches Ergebnis	19. Extraordinary result	19. Extraordinary profit or loss
20. Steuern vom Einkommen und vom Ertrag	20. Income taxes	20. Taxes on income
21. Jahresüberschuß/- Jahresfehlbetrag	21. Annual income/loss before changes in reserves	21. Profit or loss for the year
22. Auflösung unversteuerter Rücklagen	22. Reversal of untaxed reserves	22. Reversal of untaxed reserves
23. Auflösung von Kapitalrücklagen	23. Reversal of additional paid-in capital	23. Reversal of share premium account
24. Auflösung von Gewinnrücklagen	24. Reversal of reserves from retained earnings	24. Reversal of other reserves
25. Zuweisung zu unversteuerten Rücklagen	25. Allocation to untaxed reserves	25. Allocation to untaxed reserves
26. Zuweisung zu Gewinnrücklagen	26. Allocation to reserves from retained earnings	26. Allocation to other reserves
27. Gewinnvortrag/ Verlustvortrag aus dcm Vorjahr	27. Profit/Loss brought forward	27. Profit/Loss brought forward
28. Bilanzgewinn/Bilanzverlust	28. Retained earnings	28. Profit or loss

VIII. INTELLECTUAL PROPERTY LAW

The field of law relating to intellectual property is indeed a broad one. Traditionally, intellectual property includes three major legal areas, namely those of patents, trademarks and copyright and a fourth area dealing with trade secrets. Though each of these subjects is a distinctly different field of law, they do have quite a lot in common, since they are all concerned with an abstract or immaterial form of property.

Apart from the historical development of the law relating to intellectual property in England and the U.S. on the one hand and in continental Europe on the other, which shows many parallels on the legislative side, there is hardly any other field of law where concepts are so similar in both legal systems. What is most noteworthy in this respect is the fact that in all these areas of intellectual property continental legal systems have been substantially influenced by case law, which is atypical for codified legal systems. On the other hand, both Great Britain and the U.S. have had a fairly developed statutory basis for the regulation and control of intellectual property matters in addition to their common law body of intellectual property regulations. The granting and protecting of intellectual property rights has always been considered a valuable and indispensable asset and an incentive for creativity as well as inventiveness, which in turn directly benefits economic interests of a free market society. National interests led to the development of intellectual property-related law and the introduction of respective regulatory frameworks. However, with the increasing importance of international economic ties and cross-border transactions the need for harmonization of intellectual property regulations emerged. Similar needs within the individual jurisdictions as well as international conventions and organizations have contributed to a fairly broad, and to a large extent similar, body of laws and regulations in both continental European and common law legal systems.

We do not, however, suggest that substantial differences between the individual legal systems and jurisdictions do not exist, but we would rather like to point out that someone who knows his/her own country's regulatory framework concerning e.g. trademark protection, will probably have comparatively few problems in relating to and eventually understanding the concepts and terminology of Anglo-American intellectual property law.

In the following, a very brief discussion on the law of patent, trademark and copyright is presented with a focus on U.S. regulations, followed by several sample documents (two

assignment deed
license agreement
registration
certificate, legal
practicioner

assignment deeds, an excerpt from a license agreement and an excerpt from the official WIPO registration certificate) which may be helpful for the legal practitioner. Finally, a set of vocabulary covering the fields of patent, trademark and copyright law is intended to provide the reader with the terminology most commonly needed in these respective fields.

1. PATENT LAW

1.1. Origins and legal framework

In the United States, the right to grant patents and copyrights is one of the federal powers laid down in the Constitution of 1778. Article 1 Section 8, Clause 8 reads:

> *The Congress shall have power (...) To promote the progress of science and useful arts, by securing for limited times to authors and inventors the exclusive right to their respective writings and discoveries.*

Apart from the constitutional provision which vests the regulatory power for patent law matters in the Congress, the basic set of regulations is laid down in the Patent Act, 35 U.S.C.A. (United States Code Annotated) (1952).

to grant patents
federal powers

provision

Patent Act U.S.C.A.

1.2. Types and duration

Under U.S. regulations a patent is granted to prevent others from making, using or selling the patented invention. The U.S. Patent and Trademark Office, which is the official federal authority for patent and trademark-related matters, grants three types of patents, namely utility patents, plant patents and design patents. Whereas utility and plant patents are enforceable for a period of 17 years from the date of issuance, design patents only enjoy protection for a period of 14 years. Utility patents may be granted for mechanical, electrical, chemical, and/or functional aspects of an invention and/or improvements thereof. Design patents may be granted for a certain shape or appearance of an article of manufacture provided that it is original, novel or ornamental. It may, however, not be granted merely for functional aspects of a product. Plant patents may be granted for newly created plants. Recently, there has been a discussion as to whether or not a patent could be granted on genetically manipulated and thus newly created animals.

invention
U.S. Patent and
Trademark Office
authority
utility, plant and
design patents
to be enforceable,
date of issuance,
patent period

originality, novelty

1.3. Subject matter of patents

subject matter

The Patent Act provides for a specific enumeration of the kind of things that may receive patent protection:

> *Whoever invents or discovers any new and useful process, machine, manufacture, or composition of matter, or any new and useful improvement thereof, may obtain a patent therefor, subject to the conditions and requirements of this title (35 U.S.C.A. sect. 101).*

Thus, there are basically two major categories of matters that may be subject to patent protections, namely processes and products (machines, manufactures or composition of matter). Specifically barred from patentability in the United States are subject matters such as ideas, naturally occurring substances, printed matters,

processes, products
to be barred from
patentability

laws of nature, natural forces, principles, mere chemical formulas, systems of book-keeping, fundamental truths, methods of calculation, etc.

prerequisites

1.4. Prerequisites for protection

to be eligible for

utility
non-obviousness
ordinary skill

disclosure

specifications

license
patentholder
owner
termination

In order to be eligible for patent protection any process or product for which protection is sought needs to show or meet the requirements of utility, novelty, and originality, needs to be operative and must not be obvious to a person of ordinary skill in the art to which the patent is directed. Finally, the invention must be sufficiently disclosed to the effect that any person of ordinary skill is enabled to manufacture a product or put into operation a process solely based on the specifications made in the description of the patent, which may legitimately be done upon obtaining permission to do so (license) from the patentholder/owner for the life of the patent or unrestrictedly upon the termination of a patent.

ownership

1.5. Ownership

life of patent

right to use, make or
sell

working the patent
exploitation
compulsory licensing,
anti-trust

Sect. 261 of the Patent Act provides that during the life of the patent the owner has the complete right to determine who, if anybody, will have the right to use, make or sell the patented item. Since there is no requirement under American law (as opposed to many continental legal systems) that the patentee put the patent to use ("working" the patent), the inventor also has a right to determine where and how the patent will be initially exploited. Compulsory licensing, an instrument by means of which an inventor seeking patent protection may be forced to allow others to use the patent is, just like working the patent, no absolute requirement under American law. Compulsory licensing may, however, be available under certain anti-trust regulations.

application,
procedures
Patent and
Trademark Office
patentee
patentability
search
drafting the
application

filing, public
use, offering for sale,
disclosure,
publication

reproduction

1.6. Patent application/Procedures

Before applying to the Patent and Trademark Office for patent protection the (prospective) patentee will first carry out a patentability search to determine if the patent has already been granted for his/her invention. The next step is to draft the application which is a highly formalized procedure and will generally have to be done by specialists. The application will have to be filed within one year following the public use or offering for sale of the invention in the United States or the disclosure of the invention in any publication anywhere in the world. A patent application basically consists of two major parts, namely a detailed description of the invention, which must enable a person of ordinary skill to reproduce the invention without difficulties and a set of so-called claims. The claims define the inventor's rights and assert that the invention fulfills all requirements necessary for patent protection (originality, novelty, utility and non-obviousness). The claims will define the scope of coverage of the patent, which is why patentability will rise or fall upon the claims.

After an application has been filed, it will be assigned to a patent examiner, who is an expert in the area of the invention. This examiner will make an initial examination and may already at that stage reject the application. Upon notification of such rejection the applicant has the right to apply for re-examination after having provided additional arguments/evidence or after having modified his/her claims. Once claims have been rejected twice and/or a final notice of rejection has been issued, the applicant has a right to appeal to the Patent Office's Board of Appeals, which may affirm, reverse or modify the examiner's decision. Unfavorable decisions of the Patent Office's Board of Appeals may be appealed in the Court of Appeals for the Federal Circuit or in the U.S. District Court for the District of Columbia.

to be assigned to
patent examiner
expert, initial
examination, reject,
notification,
rejection, applicant,
reexamination

final notice of
rejection, appeal,
Patent Office's Board
of Appeals, to affirm,
to reverse, to modify

If the examiner agrees on the patent claims or if any of the aforementioned authorities/courts render an affirmative decision, a notice of allowance will be issued and the patent will thus be granted.

1.7. Infringement

The Patent Act provides for the definition of three types of patent infringement: direct, indirect and contributory infringement. Direct infringement may be defined as an act committed by a person who without permission makes, uses or sells the patented invention. If a person actively induces or encourages another to commit a direct infringement, s/he would thus be an indirect infringer of the patent. Contributory infringement can be committed by the sale of a component which by itself is not subject to patent protection but can only be used in connection with a patented invention. Whereas a direct or indirect infringer will be liable regardless of whether s/he has knowingly committed the act of infringement, a contributory infringer may be excused if s/he has committed the act unknowingly. There are certain concepts and strategies of defense relating to the charge of a patent infringement, such as the misuse doctrine. Misuse can be described as an attempt to illegitimately extend a patent in order to obtain a kind of monopoly in a market.

direct, indirect and
contributory
infringement, to
commit an act

to be liable

strategies of defense,
misuse doctrine
illegitimate, monopoly

1.8. Remedies

Under U.S. regulations, remedies for infringement are injunctive relief, damages, attorneys' fees in exceptional cases, and costs. Injunctive relief is a (preliminary) remedy available under equity law and may involve a broad range of court orders aimed at immediate relief stopping or preventing the infringer from committing acts of infringement. Damages are awarded on the basis that

regulations
injunctive relief,
damages
equity law
court orders

to award damages

royalty

punitive
prevailing party

they are adequate to compensate the plaintiff but in no case less than what would constitute a reasonable royalty. Apart from that, courts also have an option to award a multiple of the actual damages suffered (the ceiling would be to treble the amount) which contains a punitive element. Attorneys' fees will only be awarded to the prevailing party in exceptional cases such as an intentional infringement.

2. TRADEMARKS

2.1. Origins and legal framework

The concept of trademarks can be traced back to the medieval period when members of a guild started to affix the mark or sign of their respective guild to the goods they sold in order to identify the goods as a product of guild or craftsman. Soon the use of marks and labels also became a means to indicate certain quality standards and thus gave the producer an opportunity to gain a competitive edge over others. Thus, trademarks originated as devices to identify the producer of goods for sale in a certain market place.

In the U.S. Constitution, the right to regulate trademarks is not specifically enumerated amongst the rights conferred upon Congress (as opposed to patents and copyrights). Since the regulation of trademark-related rights is not specifically listed in the Constitution, this field of law and the power to regulate it, respectively, is vested with the States. Congress tried to federalize trademark regulations and even passed a Federal Statute to this end, but this Statute was declared unconstitutional, which is why Congress had to limit itself to the passing of a Statute regulating inter-state matters relating to trademark law. This Statute is called the Lanham Act and can be found at 15 U.S.C.A. Section 1051 et seq. The Lanham Act defines trademark as "any word, name, symbol or device, or any combination thereof, adopted and used by a manufacturer or merchant to identify his goods and distinguish them from those manufactured or sold by others".

2.2. Types of marks

Protection may be granted to trademarks or service marks, which designate the source of goods or services and symbolize the goodwill associated with the product or service. The creation and protection of marks are governed by the Lanham Act (on a federal level), State regulations, and by common law.

A tradename, which is the business name used in association with a business entity, is excluded from registration under the Lanham Act. It may, however, be protected under the common law through use.

Marks should be arbitrary or fanciful but are, however, often to a certain extent descriptive of the product. Generic terms or descriptive ones are not registrable unless and until the term in question becomes distinctive of the goods or services of a certain producer in commerce. In such case, protection would be granted as a result of what is called the secondary meaning or acquired distinctiveness.

309

2.3. Prerequisites for protection

prerequisites

creation and
establishment of
rights, date of first use

A precondition for the creation and establishment of rights in a mark is that the mark must be used. The date of first use is decisive with respect to the creation of common law trademark rights.

2.4. Application for registration under the Lanham Act/Procedures

application for
registration,
procedures

owner

to apply for

classes of goods and
services
date of first use

optical appearance,
logo, graphical
presentation, drawing
to file an application
with, Examining
Attorney, search of
records, objections

final action
to refuse, applicant
Trademark Trial and
Appeal Board, U.S.
Court of Appeals for
the Federal Circuit
Official Gazette

to initiate opposition
proceedings
cancellation
proceedings

The owner of a trademark or service mark may apply for registration under the federal system after use has been established in inter-state commerce. Registration is sought for certain classes of goods and services. The application needs to contain a statement as to the date of first use of the mark and the date of first use of the mark in inter-state commerce. If the visual appearance of the mark is of importance (logos, graphical presentation, etc.) a drawing of the mark has to be included in the application as well. The application is filed with the U.S. Patent and Trademark Office, where an Examining Attorney will consider the application in light of the rules and regulations and will carry out a search of the records of the Office. Objections to the registration, which may result either from the search or from applicable rules and regulations may lead to a final action issued by the Examining Attorney refusing registration. If such final action has been issued, the applicant has a right to appeal to the Trademark Trial and Appeal Board and the U.S. Court of Appeals for the Federal Circuit. If, in turn, the Examining Attorney has no objections and has approved the registration of the mark, it will be published in the Official Gazette. Within 30 days after publication, any person or entity who believes that registration of the mark would cause damage may initiate opposition proceedings. When this period has expired, a party who believes that the registered mark infringes its rights may commence cancellation proceedings by filing a petition to the Trademark Trial and Appeal Board.

Principal Register
Certificate of
Registration
prima facie evidence,
perpetual,
incontestable

to file an affidavit

renewal

expiration date

Upon registration in the Principal Register the owner of the mark receives a Certificate of Registration from the U.S. Patent and Trademarks Office. The registration constitutes prima facie evidence of the validity of the mark which will become perpetual and incontestable after the expiration of five years following registration. A prerequisite for this is, however, that the owner of a registered trademark files an affidavit of use between the 5th and the 6th anniversary of the registration and that s/he has not failed to stop unauthorized use by others. Trademark rights exist for a period of 20 years, however, renewal of registration may be sought for an unlimited number of times provided that application for renewal is filed during the six months period immediately preceding the expiration date.

2.5. Infringement

Under common law as well as under statutory regulations, the basic test for the existence of infringements is the "likelihood of confusion". This concept is closely linked to the concept of distinctiveness which is a prerequisite for the creation of trademark rights. When the likelihood of confusion is tested, two trademarks are compared in light of the degree of similarity of the marks with respect to appearance, connotation, sound, and impression; the similarity of the goods and services marketed under the competing marks; the similarity of the markets ("trade channels"); the strength of the mark; the degree of care likely to be exercised by the purchasers (impulse or considered purchases); actual cases of confusion and other aspects.

2.6. Remedies

In a case involving trademark infringement under the Lanham Act, statutory remedies are available, namely injunctive relief, an accounting for profits, damages, including the possibility of treble damages when appropriate, attorneys' fees under certain circumstances, and costs (15 U.S.C.A. Section 1117).

copyright

3. COPYRIGHT

3.1. Origins and legal framework

Copyright Act

Unlike the rights relating to the regulation of trademarks, the U.S. Constitution expressly conferred the power to regulate copyright matters upon Congress. Article I, section 8, clause 8 of the Constitution states: "The Congress shall have Power ... To promote the Progress of Science and useful Arts, by securing for limited Times to Authors and Inventors the exclusive Right to their Writings and Discoveries". Pursuant to the constitutional clause Congress enacted various copyright statutes, the latest of which being the

statutory protection

Copyright Act, 17 U.S.C.A., which awards federal statutory protection to all original works from the moment of their creation.

scope of protection

3.2. Scope of protection

original works of authorship

Under the 1976 Act, copyright protection is available for original works of authorship as soon as a work is recorded in some concrete way. Works of authorship include literal works, musical works, dramatic works, pantomimes and choreographic works, pictorial, graphic and sculpture works, computer programs, motion pictures and other audiovisual works and sound recordings.

Whereas patent protection applies to an application of an idea and whereas trademark protection extends to any feasible and used device for indicated origin of goods and services, copyright

original expression of an idea

protection centers fundamentally upon the original expression of an idea. Copyright protection is, however, not available for any "idea, procedure, process, system, method of operation, concept, principle or discovery..." (Section 102 (b) of the 1976 Copyright Act). Thus, only the particular expression of a work of authorship

copyrightable

is copyrightable, not however, the underlying idea.

copyright owner

The copyright owner is entitled to certain exclusive rights such as the right to make copies of the work. His/her rights may be trans-

assigns
work for hire

ferred to his/her assigns or may be vested in his/her employer if the work is "a work for hire". Exclusive rights including the right

derivative works

to reproduce the work, to prepare derivative works, to distribute copies by sale or other transfer of ownership, to perform or to display the work publicly may be transferred or assigned by assignment or license. Such license or assignment must be evidenced by a writing if it is granted on an exclusive basis.

Transfers may be revoked or terminated beginning 36 years from

execution of a grant

the date of execution of the grant. Copyright protection is available for the lifetime of the author plus 50 years.

formalities

3.3. Formalities

Unlike patent or trademark protection which only takes effect after registration, copyright protection comes into effect the very

*moment the author puts down his idea in a tangible medium. In
order to take full effect, however, a notice of copyright must be
placed on all published copies from which a work can be visually
perceived. This notice requirement is met when the author puts an
encircled letter "C" or the word "Copyright", the year of publication and the name of the owner of the copyright on all published copies.*

notice of copyright

*Copyrighted works may also be registered although such registra-
tion does not change the legal status of the copyright owner as already mentioned. Copyright registration is nonetheless mandatory
for the commencement of infringement actions. The registration
procedure involves filing an application with the U.S. Copyright
Office.*

mandatory
infringement action

3.4. Infringement

infringement

*Any violation of the copyright owner's exclusive rights constitutes
an infringement. A further infringement occurs when a party imports copyrighted materials into the United States without permission of the copyright owner to do so if the work was acquired outside the U.S.*

3.5. Remedies

*Remedies for copyright infringement are injunctive relief (both
preliminary and permanent injunctive relief), damages and profits
(actual damages, profits and statutory damages), impoundment
(disposition, possible destruction of infringing copies and equipment used to produce them), criminal penalties, attorneys' fees
and costs.*

injunctive relief
damages, profits
impoundment,
disposition,
destruction,
equipment, criminal
penalties

PRAXISTEIL ZUM IMMATERIALGÜTERRECHT

1. PATENT LAW

ASSIGNMENT

For good and valuable consideration, the receipt and sufficiency of which are hereby acknowledged, each undersigned inventor has sold and assigned, and by these presents hereby sells and assigns, unto

(name and address of assignee) (hereinafter ASSIGNEE) all right, title and interest for the United States, its territories and possessions in and to his/her invention relating to the snow-removal equipment commonly referred to as the "Snow-Blow" as set forth in his/her United States Patent Application

– executed concurrently herewith

– executed on _____

– Serial No. _____ filed _____

in and to said United States Patent Application including any and all divisions or continuations thereof and to any and all Letters Patent of the United States which may issue on any such application or for said invention, including any and all reissues or extensions thereof, to be held and enjoyed by said ASSIGNEE, its successors, legal representatives and assigns to the full end of the term or terms for which any and all such Letters Patent may be granted as fully and entirely as would have been held and enjoyed by the undersigned had this Assignment not been made.

Each of the undersigned hereby authorizes and requests the Commissioner of Patents and Trademarks to issue any and all such Letters Patent to said ASSIGNEE, its successors or assigns in accordance herewith.

Each of the undersigned warrants and covenants that s/he has the full and unencumbered right to sell and assign the interests herein sold and assigned and that s/he has not executed and will not execute any document or instrument in conflict herewith.

Each of the undersigned further covenants and agrees that at any time upon request of said ASSIGNEE, its successors, legal representatives or assigns s/he will communicate to said ASSIGNEE, its successors, legal representatives or assigns all information known to him/her relating to said invention or patent application and that s/he will execute and deliver any papers, make all rightful oaths, testify in any legal proceedings and perform all other lawful acts deemed necessary or desirable by said ASSIGNEE, its successors, legal representatives or assigns to perfect title to said invention, to said application including divisions and continuations thereof and to any and all Letters Patent which may be

ABTRETUNGS-VERTRAG
Abtretung gegen Vergütung, Bestätigung des Erhalts ausreichender Gegenleistung
Empfänger

Erfindung

Antrag an die Patentbehörde

Erteilung auf Grund des Antrags

Unterzeichner

Bestätigung des Unterzeichners über sein uneingeschränktes Recht

Verpflichtung zur Weitergabe aller notwendigen Informationen

315

granted therefor or thereon including reissues or extensions, in said ASSIGNEE, its successors or assigns or to assist said AS-SIGNEE, its successors, legal representatives or assigns in obtaining, reissuing or enforcing Letters Patent to the United States for said invention;

Vollmachtserteilung
zur Vornahme von
Vertragsergänzungen

Each of the undersigned grants the firm of ... the power to insert in this Assignment any further identification which may be necessary or desirable to comply with the rules of the U.S. Patent and Trademark Office for recordation of this Assignment.

Unterschriften der
Erfinder

_____ date _____
(Name)

_____ date _____
(Name)

Zeuge

Witness: _____
(Name)   _____

Rechtsbelehrung über
die Beglaubigungs-
formalitäten und deren
prozessuale
Bedeutung

Note: **Prima facie** *evidence of execution may optionally be obtained by execution of this document before a U.S. Consul or before a local officer authorized to administer oaths whose authority is proved by a certificate from a U.S. Consul.*

2. TRADEMARKS

2. Markenrechte

ASSIGNMENT OF REGISTERED TRADEMARKS

MARKEN-
ABTRETUNG

WHEREAS, MIRACLE CORPORATION, a corporation duly organized and existing under and by virtue of the laws of Arizona, located and doing business at 47 Durrant Way, Farnborough, Arizona 12345, is the owner of the registered trademarks listed in the attached Exhibit A;

Identifizierung des
Marken(rechts)-
inhabers

WHEREAS, PHANTASY INC., a corporation duly organized and existing under and by virtue of the laws of the Commonwealth of Virginia, located and doing business at 232 Ivy Drive, Charlottesville, Virgina 22901, is desirous of acquiring said trademarks and the registrations thereof;

Identifizierung des
Erwerbers der
Markenrechte

NOW, THEREFORE, in consideration of and in exchange for the sum of One thousand Dollars ($ 1,000) and other good and valid consideration receipt of which is hereby acknowledged, said MIRACLE CORPORATION does hereby assign unto PHANTASY INC. all right, title and interest in and to the trademarks and the said registrations, together with the goodwill of the business symbolized by the trademarks.

Gegenleistungs-
klausel*
Abtretungspreis

This Assignment is executed at Farnborough, Arizona, this 9th day of July, 1990.

MIRACLE CORPORATION

_____

Henry H. Lonesome, III
Its Secretary

State of Arizona
County of Wonderland

On this 9th day of July, 1990, before me, the undersigned, a Notary Public, personally appeared Henry H. Lonesome, III, to me personally known, who, being by me duly sworn, did say that he is the Secretary of MIRACLE CORPORATION, the corporation executing the foregoing instrument; that the seal affixed thereto is the seal of the corporation (or that there is no seal); that the instrument was signed (and sealed, if there be a seal) on behalf of the corporation by authority of its Board of Directors; and acknowledged the execution of the instrument to be the voluntary act and deed of the corporation by it and by him voluntarily executed.

notarielle Beglaubi-
gungsklausel, mit
eidesstättiger
Erklärung über die
Amtsinhabung und die
ausdrückliche
Ermächtigung durch
den Vorstand

_____

Alice M. Ancatsh
Notary Public

3. Copyright

3. COPYRIGHT

Excerpt from a Software License Agreement

Auszug aus einem
Software-Lizenz-
vertrag

Identifizierung der
Vertragsparteien

Baker Systems, Inc. (Baker), a Kentucky corporation, of 5000 Co-logne Avenue, Lexington, Kentucky 52727 and Smith Corporation (Customer), an Ohio corporation, of 5064 Hopevalley Drive, Cincinnati, Ohio 90000, agree as follows:

detaillierte Beschrei-
bung der Lizenz nicht
exklusiv und nicht
übertragbar
Anhang

I. License

1.1. Baker grants to Customer, subject to the terms and conditions contained in this Agreement, a non-exclusive and non-transferable license to use the proprietary computer software programs and related materials (Systems) described in any Schedule of Systems (Schedule) executed pursuant to this Agreement.

Wirkung durch Unter-
zeichnung eines
Lizenzvertrages samt
Anhang

1.2. The Systems must be licensed by the execution of a Software License Agreement and a Schedule. Once a Software License Agreement has been executed, Systems may be licensed upon execution by Baker and Customer of Baker's then current Schedule. No letter, purchase order, or other notice will establish a license to use the Systems.

ausschließlich interner
Gebrauch

1.3. Customer shall have the right to use the Systems solely for its own internal operation at the Designated Location and on the Designated Central Processing Unit (CPU) described in the Schedule.

im Falle zeitweiliger
Unbenutzbarkeit des
Systems des Kunden
Erlaubnis, auf ein
anderes auszuweichen

1.4. When the Designated CPU is temporarily inoperable, Customer may transfer the use of the Systems to a backup CPU until operable status is restored to the Designated CPU. In addition, Customer may make sufficient copies of the Systems for backup purposes.

Bestimmung über die
Lizenzgebühr

1.5. License charges are set forth on the Schedule. Rental License Charges and Annual Renewal License Charges are subject to change on 90 days prior written notice to Customer. If any change in these charges is unacceptable to Customer, Customer may terminate the license for the Systems for which the charge was changed as of the effective date of the change by giving 45 days prior written notice to Baker.

*EXCERPT FROM THE INTERNATIONAL DEPOSIT
CERTIFICATE OF THE WORLD INTELLECTUAL
PROPERTY ORGANIZATION*

international deposit
certificate

INTERNATIONAL DEPOSIT CERTIFICATE

*(pursuant to the terms of the Hague Agreement concerning the
International Deposit of Industrial Design)*

pursuant to the terms
of

*The International Bureau of the World Intellectual Property Or-
ganization (WIPO) hereby certifies that the particulars given below correspond to the recordings made in the International Register of Industrial Designs at the date of the international deposit,
under the Hague Agreement Concerning the International Deposit
of Industrial Designs.*

to certify, particulars,
recordings, industrial
design, deposit

(... Particulars ...)

Notes by the International Bureau

*1. This international deposit has been published in the Interna-
tional Designs Bulletin, issue No. xxx(1989 (...).*

published
official bulletin

*2. The States listed under the heading "States concerned" are the
States in which the international deposit has effect. The States
listed in section I are those States in respect of which the Hague
Agreement as revised at The Hague on November 29, 1960 (1960
Act), applies. The States listed in section II, if any, are those States
in respect of which the Hague Agreement as revised in London in
1934 (1934 Act) applies.*

to have effect

as revised
to apply

*3. In each of the States concerned, the effect of the international
deposit is the same as that of a deposit filed directly with the appropriate national or regional Office on the date of the international deposit or on that of the priority claimed, subject to the special rules established by the Hague Agreement, particularly as regards the term of protection.*

to file

to claim priority
subject to
term/period of
protection

*4. The term of protection for all States concerned is five years from
the date of international deposit. The international deposit may be
renewed, however, at least once for each of those States for an additional five-year period. For the States concerned listed in section
I, whose legislation allows a term of protection of more than ten
years for national deposits, an international deposit may be renewed a number of times for an additional five-year period each
time, with effect in each of those States until expiry of the total term
of protection permitted for national deposits under the domestic
legislation of that State. For the States listed in section II, if any,
renewal may be effected twice, for an additional five year period
each time.*

to renew

legislation

expiry

to effect renewal

*5. Renewal may be effected during the final year of the current
five-year period.*

registered
representatives

to obtain renewal

6. Six months before expiry of the current five-year period, the International Bureau sends the owner, and the registered representative if any, a letter reminding him/her of the date of expiry and informing him/her of the steps to be taken to obtain renewal. (...)

INTELLECTUAL PROPERTY LAW TERMINOLOGY

TERMINOLOGIE ZUM IMMATERIAL-GÜTERRECHT

abandonment of mark	Aufgabe einer Marke
access	Zugang (zum Original)
accounting for profits	Rechnungslegung
administrative proceedings	Verwaltungsverfahren
administrative procedure	Verwaltungsverfahren
agency	Behörde, Amt
amend an application	einen Antrag ergänzen
animals	Tiere
appeal	Berufung, Rechtsmittel
appeal	berufen, Rechtsmittel erheben
appeal a decision rendered by an agency	eine verwaltungsbehördliche Entscheidung bekämpfen
applicant	Antragsteller
application	Antrag
appropriation	Zuerkennung, Zuordnung
appurtenant to commercial activity	abhängig von der Verwendung im Geschäftsverkehr
arbitrary mark	Phantasiemarke, keine beschreibende Qualität
artistic quality	künstlerisches Potential
assign	abtreten
assignee	Übernehmer
assignment	Abtretung
assignment deed	Abtretungsurkunde, Abtretungsvertrag
assignment of all rights (pertaining) to patent	Abretung aller Patent(nutzungs)rechte
assignment of mark	Markenabtretung
assignor	Abtretender
attorney's fees	Anwaltskosten
bar	ausschließen
bar appropriation	Zuteilung/Eintragung ausschließen
bar later use	späteren Gebrauch ausschließen
barred from registration	von der Registrierung ausgeschlossen
Board of Appeals (US)	Berufungsinstanz
cancellation proceedings	Nichtigkeitsverfahren
candor	Aufrichtigkeit (Pflicht zur vollständigen Offenlegung aller relevanten Umstände)
cause of action	Klagsgrund
certification mark	Qualitätsauszeichnungen*
charge of infringement	Vorwurf des Patenteingriffs
cite (a) reference(s)	bereits eingetragene Patente anführen, Ähnlichkeitsprotokoll
claims	Patentansprüche
coin a mark	eine Marke prägen
collective mark	Gruppenmarke* (vgl Verbandsmarke, Konzernmarke)

colo(u)r	Farbe
commercial activity	Geschäftsverkehr
common terms	allgemeine Begriffe (Freihaltebedürfnis*)
communication	Schriftverkehr, Verständigung
composite mark	zusammengesetze Marke
compulsory licensing	Zwangslizenz
computer program(me)s	Computerprogramme
conduct a search of past patents	eingetragene Patente recherchieren
confiscation	Einziehung
confusingly similar	verwechslungsfähig ähnlich
constructive notice	Publikationswirkung* (schließt späteren gutgläubigen Erwerb/Gebrauch sowie jede territoriale Einschränkung aus)
contest a patent	ein Patent anfechten
contest a patent by a request to the Patent Office to re-examine	ein Patent anfechten mittels Antrag auf neuerliche Prüfung an das Patentamt
contest a patent by an infringement suit	ein Patent anfechten im Zuge einer Patenteingriffsklage
contributory infringement	Patenteingriff durch Verkauf von ausschließlich im Zusammenhang mit patentgeschützten Waren verwendbaren Produkten
copyist	Person, die etwas kopiert
copyright	Copyright, Urheberrecht*
Copyright Act 17 U.S.C.A. (1976) (US)	gesetzliche Grundlage (publiziert im United States Code Annotated)
copyright claimant	Anspruchswerber
copyright infringement	Urheberrechtsverletzung
copyright infringement action	Urheberrechtseingriffsklage
copyright infringement suit	Urheberrechtseingriffsklage
copyright notice	Anzeige- bzw. Hinterlegungspflicht betreffend geschützte Objekte (an Copyright Office und Library of Congress) als Voraussetzung für die gerichtliche Durchsetzung von Ansprüchen
Copyright Office (US)	für Copyright-Sachen zuständige US-Behörde
copyright owner	Copyright-Inhaber
copyrightability	Copyright-Schutzfähigkeit
copyrightable matter(s)	schutzfähige Objekte
costs	Kosten
court	Gericht
creative effort	künstlerische Leistung, Werkhöhe*
criminal penalties	Strafen
damages	Schadenersatz
deception	Täuschung
declaratory judgement that patent is invalid	Feststellungsurteil über Patentnichtigkeit
deny patentability	Patenfähigkeit verneinen
deposit (with Copyright Office and Library of Congress)	Hinterlegung

derivative works	abgeleitete Werke
descriptive mark	beschreibende Marke
descriptive terms	beschreibende Begriffe
descriptiveness	beschreibende Eigenschaften
design	Bildmarke*
destruction	Vernichtung
device	(Darstellungs-)Mittel
direct infringement	unmittelbarer Patenteingriff
discretion	Ermessen
display	Ausstellung
distinctiveness	Unterscheidungskraft
distribution	Vertrieb
equitable relief	Rechtsbehelf nach Billigkeit*
evidentiary proof	Bescheinigungsmittel, Beweismittel
examination	Prüfung
examiner	Prüfer
exclusive license	Exklusivlizenz
exclusive rights of derivative work	Exklusivrechte an abgeleiteten Werken
exclusive rights of display	Exklusivrechte an der Ausstellung
exclusive rights of distribution	Exklusivrechte am Vertrieb
exclusive rights of performance	Exklusivrechte an der Aufführung
exclusive rights of reproduction	Exklusivrechte an der Vervielfältigung
exclusivity	Exklusivität
expression of an idea	Ausdruck einer Idee
fair use	zulässige Nutzung (zB für akademische Zwecke oder Unterrichtszwecke)
fanciful mark	Phantasiemarke
Federal jurisdiction	Zuständigkeit der Bundesgerichte (US)
final refusal	endgültige Ablehnung
fine arts	schöne Künste
first use	Erstgebrauch (Beginn der Schutzdauer)
fixation	schriftliche Niederlegung/Aufzeichnung
generic mark	Begriffe mit allgemeinem Freihaltungs- bedürfnis (z.B. Löffel), Freizeichen
good will	Goodwill
grant a patent	ein Patent erteilen
illegal copies	Raubkopien
impermissible copying	unzulässiges Vervielfältigen
impoundment	Verfall
improvements	Verbesserungen
incontestability	Unanfechtbarkeit
indirect infringement	mittelbarer Patenteingriff (durch Bestimmung eines Dritten)
individual license	Einzellizenz
infringement action	Patenteingriffsklage
infringement suit	Patenteingriffsklage
injunctive relief	einstweilige Verfügung*
intellectual property law	Immterialgüterrecht

interference proceedings	Zwischenverfahren bei gleichzeitiger Abhängigkeit von zwei oder mehreren gleichen Patentanmeldungen
invalid patent	nichtiges Patent
invention	Erfindung
irreparable harm	unwiderbringlicher Schaden
issue a patent	ein Patent erteilen
issue of final refusal	Ausfertigung der endgültigen Ablehnung
joint invention	gemeinsame Erfindung
judicial review	Überprüfung durch die ordentlichen Gerichte
Lanham Act 15 U.S.C.A (1946)	gesetzliche Grundlage USA, publiziert im United States Code Annotated (U.S.C.A.)
Library of Congress (US)	Bibliothek des US-Kongresses (größte Bibliothek der Welt)
license	Lizenz
license agreement	Lizenzvertrag, Lizenzvereinbarung
license fee	Lizenzgebühr
life of patent	Patent(schutz)dauer
likelihood of confusion	Verwechslungsgefahr
logo	Wortbildmarke*, Bildmarke*
mark	Marke
membership mark	Mitgliedsmarke* (vgl Verbandsmarke)
mistake	Irrtum
misuse	Verteidigungsstrategie gegen Vorwurf des Patenteingriffs - unzulässig weite Ausbeutung des Patents
musical compositions	Kompositionen
name	Wortmarke*
non-exclusive license	nicht exklusive Lizenz
non-use	Nichtgebrauch, Nichtverwendung
nonobviousness	Postulat, daß Erfindung nicht von jedem technisch Begabten gemacht hätte werden können (Nichtoffensichtlichkeit)
notice requirement	Hinterlegungspflicht als Prozeßvoraussetzung
novelty	Neuheit
Official Gazette (US)	Offizielles Publikationsorgan
opposition proceedings	Widerspruchsverfahren über Antrag eines Dritten binnen 30 Tagen nach Veröffentlichung einer Markenregistrierung (US)
originality	künstlerische Eigenständigkeit/Originalität
owner of a patent	Patentinhaber
paintings	Gemälde
patent	Patent
patent application	Patentantrag

patent infringement	Patenteingriff
patent law	Patentrecht
Patent Office (US)	Patentamt
patent pending	anhängiges Patentverfahren
patent protection	Patentschutz
patent validity	aufrechter Bestand eines Patents
patentable	patentfähig, patentierbar
patentee	Patentinhaber
patenting process	Patentverfahren
pecuniary interest	finanzielles Interesse
performance	Aufführung
period of patent	Patent(schutz)dauer
petition for re-examination	Antrag einer dritten Partei auf neuerliche Prüfung
photocopying	Fotokopieren
phrase	Wortgruppenmarke*, Satzmarke*
pirate	Person, die Raubkopien herstellt
plagiarism	Raub von urheberrechtlich geschützten Werken
plagiarize	plagiieren, ein Plagiat herstellen/begehen
plants	Pflanzen
potential patentee	Patentwerber
prerequisites	Voraussetzungen
presumption of abandonment	rechtliche Vermutung der Aufgabe (einer Marke)
presumption of patent validity	Rechtsvermutung des aufrechten Patentbestands
prints	Drucke
priority	Priorität
priority of invention	Erfindungspriorität, Ersterfindung
priority of use	Priorität der Benutzung, Erstbenutzung
proceedings	Verfahren
process	Verfahren
processes	Vorgänge
product	Gegenstand, Muster
profits	Gewinn
public domain	öffentliche/allgemeine Nutzung*/ Zugänglichkeit
publication in the Official Gazette of the Office (US)	Veröffentlichung im offiziellen Publikationsorgan (US)
punitive damages	Schadenersatz mit Strafcharakter
re-examination	neuerliche Prüfung
re-issue	neuerliche Erteilung eines Patents mit ex-tunc-Wirkung unter Einbeziehung geänderter Umstände
recorded choreography	Choreographieaufzeichnungen
refuse an application	einen Antrag ablehnen
Register of Trademarks	Markenregister
registrability	Registrierfähigkeit, Eintragungsfähigkeit
registrant	registrierter Markeninhaber
registrar	Registerbeamter

325

registration	Registrierung, Eintragung
rejection of an application/claim	Zurückweisung eines Antrags/Anspruchs
remedies	Rechtsbehelfe
renew a patent	Verlängerung des Patentschutzes (nicht möglich)
reproduction	Vervielfältigung
royalty	Lizenzgebühr
search	Recherche
self-executing right	originäres Recht* (die Eintragung wirkt nicht konstitutiv, sondern ist lediglich Prozeßvoraussetzung)
service mark	Dienstleistungsmarke
similarity	Ähnlichkeit
specification	Patentbeschreibung
standing	Antragslegitimation, Klagslegitimation
statutory (punitive) damages	Schadenersatz mit Strafcharakter
statutory bar	gesetzliche Ausschließungsgründe
strength of mark	starke Marke* (vgl starkes Zeichen)
submit an application	Antrag einbringen
substantial similarity	wesentliche Ähnlichkeit/Übereinstimmung
suggestive mark	sekundär beschreibende Marke
Supplemental Register (US)	„B-Register"* (Marken, die aufgrund mangelnder Unterscheidungsfähigkeit nicht ins eigentliche Markenregister eingetragen werden können, können ins B-Register eingetragen werden und nach 5 Jahren unter gleichzeitigem Nachweis der Verwendung (vgl Verkehrsgeltung) neuerlich zur Eintragung ins A-Register angemeldet werden) (US)
termination of transfer	Beendigung der Werknutzungsberechtigung
terms of the claim	Patentanspruchsbedingungen
trademark	Marke
trademark infringement	Markenrechtsverletzung, Markeneingriff
Trademark Trial and Appeal Board (TTAB) (US)	Berufungsinstanz in Markensachen (US)
transfer	Übertragung
types of patents	Patentarten
use of mark	(Be)Nutzung einer Marke
utilitarian objects	Gebrauchsgegenstände
utility	Nützlichkeit
videotapes	Videos
working the patent	Benützung des Patents
works for hire	Auftragswerke
writings	literarische Werke

TERMINOLOGIE ZUM IMMATERIAL-GÜTERRECHT

INTELLECTUAL PROPERTY LAW TERMINOLOGY

ablehnen	*to deny, to reject, to refuse*
abtreten	*to assign*
Abtretender	*assignor*
Abtretung	*assignment*
Abtretung einer Marke	*assignment of a mark*
Abtretungsvertrag	*assignment deed, assignment contract*
ähnlich	*similar*
Ähnlichkeit	*similarity*
Ähnlichkeitsprotokoll	*official report on findings of similar marks*
Ähnlichkeitsprüfung	*search (for similar marks)*
Amt	*office, agency*
Anfechtung	*challenge*
anhängiges Verfahren	*patent pending*
Anspruch	*claim*
Anspruchswerber	*claimant, applicant*
Antrag	*application*
Antrag auf neuerliche Prüfung	*application for re-examination*
Antrag ergänzen	*to amend an application*
Antragslegitimation	*standing*
Antragsteller	*applicant*
aufrechter Bestand	*valid patent*
Auftragswerk	*work for hire*
ausschließen	*to exclude, to bar*
Behörde	*authority*
Benützung einer Marke	*use of a mark*
Berufung	*appeal*
Berufung einlegen	*to appeal*
Bescheinigungsmittel	*evidentiary proof**
beschreibender Begriff	*descriptive term*
Beweismittel	*evidence, proof**
Bildmarke	*image, logo, design**
Dienstleistungsklasse	*class of services*
eingetragen	*registered*
eingetragene Marken	*registered trademarks*
eingetragene Patente	*registered patents*
Einspruchsverfahren	*opposition proceedings*
einstweilige Verfügung	*injunctive relief*
eintragen	*to register*
Eintragung	*registration*
Eintragungsfähigkeit	*registrability*
Einziehung	*confiscation of a patent*
entgangener Gewinn	*lost profits*
Entscheidung	*decision*

327

Erfindung	*invention*
Ermessen	*discretion*
Erstgebrauch	*first use, priority of use*
exklusive Lizenz	*exclusive license*
Exklusivität	*exclusivity*
Exklusivlizenz	*exclusive license*
Exklusivrechte	*exclusive rights*
Feststellungsurteil	*declaratory judgement*
fotokopieren	*to photocopy*
Freihaltungsbedürfnis	*requirement to bar common/generic terms from protection to allow general access/use**
Freizeichen	*generic mark*
Gebrauch	*use, working*
Gebrauchsgegenstände	*utilitarian objects*
gemeinsame Erfindung	*joint invention*
Geschäftsverkehr	*course of business*
Hinterlegung	*deposit*
Immaterialgüterrecht	*intellectual property law*
Klagsgrund	*cause of action*
Klagslegitimation	*standing*
Konzernmarke	*collective mark**
Kosten	*costs*
künstlerische Eigenständigkeit	*originality*
künstlerische Leistung	*artistic effort/achievement*
Lizenz	*license*
Lizenzgebühr	*license fee, royalty*
Lizenzvertrag	*license agreement*
Löschungsantrag	*application for cancellation*
Löschungsverfahren	*proceedings for cancellation*
Marke	*mark, trademark*
Marke löschen	*to delete a mark, to cancel a mark*
Markenanzeiger	*Official Gazette of the Trademark Office* (US)*
Markeneingriffsklage	*trademark infringement suit*
Markeninhaber	*trademark holder/owner*
Markenrecht	*trademark law*
Markenrechtsverletzung	*trademark infringement*
Markenregister	*register of trademarks*
Musterschutz	*protection of designs*
nicht exklusive Lizenz	*non-exclusive license*
nichtig	*invalid*
Nichtigkeit	*invalidity*
Nichtigkeitsabteilung	*Cancellation Department**

Nichtigkeitsantrag	*application to revoke*
Nichtigkeitsverfahren	*proceedings for nullification, revocation of patent by court*
Nutzung	*use, exploitation, working*
öffentliche Zugänglichkeit	*public domain*
Originalität	*originality*
Patent	*patent*
Patent anfechten	*to challenge a patent*
Patent benützen	*to use, to work, to exploit a patent*
Patent erteilen	*to grant a patent, to issue a patent*
Patentamt	*Patent Office (US)*
Patentantrag	*patent application*
Patentanwalt	*patent attorney (US), patent agent (UK), patent lawyer*
Patentarten	*types of patents*
Patentbenützung	*use/working/exploitation of a patent*
Patentbeschreibung	*patent specification*
Patenteinbrigungsverfahren	*opposition proceedings*
Patenteingriff	*patent infringement*
Patenteingriffsklage	*patent infringement suit, infringement action*
patentfähig	*patentable*
Patentfähigkeit verneinen	*to deny patentability*
patentierbar	*patentable*
Patentinhaber	*holder of a patent, owner of a patent, patentee*
Patentrecht	*patent law*
Patentschutz	*patent protection*
Patentschutzdauer	*term/duration/period of patent*
Patenturkunde	*letters patent*
Patentverfahren	*patent procedure*
Patentversagung	*denial/refusal/rejection of patent*
Patentwerber	*patent applicant, prospective patentee*
Phantasiemarke	*fanciful mark*
Plagiat	*object of plagiarism*
Priorität	*priority*
Prüfer	*examiner*
Prüfung	*examination*
Raubkopie	*illegal copy*
Recherche	*search (for prior patent specifications, marks, etc.)*
recherchieren	*to search, to investigate*
Rechnungslegung	*accounting*
Recht zum Vertrieb	*right of distribution*
Recht zur Aufführung	*right of performance*
Recht zur Ausstellung	*right of exhibition/display*
Recht zur Sendung/Übertragung	*right of broadcast*
Recht zur Veröffentlichung	*right of publication*
Recht zur Vervielfältigung	*right of reproduction*

Recht zur Werknutzung	*right of use**
Rechtsbehelfe gegen Eingriffe	*remedies in case of infringement*
Rechtsmittel gegen verwaltungsbehördliche und gerichtliche Entscheidungen	*means of recourse against administrative and court decisions*
Register	*register*
Registerbeamter	*registrar*
registrieren	*to register*
Registrierfähigkeit	*registrability*
Registrierung	*registration*
Sachbearbeiter	*examiner*
Schadenersatz	*damages*
Strafen (strafrechtlich)	*criminal sanctions, e.g. fines*
Tantiemen	*royalties*
Übertragung	*transfer*
Unanfechtbarkeit	*incontestability*
Unterscheidungskraft	*potential for distinction**
unzulässiges Vervielfältigen	*illegal reproduction*
Urheberrecht	*copyright**
Urheberrechtsklage	*copyright infringement suit*
Urheberrechtsverletzung	*copyright infringement*
Verbandsmarke	*collective mark*, certification mark*, trademark for use by members of a trade association*
Verfahren	*proceedings, procedure*
Verfall	*impoundment*
Verlängerung der Schutzdauer	*renewal of protection, extension of protection period*
Veröffentlichung	*publication*
verwaltungsbehördliche Entscheidung	*administrative decision*
Verwaltungsverfahren	*administrative proceedings*
verwechslungsfähig ähnlich	*confusingly similar*
Verwechslungsgefahr	*risk of confusion*
Voraussetzungen	*requirements, prerequisites*
Warenklasse	*class of goods*
Werkhöhe	*eligibility for protection, artistic effort/achievement*
Werknutzungsvertrag	*contract for the use of a work of art**
Wortbildmarke	*combined name and image mark/logo*
Wortmarke	*name (mark)**
zulässige Nutzung (eines urheberrechtlich geschützten Werkes)	*permissible use, fair use (US)**
Zwangslizenz	*compulsory license*

KPMG *Austria – The Advisory Firm*

KPMG Austria is Austria's leading group of **Certified Public Accountants** (CPA), specialised in audit, tax consultancy and management consulting with 20 offices throughout Austria. With a staff of about 650 employees (40 partners and more than 400 professionals) the full service range of business consultancy is rendered to clients, both on local, national, and international level. Being a member of the international KPMG group that is a top of the Big Six in Europe with representations in 136 countries and 72,500 employees worldwide, KPMG Austria takes advantage of leading quality standards and expertise in various fields of business consultancy.

The services offered by KPMG Austria cover audit and related services, according to both national, international, and Anglo-American standards, furthermore **tax consultancy,** among others with special regard to international tax planning concepts, and management consulting, focussing on the implementation of accounting systems, SAP and others. Furthermore services of the so-called general practice, i.e. bookkeeping, accounting, payroll accounting, cost accounting and budgeting, are rendered. Apart from the "classical" services of audit and tax consultancy, KPMG Austria is specialized in corporate finance, i.e. analysis and qualified opinion related to mergers and acquisitions, and corporate recovery, i.e. audit and consultancy related to insolvencies.

In order to consider all aspects relevant to the client and his/her business a specialization in industry groups such as Banking & Finance; Insurance; Manufacturing, Wholesale, Retail & Distribution; Building & Construction; Information, Communication & Entertainment; Energy, Environment & Natural Resources; Health Care & Life Sciences; Government & Non Profit Organisations; and Transportation was established on a world-wide basis to facilitate an in-depth expertise. All assignments are supervised by a lead partner who ensures that all performances are delivered according to KPMG quality standards. Therefore continuing education and training in latest developments of audit, tax, and industries are obligatory for all auditors and consultants. According to these principles an interdisciplinary approach is provided to realize synergies for the client's benefit through services performed by KPMG, the Advisory Firm.

STICHWORTVERZEICHNIS

TRANSLEX

MMAG. FRANZ J. HEIDINGER, LL.M.
ST. ULRICHS-PLATZ 4
1070 WIEN

TEL.: 526 84 78 OD. 403 65 12/17
MOBILTEL: 0663 813 019
FAX.: 526 84 89

UNSER SERVICE FÜR IHRE KANZLEI:

* ÜBERSETZUNGEN
* BEGLAUBIGUNGEN
* DOLMETSCHUNGEN
* BERATUNGEN
* FACHSPRACHKURSE
* VORBEREITUNGEN FÜR SEMINARE
  UND TAGUNGEN
* PUBLIKATIONSASSISTENZ

UNSER QUALITÄTSANSPRUCH:

* WIR SIND JURISTEN UND
  FACHSPRACHSPEZIALISTEN
* STRENGSTE DISKRETION
* PERSÖNLICHE BETREUUNG
* VERLÄSSLICHKEIT

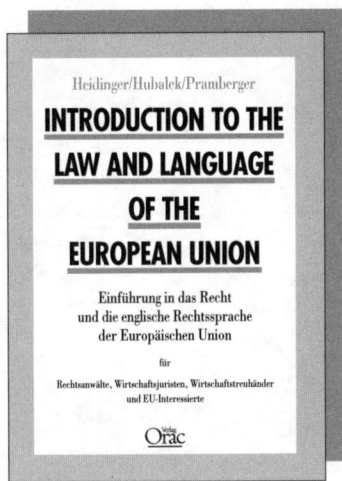